William H. Kingston

The Three Commanders

William H. Kingston

The Three Commanders

ISBN/EAN: 9783337810177

Printed in Europe, USA, Canada, Australia, Japan

Cover: Foto ©ninafisch / pixelio.de

More available books at **www.hansebooks.com**

THE THREE COMMANDERS

BY

W. H. G. KINGSTON

AUTHOR OF
"FROM POWDER MONKEY TO ADMIRAL," "THE THREE MIDSHIPMEN," ETC.

NEW EDITION

ILLUSTRATED IN COLOUR BY T. C. DUGDALE

LONDON
HENRY FROWDE
HODDER AND STOUGHTON
1912

LIST OF ILLUSTRATIONS

Facing page

"AS THE PINNACE RANGED UP ALONGSIDE, SEVERAL SHOTS WERE FIRED" (see p. 76) . *Frontispiece*

"AWAY ALL HANDS DASHED RIGHT UP TO THE WALL, AND ... JUMPED DOWN INSIDE" 128

"IN A FEW MINUTES THEY FOUND HIM, SEATED IN FRONT OF HIS TENT, IN A WASHING TUB" . . 238

"'LEND A HAND, ALL OF YOU,' CRIED THE NAVAL OFFICER" 286

"'NOW, UP GOES THE BRITISH ENSIGN, AND THE FORT IS OURS!'" 314

"TO THEIR DISMAY, THEY SAW THE SHIP RUNNING AWAY FROM THEM" 402

"AWAY ALL HANDS DASHED RIGHT UP TO THE WALL. AND . . . . JUMPED DOWN INSIDE."

"NOW, UP GOES THE BRITISH ENSIGN, AND THE FORT IS OURS!"

"TO THEIR DISMAY, THEY SAW THE SHIP RUNNING AWAY FROM THEM."

THE THREE COMMANDERS

―♦―

CHAPTER I

Murray's Highland Home—A Visit from Admiral Triton—Adair and his Nephew appear — Murray appointed to the *Opal*, Adair First Lieutenant—Preparations for Departure—Admiral Triton and Mrs. Deborah invite Mrs. Murray to stay at Southsea — The *Opal* and her Crew—A Poetical Lieutenant—Parting between Miss Rogers and Adair—The *Opal* sails for the East Coast of Africa.

ALICK MURRAY had not over-praised the Highland home of which he had so often spoken when far away across the wide ocean. The house, substantially built in a style suited to that clime, stood some way up the side of a hill which rose abruptly from the waters of Loch Etive, on the north side of which it was situated. To the west the hills were comparatively low, the shores alternately widening and contracting, and projecting in numerous promontories. The higher grounds were clothed with heath and wood, while level spaces below were diversified by cultivated fields. To the east of the house, up the loch, the scenery assumed a character much more striking and grand. Far as the eye could reach appeared a succession of lofty and barren mountains, rising sheer out of the water, on the calm surface of which their fantastic forms were reflected as in a mirror. Across the loch the lofty summit of Ben Cruachan appeared towering to the sky. The scenery immediately surrounding Murray's domain of Bercaldine was of extreme beauty. At some little distance the hill, rising abruptly, was covered with oak, ash, birch, and alder, producing a rich tone of colouring; the rowan and hawthorn trees mingling their snowy blossoms or coral berries with the foliage of the more gigantic natives of the forest, while the dark purple heath, in tufted wreaths, and numerous wild-flowers, were interspersed amid the rich sward and underwood along the shore beneath. Behind the house were shrubberies and a well-cultivated kitchen-garden, sheltered on either side by a thick belt of pines; while in front a lawn, also protected by shrubberies from the keen winds which blew down from the mountain heights, sloped towards the loch, with a gravel walk leading to the landing-place. Murray had added a broad verandah to the front of the house, to remind himself and Stella of Don Antonio's residence in Trinidad, where they had first met. Indeed, in some of its features, the scenery recalled to their memories the views they had enjoyed in that lovely island; and though they confessed that Trinidad carried off the palm of beauty, yet they both loved far better their own Highland home.

It was a lovely summer day, and Stella was sitting in the verandah with a small stranger, whom her faithful black maiden, Polly, had just placed in her lap. She was fully employed in bestowing on him those marks of affection which a loving mother delights in affording to her first-born. Alick stood by her side, watching her and their child with looks of fond pride. He had just come in from the garden, which it was one of his chief occupations to tend, and had taken off his gardening gloves, that he might pat his child's cheek and tickle its chin to make it coo and smile. He might have been excused if he was proud of his boy, for he was a noble little fellow,—a "braw chiel," as he was pronounced to be by his grand-aunt, Mistress Tibbie MacTavish, who had presided at his birth,—and likely to do no discredit to the name of Murray.

"The cutter ought to have been back by this time," said Alick at length, looking at his watch; "Archie has had a fair tide from Oban, and a leading wind up the loch. I hope that he has not managed to run the *Stella* ashore. Ben Snatchblock knows the coast, and he himself should be pretty well acquainted with it."

"Perhaps Mr. Adair did not arrive at the time expected, and Archie would, of course, wait for him," observed Stella.

"That may be the case," said Alick, taking the telescope from a bracket on the wall, and looking through it down the loch. "There is no sail in sight like her, but I see a four-oared boat, which has just passed Bunaw Ferry, pulling up the loch. Can Adair by any means have missed the cutter, and be making his way alone to us?"

"Probably she contains a party of tourists on an excursion," said Stella.

"She is, at all events, steering for Bercaldine," observed Murray; "if she does not bring Paddy Adair, you will have the opportunity of exhibiting the small Alick to some other visitor. I will go down to the pier to receive him, whoever he is, with due honour." Saying this, Murray, having bestowed a kiss on his wife's brow, and given another tickle to his baby's chin, which produced an additional coo of delight, hurried down to the landing-place, towards which the boat was rapidly approaching. He had his telescope in his hand. He stopped on the way to take another look through it.

"It is not Terence, but—who do you think?—our old friend, Admiral Triton!" he shouted out, as he looked back to his wife; and then hurried on to the landing-place, that he might be there before the admiral could step ashore. In a few minutes he was receiving the old man's hearty grasp of the hand, as he helped him out of the boat.

"I had long promised to pay a visit to some friends in the Highlands, and I determined to make a trip a few miles farther and take you by surprise, for I knew that I should be welcome at whatever time I might arrive," said the admiral.

"Indeed you are, my dear sir," answered Murray; "most sincerely I say it. We are flattered by your visit."

"Give me your arm, my boy, for I don't walk up hill as easily as I used to do a few years back," said the admiral, leaning somewhat heavily on the young commander as he stumped along with his timber toe. "Stay! by the bye, I must dismiss my crew," he exclaimed, stopping short.

"Let them come up to the house first, admiral," said Murray; "they would consider otherwise that we were forgetful of Highland hospitality at Bercaldine. You will find your way up to the kitchen, my lads, by yonder path," he added, turning round to the boatmen. "The cook will have a snack for you before you pull back to Oban."

The men touched their bonnets, and gratefully grinned their assent to the laird's proposal, as they tumbled out of the boat; while Murray conducted Admiral Triton by the centre path, which led through the grounds to the house.

Mrs. Murray, having deposited the wee Alick in the arms of Polly, stood ready to receive them.

"I am delighted to see you looking so bright and blooming,

my dear Mrs. Murray!" exclaimed the old admiral, shaking her warmly by the hand; "it shows that the Highland air agrees with you, notwithstanding your long sojourn in the West Indies."

"Except in being more bracing, the climate differs but little from that to which I was accustomed in the north of Ireland till I grew up; and I was scarcely long enough in the West Indies to become acclimatised," answered Stella, and a shade passed over her countenance as she recollected the trying scenes she had gone through during the time to which the admiral referred.

He observed it, and changed the subject. "And so you are expecting to see our old shipmate, Terence Adair?" he remarked, as he sat himself down in a chair which Murray placed for him. "I shall be heartily glad to shake him by the hand again, and to talk over old times. I haven't forgot his making me carry his portmanteau for him, the rogue!" and the admiral chuckled and laughed, and told Stella the story while he rubbed his hands. "I made him pay, though. He thought he was going to do me out of that, but I was too sharp for him. Ha! ha! ha!" and he laughed till the tears ran down his cheeks. He was becoming more garrulous than before—another sign of advancing age, which Murray was sorry to observe. He told many of his old anecdotes, laughing as heartily at them as ever. He was interrupted by the appearance of Polly, who had been watching for an opportunity of introducing the baby, which she now brought to its mamma.

The admiral started up on seeing it. "What! I hadn't heard of this small stranger!" he exclaimed; "is it a boy or a girl? A fine little creature, at all events! I congratulate you, my dear Mrs. Murray, with all my heart. A sailor's wife is all the better for a few small ones to occupy her thoughts when her 'guid mon,' as you call him in Scotland, is away from home; though I suppose you have no intention of letting Murray go to sea again just yet?"

"I hope not, indeed," answered Stella, turning pale at the thought. "There are numberless officers who have nothing to do on shore, and he has plenty to occupy him."

"But he ought to take a trip to sea, to prevent himself from growing rusty," said the admiral. "We want the best officers to command Her Majesty's ships, and he is among them. You will not contradict me on that point?"

"I am sure he is," said Stella, with a sigh.

"Then, in case the Admiralty require his services, you will not dissuade him from accepting an appointment?"

"Oh, admiral, are they going to send him to sea?" exclaimed Stella suddenly.

"Not that I know of," answered the admiral. "I have not been let into their secret intentions, and I don't wish to act the part of a bird of ill-omen; though I confess that, were he to have the offer of a ship, I should advise him to accept it."

Stella's lips quivered. She had thought herself very heroic, and that she should be ready to sacrifice her husband for the good of his country; but when it came to the point, she could not bear the idea of parting from him.

Alick had gone round to see that the boat's crew were attended to. On coming back, he took another glance through his telescope down the loch. "Here comes the *Stella*; we shall soon have Terence Adair with us!" he exclaimed.

"What brought him home?" asked the admiral. "Surely he went out with Jack Rogers to India?"

"He got an ugly wound in cutting out a piratical junk in the Indian seas," said Murray. "It was a near thing for him, and the doctors insisted on his returning home as the only chance of saving his life; so he wrote me word in a few lines. But he is not much addicted to letter-writing; I, therefore, know no particulars. He will give us the account when he arrives."

Murray stood watching the cutter, while the admiral continued talking to Stella. The little craft, a vessel of about twelve tons, had been built by the young commander soon after he settled at Bercaldine. What naval officer, who has the means in his power, would fail of possessing a vessel of some sort? She was not only a pleasure-yacht, but was useful as a despatch-boat to bring the necessary stores for the house from Oban, and served also for fishing in summer and for wild-fowl shooting in winter. She was a trim yacht, notwithstanding her multifarious employments. Ben Snatchblock, who acted as master, with a stout lad as his crew, was justly proud of her. He boasted that nothing under canvas could beat her, either on a wind or going free, and that in heavy weather she was as lively as a duck. Not a better sea-boat could be found between the mainland and the Hebrides. Indeed, she had often been pretty severely tried; and on one occasion Murray had had the satisfaction of preserving the crew of a wreck on a dangerous reef, when no other craft was at hand to render them assistance. He had, of course, named his yacht the *Stella*; for what other name could he have thought of giving her? He now watched her with the interest which every seaman feels for the vessel he owns, as, close-hauled, she stood up the loch. Now a breeze headed her, and she had to make a couple of tacks or more to weather a point. Now she met a baffling wind, and it seemed impossible that she would do it. "Keep her close, Archie!" exclaimed Murray, as if addressing his cousin; "now keep her full again and shoot her up round the point. That will do it, lad. Capital! Another tack and you will have the wind off the shore; that is only a flaw. Put her about again. With two more tacks you will do it."

The breeze freshening and proving steady, in a short time the *Stella* was near enough to enable Murray to distinguish Terence Adair and another person, in addition to those who had gone away in the yacht. As the jib and foresail were taken off her, she shot up to the buoy. Murray hastened down to the landing-place, in time to meet Adair and the stranger, whom Archie pulled on shore in the punt.

Adair sprang to land with much more agility than the old admiral had exhibited, and was warmly greeted by Murray. "As you told me that Archie was staying with you, I brought that broth of a boy, my nephew, Gerald Desmond, to bear him company and to help keep him out of mischief," exclaimed Adair, turning round and pointing to his nephew, who hung back till his uncle had offered some explanation as to the cause of his appearance uninvited.

"Desmond, you have grown such a strapping fellow that I didn't recognise you," said Murray, putting out his hand. "You are welcome to Bercaldine; and we can easily stow you away in some odd corner or other, notwithstanding your inches. Will you come up to the house with us, or will you wait for Archie?"

"I will wait for Archie, sir, thank you," answered Gerald; and Murray and Adair walked on.

"We have had sad times at Ballymacree," said the latter, speaking in a much graver tone than usual for him. "Gerald only arrived a couple of weeks ago. Although he has grown so much, the climate of the China seas has played havoc with his constitution, and I didn't like to leave him in a house of mourning. His mother died while he was away, and my poor sister Kathleen caught cold, and went off in a rapid consumption a few days after he arrived."

"Your sister Kathleen! to whom Rogers was engaged!" exclaimed Murray; "I am truly sorry to hear it. What a blow for him, too, poor fellow! You said nothing about this in your letter, though I saw that you were in mourning."

"Faith, I hadn't the heart to do so," answered Terence. "I knew that I'd have to tell you all about it, and so I thought it better just to ask the question whether I might come and see you, without saying more, knowing very surely what your answer would be, if I didn't get it—which I didn't, seeing I left home before it arrived; but I suppose it's all right, as Archie said that you were expecting me?"

"Of course, my dear fellow," said Murray. "Poor Jack! Have you written to him?"

"No, but Kathleen did, while she had strength to hold a pen; and her mother put in a few words to tell him that all was over. On my life, I couldn't have done it. Things have gone badly, too, at Ballymacree in other respects. The old place must go, after all; and it will break my father's heart, I am very certain. If we had had a good rattling war, and I had picked up lots of prize-money, I might have saved it. But that is not to be thought of. And then, my dear Murray, a little private affair of my own, which has put me out sadly. I wrote, when I first came home, to Lady Rogers, asking leave to pay a visit at Halliburton Hall. I got an answer from Sir John, very kind and very polite. At the same time, he gave me to understand that he considered it better I should not make my appearance there; in other words, that I wasn't wanted. I fancied that Lucy had begun to care for me, and so Jack thought, I suspect, from what he said when I confessed to him that I was over head and ears in love with his sweet little sister, and had for her sake kept my heart intact, notwithstanding the fascinations of all the charming creatures we met with in the West Indies. So in truth, Murray, I am about as miserable a fellow as any in the three kingdoms just now."

"I am very sorry to hear what you tell me," answered Alick. "We will do our best to cheer you up; and our old friend, Admiral Triton, who arrived a couple of hours ago, will, I am very sure, lend a hand in the good work."

Terence, having unloaded his heart of his griefs, had considerably regained his usual spirits by the time he had got up to the house, and had shaken hands with Stella and the admiral. While he was talking to the latter, Murray hinted to his wife not to ask questions about his family or the Rogers', telling her briefly what had occurred. The admiral immediately attacked Terence about the old story of the portmanteau, and that led him into a whole series of yarns, laughing so heartily himself at them, that Adair was compelled to laugh also.

"You must give me a cruise in the *Stella* to-morrow, Murray," he said; "she will be far the best style of locomotion for me, for these mountains of yours don't suit me—and yet I should like to see something of the magnificent scenery surrounding you." The proposal was at once agreed to, and Stella said that she should like to go also.

Archie and Desmond now arrived, and paid their respects to the admiral. Desmond was introduced in due form to the young heir of Bercaldine.

"Faith, Mrs. Murray, he'll be after making a fine young midshipman one of these days," said Gerald, patting the baby's cheek. "Won't you just let Archie and me take him to sea with us next time we go afloat? We'll watch over him as carefully as any she-nurse can do on shore, and teach him all manner of tricks."

"I daresay you would," said Stella, laughing. "His nautical experiences must be confined at present to a cruise on board the yacht now and then in fine weather, though I don't forget the good care you took of Master Spider on board the *Supplejack*. By the bye, what became of your pet, may I ask?"

"Tom Rogers and I took him with us on board the *Niobe*. He was making immense strides in civilisation, having taken to sleeping in a hammock under bedclothes, and learned to drink tea in a teacup, when he was lost at sea in a gale of wind rounding the Cape. Tom tried to write a poem to his memory, but broke down, declaring that his feelings overcame him; though in truth he couldn't manage to make even the two first lines rhyme, so that that might have had something to do in the matter."

While Gerald was rattling on, Archie produced the letter-bag, which he had hitherto forgotten to give to Commander Murray. It contained several letters for him, as also others forwarded by his navy agent to Lieutenant Adair. Among them were two long, official-looking despatches, with the words, "On Her Majesty's Service," printed outside. Murray looked somewhat grave as he read his; at the same time, an expression arising from gratified pride appeared on his countenance.

Terence tore his letter open. "They don't intend to let me rest on shore, at all events. I expected to have my promotion, however; but instead, their lordships send me off to sea again. I am appointed to the *Opal*, just commissioned at Portsmouth, as first lieutenant. I ought to be highly flattered; and, Desmond, my boy, you are to go with me."

"The best thing that could happen to you; I congratulate you," said the admiral. "And what news does your despatch contain?" he continued, to Murray. Without answering, Alick put the letter into the admiral's hands, and, taking his wife's arm, led her into the garden, where they were concealed from sight by the shrubbery.

"It will be a blow to her," said the admiral, as he glanced over the official document; "still it is flattering to Murray, and, unless he has resolved to give up the service altogether, I could not wish him better luck. You and your old shipmate are not to be parted, Adair. He is appointed to the command of the *Opal*, and I have a notion that she will be stationed at the Cape, and probably sent to the East Coast of Africa, where there is work to be done, and prize-money to be picked up, not to be got every day in these piping times of peace. It is no easy matter, however, to catch those slippery Arab slavers, so you mustn't count your hens before they are hatched. Still, the *Opal* is a fast craft, and if any man can do what is to be done, Murray will do it."

"At all events, I am delighted to hear that I am to serve with him. I was anxious to be off to sea as soon as possible, and it makes amends to me for my disappointment in not getting my promotion."

"I say, Archie, I suppose that you will be appointed to the same craft?" exclaimed Desmond.

"Nae doot about it, mon," answered Archie; "I've a notion it's the doing of our cousin, Admiral M'Alpine, who returned home not long ago from the West Indies, and would of course have been looking after our interests, for he is a very kind man."

"I suspect that Mrs. Murray considers it a very cruel kindness," observed the admiral; "but every sailor's wife must be prepared to be parted from her husband, and to make the most of him when he is on shore."

"He is a lucky fellow who has got a wife to be parted from," said Terence, thinking of Lucy; "at all events, when he is away, he can look forward to the happiness of being again united to her, instead of having to come home, as is the lot of some of us, without anyone who cares for him to give him a welcome; so the favours of Heaven are very fairly divided, and in my opinion Murray has the best of it, though it may give him and his wife a severe pang to part from each other."

"Here they come, and we shall learn how they have settled the matter," observed the admiral; "but as duty has ever been my friend Murray's guiding star, I am very sure that he will not allow his inclination to prevent him from acting as he thinks right, and, unless I am mistaken as to his wife's character, she will not utter a word to prevent him."

No one would have supposed from the countenances of Alick and Stella how much their hearts were agitated. "I am sorry, admiral, we must give up our projected cruise for to-morrow, and cut yours and Adair's visit short, as we shall have much to do in preparing to leave Bercaldine, though I must beg you to stay as long as we remain," said Alick, quite calmly. "We must treat you without ceremony; and I know, Adair, that you and Desmond will lend a hand in setting things in order for our departure."

"Then you have made your mind up to accept the command of the *Opal*?" said the admiral. "I said it would be so; I was sure of it. I must compliment Mrs. Murray, for there are some wives, who don't love their husbands a jot the better, who would have turned the scale the other way. Duty, my lads, duty should carry everything before it," continued the admiral, turning to the midshipmen. "Learn a lesson from your superiors, and never let anything induce you to swerve from duty!"

Murray, of course, had an immense amount of work to get through. It was at once settled that Stella should accompany him to Portsmouth, and should take up her residence in the neighbourhood during his absence. Bercaldine was to be let, and a tenant had to be found, arrangements made with the factor and grieve, and other retainers; various articles to be stored up, and others to be carried with them; the *Stella* to be laid up, and the horses to be sold.

A couple of days thus passed rapidly away, and, all working with a will, the party were ready to start. The rays of the sun, just rising above the lofty summits of the hills, glanced down the loch as they assembled on the landing-place with their dependents, and every cotter on the estate from far and near, who had come to bid them farewell. Many a tear was shed by the females of the family, as Mrs. Murray, the baby and Polly, with the gentlemen of the party, embarked on board the *Stella*, which was to convey them to Oban. The men waved their bonnets, and uttered a prayer in Gaelic that the laird and his good wife and the "bairn" might be brought back to them in safety.

Sail was made, and the little craft glided away from her moorings with a fair breeze down the loch. Mrs. Murray looked with fond regret at the lovely home she was leaving, though no longer the home it had been to her without her husband. The admiral, of course, did his best to keep up her spirits; and whatever Alick might have felt, he was as cheerful as if they were merely making a day's excursion. The scenery around the home he loved so well looked even more attractive than ever. On the port hand Ben Cruachan rose proudly amid the assemblage of craggy heights which extended to the eastward along the shores of the loch. The ruins of Ardchattan Priory, covered with luxuriant ivy, and o'er-canopied by lofty trees, soon came in sight on the starboard side.

"The monks of old, wise in their generation, chose pleasant places for their residences," observed the admiral, pointing to the ruins.

"They must have been of great benefit to the surrounding population in those turbulent times," said Mrs. Murray. "I have sometimes thought that it would be well if they still existed in districts where no landed proprietors live to look after the people."

"Very well in theory, my dear madam," said the admiral; "but we must take into consideration what human nature really is. Monks in many instances proved themselves to be arrant knaves, and among every assemblage of mortals such will ever be found in time to leaven the whole mass. These and friaries and convents were not abolished a day too soon; and, advanced as the present generation esteems itself, I am very sure that if we were to shut up a dozen men together, picked from among the most learned and enlightened students at our universities, or the same number of the most charming women to be found, and insist on their living as celibates to the end of their days, and devoting themselves to a certain routine of strict forms and ceremonies, they would very soon come to loggerheads, and do more harm to themselves and others than they could possibly do good. The wisest men in all the nations of Europe have seen the necessity of abolishing the conventual system, and I cannot suppose that English men and women are more likely to be holy and immaculate than the people of other countries. The whole thing is an illusion; and I am very sure that the system, if, as according to the wishes of some, it should again prevail in England, would only tend to the corruption of those who are beguiled by it, and to the dishonour of true religion."

"You are right, admiral, and certainly my wife does not advocate the re-establishment of monasteries in this country," remarked Alick.

"Oh no, no! I was thinking rather of the past," said Stella; "and probably, if we could look into the interior of convents in their best days, we should see much to grieve and shock us."

The tide was on the ebb, and as the cutter passed through the narrows at Connel Ferry, she pitched and tossed in the turbulent current, here forming a perfect race, in a way which put a stop to further conversation. The breeze being steady, she, however, with Murray's skilful handling, ran through and glided forward on her course. Now Dunstaffnage Castle, standing on a slight elevation near the shore, came in sight—a picturesque ruin, its high walls and round towers rising boldly against the sky. Farther on appeared Dunolly Castle—an ivy-clad, square keep, in former times the seat of the Macdougals of Lorne; and now the cutter entered the bay of Oban, with the long island of Kerrera on the right, and brought up amid a fleet of small craft and coasters. A steamer on her way to Glasgow was waiting for passengers, and the party had just time to get on board before she began paddling on to the southward.

"You will take good care of the craft, Dougal," said Ben Snatchblock, as he handed over his command to the old Highland skipper, into whose charge Murray had given the yacht: "cover her over carefully, and keep the sun from her in summer and the snow in winter, and we'll have many a cruise in her yet when we come back from the East Indies."

"Dinna fash ye, mon; she'll no' take harm under my charge," said Dougal.

"Dougal has been somewhat jealous of Ben on account of his having been appointed to the yacht instead of himself," remarked Alick.

Glasgow was reached before nightfall, and the next morning the whole party started by train for the south. Admiral Triton insisted on accompanying his friends to Portsmouth. "My sister Deborah and I have taken a house on Southsea Common for three years, and you and your wife and bairn must be our guests, and we have a room for Archie till it is time for him to take up his berth on board. You will cheer us up, and we old people want companionship, for I can't get about as I once did; and the young fellows fight shy of me and don't laugh at my yarns, as you and Jack used to do; and I say, Murray, if you want to do me a favour, you will let your wife stay on as our guest. The boy will be a great amusement to us both. We'll not spoil him, depend on that. I then can come and go as I like. And when I am away, she'll help to keep my good sister alive and cheerful. When Deb hasn't me to look after, she's apt to get out of spirits, and to be thinking about her own ailments—fancied more than real, for she is as hearty as she can expect to be at her age; while, if she has a guest and a little child to occupy her thoughts, she'll be perfectly happy and contented; so, you see, you'll be doing her and me the greatest possible favour. Don't say no, but settle the matter at once."

Murray, of course, thanked the admiral very heartily. He was sure that the invitation was given from the kindest of motives, and he fully believed that Stella would contribute greatly to the happiness of the old man and his sister, who, without kith or kin, required someone to solace them in their declining years. He seemed truly grateful when Murray, after talking the matter over with Stella, accepted his kind proposal.

"She mustn't consider herself a mere visitor, but must be as much at home as if Deb were only her housekeeper—that is just what Deb will like. And I must be looked upon as their visitor when I come back from paying a visit to any of my friends who are still willing to receive me; though the only people on whom I can now depend to give me a hearty welcome are Sir John and Lady Rogers; they don't get tired of my yarns, and Sir John laughs at them as heartily as he did many a long year ago."

So the matter was settled; and, on reaching Portsmouth, Murray and Stella accompanied the admiral to his very comfortable house at Southsea, at the entrance door of which Mrs. Deborah Triton—she had taken brevet rank—stood with smiling countenance ready to receive them. It overlooked Spithead and the Isle of Wight, with the Solent stretching away to the westward; the entrance to Portsmouth harbour, with steamers and vessels of all sizes running constantly in and out, being seen at no great distance off across the common. But Sister Deb, as the admiral generally called her, is more worthy of a description than the house. She was remarkably like her brother, except that she had two feet, whereas he lacked one; and that her still plump face was free from the weather-beaten stains contracted by his honest countenance during his days afloat. Her figure was short and round, exhibiting freedom from care—it was such, indeed, as only a good-natured person could possess; but her face was the index of her mind and heart. That bore an unmistakable expression of kindness, gentleness, and good-temper, which perfect faith in the simple truths of Christianity could alone give. Murray felt perfectly confident that his wife and child would be in good keeping during his absence, and his heart felt lightened of one of its chief cares.

Next morning, Murray, accompanied by Archie, went on board the *Opal*, which, having just been brought out of dock, lay alongside the hulk. She was still in the hands of the riggers, who, busy as bees, swarmed in every part, rattling down the rigging, swaying up the topmasts, and getting the yards across. Her appearance in that condition was not attractive; but as he surveyed her with a seaman's eye, he felt satisfied that she was a fast craft, and well calculated for the service on which she was to be sent.

"I have no wish to command a steamer, but I cannot help fancying that a pair of paddles would be more likely to catch the Arab dhows we are to go in search of than is the fastest craft under canvas," he observed to Adair, whom he found on board.

They at once set to work to collect a crew, in which business Ben Snatchblock was especially active. Ben a few days afterwards received, to his satisfaction, his warrant as boatswain, his zeal being considerably enlivened thereby. He, before long, managed to pick up a number of prime hands from among his old shipmates, on whom he could thoroughly depend. The gunner and carpenter joined the same day he got his warrant. The former, Timothy Ebbs, was a little man, but he had a big voice and a prodigious pair of black whiskers, which, sticking out on either side of his face, gave him a sufficiently ferocious aspect to inspire ship-boys and other young members of the crew with the necessary amount of awe; while the able seamen respected him for his tried courage and undoubted nautical experience. Adair was very glad to find that Jos Green was appointed as master, as he had known him well when he was second master of the *Tudor*, in the West Indies, and a more merry, kind-hearted, better-disposed fellow never stepped. Jos, it was said, never went anywhere without finding friends, or came away without having made fresh ones. Adair, Archie, and Gerald, with all the officers who had as yet been appointed to the corvette, took up their quarters on board, and the work of fitting out made rapid progress.

"I wonder whom we shall have for our second lieutenant?" said Gerald, as they were sitting in the berth; "an old shipmate or a new one? I hope we may get a good sort of a fellow. I should like to have old Higson. What a good-natured chap he was!"

"That was when he was first promoted; he may have grown rusty by this time, at not getting another step," observed Archie. "He is older than the captain, and yet junior to Mr. Adair."

On going on deck soon afterwards, an officer came up the side, who introduced himself to Terence as Lieutenant Frank Mildmay, come to join the *Opal* as second lieutenant. No two persons could be more dissimilar than the first and second lieutenants of the corvette. He had a smooth face with pink cheeks, whiskers curled to a nicety, and hair carefully brushed. His figure was slight and refined, and he wore lilac kid gloves, his appearance being certainly somewhat effeminate; indeed, he looked as if he had just come out of a bandbox.

"He'll never set the Thames on fire," observed Paddy Desmond to Archie. "Faith, the men will be after calling him Mr. Mild*man*, unless he condescends to dip those delicate paws of his into the tar-bucket."

The men probably looked on their second lieutenant with much the same feelings as did the two midshipmen; while he, regardless of what they thought of him, accompanied Adair into the gun-room to make himself acquainted with the rest of his messmates. The remainder of the gun-room officers and midshipmen joined the next day, and, the complement of the crew being made up, the corvette, casting off from the hulk, took up her moorings in the middle of the harbour. Of the new-comers, two small midshipmen, who had never before been to sea, Paddy Desmond immediately designated one "Billy Blueblazes," in consequence of his boasting that he was related to an admiral of that name, while the other was allowed to retain his proper appellation of "Dicky Duff," Paddy declaring that it required no reformation. An old mate who was always grumbling, and two young ones who had just passed their examination, with an assistant-surgeon, two clerks, and a master's assistant, made up the mess; and pretty closely stowed they were in the narrow confines of the berth. The only other person worthy of note was the third warrant-officer, the carpenter, who rejoiced in the designation of Caractacus Chessle, the name of the British hero having been bestowed on him by his father, who had once on a time been a stage-player. He was as tall and bulky as the gunner was short and wiry; indeed, the three warrant-officers formed a strange contrast with each other.

Murray frequently came on board to see how things were getting on, but never interfered with Adair's arrangements. He was sometimes accompanied by Admiral Triton, who seemed to take almost as much interest as he did in fitting out the ship. The sails were now bent, and Murray waited in daily expectation of receiving his sailing orders. Meantime, the kind admiral and his sister were moved with the thoughts of poor Stella's approaching bereavement, and, knowing nothing of Adair's attachment, he got Deb to write to Lady Rogers, inviting one of her daughters to pay them a visit, and assist in taking care of Mrs. Murray. As it happened, he said nothing of the first lieutenant of the *Opal*, and Sir John and her ladyship, supposing that Adair was at Ballymacree, made no objection to Lucy's accepting the invitation. She accordingly, much to Murray's satisfaction, arrived the very day the ship was ready for sea. It so fell out that Adair, who had managed to escape from his multifarious duties, and was not aware of her coming, called to pay a farewell visit at the house. He was ushered into the drawing-room, where a lady was seated with a book in her hand, though her eyes were oftener cast over the blue ocean than at its pages.

The servant announced his name; the lady rose from her seat, and gazed at him with a look in which surprise was mingled with pleasure, a rich blush suffusing her countenance. "Mr. Adair!" she exclaimed, holding out her hand, which Terence took, and seemed very unwilling to relinquish. Nor did she withdraw it.

"I thought you were at Ballymacree," she said. "I was very sorry that papa thought it right not to accept your proposal to pay us a visit at Halliburton while Jack was absent, but, believe me, he did not intend to be unkind."

"I felt that, though it made me very unhappy," answered Terence; "but did you wish me to come?"

"Yes," said Lucy, "I should have been very glad to see you; I should not be speaking the truth if I did not say so."

"Then, if I get my promotion and come back with lots of prize-money, may I hope"—

"Pray don't speak about that," answered Lucy, growing agitated; "I can make no promise without papa's sanction, and I have already said enough to show that I am not indifferent to you."

Terence was an Irishman, and Irishmen are not wont to be bashful, but at that moment Alick and Stella entered the room, not failing to remark the confusion their appearance created. Terence, of course, explained that he had called, not expecting to see Miss Rogers, but had come to pay his respects to Mrs. Murray. She tried to send her husband out of the room, intending to follow, but he would not take the hint; and Terence, who had but a short time to spare, was compelled at length to pay his adieux without eliciting the promise he wished from Lucy. She looked very sorry when he had gone, but probably was the better able, from sympathy, to afford consolation to poor Stella, when the moment for her parting with her husband arrived. That moment came the very next day. It need not be dwelt on. Stella's lot was that which numberless wives of naval officers have to endure; but, though widely shared, her grief was not the less poignant as she watched with tearful eyes through the admiral's spy-glass the corvette under all sail standing down the Solent.

CHAPTER II

Crossing the Equator—Billy Blueblazes looks out for the Line, but does not see it—He and Gerald mastheaded—Tristan d'Acunha: Jos Green, as usual, "meets with a Friend"—The Opal at the Cape—Sails for Madagascar—Commodore Douce of the Radiant—A Boat Expedition up the Angoxa River—The Slavers' Stronghold—Mildmay's Sonnet interrupted by the Guns of the Fort—Attack on the Slave Dhows—The Commodore is landed by Tom Bashan—Capture of the Fort—Crossing the Bar.

HER MAJESTY'S corvette *Opal*, under all sail, was slowly gliding across the line, for which Dicky Duff and Billy Blueblazes were eagerly looking out, Paddy Desmond having assured them that if they watched fast enough they would be sure to see it. Mr. Mildmay, being addicted to poetry, was busily engaged in writing a sonnet on the subject, which, however, did not corroborate Gerald's statement, as it began, "Ideal cincture which surrounds the globe"; but as he was interrupted by Ben Snatchblock's pipe summoning the crew to exercise at the guns, the second line was not written, when Jos Green caught sight of the MS. which he had left on the gun-room table.

"I say, Desmond, Dicky and I have been looking out this last hour or more for the line, and haven't sighted it yet," said Billy.

"Of course not; and you never will on deck. You should go to the foretop-gallant-masthead; you will see it clearly from thence, if you keep your eyes open wide enough; but if not, you have no chance."

"But if we do, we shall miss Neptune's visit. I suppose he'll be on board us before long?" answered Billy.

"Of course he will, if he doesn't happen to be otherwise engaged; but he has plenty of work on hand just now, and is just as likely as not paying a visit to some other ship away to the eastward. You see, he can't be everywhere at the same time. Or maybe his children have got the measles or whooping-cough, and of course he wouldn't like to leave them, especially if his wife happens to be out marketing. He's a domestic old fellow, and the best of husbands and fathers. So you youngsters mustn't depend on seeing him; and lucky for you, too; for his barber would be after shaving your chins off, seeing you've nothing else round your faces for him to operate on."

Paddy, the rogue, knew very well that the commander did not intend to allow the once usual frolics and gambols to take place; the time-honoured custom having, of late years, been generally abandoned on board Her Majesty's ships of war, as has the barbarous custom of burning Guy Fawkes been given up on shore by the more enlightened of our times; albeit the fifth of November and the lesson it teaches should never be forgotten.

The two midshipmen, who mustered a binocular between them, thus instigated by Paddy, made their way aloft, where, for their own pleasure, they remained looking out for Mr. Mildmay's "ideal cincture" with the utmost patience, though they would have grumbled greatly had they been ordered up for punishment. At length they were espied by the first lieutenant. "What are you two youngsters doing up there aloft?" he shouted.

"Looking for the line, sir," was the answer, in Billy's shrill voice.

"Then remain till you see it, or till I call you down!" cried Adair. "I say, Gerald, you've been after bamboozling those youngsters," he added, as he caught sight of a broad grin on his nephew's face. "Go up to the maintop-gallant-masthead, and assist them in looking out for the line. Perhaps you will sight it sooner than they will, and it will help you to correct your day's work."

Gerald, pulling a long face, began to ascend the rigging, greatly to the amusement of Archie and his other messmates.

"I say, Adair, you're somewhat hard upon the youngsters," observed the commander, who had just then come on deck. "You remember that Rogers and you and I thought ourselves severely dealt with when we three had to grace the mastheads of the old *Racer*."

"Faith, but I think we were rightly punished, and that's the reason I sent Desmond aloft, and allowed the other youngsters to remain where they had gone of their own accord."

"You forget that the sun is somewhat hot, and they may come down by the run and knock their brains out; so don't you think it would be better to call them down presently, and give

Master Gerald a lecture on the impropriety of playing on the credulity of his younger messmates?"

Of course Adair did as the commander wished, though he had some difficulty in keeping his countenance when he called up the three youngsters before him to receive his lecture.

"Remember, Master Desmond, if you begin by bamboozling, you may end by practising more serious deceptions on your fellows; so let me advise you in future to restrain your propensity in that direction," he wound up by saying, with as grave a countenance as he could command. He then informed the youngsters that the line was only imaginary, to denote the sun's course round the globe.

"An 'ideal cincture,' you will understand, youngsters," observed the master, who had heard Adair's remarks, giving at the same time a nod to Mr. Mildmay, who blushed an acknowledgment of being the author of the poetical simile.

The two youngsters were very greatly disappointed when they found that they had got some way to the south of the line without having made acquaintance with Neptune and his charming family.

Rio was at length reached, and Gerald and Archie had time to pay visits, in company with the good-natured master, to many of the localities with which they were acquainted when there before, though unable to get up the harbour, as they wished to call on the officious old magistrate, the Juiz da Fora who had imprisoned them and Higson. They remained, however, only long enough to take in a stock of fresh provisions and water, and then steered eastward across the Atlantic to the Cape of Good Hope.

About sixteen days after leaving Rio, land was sighted.

"What, have we got to the Cape already?" exclaimed Desmond, who heard the cry from aloft.

"No, my lad; if you had been attending to your day's work you wouldn't have asked the question," answered Green. "The land ahead is the island of Tristan d'Acunha, not the most delectable of spots for the residents, though I believe there are some on it. We are going to put in to get some more fresh mutton and beef, with any vegetables they are able to spare."

"Hands shorten sail and bring ship to an anchor!" shouted Adair soon afterwards, and the corvette brought up before a green slope, spotted with small whitewashed buildings, the hill becoming more rough and craggy till it reached an elevation of eight thousand feet above the sea. The other side of the island, as they afterwards discovered, rose sheer out of the water in a vast precipice to the summit. Between the anchorage and the shore was a prodigious mass of enormous seaweeds, inside of which the water was perfectly calm, forming a safe harbour for small craft. Off it appeared two small islands, known as Inaccessible and Nightingale. To the latter, Billy and Dicky Duff were anxious to go and catch some of the birds, from which, as they were informed by the irrepressible Paddy Desmond, the island took its name. Its feathered inhabitants are, however, only the wild sea-fowl which seek their prey from among the denizens of the ocean.

"You will not find any friends here, Jos, I suppose?" said Adair to the master.

"It is possible, as I have never been off the place before," answered Jos; "but still I am never surprised at meeting someone who knows me. Once, when pulling up the Nun, in Africa, on the first visit I paid to that delectable stream, as I happened to be remarking that I had no friends there, at all events, a black, who had swum off from the shore, put his head over the bows and exclaimed, 'Massa Green, glad to see you. What! sure you 'member Jiggery Pop, who served aboard the *Frisky*, at the Cape?' And sure enough I remembered Jiggery well, seeing that I had once picked him out of the water when he was near drowning, and he had served me the same good turn."

While Jos was narrating this anecdote, a boat, pulled by half a dozen stout seamen in blue and red shirts, was coming off from the shore to the ship. Without ceremony they stepped on board, when one of them, coming aft, touched his hat to the master. "You'll remember me, sir. Served with you aboard the *Pantaloon*. I'm Jerry Bird."

"Glad to see you, Jerry; you saved me from being cut down when we had that affair out in the Pacific."

"No, sir, I think it was t'other way," said Jerry; "I haven't forgotten it, I can tell you, sir."

"Well, it was one or the other," observed Green. "Tell me what brought you to this out-of-the-way place?"

"Couldn't help it, sir—ship cast ashore, and I was the only one to get to land alive, and have been living here ever since; but, if so be the captain will ship me aboard, I'll enter at once."

As Jerry was a prime hand, the offer was not likely to be refused, and he was entered accordingly.

A boat with several officers visited the shore, making their way, not without difficulty, through the floating breakwater of seaweed. The inhabitants, consisting of about forty men, women, and children, gathered on the beach to welcome them in front of their little stone-boxes of dwellings which were scattered about here and there. They appeared to be a primitive race, the descendants of two old men-of-war's men, who, having been discharged from the service at the end of the last century, had lived there ever since with wives whom they had brought from the Cape, their respective children and grandchildren having intermarried. Their wealth consisted in bullocks and flocks of sheep, which, having increased in the same proportion as their owners, were now very numerous. Their carcases, as well as the skins and wool, were exchanged for such luxuries as they required with the skippers of ships calling off their island. Here the old patriarchs, with their families, had dwelt for well-nigh half a century or more, knowing little of what was going forward in the world, and by the world unknown.

The *Opal*, having supplied herself with a stock of fresh provisions, once more weighed anchor, carrying off Green's old shipmate, Jerry Bird, who seemed heartily glad to get away from his friends, whom he described in no very flattering colours. After a run of twelve days, the *Opal* came in sight of the Cape, but it was night before she dropped her anchor in Simon's Bay. Dark masses of land were seen towering above her mastheads, and rows of light streaming from the main-deck ports of two frigates, between which she took up her berth; while the sound of bugles coming across the water betokened the neighbourhood of troopships, with redcoats on board, bound out to India, or returning home. It reminded those whose thoughts were with the loved ones in Old England, to lose no time in sitting down to their desks. Of course the commander wrote to his wife, and Adair humbly requested that he might be allowed to enclose a letter to Lucy, in case, as he observed, she might still be staying with Mrs. Deborah Triton. They both also wrote to the kind old admiral.

As the morning broke, a ship was seen standing out of the harbour, and a boat sent with a well-filled letter-bag to overtake her. How hard the crew pulled! for they knew by the commander's manner that he intended that letter-bag to be put on board. They did it, however,—as British seamen generally do whatever they are ordered,—though at no small expenditure of muscular strength, and, of course, received, well pleased, a glass of grog on their return on board.

The *Opal* remained but a short time at the Cape. Murray received orders to follow the *Radiant*, one of the frigates seen on the night of her arrival, to the Mozambique Channel, as soon as she had filled up with water and other stores.

The corvette made but a short stay, and again sailed for St. Augustine's Bay, at the southern end of Madagascar, which island was sighted in little more than a fortnight. The *Radiant* was found at anchor in the bay, Commodore Douce, who commanded her, having put in to water the ship.

Murray went on board to pay his respects and receive his orders, and numerous visits were exchanged between the two ships. The commodore, a remarkably small man with a fiery countenance, overshadowed by a prodigious cocked hat, was walking the deck with hasty strides as Murray came up the side.

"I have been expecting you here for three days, at least, Commander Murray," he exclaimed, as Alick made his bow. "There is work to be done, and the sooner it is done the better. I have received notice that a piratical band of Arabs, who have long had possession of a strong fort up the river Angoxa, have a number of barracoons full of slaves and several dhows lying under the protection of their guns. I have resolved to make a dash up the river to cut out the vessels, capture the slaves, and destroy the fort."

"I am very glad to hear it, sir," answered Murray, "and will send my boats on shore to procure water immediately, so that we may be ready to sail with as little delay as possible. The men, when they hear the object, will work with a will, you may depend on that, commodore; and I trust that the crew of the *Opal* is not to be surpassed in smartness by that of any other ship in commission. I think that you will acknowledge that when you have an opportunity of judging."

"Well, well, you brought-to in very good style, I must confess that," answered the commodore, who, though inclined to be irascible, was quickly appeased. "When you send your boats on shore, let the officers in command keep an eye on the natives, and take care that none of the crew stray. The people about here are treacherous rascals, and would murder anyone they could catch hold of without any provocation. I'll send three of the frigate's boats to assist you, and order the crew of one of them to remain on guard while the others are filling the casks."

The news which Murray took when he returned on board made everyone alive. In a few minutes the boats were ready to shove off. The brown-skinned natives kept hovering about all the time, seeing the sailors engaged in filling the casks; and it was very evident that, had they dared, they would have treated their visitors as the commodore had thought probable. Not long before, in the bay, a short distance to the northward, the inhabitants had murdered an officer and boat's crew, without, as far as could be ascertained, the slightest provocation. Murray was therefore thankful when his boats returned safely on board.

Leaving St. Augustine's Bay, the frigate and corvette sailed across the Mozambique Channel, and came to an anchor off the mouth of the Angoxa. During the passage, every possible preparation was made for the intended expedition; the firearms were looked to, cutlasses sharpened; the surgeons packed up their instruments, bandages, and medicines. The Arabs were not fellows to yield without a determined struggle, and some sharp fighting was expected. About midway across the channel, a thin wreath of smoke was observed to the southward. "A steamer in sight, standing this way, sir," reported Adair to the commander. "The commodore has made the signal to heave-to."

In a short time the steamer got near enough to allow her number to be made out. "The *Busy Bee*," reported Archie, who was acting as signal midshipman. The commodore directed her to join company; her boats would be an important addition to the proposed expedition. The three vessels now stood on to the mouth of the river, off which they brought up, for the depth of water on the bar was not sufficient to allow even the *Busy Bee* to enter. The boats were therefore immediately lowered, those considering themselves most fortunate who had to go in them; and it was hoped that by pulling up at once the Arabs might be taken by surprise. The frigate sent four boats, the corvette three, and the steamer two of her paddle-box boats and a gig. The larger boats were armed with guns in their bows, capable of carrying shell, grape, and canister, as well as round shot. The crews were provided with muskets, pistols, and cutlasses; and all formed a pretty strong body, against which the Arabs were not likely to make any effectual stand. All hands were in high spirits—there is nothing Jack enjoys so much as an expedition on shore, whether for fighting or for a game of cricket. Provisions for three days were stowed away in the boats, with plenty of ammunition, and numerous articles, including pots and pans for cooking, blanket-frocks and trousers, blankets and other means for making themselves comfortable at night. The surgeons did not forget a supply of quinine to mix with the men's grog, the only way in which they could be induced to swallow the extract, albeit the only reliable preventive for fever.

Jos Green was much disappointed at being compelled to remain in charge of the corvette. "I fully expected to find some old friend or other among the Arabs or captured slaves; however, give my kind regards to anyone who knows me, and say I shall be happy to see them on board," he exclaimed, as Terence went down the side.

Murray went in his gig, accompanied by Archie; Adair had command of the pinnace, a mate and Desmond going with him; Mr. Mildmay commanded the cutter, accompanied by Billy Blueblazes; and Dicky Duff was in the boatswain's boat. The commodore led the expedition in his own gig, in the stem of which sat, as coxswain, Tom Bashan, noted as the biggest man in the fleet—even the carpenter of the *Opal* looked but of ordinary size alongside him. He had followed Captain Douce from ship to ship, and had often rendered his commander essential service, when the little man might otherwise have come to serious grief. Bashan had the affection for his chief which a nurse entertains for the child under her charge, and considered it his especial duty, as far as he had power, to keep him out of harm—not that the commodore ever suspected that his subordinate entertained such a notion; he always spoke of him as an honest, harmless fellow, who knew his duty and did it.

The bar being tolerably smooth, the boats crossed without any accident, the crews giving way with a will up the river. The tide was flowing, so they made rapid progress.

"This is something like our expedition up the San Juan de Nicaragua," observed Desmond to Adair. "Except that we had white fellows to fight instead of Arabs, and a hot stream to pull against instead of having the tide with us."

"The tide will turn before long," answered Adair; "and if the boats get aground we may find these same Arabs rather tough customers. However, we must look out to avoid the contingency, and if we can take the fellows by surprise, we may manage to get hold of a good number of slaves."

The tide before long, as Adair predicted, began to ebb, and the boats made much slower progress than before. It was nearly nightfall when they got up to Monkey Island, inside of which the commodore ordered them to anchor; the boats being brought up close together, the awnings were spread, the mainbrace spliced, and other preparations made for passing the night. An extra allowance was served out to induce the men to swallow the quinine mixed with it; for though some made wry faces, their love of grog induced them to overcome their objection to the bitter taste.

After the grog, songs were sung alternately by the crew of each boat, the commodore, who had nothing of the martinet about him, being always ready to encourage his men to amuse themselves harmlessly; and they were yet too far off from the fort to run any risk of their approach being betrayed by their voices.

"Sweethearts and wives," sung out a voice from one of the boats, and was taken up by the rest, as the last drop of grog was drained. Murray and Adair drank the toast heartily, though in a less demonstrative manner than their companions, who possibly might have been very little troubled with the thoughts of either wives or sweethearts. No one for the time dwelt on the somewhat serious work on which they were likely to be engaged the next day. At length, each man looked out for the softest plank he could find, and turned in to sleep, the officers enjoying no more luxurious couches than their inferiors; to some poor fellows it might be the last rest they were to take here below.

A look-out, however, was kept, in case any of the Arab dhows should slip down the river. Two of the gigs were sent alternately ahead to watch for any craft which might come in sight. None, however, were seen, and just as the first streaks of daylight appeared in the sky, the commodore gave the order to "pipe to breakfast." Fires were lighted on the island, and cocoa and coffee warmed up, while another dose of quinine was served out to each man.

The operation did not take long, and once more the flotilla advanced, the tide carrying them rapidly up the river. About noon, as the sun was beating down with tremendous force, Angoxa came in sight, with, as the commodore had expected from the information he had received, several dhows at anchor before it under the protection of its guns. Directly the boats rounded the last point, which had before concealed their approach, the red flag was hoisted above the fort, and at the same time the loud sounds of the beating of tom-toms and drums commenced, continuing incessantly, as if to intimidate the English tars and induce them to pull back again to their ships.

The men laughed. "What a row them niggers do kick up! I wonder whether they think we're going back frightened by all their tom-tomming. We'll show them presently that we've got some chaps aboard which will bark not a little louder and do a precious deal more harm," exclaimed Ben Snatchblock, who accompanied Mr. Mildmay in one of the *Opal's* boats. That young officer took things very coolly. He was observed with his notebook jotting down his thoughts, but whether in the form of a poetical effusion or not, Billy Blueblazes, who was beside him, could not ascertain, though he tried hard to do so.

"The great Wolfe recited poetry when about to die in the arms of victory on the heights of Abraham," observed Mr. Mildmay to the midshipman; "do you recall the lines to your memory, Billy? What were they?"

"I think, sir, they were something about 'the curfew tolling the knell of parting day,' but I can never recollect more of the poem."

"Ah! so they were—let me see," and the lieutenant bit the end of his pencil. "'As Britain's tars who plough the mighty deep.'"

"'Sheep' or 'sleep' come in rhyme with 'deep,'" suggested Billy.

"Be silent—I want a grander term," said the lieutenant. "'Where waves on waves in wild confusion leap'—that's fine isn't it?"

"Yes, sir," said Billy. "We're up an African river, and are going to lick a lot of blackamoors; you'll have a difficulty in bringing blackamoor into your lines, I've a notion."

"Of course I should call them Arabs, their proper designation, when I get as far," replied Mr. Mildmay.

Just then the boat grounded, as did several others near her, and there the whole flotilla lay in sight of the fort, outside of which appeared a number of barracoons, but whether full of slaves or not it was impossible to say. The unavoidable delay of the leading boats enabled the others to overtake them; and as the tide rose, their crews shoved them over the shoals, and once more they advanced in line abreast. Their progress was slow; again several of the larger boats grounded, and the whole, consequently, had to wait till the rising tide floated them. The next time they grounded, the Arabs seemed to have discovered that they were within range of the eight guns mounted on the fort, as well indeed as the muskets of the large party sent out along the bank. The latter, as well as the guns in the fort, now began blazing away, shot and bullets flying thickly over and around the boats. Mr. Mildmay at this juncture thought it as well to put his notebook into his pocket. The boats' guns, however, were not to be idle; the commander gave the order to fire, and immediately they opened with spherical case-shot, grape and canister, the former thrown with great accuracy into the middle of the fort, while the latter quickly sent some of the swarthy heroes under shelter, and put the greater number to flight. Several of the men in the boats had been hit, which excited the eagerness of the crews to get at the foe. The first thing, however, to be done was to destroy the dhows. As the boats worked their way up over the shoals towards them, a hot fire was opened from those lowest down. This was quite sufficient to show their character, and the marines and small-armed men began peppering away at every Arab turban or cap of which they could catch sight, while the shells and grape prevented the enemy from returning to their guns in the fort. The tide, rushing in more rapidly than before, quickly enabled the smaller boats, led by Adair, to get up to the dhows. He was the first on board the largest, a craft of a hundred tons or more. Her crew, having had no time to escape, fought desperately. Some were cut down, and the rest driven overboard, not a human being remaining alive on board. She was at once set on fire, and the rest of the dhows were attacked in the same manner in succession. On board, some resistance was offered, but the crews of others, leaping overboard, attempted to save themselves by swimming to the shore. As there was no object in carrying any of them off, they were all burned, there being no doubt of their piratical character.

Though the guns in the fort were for the time silenced, they were still capable of mischief, and the commodore wisely resolved entirely to destroy the hornets' nest. "We must land, Commander Murray, and drive the enemy into the woods, burn their stockade, spike their guns, and tumble them into the river," he shouted. The first part of the business, on which the rest depended, was not so easily accomplished. The banks shelved so gradually that the boats grounded when still some twenty yards or more from the shore. The rising of the tide would in time carry them nearer; but in the interval they were exposed to a galling fire from the enemy, who were under shelter both in the fort and in several other spots along the bank; while, in all probability, before the fighting on shore was over the tide would again ebb and leave the boats high and dry, exposed to the attacks of the numerous bands who were gathering on the spot in the hope of wreaking their vengeance on their foes. Still the plucky little commodore, in spite of all risks, was determined to carry his plan into execution. The commanders of the boats received orders to sweep round in line, run their bows as far up as they could, and while the enemy were driven from the banks by showers of grape and canister, the marines and small-armed men were to land and attack them with the bayonet should they attempt to make a stand.

The order was quickly obeyed; the guns from the larger boats sent forth so deadly a shower of missiles that the Arabs, who were coming down in force to dispute their landing, took to flight, leaving many dead and wounded. The difficulty was now to get on shore; the bottom was likely to be muddy, the water tolerably deep. Murray and Adair, with their boats' crews, were among the first to gain a footing on dry land. The commodore was eager to be up with them, but, at the same time, was very unwilling to get wet. Tom Bashan, having stepped out into the mud, received orders from his chief to lift him on his shoulders and carry him on shore. Tom, who had his musket in his right hand, did as he was ordered by taking the little commodore up with his left arm and placing him behind his back, where the brave leader of the expedition sat, his head just above Tom's grinning countenance, while he waved his sword with no little risk of cutting off his coxswain's nose, shouting in his eagerness, "On, my lads! on! form on the beach as you land—skirmishers to the front. Now let the brown-skinned rascals see what British sailors are made of!"

The marines, who had landed by the time the commodore had been deposited by Tom on the ground, formed in good order, with parties of bluejackets on either flank. The Arabs appeared to be taken completely by surprise, never apparently supposing that the British would leave their boats. They had halted at some distance, and looked a formidable body, ten times more numerous than those who were about to attack them; while the commodore, nothing daunted, waving his sword and dashing forward, shouted, "Charge, my lads! charge!"

The British bayonets gleamed brightly in the sun, as, with steady tramp, the line of redcoats and bluejackets advanced at the charge. The Arabs fired a round, the scimitars of their leaders flashing for a few seconds, and then, unable to face the bristling wall of bayonets, their courage gave way, and they fled helter-skelter for safety towards the neighbouring woods. The English pursued them for some distance, firing as they advanced, and halting only to give sufficient time to reload. If they advanced too far, as the fort was yet unsubdued, there was a risk of a sally being made from it and the boats being destroyed. The commodore, carried away by his ardour, had already gone farther than was wise. Discovering his error, he ordered his followers to fall back as rapidly as possible on the boats.

Just then a strong body of men were seen issuing from the fort. Not a moment was to be lost, or they might reach the boats. The commodore was pretty well blown by his recent exercise, but, putting forth all his strength, he led his men back even faster than they had come. As soon as the enemy saw their approach, they hastily retreated within the stockades.

"Now, my lads," cried the commodore, "we have the last part of the business to accomplish. Before a quarter of an hour is over, we must be inside that fort. I know that you can do it, and will do it."

The men replied by a loud cheer, and advanced, in high spirits at their previous success, towards the stockades. The Arabs, who had seen their friends beaten, lost heart from the first; and though they defended the stockades for some minutes with considerable bravery, they quickly took to flight as the bluejackets came tumbling down over their heads, cutlass in hand. In a few minutes the place was won, the garrison escaping by a western gate, as the English forced their way in over the eastern side. The commodore's first impulse was to follow the enemy, but there were still too many people in the fort to make such a proceeding safe. The non-combatants, women and children, received orders to take themselves off with such of their personal property as they could carry, an act of leniency which surprised them not a little. In a short time not a single inhabitant remained behind.

The guns were then spiked and dragged to a part of the fort directly over the stream, into which they were tumbled, and from whence it would give the Arabs no small amount of trouble to fish them out again. The place was next set on fire in every direction, when the party, each man carrying such booty as he had managed to pick up, left the fort to the destruction awaiting it. The flames spread amid the wooden and thatch-roof buildings, till the surrounding stockades caught fire, and the whole hornets' nest was one sea of flame.

The barracoons, from which the slaves had, as it was expected, been removed, were treated in the same manner, when the commodore, highly satisfied with the result of the expedition, ordered the men to embark. To get the heavy boats afloat, however, was no easy matter; the tide had already begun to ebb; it seemed very doubtful whether they could be got off, till the crews, putting their shoulders under the gunwales, lifted them by sheer strength into deeper water. Before a single man attempted to get on board, the gallant commodore, who, though not afraid of the hottest fire, had an especial dread of getting wet, was again carried for some distance on Bashan's shoulders, till he was safely deposited in the sternsheets of his boat, where the giant, with dripping clothes, followed him.

Further delay would have been dangerous, as, the channel being unknown, the boats might at any moment get aground, and be left there by the rapidly-falling tide. It was, besides, important, for the sake of the wounded men, to return as soon as possible to the ships. Although not a man had been hit on shore, either when attacking the enemy in the open or storming the fort, during the first part of the day several casualties had occurred; two poor fellows had been killed, and six others had been wounded, one very severely. Excepting, however, on board the boat in which the dead bodies lay, the men were in as high spirits as usual, exulting in the success of the expedition. Now and then they restrained their mirth, as first one and then another of the boats grounded, and there seemed a probability that the rest would share their fate. They, however, were got off, and the flotilla continued its course down the stream, one boat following the other in line.

They reached their anchorage inside Monkey Island soon after darkness came on. Though the water was here of sufficient depth, even at low tide, to allow the boats to keep afloat, and, the dhows having been destroyed, they could not be assailed from above, still their dangers and difficulties were not over; for, should their position be discovered, a force might gather on the banks, and cause them considerable annoyance. During the night, therefore, the men were ordered to keep their arms by their sides, ready for instant use—it being impossible to say at what moment they might be attacked.

The bar, also, had to be crossed. It was sufficiently smooth when they came over it, but how it would be on their return was the question. Those who had before been on the coast declared that they had frequently seen a surf breaking over it in which even a lifeboat could scarcely live.

"Faith, Archie, we've had a jolly day of it," remarked Desmond, whose boat was lying alongside that of the commander of the *Opal*; "if this is the sort of fun we're generally to have, I'm mighty glad we came out here."

"Small fun for the poor fellows who have been shot," answered Archie; "I hear one of them groaning terribly; the sooner we get back to the ships the better for them."

"Faith, it isn't pleasant to have a shot through one, and I hope that won't be our lot," said Desmond. "I only wish Tom Rogers was with us. From what I hear, the boats of the squadron are constantly sent away on separate cruises to look after slavers, and it would be capital if we could get sent off on a cruise together—much more amusing than having to stick on board the ship with the humdrum, everyday routine of watches and musters and divisions."

To this, of course, Archie agreed. The youngsters, forgetting that their commander was close to them, were chattering away in somewhat loud voices, when Murray ordered them to knock off talking, and to turn in and go to sleep. The night passed away quietly, and all hoped to get on board their respective ships at an early hour the next morning.

After the men had breakfasted on the island, the squadron of boats, led by their gallant commodore, pulled down with the ebb towards the mouth of the river, up which a stiffish breeze was blowing, just sufficient to ripple over the surface of the water glittering in the rays of the rising sun. On either hand rose a forest of tall trees, their feathery tops defined against the clear blue sky. In a short time the ships could be discerned in the offing, rolling their masts ominously from side to side, while ahead rose a threatening wall of white foam, extending directly across the river's mouth. The crew of the commodore's boat ceased pulling, and the other boats as they came up followed their example.

"Here we are, caught like mice in a trap, gentlemen!" exclaimed Adair, as Murray and the commander of the *Busy Bee* came up alongside him.

"It will be madness to attempt forcing the boats through yonder breakers; the largest would be swamped directly she got among them," observed Murray. "It's now nearly low tide; but perhaps at the top of high-water they may prove less formidable, and we may be able to get out. We shall, at all events, have to wait till then."

As the boats, during this conversation, had been carried somewhat close to the dangerous breakers, the commodore ordered them to pull round and to make their way some little distance up the river, where the men could lie on their oars and wait for an opportunity of crossing the bar. Many an eye was turned towards the shore, where a game of leap-frog or some other amusement could be indulged in, but not a spot appeared on which they could land. The sun rose higher and higher in the sky, his rays beating down on their heads and blistering their noses and cheeks, while the stock of water and other liquids which had been brought rapidly diminished.

"I hope that we shall be able to get out when the tide rises," said Desmond to Adair; "if not, I've a notion that we shall be pretty hard pressed."

"So have I," said Adair; "but it is possible that the bar may remain in its present state for several days together, and, if so, we shall have to forage on shore for whatever food we can pick up. It may not be so easy to find pure water, though."

"For my part, I should be ready to drink ditch-water," exclaimed Desmond; "I never felt so thirsty in my life."

Many others were in the same condition as Paddy, but no one complained. A small quantity only remained, which was willingly given up for the use of the poor wounded men, who of course suffered greatly. Hour after hour passed by, and anxious eyes were cast at the white wall of surf, which cut them off from the blue ocean beyond; its summit, dancing and leaping, glittered brightly in the sun's rays.

At length, the tide rising, the breakers appeared to decrease somewhat in height. "I think, sir, that I could carry my gig through," said Murray, "and, if so, the heavier boats may be able to follow."

"You may make the attempt, provided all your people can swim, for your boat may be swamped," said the commodore;

"but as the tide is rising, you will be drifted back, and we must be ready to pick you up."

"All my boat's crew are good swimmers," said Murray, "but I hope they will not be compelled to exercise their powers."

Murray, having placed the remainder of the stores, with all unnecessary weight, on board the larger boats, prepared to make the bold attempt; Adair and Snatchblock following him, as close as they could venture, to the inner line of breakers. Standing up and surveying the bar for some minutes, he at length selected a part where the rollers which came in from the ocean appeared to break with less violence than on either hand.

"Give way, my lads," he cried suddenly; and the crew bending to their oars, the boat shot quickly up the foaming side of the first of the formidable watery hills which had to be passed before the open sea could be gained. His progress was watched with intense eagerness by those in the other boats. Now she was lost to sight, as she sank into a valley on the farther side of the inner roller; now she rose to the foaming summit of the next.

"He'll do it!" cried the little commodore, standing up in the sternsheets, that he might the better watch the progress of the young commander's boat, and clapping his hands like a midshipman. The more dangerous part of the bar, however, had not yet been reached; still Murray continued his course. Now the summit of another roller was gained, the white foam hissing and sparkling over the boat, and almost concealing her from sight.

"She's capsized after all, and they'll have a hard swim of it," shouted someone.

"No, she isn't," cried another voice; "I see her bows rising up on the outer roller. In another minute she'll be clear of them."

"Bravo! well done!" exclaimed the commodore, dancing with delight; "she's through it, and will soon be on board the *Busy Bee*."

The officer in charge of the steamer, it should be said, not finding the boats at the time expected, had, according to orders, got up steam and stood in to ascertain what had become of them.

"Now, my lads," cried the commodore, "what the gig has done we can do. I'll bring up the rear, and be ready to help any boat which may meet with an accident. The post of most danger is the post of honour, which I claim for myself; for those in the last boat will have less chance of being rescued than any of the rest."

Adair was the next to attempt the hazardous experiment. His boat was half filled, but he got through without being swamped, and the water was baled out. The rest in succession followed, each officer waiting for a favourable opportunity to steer through the line of surf.

CHAPTER III

Mozambique—Visit to the Governor—Hamed, the Interpreter—Escape of a Slave to the *Opal*—Preparations for Sharp Work—A Slave Dhow in Sight—Her Wreck—Adair after her through the Breakers—Several of the Slaves rescued—Ben Snatchblock attempts to comfort them—His Efforts not appreciated—Return to the Ship—Horrible State of the rescued Blacks.

WHILE the frigate stood to the northward, and the *Busy Bee* buzzed across to Madagascar, the *Opal* stood for Mozambique, where Murray had to obtain an interpreter, to pick up all possible information regarding the movements of slavers. Two days afterwards the corvette came to an anchor off the chief settlement of the Portuguese on that coast.

The town stands on an island, about a mile and a half in length, situated on a deep inlet of the sea, into which several small rivers fall. The harbour is of considerable size, its entrance guarded by a fort, beyond which appeared an avenue of trees on a gentle slope, then a collection of flat-roofed whitewashed houses, then the palace of the Portuguese governor, with pink walls, and a considerably dilapidated cathedral, below which a stone pier, with buttresses of a sugar-loaf form, runs out into the sea.

"Not a very attractive-looking place," observed Terence to his brother lieutenant, as they viewed it from the ship.

"Yet it speaks of the bygone magnificence of the once proud Lusitanian," answered the poet. "I must write some lines on the subject. The place is not without interest."

"Those dhows, and low, dark, piratical-looking schooners, have considerably more interest to us, however," said Adair; "they are not employed in any honest calling, depend on that; and there lie two Spaniards and a Yankee. If they have no slaves on board, they will have before long, and we must do our best to catch them. We must depend on our own wits, though, for it's impossible to get any correct information from the Portuguese officers—they are most of them as arrant slave-dealers as the Arabs themselves. That man-of-war schooner, for instance, is much more likely to help the slavers to escape than to assist us in catching them, and is very likely often employed in bringing off a cargo of ebony from the shore."

The schooner he pointed at was a handsome vessel, with a thoroughly piratical look about her. However, she formed a strong contrast to the Arab dhows by which she was surrounded. They were of all sizes, the largest measuring, perhaps, three hundred and fifty tons.

"If I had to describe a dhow, I should say that her shape was like half a well-formed pear, cut longitudinally," observed Adair, looking towards the large craft over the quarter, which lay at some little distance, and was preparing apparently to put to sea. "See, her bow sinks deeply in the water, while the stern floats lightly upon it. Large as that craft is, she is only partially decked. She has cross-beams, however, to preserve her shape, and on them are laid flat strips of bamboo, which enable the crew to make their way from one end to the other. At the after-part she has a large house, lightly built, the roof of which forms a poop, while the interior serves, I have no doubt, for the cabin of the skipper, and probably for his wives and children, as well as his passengers and the whole of his crew. She has a heavy, rough spar for a mast, tapering towards the head and raking forward. The sail which they are now just hoisting is, in shape, like a right-angled triangle, with a parallelogram below its base; the hypothenuse or head of the sail is secured to a yard, like an enormous fishing-rod; the halyards are secured to it about a third of the way from the butt-end, and it is hoisted close up to the head of the mast. A tackle brings down the lower end of the yard to the deck, and serves to balance the lofty tapering point, while the sheet is secured to the lower after-corner of the sail. Though many of the smaller dhows have only one mast, that big fellow has two, with a sail of the same shape as the first, but more diminutive. The larger sail is of preposterous proportions, and it seems wonderful that she can carry it without being capsized. It appears to be formed of a strong soft cotton canvas, of extreme whiteness. Those vessels don't tack, but when beating to windward wear by putting up the helm and taking the sheet round before the yard and bringing it aft again on the other side; the deepest part of the dhow being, as you see, under the foremast, it forms a pivot round which the shallow stern, obeying the helm, rapidly turns. Clumsy as they look, I hear that these craft are wonderfully fast, and, with the wind free, will put us on our mettle to overhaul them."

"I should like to judge for myself on that point," observed Mildmay. "Fellows who have allowed prizes to escape them always declare that the craft they have chased is faster than anything afloat."

"I hope we shall have the chance before long," said Adair; "we must keep a bright lookout from the ship and try to do what we can. The commander intends running down the coast, and then despatching all the boats which can be spared to look into the creeks and harbours, and other hiding-places in which any slavers are likely to take shelter. I should like to go on such an expedition myself, if the commander can spare me, shouldn't you?"

"No, thank you," answered Mildmay; "I've no fancy for going away and sleeping in an open boat, without a change of linen or any of the necessaries of life."

"Well, then, I'll leave you to do my duty on board, and volunteer to command the first expedition sent away," said Adair; "you'll take good care of the ship in the meantime."

"Ah, yes!—though I have never aspired to the post of first lieutenant,—to oblige you," said Mildmay.

"Thank you," answered Adair, laughing.

In the afternoon the captain and lieutenants went to pay their respects to the Portuguese governor, and Desmond and Archie were invited to accompany them. Landing on the stone pier before described, they made their way along the narrow, dirty streets, which literally swarmed with slaves. There were faces of every form, if not of colour, for all were black as jet; their faces disfigured in every variety of manner, some with liprings, others with rings in their noses, and some with pieces of bone stuck spritsail fashion through the cartilage. Some, instead of bone, wore brass-headed nails, while many had pieces of bone through their ears. The faces of others were fearfully gashed, a yellow dust filling up the grooves.

Mozambique, indeed, is the chief slave-mart of the Portuguese, and thousands of unhappy beings are kidnapped and brought there from all parts of the interior, ready to be shipped to any country where slave-labour is in demand.

The English officers found the Portuguese governor seated in a broad verandah, in an easy chair, smoking a cigar, and enjoying the sea-breeze, while sheltered from the hot sun. He received them courteously, begging them to be seated, and ordering coffee and cigarettes, which were immediately brought by his slaves, the latter accompanied by a plate of hot charcoal, from which to light them. He expressed himself gratified by their visit, and assured them that his great desire was to put down the slave-trade; but, shrugging his shoulders, he acknowledged that it was no easy matter. "In spite of all I can do," he added, sighing, "my subordinates will indulge in it. What can be expected? They do not like the country, and are naturally in a hurry to make their fortunes and get away again. It is a second nature to the Arabs, and their chief mode of existing; and as long as the French and Brazilians and Cubans will buy slaves, what can prevent it? The former, to be sure, ship them as emigrants and free Africans, though not a negro would leave his country if he could help it."

The governor was so frank, and apparently so sincere in his offers of assistance, that Murray told him one of his chief objects in coming to Mozambique was to obtain an interpreter who could thoroughly be trusted.

"I know the man for you," said the governor; "though not a beauty, he is worthy of confidence—knows the whole coast and the tricks of the slave-dealers, and would obtain for you all the information you require. I'll give directions to have him sent on board, and you can there make any arrangements you think fit."

Murray having thanked the governor for his courtesy, he and his party took a walk round the island. "Faith, for my part, I'd rather be first lieutenant of the *Opal* than governor-general of all the Portuguese settlements in the East put together," exclaimed Adair; "for of all the undelectable places I ever set foot in, this surpasses them in its abominations."

Soon after they returned on board, an individual, who announced himself as the interpreter sent by the governor-general of Mozambique to serve on board Her Majesty's war-ship, came up the side.

"And what's your name, my fine fellow?" asked Murray, as he eyed the unattractive personage. The governor had certainly not belied him when he described him as destitute of good looks. On the top of his grisly head he wore a large white turban. His colour might once have been brown, but it was now as black as that of a negro, frightfully scarred and marked all over. He had but one eye, and that was a blinker, which twisted and turned in every direction when he spoke, except at the person whom he was addressing. His lips were thick, his nostrils extended—indeed, his countenance partook more of the negro than of the Arab type. His feet were enormous, with toes widely spread. He wore a loose jacket, striped with blue, over a dirty cotton coat reaching to his knees, and huge blue baggy trousers.

"Me Haggis ben Hamed at your sarvice, Señor Capitan," he answered, making a salaam; "me undertake show where you find all the slaves on the coast, and ebbery big ship and dhow that sails."

"And what payment do you expect for rendering us these services?" asked Murray.

"Forty pesados for one month, sar; eighty, if I take one dhow; and hundred and sixty, if I help you to one big ship."

"Pretty heavy payment, Master Hamed," observed Murray.

"Ah, Señor Capitan, you not take one vessel without my help—you see," answered the interpreter, drawing himself up and looking very important. Murray suspected that he was right, and finally agreed to pay the reward demanded. From that moment Hamed was installed on board.

As a fair breeze blew out of the harbour, Murray was in a hurry to be off. The pilot, however, asserted that he could not venture to take out the ship except during broad daylight. The *Opal* had therefore to wait till the next morning. The pilot accordingly took his departure, promising to come off again at an early hour. Some time after sunset, Adair and the master were walking the deck, discussing the plan of their proposed boat excursion, to which the commander had agreed, when, as they turned aft, they caught sight of the dark figure of a man who had just climbed over the taffrail, and now stood quaking and shivering before them.

"Where do you come from, my friend?" asked Jos; but the stranger did not reply, except by an increased chattering of his teeth, though he put up his hand in an attitude of supplication.

"Well, no one wishes to hurt you," said Green; "come forward and let us see what you are like," and he called to the quartermaster to bring a lantern. The stranger, gaining courage from the master's kind tone of voice, followed him and Adair. He was evidently greatly exhausted.

"Bring a cup of hot coffee and some biscuit; it will restore the poor wretch, and help him to tell us what he wants," said the master.

After taking the food and liquid, the negro speedily revived, and, drawing his finger across his throat, with the addition of other signs, he intimated that his master was about to kill him, when he made his escape; and it was evident that he must have swum a distance of two miles or more at the risk of his life, to put himself under the protection of the British flag. His name, he intimated, was Pango; and that his master, if he should recapture him, would carry him off and kill him. Hamed, on being summoned, interrogated the black; and from the account he gave, Adair and Green were convinced that they had clearly understood Pango's pantomimic language.

The commander, who had not turned in, on coming on deck and hearing the case, promised poor Pango that he should be protected; and to do so effectually, at once entered him on the ship's books. The negro expressed his gratitude by every means in his power, and, being taken below by Ben Snatchblock the boatswain, was speedily, to his delight and satisfaction, rigged out in seaman's duck trousers and shirt. He was, notwithstanding, far from being at ease, dreading lest the tyrannical master from whom he had fled should discover his place of retreat, and claim him. Hamed, however, made him understand that he now belonged to the ship, and that all on board would fight for him with their big guns and small arms, and go to the bottom rather than give him up. On comprehending this, he showed his joy by capering and singing, and making a variety of demonstrative gestures, signifying that if his former owner came to look for him, he would get more than he bargained for. At length he stopped, and a shade of melancholy came over his countenance. Hamed, who, in spite of his ugliness, possessed some of the better feelings of human nature, asked him what was the matter.

He sighed, and said that he had a brother on shore who was as badly off as he had been, and that he should now be parted from him for ever, as he could never venture back to Mozambique, or set his foot on shore in the neighbourhood, lest he should be kidnapped and carried back to a worse bondage than that from which he had escaped.

Hamed, of course, could give him little hope of rescuing his brother, and advised him to turn in and be thankful that he himself had escaped. Notwithstanding poor Pango's fears, no one appeared to claim him, and the next morning he was seen among the men forward, lending a hand at all sorts of jobs, evidently anxious to make himself useful.

The pilot at length came off, announcing that the tide and wind would now serve for taking out the ship. "Hands shorten in cable!" shouted Ben Snatchblock, his pipe sounding shrilly along the decks. Pango remained forward, concealing himself behind the foremast, though he every now and then took a glance at the ill-favoured pilot, a big, cut-throat, piratical-looking individual, who was standing aft near the master, while his boat hung on alongside the quarter.

Sail was made, the anchor lifted, and the ship was gathering way, when a black sprang out of the boat alongside through a port, and tried to hide himself under one of the midship guns. The savage-looking pilot espied him, and ordered him back into the boat. Instead of obeying, he clung tightly to the gun. "Remove the man and put him back into the boat," said the commander; "but do not handle him roughly." Now, as the poor black clung with might and main to the gun, and shrieked loudly for mercy, the latter order prevented the seamen from executing the former.

"The nigger won't let go, sir," shouted the master-at-arms, Ned Lizard, "unless we cut off his hands and feet—might as well try to haul a cuttle-fish from a rock without leaving its feelers behind it."

"Let him alone, then," said Murray; and, turning to the pilot, he intimated that he must take his man himself if he wanted him, but that he must, in the meantime, look out not to run the ship on shore.

The pilot accordingly continued at his post, every now and then glaring savagely at the poor negro, and uttering a growl signifying that he would very soon have him in his power. Blackie still clung fast to the gun, casting a piteous look at the good-natured countenances of the seamen, imploring them to help him, which it was evident they would be very ready to do.

At length the ship was in the open sea, and the pilot, who had received his payment, was in a hurry to return. Approaching his slave, he ordered him to get into the boat; the latter only replied by piteous shrieks and cries, clinging as tightly as before to the gun with arms and legs, while he seized the tackle in his jaws.

"Tell the pilot, Hamed, that he must carry off the gun and all, if he wants the man; but take him by force he must not," said Adair.

No sooner had Hamed interpreted this than the pilot, drawing his dagger, would have plunged it into the back of the miserable slave, had not the master-at-arms seized his arm, exclaiming, "No, no, my fine fellow; we'll have none of that sort of thing on board here. If you want the man, as the lieutenant says, you must take him by fair means; and, if not, you must let him stay. Tell him, Hamed, if he tries that trick again, he'll be run up to the foreyardarm there before he is many hours older."

The pilot stamped and swore all sorts of Mohammedan oaths, which might have shocked even the ears of the prophet, and appealed to the commander, who intimated, in return, that if the slave sought the protection of the British flag, it would be granted him, and that it was very evident he had no desire to go back to Mozambique. At last Mustapha saw that he must make up his mind to lose his slave, and, casting a last ferocious look at him, as much as to say, "If I ever catch you on shore, my fine fellow, your skin and bones will part company," he lowered himself down into the boat.

Blackie peered through the port till he saw that she had actually let go and was dropping astern, when he jumped up, and the next instant, Pango, coming from his hiding-place, rushed aft, and the two blacks, throwing their arms round each other, burst into tears of joy. The last runaway was no other than Pango's brother, who was forthwith christened Bango. Not forgetting the pilot, they together ran aft, and waved their hands triumphantly at him, as the ship, increasing her speed, left the boat astern, he shouting and grinning with mad and impotent rage.

The corvette stood down the coast, a bright look-out being kept both for native dhows and square-rigged vessels, of which not a few Brazilians, Spaniards, and Americans were known to be engaged in the nefarious traffic. The carpenters had been busy fitting the boats, raising the gunwales of the smaller ones, and adding false keels to the larger, to enable them the better to carry sail; and all hands guessed that something was to be done, but what it was the commander kept to himself, or made known only to his lieutenants.

In spite of the utmost vigilance of the look-outs, not a vessel had been seen, till one morning, just at daybreak, as the ship was standing in for the land, the wind being to the southward, a dhow was discovered coming up before it, her canvas of snowy whiteness glittering in the rays of the rising sun. The commander, who was on deck, in a moment gave the order to lower the lifeboat; and Adair, with Ben Snatchblock and Desmond, leaped into her and pulled away for the coast, so as to intercept the dhow should she attempt to pass ahead of the corvette.

"We've caught the dhow in a trap, at all events," observed Adair, "for she's no chance with the ship on a wind. She is certain to try and run for it close inshore, when we shall as certainly catch her. Give way, my lads! she hasn't seen us as yet, and stands on with a flowing sheet, thinking that she has a good chance of slipping between the corvette and the land."

The wind being light, the corvette was making but little way through the water, and had a breeze come off the land, the dhow would have had a fair chance of escaping, had it not been for the boat ready to intercept her. The dhow, under her immense spread of canvas, glided on rapidly; and her Arab captain was probably congratulating himself on the prospect of escaping from his powerful foe, when he caught sight of the boat lying in wait for him. Heavy rollers broke on the shore, sending the surf flying up many yards over the beach. The dhow was seen suddenly to put up her helm and to steer directly for the shore.

"Good heavens!" cried Adair; "the Arab isn't going to attempt to carry his vessel through those breakers?"

"He is, though, sir," observed Snatchblock. "It's a pretty sure sign that he has got a cargo of slaves aboard. Poor beings! not many of them will reach the beach alive."

Adair immediately steered the boat towards the dhow, though he had little hope of reaching her in time to prevent her from running on destruction. Several shots were fired to make her heave-to, but the Arab crew heeded them not; and Adair had got almost within a cable's length of the breakers when the doomed vessel was seen plunging in their midst, to be cast in a few seconds on the shingly beach.

Wildly the sea broke over her, and almost as if by magic, her bulky hull, melting away, exposed to view a hundred or more black forms struggling in the water, endeavouring to make their way to dry land. Some of the unfortunate beings succeeded, but others were carried back into the surf, and, hurled over and over, were lost to sight, none of them being drifted out as far as the boat.

All this time Adair was pulling in towards the breakers. He saw that the Arab crew, who had been the first to reach the shore, were urging on the blacks to run towards a thick wood, the outer edge of which was a few hundred yards only from the beach.

"I think we can do it," he said to Snatchblock; "I have been through worse breakers than those in a less buoyant boat than ours. If we don't manage to get on shore, the Arabs will carry off every one of the slaves."

"She'll go through it, sir," answered Snatchblock, looking round at the breakers.

"We might save some of the poor wretches, at all events. Give way, my lads!" cried Adair, and the boat, urged forward by the stout arms of the crew, was speedily in the midst of the breakers. The sea struck her abaft, and washed clean over her from stern to stem; and had not Snatchblock aided Adair in hauling away on the yoke-line, she must have broached-to. A lifeboat alone could have existed amid those heavy breakers.

The next instant another sea struck her, washing over her whole length, and covering everyone in her; but as it went right over the bows, only a few inches of water remained. A third time she was deluged, and then down she sank, it seemed, into comparatively smooth water, and glided up easily on to the shelving beach.

The firearms, having been fortunately covered up, were fit for use. Calling to his men to follow, two only being left in the boat, Adair set off in pursuit of the Arabs and their captives. It seemed extraordinary that the latter should have been willing to run off when friends were at hand eager to rescue them from captivity, but they were evidently as eager to escape as their masters. The Arabs, seeing only a small number of Englishmen, would probably, as soon as they had gained the shelter of the wood, have turned round and fired, and Adair fully expected to be attacked. Fortunately, in their hurry to escape from the dhow, they had left their muskets behind them, and their only chance of safety was by flight. How the slaves, when they found them unarmed and in their power, might be inclined to treat them was a different question.

Several black forms were still seen running as fast as their legs could carry them towards the bush, and Adair and Desmond, who kept ahead, came up with two young men, looking more like skeletons than living beings. As they caught them by the arm, the poor wretches sank down on the ground, shrieking with terror. Snatchblock and the men caught three more, but it was no easy matter to induce them to run to the beach. Not one Arab was to be seen, and the remainder of the blacks disappeared among the thick bushes, where it would have been next to madness for so small a party to have followed them, not knowing what enemies might be lurking near at hand. After some persuasion the blacks were induced to come back to the beach, though trembling in every limb from terror and weakness as they walked along. Here four small children were found in the same emaciated condition as their elders, and one unhappy woman, to whom one of the children appeared to belong; she had injured her foot in landing, and had been unable to run away. From her cries and shrieks it was evident that she believed some dreadful fate was about to befall her. How many poor creatures had been lost in the surf it was impossible to say, and, as Hamed had not accompanied them, no information could be gained from the blacks.

Adair, indeed, had now to consider how they were to get off again. As from the higher ground on which he stood he looked over the wide belt of foaming breakers, it seemed almost impossible that the boat, buoyant as she was, could be forced through them. Even Snatchblock eyed them anxiously. "We may do it, sir," he remarked, "if there comes a lull; if not, we shall have to wait here till the sea goes down. The worst is the want of grub and water, and we are not likely to find either in these parts, I've a notion, unless some wild beast or other comes to have a look at us; then we may give him a shot, and try what his flesh tastes like."

The day was by this time drawing on. As not a particle of food or a drop of water had been brought in the boat, all hands were excessively hungry and thirsty. It was dangerous to separate, though, in search of provisions, as it was more than possible that the Arabs might instigate the natives to attack them. Snatchblock and Desmond, however, volunteered to go, taking different directions, each accompanied by one man. For the sake of the poor blacks, who seemed literally perishing from starvation, Adair would willingly have consented, but it would be far better, he thought, if possible, to get off to the ship. Anxiously he watched the long line of breakers, but they extended up and down the coast as far as the eye could reach, without an opening through which the boat might possibly pass. Another hour or more went by; no shade was to be obtained except at a distance, under the trees of the forest; and Adair considered that it would be dangerous to venture so far from the shore, as the natives might then have the opportunity of stealing on them unawares. They accordingly sat down on the beach watching the breakers, in the hopes, as the tide rose, that their violence might decrease, and an opening appear through which the boat might be forced. The rays of the sun struck down on their heads with terrific force, quickly drying their drenched clothes; but they would gladly have remained wet as they were, could they have found a few yards of shade beneath a neighbouring tree or rock.

The wretched blacks sat with stolid looks, as if totally unconscious that their liberators wished to benefit them. Every now and then, when they fancied that they were not observed, they cast frightened glances at the sailors. "I don't know what the poor niggers are thinking of," observed Snatchblock; "maybe they fancy that we're going to eat them, though it would be a hard matter to scrape enough off the bones of all of them to feed a young dog. I wish I knew something of their lingo, I'd try to make them understand that when we get on board we'll give them a good blow-out, and that in a week or two they'll not know themselves. I say, Sambo! we not want to mangy you, old chap," he added, to the black nearest him, and making significant signs; "we want to put some honest beef and pork flesh on that carcass of yours and fill you out, boy; then you dance and sing, and become as merry as a cricket."

The black certainly did not understand what was said, and probably misunderstood his pantomimic gestures. One of them, the farthest off from the men, had been sitting with his head sunk down between his bent knees, apparently utterly unable to move; turning his head over his shoulder, he suddenly started up, and, before anyone could seize him, darted off towards the wood.

"Come back, you silly fellow!" cried Desmond, who, with two of the men, rose to follow him; but before they had got many paces, a large party of natives armed with bows, arrows, and spears, accompanied by several of the Arab crew, rushed out from among the trees, uttering threatening shouts, as if to intimidate the Englishmen.

"Stand to your arms, my lads," cried Adair; "we must not let those fellows get near us, or we may be overpowered by numbers." Still the natives came on, some flourishing their spears, and others preparing their bows to shoot. Adair lifted his rifle. "Don't any of you fire till I tell you," he said to his men, while he took aim so as to strike the ground a few yards in front of the headmost of the party. No one was hit, but they knew enough of the effect of firearms to be aware that another bullet might find a billet in one of their bodies. Springing back, the foremost tumbling the rear-ranks over, they threw themselves flat on the ground, and began to creep away towards the shelter of the bush. Adair, shouting to them, pointed to his own rifle and to the muskets of his men, intimating that if they ventured to advance, they would have to receive their contents.

The hint, apparently, had the desired effect; for, though the Arabs seemed to be doing their utmost to induce the blacks to attack the strangers, they remained carefully hiding themselves among the trees. As, however, they might at any moment rush forward, the seamen kept their muskets ready for instant service, with a watchful eye on their movements. In the meantime, the black who had escaped had joined them. What account he had given of the white men it was impossible to say. One thing was certain, that the presence of the natives would prevent any attempt to go in search of food and water, and that if they could not get off, their sufferings from thirst and hunger would become serious. With increased anxiety, Adair cast his eye over the foaming rollers, both up and down the coast. The breeze blew strong as ever, and not a break appeared in that long line of glittering surf. The party were literally hemmed in, almost without hope of escape. They might have beaten off the natives, and made their way into the interior till they could fall in with some game and a stream of water, but then they would have had to leave the boat and the blacks unprotected. Still, to starve where they were was not to be thought of.

"Faith, I'm growing fearfully peckish," exclaimed Desmond; "if you'll let me, sir, we'll try and get hold of one of those fellows, and make him order the rest to bring us some grub; if the sea won't go down, it's the only chance we have."

Snatchblock was of Desmond's opinion, and of course the men were ready to follow them. Still, Adair was unwilling to run the risk of being overpowered. "No, no," he answered; "we can hold out some time longer, and if at last we find it impossible to get off, we can but do as you propose."

"I think, sir, the sea is going somewhat down," said Snatchblock, at length; "we might get through just a little to the right there. See, sir, some of the rollers come in with only just a slight top to them, and if we take the right moment, we may get through."

"We can but try it," cried Adair. "Lift the poor blacks into the boat; they'll not add much to her weight. Be smart about it, my lads, though."

The negroes seemed very unwilling to move, and shrieked out as if they were about to be put to death; but they were but as infants in the arms of the stout seamen. The woman clung to her child as she was lifted with it into the sternsheets. The men were carried next, and placed at the bottom of the boat with the little children between them. She was then run off into the smooth water inside the breakers, the crew jumping into her; but each time the water receded, she struck on the hard coral beneath, her admirable construction alone preventing her from being stove in. The oars were got out, and the boat pulled along till the spot Snatchblock observed was reached. Her head was then put to the sea.

"Give way, my lads," cried Adair, he and Desmond holding on to one yoke-line, while the boatswain held the other, their eyes eagerly cast towards the foaming breakers, amid which they were about to force their way. The crew put forth all their strength. The first breaker was past. Though they bent to their oars like true British seamen, the second, as it came thundering on, hurled them back; and it required all the skill of Adair and his companions to manage the boat till they reached the smooth water.

"Never say die, lads!" cried Adair, after waiting a few minutes to allow the men to recover their strength; "we'll try it again; if the ash-sticks hold, your muscles will, I am sure."

"Ay, ay, sir!" answered the crew; "we're ready."

"Then give way." The attempt was made as before, but again a mighty roller dashed back the boat, and sent her nearly up to the beach. Still Adair was unwilling to abandon the attempt. He waited as before, allowing the boat to remain where there was just water to float her.

"I am afraid we shall have, after all, to haul up the boat,

and sleep on the beach without our suppers," he observed to Snatchblock; "we can easily keep the natives at bay, and must hope for smoother water in the morning."

"If it must be so, it must," answered the boatswain, standing up, however, as he spoke, and looking seaward. "We'll tackle them this time, sir," he exclaimed suddenly; "the outer line of breakers has gone down since we shoved off."

Adair stood up. "Yes, we'll not be driven back again, lads; never fear!" he cried, dropping into his seat. The crew, with a hearty shout, bent to their oars, and the boat, urged by their strong arms, bravely breasted the foaming rollers. The first and second were past; the third came on hissing and roaring; the boat still advanced; its heavy curling crest swept her from stem to stern, but she held her way, and was ready when another came on to meet it boldly. Over it she went, throwing out the water which she had taken in, and in another minute was dancing merrily on the heaving seas outside the breakers.

Adair looked anxiously to see whether any of his sable passengers, young or old, had been washed away. In spite of the risk they had run, all were safe. The poor mother had grasped her child, and the men the other young ones. The sun was by this time sinking behind the land; the crew pulled away with right good will towards the corvette, which could be seen at a distance of three miles or so. She was standing away from the land to get a good offing during the night.

"They've seen the state of the surf, and have thought we couldn't get through it, or maybe that we were lost," observed Snatchblock.

"Shure, it'll be the greater pleasure to them when we come back," said Desmond. "Mr. Mildmay will be mighty glad to find that he hasn't to do duty as first lieutenant, though I don't know what old Sandford may wish in his heart of hearts. He might not object to be made acting lieutenant." Sandford was the senior mate on board.

"Had he thought that any accident had happened to us, the commander would have sent in a boat to ascertain the fact," said Adair.

Darkness was rapidly coming on, and by degrees the canvas of the corvette became shrouded in the mists of night. Adair, however, had taken her bearings, and by the help of the stars was able to steer directly for her. Still Desmond, who had become perfectly ravenous, could not help wishing that the commander, instead of keeping off the coast, had stood in nearer to pick them up.

The men, however, pulled away cheerily, encouraged with the thoughts of a good hot supper and a quiet snooze till the next morning. After some time, a bright light burst forth, sending a lurid glare across the ocean.

"There's the corvette," cried Snatchblock; "they hadn't forgotten us. We'll be snug on board before many minutes are over."

At last the boat reached the ship's side, and eager hands were stretched out to lift the emaciated creatures they had brought off on board. The doctor took charge of them, and administered some weak broth, while the rest of the party hurried below to obtain the more substantial viands of which they stood so much in need.

On Hamed's questioning the liberated slaves, it was discovered that Snatchblock had been right in his suspicions that the Arabs had told them, in order to induce them to escape on shore, that if captured by the white men they would be cooked and eaten. They stated that the dhow had been crammed full of slaves, many of whom had been drowned in their attempt to reach the shore, while it was probable that a still larger number would perish before they were again put on board another slave-ship by their cruel masters. Had anything been necessary to induce the officers and crew of the *Opal* to exert themselves in putting down the horrible traffic, the state of these poor negroes, and the account they gave, would have been sufficient to stir them up. One of the men and two of the children, notwithstanding all the care taken of them, died before morning. The rest quickly recovered, their skins filling out perceptibly every day with the good food they received.

CHAPTER IV

Ordered again to Angoxa—Island of Mafamale—Seine Fishing—Desmond's Victory over the Fish—The Carpenter tries his Hand, but catches a Tartar—Life on the Island—Jerry Bird's "Kettler"—Second Boat Expedition—Lightning in the Tropics—Up the River—Capture and Burning of a Dhow—Land for Provisions—Treachery of Natives—Adair and Desmond made Prisoners—Adair turns the Tables on the old Chief.

THE corvette lay becalmed, lapping her sides in the shining water, as the glass-like undulations under her keel rolled her now to starboard and now to port, the sun striking down and making the pitch bubble up out of the seams of her deck. No sail was in sight, but still a bright look-out was kept. In case any slaver bringing up a breeze might attempt to slip by inshore of her, the boats were in readiness to shove off in chase.

"A steamer to the nor'ard, sir," shouted the look-out to the second lieutenant, who reported the same to the commander. All hands were quickly up on deck. She was probably a British cruiser, perhaps bringing news for them—a mail *via* the Isthmus of Suez and the Red Sea.

At last, after various conjectures as to what she was, the *Busy Bee* made her number, and paddled up in a way which made the crew wish that they possessed similar means of locomotion. She blew off her steam when close to them, and a boat from her side brought her commander on board. He was the bearer of despatches from the commodore.

Murray called Adair into his cabin. "The commodore has received information that the Arabs are rebuilding the fort we destroyed," he said, "and so I suppose that we shall have to go up the river to do the work over again. He has directed me in the meantime to station two of our boats, with one from the *Busy Bee*, to be joined shortly by a fourth from the frigate, at the island of Mafamale, which is about seven miles from the mouth of the river. I may select the officer to command the expedition, and if you wish to go, I will appoint you, with Jos Green and Desmond and Gordon. You will look out for dhows either going up to, or coming down from Angoxa, and for others running along the coast, which are certain to pass between the island and the mainland. The corvette and the steamer will in the meantime stand down the coast, and the dhows seeing us will hope to get to Zanzibar without interruption. The plan seems to be a good one, and I trust that we shall be able to strike a more effectual blow at the slave-trade than the commodore has hitherto been able to give it."

Terence, who had been wishing for this sort of work, gladly accepted Murray's offer. The corvette stood on till she came off the island, when the pinnace and barge, well fitted for the duties they were at once to engage in, were got out. The *Busy Bee* landed a couple of water tanks, for not a drop of the necessary fluid was to be found on the island; while she and the corvette sent three months' provisions on shore, with tents, arms, and ammunition;

With three hearty cheers from the crews, responded to by their respective ships, the boats shoved off and pulled away for the island, to become their headquarters for the next three months. Its appearance was not over-attractive, for it was low and sandy, scarcely more than two miles in circumference, with a small forest of Casuarina trees on the highest part, bordered by a belt of thin grass.

One of the first boats sent on shore contained a large seine, and Jos Green was directed to haul it as soon as possible for the purpose of supplying the ship's company with fresh fish. All hands were well pleased to hear the order, and the men destined for that object quickly transmogrified themselves into fishermen with blue jerseys, tarry trousers, and red caps, looking more like lawless pirates than well-conducted men-of-war's men. Two of the smaller boats under the command of the master, who was accompanied by Desmond and Archie, then pulled in. On the north side of the island was a shelving beach, where the water was perfectly smooth and not a rock or stone to be found. It was just such a beach as to satisfy all the requirements of men-of-war's men, capable at the same time of supplying sand for holy-stoning the decks, and to afford admirable ground for hauling the seine.

The net was quickly run out, forming a wide semicircle, and surrounding, no doubt, vast numbers of fish, as they could be seen of various forms and sizes sporting in the clear water. The boats being hauled up, the work of hauling the net began. Just at that juncture several officers who had before landed came across the island to see the fun, and immediately all hands tailed on to the hauling-lines. As the net drew nearer and nearer to the land, innumerable specimens of the finny tribe could be seen leaping and springing about, mutually surprised at finding themselves brought unexpectedly in such near proximity to each other and to the shore; evidently thinking that it was time to make a dash for the more open water. Vain were the attempts of those who foolishly fancied by swimming slow and concealing themselves they might the more surely effect their escape. The bolder fish, who, leaping high, cleared the encircling net, were alone successful, some enormous fellows setting the example. Others attempted to follow them.

"We shall have them all getting off if we don't bear a hand," cried Green; "haul away, my lads."

"Better be after them and hook them out," exclaimed Desmond, suiting the action to the word, and plunging in amid the struggling fish. Archie could not resist doing the same, and presently every officer, including the commander and Adair, were up to their knees in the water, each trying to seize one or more of the monsters, who, it was evident, would, if they attempted it, clear a passage for themselves through the meshes. Desmond had fixed upon two, and down he went upon hands and knees, endeavouring to kill the creatures leaping, wriggling, and struggling to get free. As he did so, one of them, making a bolt between his legs, toppled him over on his nose, where he lay kicking and plunging, scarcely to be distinguished from the fish surrounding him. He quickly, however, got his head above water, as he did so, spluttering out, "Arrah, the baste! I haven't let him go, though," and, kneeling on the creature, he managed to work his hands under its gills, when, holding it up, he dragged it triumphantly to the shore.

One of the smaller youngsters, Billy Blueblazes, upon trying to follow his example, was literally dragged off his feet, and, had not Archie seized him and the fish which he held by the gills, might very possibly have been drowned.

The shouting and laughing and hallooing which arose on all sides would alone have been sufficient to drive the unfortunate fish out of their minds, as officers and men were plunging about here and there grasping at the larger fish right and left. At length the greater number of the monsters who had failed to escape having been captured, the men drew the seine high up on the beach, with some hundreds of fish, most, if not all of them, as Green declared, excellent eating. As soon as they had been rendered incapable of effecting their escape, the seine was again carried out; and though it might have been supposed that the fish would have avoided the spot, as many as at the first haul were speedily drawn to land, when a similar scene was enacted, and, all hands being thoroughly wet, everyone not required for tailing on at the hauling-lines plunged in as before. Among the most adventurous was the carpenter, who in his eagerness rushed forward till the water was up to his armpits; when, fancying he saw a fish of unusual size, and desirous of gaining the honour of bringing it to shore, he plunged down his hand. Scarcely had he done so, when, with a shout which might have reached almost to the ship, he drew it up again, exclaiming, "Bear a hand, mates, and help me to get rid of this imp of Satan. I'm blessed if I thought such creatures lived in the ocean."

He uttered this as he staggered towards the shore, when it was seen that his whole arm, which he held at full length, was grasped by the dark slimy tentacles of a monster which, with a beak resembling that of a bird, was attempting to strike him in the face; had the creature got hold of a smaller person, it might have succeeded in doing so. Desmond and Billy Blueblazes were at first inclined to laugh, till they got closer to the hideous creature. Several of the men with their knives open hurried forward to the assistance of the carpenter, who bravely kept his arms stretched out till they succeeded in cutting off its head; but even then those powerful tentacles retained so much vitality that it was necessary to remove them one by one. The carpenter's arm was almost paralysed, and he complained of considerable pain and irritation.

His adventure, however, did not prevent the rest of the party from continuing their chase of the larger fish, though they kept a bright look-out not to be caught by crabs, or to avoid catching hold of a squid. Though, as before, some escaped, the second haul was almost as productive as the first. The boats, being loaded with the fish, returned to the ship.

The shore party then set to work to prepare for their Robinson Crusoe life, while the *Opal* stood away to the northward. Tents were set up, a hut for the blacksmith's forge, and another for the carpenter close to the beach, before which a coral reef made a secure harbour for the boats. A third hut was built near the camp for the cook—not that any skilled one belonged to the party. The magazine was wisely placed at a distance, in case a spark from the kitchen or a tobacco-pipe might chance to find its way to the gunpowder. Everyone was in high spirits and supremely happy. As soon as the work of the day was over, the men took to playing leap-frog, diversified by bowls and quoits, which had been brought on shore. The officers had not forgotten foils and boxing-gloves, as well as books and writing-desks and drawing materials. All was not play, however; the arms had to be cleaned every morning, the men inspected, and a bright look-out kept from dawn to sunset, and even at night, when the moon afforded sufficient light to distinguish a sail at any distance gliding over the dark waters. For this purpose a platform was erected between the summits of two trees, which grew conveniently close together at the west end of the island, with steps cut in the trunk of one of them, a man-rope hanging from the top making it an easy matter to get up.

Jerry Bird, Green's old shipmate, the man who had been taken off from Tristan d'Acunha, was the wit of the party. He was the cook the first day. "Now, my boys, I'll give you a treat," he exclaimed, as he carried off the various provisions served out by the storekeeper; "don't suppose that I have lived among savages for no end of years without learning a trick or two." The fire was lighted, and Jerry put on a huge kettle to boil. He was soon busily plucking a couple of the fowls which had been obtained from the last place at which the ship had touched. It was naturally supposed that there was to be roast fowl for dinner. While the rest of the party went in various directions,—some to collect oysters, which clung to the rocks, with hammers and tomahawks to break them off; others to the look-out man up the tree; and some to lie down and read under the shade of the tents,—Jerry proceeded with his culinary operations. A frying-pan and a ladle served him instead of a gong. When dinner was ready, he commenced a loud clanging, which sounded from one end of the island to the other. The hungry party soon collected. There were rows of plates, with knives and forks and basins with spoons laid out in order, while Jerry stood, ladle in hand, before his kettle, stirring away with might and main.

"Here, Tim, stand by with a plate and basin, and take

the officers their dinner," he said. Tim Curran was one of the ship's boys who did duty as officers' servant.

As Jerry ladled out the contents of the kettle, it was seen to contain every article with which he had been furnished; the fowls and beef cut up into small bits; peas, biscuit, flour, preserved vegetables, emitting a most savoury odour. No one had cause to complain, for Jerry had added a seasoning which all acknowledged to be superior to anything they had ever tasted.

"I knew you'd like my 'kettler,'" he observed, with a self-satisfied air, as he sat down with his messmates, who gathered round him.

The rogue had wisely beforehand consulted Adair, who had approved of his proposal on the subject, and so excellent was his "kettler" pronounced, that from henceforward it was the everyday meal of the party; and though others tried to surpass him when their turn came, they all confessed that they could never do it, and it was voted that it was unequalled by the best Scotch hotch-potch, which it much resembled.

They were not long, however, allowed to lead so pleasant a life on shore. Adair sent off one of the boats across the channel to the mainland to be in readiness to pounce down on any dhows creeping up on that side, while he himself went away in the pinnace to the southward, accompanied by Gerald and Archie, leaving Jos Green in command of the island. Jerry Bird formed one of the crew, so the party on shore lost their cook. Pango also, one of the escaped slaves, went as interpreter, he having by this time acquired enough English to make himself understood and to understand what was said to him. The boat was provisioned for three weeks, and Adair hoped, by getting fresh food and vegetables from the shore, to be able to stay out longer if necessary. He had on board several articles for barter, and, in addition, a store of empty beer-bottles, for which he had heard the natives have an especial fancy.

Adair's intention was to examine every opening and indentation in the coast in which a slave dhow could take shelter. He accordingly steered for the mainland, towards the first bay to the south of Angoxa, into which it was possible one of the hoped-for prizes might have crept during the night. On reaching the bay, however, no vessel was to be seen, and the pinnace accordingly stood out again with a light breeze, which enabled her to stand down the coast. The day was passed much as men-of-war's men are accustomed to spend their time on boat expeditions; the meals were cooked in one pot, common to officers and men, whether "kettler" for dinner or chocolate for breakfast and supper. Pipes were smoked, yarns spun, songs sung, journals written up, and now and then, though not often, books were read. Regular watches were of course kept, and, as a rule, everyone took as much sleep as he could get. The life, as all agreed, was pleasant enough while the weather was fine, but it would be pleasanter to catch a few dhows, send them as prizes into port, and restore the negroes found on board to liberty.

"Faith, I wonder whether we ever shall catch one of those rascals," exclaimed Desmond, beginning to lose patience when, after three days at sea, not a single dhow had been caught sight of.

"No fear, Gerald," observed Archie; "they'll be dropping into our jaws before long if we keep them wide enough open."

At night the boat was sometimes hove-to, or when the wind was light kept slowly gliding on over the calm surface of the deep. One night Archie Gordon had the middle watch. Scarce a breath filled the sails; the ocean was like glass; not a cloud dimmed the sky, from which the stars shone forth with a brilliancy which afforded light almost equal to that of the full moon; every star, reflected in the mirror-like deep, gave it the appearance of being spangled and streaked with gold. Suddenly there burst forth over the land so vivid a flash of lightning that rocks and trees and the distant hills for a moment stood out in such bold relief, that Archie could not help fancying that the boat had been carried by some unknown current close to the beach. With a cry of surprise he aroused his companions.

"Is anything the matter?" asked Adair, starting up.

"Arrah, what's in the wind now?" exclaimed Gerald, echoing the question.

"The whole country seems on fire," answered Archie. "I can by no means make it out." As he spoke, another flash lighted up, as brilliantly as during the brightest sunshine, the distant hills and wide expanse of ocean. The flashes continued bursting forth in rapid succession, lasting fully ten seconds, with even a less interval between them. Not the slightest sound of distant thunder was heard; silence reigned over the ocean. Even the men, who had roused up their companions to gaze at the wondrous spectacle. uttered not a word. A slight flapping of the sail against the mast, as a catspaw caught it, or an increased ripple of the water against the bows, alone struck the ear.

These brilliant phenomena lasted the greater part of the night.

"It's very fine," exclaimed Jerry Bird at last; "but to my mind a sound snooze is more to the purpose than straining our eyes out by winking at it, seeing we can't say what work may be cut out for us to-morrow; and so I'm going to turn in."

His example was followed by the rest of the watch below, though the more sentimental of the officers continued gazing at it for some time longer. Adair wished that Lucy Rogers could enjoy it with him.

"I say, Archie, wouldn't Mr. Mildmay now be after writing a splendiferous sonnet if he was here?" whispered Desmond.

"Can't you try your hand, Gerald?" said Archie.

"Not I; I'm no poet. I can make a very good line to begin with, but when I come to the second, I can never manage to fit the words in properly."

"Just try now," said Archie. Thus encouraged, Desmond at length exclaimed—

"'The lightnings flashing o'er the boundless deep'"—

"Very good," said Archie.

Gerald repeated the line several times. "'Arouse the seamen from their' something 'sleep,'" he added. "I'll get Mr. Mildmay to put in a proper word instead of 'something,' for it's more than I can be after doing."

"Hold your tongues, youngsters!" exclaimed Adair, whose thoughts had been far away till they were brought back by his nephew's voice. "Turn in and get some sleep instead of chattering nonsense."

The midshipmen, obeying, coiled themselves in the stern-sheets, while Adair, who took the helm, sat indulging in a mood to which he had hitherto been a stranger.

The morning came, and soon after breakfast, as the boat was running along the coast, the entrance to a river, apparently of some size, was discovered. The sea was tolerably calm on the bar, and as it appeared a likely place for slavers to ship their cargoes, Adair resolved to run in and explore it thoroughly. The wind carried them close up to the mouth, when, it failing altogether, the oars were got out, and the crew pulled away lustily, in the hopes of at length finding a slaver which they could make their lawful prize. At this time, however, the Sultan of Zanzibar issued licences to no inconsiderable number of vessels, on the pretence that they were engaged in bringing him negroes to work on his plantations; although, were his island ten times the size that it really is, he could not have employed one-tenth of the blacks carried off to slavery. On this flimsy pretext they might therefore find a dhow full of blacks, and yet not be able to capture her. This, of course, was often the cause of great disappointment to the crews engaged in the suppression of the slave-trade.

A belt of mangrove trees running far into the water being passed, a long reach of the river was opened up, with a large dhow at the farther end of it, lying at anchor in mid-stream, apparently ready to sail. The crew of the pinnace could not restrain a shout of satisfaction. In spite of the hot sun beating down on their heads, they eagerly bent to their oars in the hopes of soon being on board her. As they approached, they saw that her sails were unbent, so that she could not have been on the point of putting to sea. On getting still nearer, about twenty fierce-looking Arabs popped their heads over the side, and in loud voices, with threatening gestures, ordered the boat to keep off, intimating that if she did not, they would fire into her. That she possessed the power of doing mischief was evident, as a three-pounder gun was seen mounted on a sort of raised deck in her bow.

Neither Adair nor his crew were likely to be deterred by the menaces of the piratical-looking fellows from boarding the dhow. With a loud cheer they dashed alongside, and quickly scrambled on her deck, cutting down several of the more daring of the band, who, not knowing what English seamen were made of, ventured to oppose them. A fine-looking old fellow, with a long white beard, who proved to be the Arab captain, exchanged a few passes with Adair, who, however, quickly disarmed him, and tumbled him head over heels into the hold, while the rest of his men leaped below to escape from their daring assailants. On following them, Adair found, to his disappointment, that there were no slaves on board. The Arab crew having been secured, Adair ordered his men to bend the sail, while he and Desmond, accompanied by Jerry Bird, searched the vessel to ascertain whether she had anything on board by which she could be legally condemned. Besides the three-pounder gun, a number of muskets, spears, and swords were found on board, with a supply of water and a large quantity of rice, in addition to which her hold was fitted with three tiers of bamboo decks, which could be intended for no other purpose than for the stowage of slaves.

Adair pointed this out to the old skipper, and made him understand that he considered the vessel his lawful prize.

"It is the will of Allah," answered the captain, who made no attempt to show either papers or colours, so it was considered evident that he did not possess them.

"There are whole hosts of people collecting on shore, sir," shouted Archie; "many of them are armed, and by the signs they are making they don't seem in a friendly mood. They've got, too, plenty of canoes, and it looks very much as if they intended to come off and attack us."

Adair hurried on deck, and could not help being of Archie's opinion. "Be sharp there with the sail," he cried.

"It's more than we can manage to bend it, sir," answered Jerry Bird; "for there's not a bit of rope-yarn or stuff of any kind we can find to do instead."

Adair and Desmond, stepping forward to lend a hand, found that the men were right. The blacks on shore, increasing in numbers, were already uttering most terrific shouts and cries, and had begun to launch their canoes. It would be impossible to defend the dhow without running the risk of losing the boat. Adair had no wish to bring on an encounter with the savages.

"We must burn the craft and make the best of our way out of the river," he exclaimed. "Get the prisoners into the boat, and we will then set the dhow on fire, and prevent her, at all events, from taking on board another cargo of ebony."

While the men were carrying out his orders, the old Arab captain, who had been left at liberty, came up to him, and made signs that there was some object of great value in the hold which he was anxious to recover. In his eagerness, as with half bent body he stretched out his hands, he seized Adair by the beard, tears actually running down his eyes.

"Can he have his wife or children stowed away anywhere?" suggested Desmond.

"It may be, but we must not let them be burned, at all events," said Adair. "Well, old fellow, go and bring them up," he added, making a significant gesture. The Arab, however, did not comprehend him, and at length, pulling out a piece of gold, he made signs that he had a box or bag full of such pieces stowed away.

"Faith, it's myself will go and help ye hunt for them," cried Desmond, about to accompany the old Arab, who was hurrying below.

"Stay," exclaimed Adair; "there is not a moment to spare. See, the canoes are coming off, and we shall be surrounded presently. I suspect it is only a trick after all, that he may induce us to remain till the tables are turned. Here, tumble the old fellow into the boat, and set the dhow on fire fore and aft."

While the men obeyed this order, Archie and Gerald, who had been lighting some bundles of tow, threw one of them down forward among the other combustible materials, while another was placed aft; and another, still larger, which Desmond ignited, was let drop into the hold. A thick smoke, followed by flames, immediately burst forth, showing that the craft had been effectually set on fire.

A good-sized canoe was floating alongside the dhow. "We will have her," said Desmond; "make her fast astern. She'll assist us in landing the prisoners, and be useful afterwards."

A whole fleet of canoes, full of shrieking savages, was now coming off towards the dhow. "Give them a shot from the six-pounder," said Adair, putting the boat's head round; "it will teach them that they had better not follow us." The missile went flying over the water, just ahead of the canoes. It appeared to have had the desired effect, for some ceased paddling, and others went back as fast as they could make way towards the shore; while the pinnace, with the canoe in tow, proceeded down the harbour.

Night had now come on; the flames, which rose from every portion of the burning dhow, their glare extending down the river and casting a ruddy light against the tall trees on either side, enabled them, without difficulty, to make their way towards the ocean. The cut-throat-looking Arabs, with their venerable captain, appeared to be very uneasy in their minds, not knowing what was to be done with them; perhaps supposing that their captors were carrying them out to sea to drown in deep water. They were evidently much relieved when, a point some little way down the river being reached, Adair intimated to them that they were forthwith to be put on shore. As many as the canoe would hold were tumbled into her, and they, being quickly landed, she returned for another cargo. The old skipper was the last. As he gazed at his burning vessel, he wrung his hands, mourning his hard fate.

"Very hard for you," observed Archie; "but it would have been harder for the unfortunate blacks you would have carried off into slavery."

During this time the natives, gaining courage, were coming down the river in vast numbers, beating their tom-toms and shouting and shrieking. They could be easily beaten off, provided they were not allowed to get too near; but Adair had no wish to shed blood, and therefore, having completely destroyed the dhow and got rid of the prisoners, he stood on down the river. The bar was fortunately as smooth as when they entered, and running out, the pinnace, with the captured canoe, was soon in the open sea. The latter was light enough to take on board should bad weather come on; but, as she would inconveniently occupy much space, she was allowed, while the sea remained calm, to tow astern.

"Well, we've done something," said Desmond, as, the boat having got a good offing, all hands were piped to supper; "only I wish we'd got hold of that box of gold."

"I very much doubt the existence of the box of gold," said Adair; "the object of the old Arab was to delay us till his friends could come to his assistance, and cut our throats. However, if I am right, he acted his part to admiration."

The pinnace continued her cruise. Happily the weather remained fine, and no one had to complain of hardship, though all hands would have been glad to get a run on shore, instead of being cramped up day after day in the boat. As their water was, however, running short, they at length stood into a small bay which offered a safe landing-place. The canoe was found very useful in conveying them on shore, while the pinnace brought up a short distance from the beach. Several natives came down, who appeared friendly, and showed Adair and Desmond, who had landed, a spring of water where the casks could, without difficulty, be filled and rolled down to the canoe. While four of the men remained in the boat with Archie, the rest brought the casks on shore, and all went on well. A supply of water was taken on board, and trifling presents, as an acknowledgment of the services they had rendered, given to those who appeared to be the leading men among the natives. Hands were shaken, and the party embarked.

"We must mark this spot," observed Adair, as they once more made sail; "the natives appear to be good sort of fellows, and we'll pay them another visit on our way northward."

The balmy weather which had hitherto prevailed was not to continue. The south-west monsoon had begun to blow, and the sea got up, washing over the bows and flying-deck, and giving ample occupation to all hands in baling out the water as fast as it broke on board. It was impossible to spread the usual awning drawn over the boat in ordinary rainy weather, or when at anchor, as it would have been blown away in an instant; and all that could be done was to keep her jogging on under close-reefed sails. It was somewhat trying work, as the fire could not be lighted to cook, and the party had therefore to subsist on raw salt pork and biscuit, washed down with cold grog. Everyone, of course, was wet to the skin; but when the sun again burst forth, their clothes were speedily dried. The boat behaved admirably, rising over the seas like a duck. Two days the gale lasted, and then the weather again cleared.

"If we get any more downpours, I don't intend to let my clothes get wet," said Desmond.

"How are you going to prevent that?" asked Archie.

"Why, by stowing them away in the locker and jumping overboard," answered Desmond. "It's the wisest plan, depend on it. That's the way the nigger boatmen manage in the West Indies, and it will answer here just as well."

"Not if it is blowing hard, as it has just been doing," said Archie.

"No," replied Gerald; "but if it's tolerably calm, we can easily get on board again when the rain is over."

Adair, who had heard of the plan being adopted by other boats' crews, had no objection; and the next day, when the clouds again gathered and sent down a deluge, such as only falls in the tropics, all hands, with the exception of two, who remained to take care of the boat, stripped off their clothes and jumped overboard, swimming about and amusing themselves till the rain was over. They did the same half a dozen times during the day, whenever a torrent descended from the clouds, and then again clambering on board, after rubbing themselves over, put on their dry garments. The only wonder was that no one was carried off by a shark, but probably, as they were splashing about and making a loud noise all the time they were in the water, the savage monsters were kept at a distance.

The weather again permanently cleared up. Several dhows were chased and overtaken. The first they boarded had, in addition to her brown-skinned Arab crew, an equal number of black seamen, who were pulling and hauling and making themselves very busy; while she also had a large party of black passengers, who sat ranged round the deck mute as statues, dressed up in Arab costume, each man having with him two or three wives and several children.

The captain, or "negoda," as he was called by the Arabs, met Adair with a smiling countenance as he stepped on board, and expressed himself in choice Arabic as highly delighted to see the English officer.

"Well, my friend, who are all those black fellows there?" asked Adair, pointing to the negroes, who were jumping about and tumbling over each other as they ran from side to side.

The negoda or skipper made signs as if hauling on a rope. "Oh, they are your crew, are they?" said Adair; on which the skipper nodded his head as if he had really understood the question.

"And who are those ladies and gentlemen seated so comfortably on the deck?" continued Adair. The skipper signified that they were coming from some place in the South, and bound to Mozambique or Zanzibar to join their relatives. He did this by pronouncing the names of those places, talking away all the time, and transferring a piece of money from one hand to the other, as if to show that they had paid their passages.

"Now let me see your papers," said Adair, moving his hand as if holding a pen and writing. The Arabs being accustomed to signs, the negoda at once understood him, and produced from a case some documents written in Arabic characters, which were about as comprehensible to the English officer as the words which the voluble skipper was pouring forth into his ear. The papers might be, for what he could tell, bills of sale for the negroes on board, or directions to the skipper how to avoid the English boats and cruisers, with the hint, should he find himself strong enough, to knock every Briton he could fall in with on the head. Adair, it is true, had his suspicions that all was not right, but how to ascertain this was the question.

Pango, who knew the true state of the case, was evidently very much troubled in his mind on the subject; but in vain he tried to explain his ideas while he sat in the boat, wriggling and twisting his body, and making such extraordinary grimaces as he tried to get out his words, that the rest of the crew burst into fits of laughter, which effectually prevented him from giving the information he possessed.

Had Hamed come in the boat, the case would have been

different, and Adair resolved, if possible, not to go cruising again without the interpreter.

The skipper had no objection to his examining the vessel, though he seemed highly pleased on seeing his visitors about to take their departure. He and several of his crew shook them warmly by the hands, and showed an especial eagerness to assist them into the boat.

As the dhow stood away to the northward, both Gerald and Archie declared that they heard shouts of laughter proceeding from her; but Adair was of opinion that the Arabs were not wont to indulge in such exhibitions of hilarity, though he had very strong suspicions that he had been humbugged.

The southern limits he had designed for the cruise having been reached, Adair put the boat's head to the northward, intending, as before, to search all the inlets and creeks; for although no birds had been entrapped on their previous visit, some might be caught on a second. He was half inclined to suppose that the slave-trade could not be carried on to the extent which was reported, for so many of the dhows boarded had no slaves or fittings for the reception of slaves, while others were carrying only black passengers, seized with the desire apparently to see the world. Adair was sorely puzzled. "I wish we had brought Hamed with us," he repeated for the twentieth time; "he would have cleared up the difficulty, and enabled us to obtain more information than we are likely now to pick up."

As they were again in want of water, by the time they came off the pretty little village where they had before been received in so friendly a manner, he determined to pay it another visit. The pinnace was accordingly steered into the bay, and anchored a short distance from the shore. Adair and Desmond landed in the canoe, accompanied by two men and as many breakers as she could carry. While the two men paddled back for more, he and his nephew walked up to the village. The primitive-looking palm-leaved thatched huts were picturesquely situated an eighth of a mile or so from the beach, under the shade of a grove of lofty cocoa-nut trees. The chief man, with a party of his followers, came out to meet them, and invited them into the principal hut, used apparently as a guest-house. The chief made signs that the women were preparing food, and begged their guests to rest till it was ready. Adair was inclined to accept the invitation.

"There seem to be a good many of the fellows collected, considering the size of the village, and I see that they are all armed," observed Desmond; "the chief, too, is evidently mighty eager for us to go into the hut. They may be very honest, but they may mean mischief."

"I am inclined to agree with you," answered Adair; "we must be on our guard, at all events, though I don't suppose they will venture to commit any act of violence."

He, accordingly, when the chief again pressed him to enter the hut, made signs that he was in a hurry, and could not accept his hospitality. He and Desmond, however, stood talking, or rather exchanging pantomimic gestures with the chief for some time, while the men were engaged in filling the casks and carrying them back to the boat. Desmond, who had returned a short distance towards the shore, to a spot whence he saw that the canoe was shoving off with her last cargo, on turning back to tell his uncle, what was his dismay to see a dozen savages throw themselves upon him, and, seizing his arms, hold him in a way which prevented him from offering the slightest resistance! Desmond, who had on his sword, as well as a rifle in his hand, was rushing back to render what help he could, regardless of the danger he ran, when another party of the natives, concealed behind the trees, suddenly sprang out upon him; and before he saw them, they had seized him and thrown him down on the ground. He struggled to free himself, as every Irishman would do, especially an Irish midshipman, but in vain. Some seized his legs, and others his arms, while one of the party threw a piece of cloth round his mouth to prevent him from crying out. He managed to get that off, however, and shouted at the top of his voice, in the hopes that the men in the canoe would hear him. Finding that all attempts to escape were hopeless, he submitted with as good a grace as he could, and was placed by his captors on his feet.

Adair was, in the meantime, trying to make the chief say why he had committed the outrage, and threatening him with the vengeance of Her Majesty's fleet in those seas if he and the midshipman were not immediately released. The chief might possibly not have understood a word he said. At all events, he was not moved by his threats.

"Now, you scoundrel, what do you intend to do with us?" asked Adair. The chief seemed to understand the question, possibly from the tone in which it was put, and, pointing his musket first towards him, and then at Desmond, gave him to understand, by a sign not to be mistaken, that he intended to shoot them both. Things were now, indeed, becoming serious. They were just out of sight of the boat, and it was a question whether the men in the canoe had heard Desmond's shouts. If not, probably more of the men would come on shore to look for them, and would to a certainty be made prisoners, and in all likelihood murdered.

"What is to be done?" asked Desmond. "I'll give another shout, even though the rascals may gag me for doing so."

After remaining perfectly quiet and apparently resigned to his fate, raising his voice to the highest pitch, he shouted out, "Help! help!" He had only time to utter these words, when a big negro standing near him clapped his hand before his mouth, and effectually prevented him from uttering another sound.

"Never fear, Desmond," said Adair; "I think they must have heard that shout, and Gordon will to a certainty suspect what has happened to us."

While a number of negroes collected round their captives, regarding them with savage looks, the chief and some of his principal men assembled to hold a consultation as to what was to be done with them. An immense amount of jabbering took place, and Desmond, who was closest to the circle of councillors, looked anxiously at their countenances to ascertain, if possible, what decision was likely to be arrived at. He gazed in vain—nothing could he learn from the expression of the hideous faces of those who might at any moment determine to shoot him and his uncle.

"It's all owing to not having Hamed with us," sighed Adair; "or even had we brought Pango on shore, he would probably have suspected the old rascal of a chief, and warned us in time; but cheer up, Desmond, I don't think the black villains will dare to kill us. I'll try and make them understand that if they do, a terrible vengeance will be wreaked on their heads."

"That won't help us out of the scrape, I'm afraid," said Desmond; "but they are getting on their feet, and I suppose we shall soon know."

In a short time the chief and his advisers, having come to a resolution what to do, approached their prisoners, and, with very little ceremony, seizing them by their collars, two on each side of them, dragged them along towards the beach till they reached a couple of trees, whence the boat was clearly visible. The canoe had returned on board, and Adair observed that the men had got out their arms and were pulling her in towards the shore, while Jerry Bird, who acted as gunner, was standing on the forecastle, busy apparently in loading the gun mounted on it; the greater portion of which was, however, covered up with a piece of tarpaulin, so that the natives might not discover what was there. The rest of the crew not pulling had their muskets in their hands ready for use. All this was seen at a glance.

Directly they arrived at the two trees, the savages without further ceremony bound Adair to one, and Desmond to the other, facing the boat; while the chief and several of his followers, who were armed with muskets, levelled them at their heads.

"By my faith, we're in an unpleasant position," exclaimed Desmond. "Sure the fellows can't be after blowing our brains out."

"They most certainly will, if Archie ventures to open fire on them; but I don't think he'll do that while we're alive," answered Adair. "Had Hamed been with us, we could have learned what they want. As it is, I'm afraid that there is as little hope of our understanding them as there is of their making out what we say. However, I'll try." Though Adair was lashed to the tree, his arms were left at liberty, and beckoning to the chief, he tried to make him signify what it was he wanted. At length he seemed to understand Adair's question, and, going through the action of rolling a cask down the beach, he put on an angry look, and then, holding his musket and a piece of cloth in his hand, he showed that he wanted those articles in payment for the water carried off.

"The rascal!" exclaimed Adair; "however, it's better to pay them than run the risk of being shot," and, shouting to Archie, he directed him to send two of his men on shore with the articles demanded, there fortunately being still a supply of cloth on board, which had been brought for bartering with the natives.

"Let the small-armed men cover the men while they are landing," he again shouted, "and let them leave the things on the beach, and take good care that the natives don't seize them."

Archie heard the order, and soon afterwards the canoe came towards the beach, bringing an old musket and a few yards of calico.

The chief, eager to possess himself of the treasures, hurried down to the water, while the men in the canoe, as directed, paddled back to the boat. When the chief had got possession of them, he, like Pharaoh, hardened his heart, and refused to liberate his captives, insisting on having a further ransom. Adair was very much inclined to refuse, and shook his head to show that he would pay no more. On this the chief levelled his musket, with significant gestures, showing that he intended to persist in his demand.

"We must yield to the fellow," said Adair; "it would be folly to run the risk of being shot for the sake of maintaining our dignity."

"I don't think that musket would be after shooting us," observed Desmond, with perfect calmness.

"Why so?" asked Adair.

"Because it happens not to have a lock," answered Gerald; "and, as far as I can see, it is the best of the lot."

"So far that is satisfactory," said Adair; "as the fellows can't injure those in the boat; but, notwithstanding that, they may give us club-law or run their daggers into us, so it won't do to try them too much." Adair asked the chief what he wanted in addition to the things he had received, but he could not make out the meaning of the old fellow's reply. He therefore directed Archie to send some large rings and beads, and a few other articles used to trade with the natives. On these being received the chief seemed tolerably well satisfied, and ordered his men to release the prisoners, putting out his hand as if he had acted in no extraordinary manner, and wished to part good friends. Adair, not to be outdone, shook his hand, and, taking him by the arm, walked with him slowly down towards the beach.

"Stick close to his other side, Desmond," he said. "I'm going to play the old fellow a trick he little thinks of."

The chief seemed to have no suspicions of Adair's design, and was evidently anxious to do away with the effect his conduct had produced. When they had got about half-way to the beach, however, on finding himself at some distance from his followers, he stopped, when Adair, suddenly pulling out a pistol from his pocket, which the natives had not discovered, held it to the old fellow's head, and made him understand that he would shoot him through the brain if he refused to come on to the canoe, or if any of his people approached to his assistance. Archie, seeing what had occurred, had sent in the canoe, which had just reached the beach with a couple of hands. He had likewise brought the gun to bear on the mass of natives, who stood very much astonished at the sudden change of circumstances. Some way from the water, the old chief, fully believing that the English officer would put his threat into execution, sang out to his followers to keep quiet, and not to attempt to rescue him.

"Come along, old fellow, come along," cried Desmond, hauling away at the arm of the reluctant chief, who had, by the bye, fastened Adair's sword-belt round his waist. The old man, who exhibited but little heroism on the occasion, trembling in every limb, turned an imploring glance at the lieutenant, to entreat him not to pull the fatal trigger.

"Now, Desmond," cried Adair, "trip him up by the heels as soon as we get to the canoe, and we'll give him a lesson neither he nor his followers will forget in a hurry."

The two men in the canoe, guessing what their officers intended, kept her afloat; and Adair and Desmond with a sudden jerk running the old chief into the water, the latter tripped up his heels, and, before he knew where he was, he was hauled on board and stowed away in the bottom.

"Shove off," cried Adair, as he and Desmond sprang into the stern; and the next instant they were paddling away in the canoe, before even the natives on shore had clearly comprehended that their chief was being spirited off. He groaned and shrieked, without exciting the slightest compassion, and was soon lifted crop and heels on board the boat. Archie had already begun to weigh anchor; the sails were hoisted, and the wind being off-shore, the boat stood out to the offing, leaving the natives lost in wonder as to what had become of their chief.

"Thank you, Gordon; you behaved admirably under the circumstances," said Adair.

"I am glad of your good opinion, sir," answered Archie; "but, if you will allow me to say so, I think you and Desmond acted still more admirably."

The crew, of course, were loud in their expressions of admiration at their officers' conduct.

"Now we've got him, what are we to do with him?" asked Desmond.

"Treat him well, and send him back a wiser if not a better man than he was," answered Adair. "We'll carry him with us on board the *Opal* as a proof of the transaction, and perhaps, after a few months' stay on board, he will have learned better manners."

The old chief, however, did not seem at all to approve of the change of his circumstances, and at first it was thought that he was going to give it up as a hopeless case, and die of vexation.

Jerry Bird, however, patted him on the back. "Don't take on, old fellow, in this fashion," he said, in a consoling voice; "you thought you were going to play the lieutenant a trick, and, like many a better man, you found you caught a Tartar. What's the odds? we'll give you as much pork and biscuit as you can eat, and a glass of grog to cheer you up, and you'll come all right by and by."

Whether it was the words of this address, or the tone in which it was uttered, need not be discussed; but it seemed to have the effect of bringing the old chief round, and when a basin of "kettler" was served out to him, he did not inquire what were the ingredients, but gobbled it up with evident gusto. He smacked his lips, also, after tasting the pannikin of grog which Jerry offered him, and though he put it down again once or twice, as if doubting about the matter, he finally drained it to the dregs.

"I thought as how you'd like it," said Jerry, patting him on the back; "you shall have another presently, and you won't have to say that we treated you with scant hospitality. That ain't our way aboard ship."

Adair, however, interfered, and prevented the men from giving the old chief as much liquor as they were ready to bestow on him, lest he might get drunk, and take it into his head to run a-muck or jump overboard. He had taken enough, however, to send him fast asleep in the bottom of the boat, where he lay, as Jerry observed, "like a porpus in a gale of wind."

CHAPTER V

Three Dhows chased—One is captured and left in Charge of Desmond and Archie—Frightful Condition of Slaves on Board—Horrible Cruelties practised by Arabs—Jerry Bird sets the Slaves dancing to keep up their Spirits—Desmond's Watch—He and Archie thrown Overboard.

AS the breeze continued light and favourable, the boat ran on all night under easy sail. A bright look-out was kept, however, in the possibility of meeting a dhow creeping along-shore. Just as morning dawned, and they arrived abreast of a deep bay which Adair intended to explore, three dhows were seen standing out from under the land, with their wide spread of canvas wooing the light breeze. It was pretty evident that the boat had been discovered. Adair therefore ordered the crew to lower the sails, and to take to their oars, which they did with right goodwill, hoping to catch two, at least, of the strangers in sight.

The smallest and leading vessel showed Arab colours. A shot across her fore-foot quickly made her haul them down. The other two exhibited no bunting. From the efforts they were making to escape, it was pretty evident they were full slavers. As soon as Adair reached the first dhow, he leaped on board; but a glance told him that she was a legal trader, with not a slave in her, as far as he could judge; although there were several black men, whom the negoda affirmed belonged to the vessel.

"We'll give you the advantage of believing you," said Adair, jumping back into his boat, which pulled away to the nearest of the other vessels. Just then she lowered her sail.

"Hurrah!" cried Desmond; "she has given in."

"Not a bit of it," answered Adair; "see, she is going to set a wider spread of canvas than before."

He was right. Presently a long tapering yard rose to the head of the stern, the sail swelling out like the balloon jib of a racing yacht, and shining brightly in the rising sun.

"Should the breeze increase, she will walk away from us like greased lightning, as the Yankees say," observed Adair.

"We'll hope, then, it will remain calm," said Archie. As it was, though the men strained at their oars, it taxed their utmost strength to gain on her. Still, they were gaining. Desmond and Archie stepped forward to assist Jerry in getting the gun ready to fire a shot as soon as they got near enough to make her heave-to. Light as was the breeze, the dhow continued to slip rapidly through the water. It was evident, however, that the boat was gaining on her, and the men redoubled their efforts.

"Shall we fire, sir?" asked Archie. "We might manage to bring down her sail."

"Fire over her," answered Adair; "a shot might chance to hurt some of the poor slaves, instead of the rascally Arabs."

Jerry elevated the gun, and pulled the trigger. Away flew the shot right through the dhow's huge sail; but her crew, looking to windward, fancied that the breeze was about to freshen. The gun was quickly sponged and again loaded.

"Try another shot," cried Adair; "if you can hit the yard or mast, it will save us a long pull."

Jerry willingly obeyed; but again the shot, though well aimed, only went through the sail.

"Very good practice," said Adair, "but just let it be a little better."

Jerry Bird, though watching the chase, could not help now and then taking a look at the countenance of the old chief,—Mustapha Longchops, the sailors called him,—but whether he wished the dhow to escape or not, it was difficult to say. Jerry had again got the gun ready, and, putting it on the breech, he exhorted it this time to do its duty. Again he pulled the trigger, when the next instant down came the long yard by the run on deck. The midshipmen uttered a hearty cheer, taken up by Adair and the crew, and in a few minutes they were alongside the vessel.

The Arabs, however, seeing only a single boat, and unsupported, had made up their minds, it seems, not to yield without a struggle. Some twenty savage-looking fellows, some armed with two-handed swords, others with muskets and assegais, stood ready to defend their vessel. As the pinnace ranged up alongside, several shots were fired and assegais hurled at them, one of which, whizzing close to Adair's ear, stuck quivering in the sternsheets as he was springing up the side. The dauntless seamen, however, were not to be stopped by their show of weapons and threatening gestures. In spite of the Arabs, who cut and slashed right and left with their two-handed swords, several of the bluejackets were about to spring up the vessel's side, when one of the former, aiming a blow at the head of the boat-hook, with which Jerry Bird was holding on, cut it right through; and at the same instant some of the Arab crew, who had in the meantime been bending on fresh halyards, hoisted away on the sail, the dhow forging ahead.

"Fire at those fellows!" cried Adair to the small-armed men; who, letting fly with their muskets, bowled over three at once. The oars were meantime again got out, and the sail having come down on deck, the boat once more dashed up, this time making for the starboard bow. Jerry took the precaution of making fast with a stout rope; and, led by Adair, all hands were quickly on board, two more of the Arabs being shot down.

The others, however, still bravely attempted to defend their vessel, wielding their weapons with the same vigour as before; but, desperate as they were, they could not withstand the British cutlasses, and were driven aft for refuge in the cabin, crying out for mercy. All this time shrieks and groans arose from the hold, while the vilest of odours, a mixture of everything abominable, pervaded the vessel, leaving not a doubt, even had the crew not attempted to defend her, that she was a full slaver, and a legal capture.

"Hand over your arms," cried Adair, "and we'll spare your lives." It is possible some one among the Arabs might have understood English; at all events, the whole of the crew soon hurried up and handed over their swords and other weapons to the victors.

"Tumble their arms into the pinnace," said Adair; "we must have that other dhow. Gordon and Desmond, I'll leave you with five men to manage these fellows, while I go in chase of her. If I take her, keep close to me. Signalise should they show any inclination to be mutinous, and I'll bear down and help you. I'll leave you the canoe; we shall make better way without her." Saying this, Adair shoved off and pulled away in chase of the third dhow.

The first care of the midshipmen was to complete the task in performing which the three Arabs had been killed, and to hoist up the sail, aided by several of the crew, whom they compelled at the point of their swords to lend a hand; while, one of the seamen being sent to the helm, the dhow steered after the pinnace in hot chase of the still uncaptured slaver, the canoe, which had hitherto been alongside, being stowed astern.

The deck of the dhow, on board which the midshipmen found themselves, presented a horrible appearance. The three men who had first been shot lay stiff and stark, weltering in their blood at the foot of the mast. Farther off sat the negoda, with a shot through his leg and another in his body, glaring fiercely at them; while another man lay not far off, writhing in agony, with life ebbing fast. The rest of the crew, greasy, dirty ruffians, with close-fitting turbans and caps on their heads, baggy trousers, and vests covering their bodies, stood about with sulky, hang-dog looks, regarding the victors.

"We must keep an eye on these fellows," said Jerry Bird to Archie; "they'll not mind cutting our throats if they have the chance."

"Little doot aboot that," said Archie; "but hallo! here's our old friend Mustapha Longchops. How did he get on board?"

It was very evident that the old chief must have scrambled up after the seamen boarded, and stowed himself away till the fight was over. What was his object in so doing was difficult to ascertain.

"It wasn't with any good intention, I've a notion," said Desmond; "however, we'll be up to him."

"I think, sir," said Jerry Bird, "we may as well see if they've got any more arms stowed away. If they have, the sooner they're hove overboard the better; for if they get hold of them, the Arabs would prove somewhat ugly customers on a dark night."

Jerry's advice was followed. While two of the hands kept an eye on the crew on deck, Jerry and Desmond, with the rest, searched the after-cabin, and discovered no less than a dozen muskets, several pistols and swords, and some formidable-looking knives or daggers, which would have proved deadly weapons in the hands of the Arabs. They were all quickly hove overboard, greatly to the disgust of their former owners. They were, however, not the only articles discovered.

"Hallo! what's this?" cried Jerry, drawing out a box from the locker; "it seems pretty heavy for its size. Shouldn't be surprised to find it full of gold."

Desmond, who was superintending the search, laughed. "We can scarcely expect such good luck as that," he answered.

"We'll try, sir," said Jerry, prizing open the top with one of the daggers which he had retained. "Hurrah! I was right, sir," he sang out; "golden pieces every one of them, four or five hundred, at least!"

"No doubt about it," observed Desmond, examining the box; "it is not ours, however, after all. We must hand it over to the commander as part of the cargo found in the prize, as well as every other article of value; though we shall get our share in due time."

"To be sure, sir, to be sure," answered Jerry, with a sigh. "At first I thought you and Mr. Gordon, and the rest of us, might pocket it; but it's all right—we must share and share alike."

Desmond ordered the box to be stowed away in the forepart of the cabin, which he and Archie intended to occupy. The Arab captain cast a longing glance at his treasure as it was carried away, possibly regarding the present possessors with no friendly feeling. The discovery induced the seamen to make a further search, and jewellery, pieces of cloth and silk, and numerous rich Arab garments were brought to light, sufficient altogether to fill a considerable portion of the cabin.

"Now let's look after the slaves below," said Archie; "the poor fellows must have been in a fearful quandary while the fighting was going forward."

Whatever feeling of pity the condition of the wounded Arabs might have excited in the breasts of the English was removed when they came to examine the hold. Indeed, the horrible state of the unhappy beings surpasses all description. Upwards of two hundred human beings were found stowed away in the hold of the craft, which could not have measured more than a hundred tons. On a bamboo deck, scarcely raised high enough above the keel to be free of the abominably-smelling bilge-water which occupied her lowest depths, lay some eighty or ninety men, doubled up, and packed so closely together that it was utterly impossible for them to stretch their legs; while there was not room enough for them to raise their heads without touching the deck above. They were stowed away, indeed, literally, as Jerry Bird observed, "like herrings in a cask." Above them were an equal number of women huddled together, doubled up in the same fashion, the space being insufficient for them to sit or recline. On the highest deck were penned away a still larger number of children of various ages, ranging from six years old to twelve or thirteen, girls and boys, with even less space allowed them, in proportion to their size, than their elders. The miserable wretches were evidently suffering fearfully from starvation and dysentery. Many were too weak to move, and several on the point of breathing their last. Five or six of the women had infants in their arms but a few weeks old. As one of the mothers was brought on deck, she exhibited her child with its head crushed in, which she intimated had been done, just after the boat had been discovered in pursuit, by one of the Arabs, because the child had been crying somewhat lustily.

"Let's see the fellow who did it," exclaimed Desmond, "and we'll pay him off for his barbarity."

The woman understood him, and looked about among the crew till her eye fell on the wounded Arab, who still lay writhing on the deck.

"Is that he?" asked Desmond. "Well, he has got his due, and little pity any of us can feel for him."

The midshipmen, with their cargo of slaves and villainous prisoners, found themselves in a very trying position, requiring the full exercise of all their wits and energies. Probably, had Adair had time to consider, he would not have left them with so small a force on board; but his eagerness to overtake the other dhow prevented him from reflecting on the difficulties and dangers they would have to encounter.

Their first care was to try and ameliorate the condition of the slaves. Search was made for such food and water as the dhow contained, and the Arabs were ordered to prepare a hearty meal for them—a task they set about with no very good grace. The only provisions they discovered were rice and millet seed, with scarcely drinkable water, and of these in most limited portions, on which the slaves would have had to subsist till the termination of their voyage. No wonder that many had died, and that nearly all looked more like living skeletons than human beings.

"If we'd had Dick Needham on board, he'd have told us how they managed with slavers captured on the West Coast," observed Archie.

"I'll tell you," said Jerry Bird; "I've seen many a one taken. The best way is to get up forty or fifty at a time on deck and set them dancing. It seems to put new life into them, bad as they may be."

The midshipmen followed Jerry's advice at once, and released fifty of the men, who crawled up and squatted down on either side of the deck. A mess of rice, with a little water, was then served out to each of them. They eagerly swallowed the food, cramming it into their mouths like monkeys, but with less intelligence or animation in their countenances than those creatures exhibit.

"They don't look as if they had much dancing in them," observed Gerald.

"Stay a bit," said Jerry; "we'll soon see," whereon he began skipping about, snapping his fingers and singing. Then he took hold first of one and then of another, and in a few seconds more than half of them were dancing like magic on their feet, imitating his movements; many more of them seeming willing to join in the sport, had they possessed the requisite strength. They sang and laughed and jabbered away as if they had not a care in the world.

"Faith, they look more like dancing skeletons than anything else," said Gerald, watching the poor fellows. The voices of many of them were also so faint as scarcely to be audible, in spite of their efforts to sing out; indeed, it seemed a wonder that they could utter any notes except those of wailing and despair.

Of course, an anxious eye had been kept on the pinnace and the vessel she was chasing. "She's up to her," cried Desmond, who was looking through his glass; "she struck without a blow, and there go our fellows tumbling on board. Little doubt, however, about her being a slaver, though, as they must have seen the way in which we got hold of this craft, they thought it as well to save their bacon, and make the best of a bad job."

It was evident that Adair had got easy possession of the third dhow, as the sail, which had at first been lowered, was quickly hoisted again, while the pinnace was dropped astern. He appeared to consider that all was going well on board the first capture, as he did not shorten sail to allow her to come up. Perhaps he was too busy with the Arab captain and the slaves to think about the matter.

The first gang of blacks, having enjoyed themselves for some time in their own fashion, were ordered below. The women were next got up. Poor creatures! there was very little dancing power in them; many of them being mothers who had lost their children, and others with dying infants in their arms, many of them in the last stage of sickness. Still, some of them, on being set to work, began skipping about, clapping their hands, laughing and singing, at no little risk of breaking in the frail deck; for, in general, being fatter, they were heavier than the men. The Arabs looked on with evident disgust, not comprehending the object of the English in expending so much food, and allowing the negroes to move about, thereby increasing their appetites. The poor children were the last to appear on the stage, and they were all turned out together, looking more like apes than human beings. Having been on the highest deck, with some ventilation from above, they were less in want of air than the grown-up people, though they seemed to enjoy the exercise allowed them even more than the rest; but not a particle of the animation of childhood was discernible among any of them. From the way they moved about, they seemed to fancy that their dance was but a prelude to their being put to death to fill the cooking-pots of the white men, which their Arab captors had told them would be their lot.

All hands had been so busy that no one had thought of eating themselves. It was then discovered that a bag of biscuit alone had been brought on board and a bottle of rum, which one of the men in the pinnace had handed up to Jerry just as she was shoving off. This was, however, better than nothing, and they hoped before long to be up with the other prize, and to obtain more substantial fare. The day was now drawing to a close. The wind continued light as before, and the two dhows retained their relative positions; the last taken being about half a mile on the port bow of the other. The four dead bodies were hove overboard (for the badly-wounded wretch had followed his companions to the other world).

Archie and Gerald had done their best to bind up the hurts of the negoda, who had been placed in the cabin with such care taken of him as circumstances would admit. They tried to make him understand that, as soon as they could fall in with a surgeon, his wounds would be better dressed. The Arab crew, being tired, coiled themselves away in different parts of the vessel, while Mustapha Longchops had seated himself at his ease near the skipper. Thus the management of the dhow was left entirely to her captors.

Archie and Desmond consulted together as to whether they ought to clap the crew in irons, or, rather, to lash their arms and legs together, thus putting it out of their power to commit mischief. They settled, however, as Adair had said nothing about it, to allow them to remain at liberty. Archie, of course, took one watch and Desmond the other, with the crew divided between them. As the night advanced, the wind increased, and the dhow made rapid way through the water, steering after Adair's prize. No moon was shining, clouds gathered in the sky, and the night became darker than usual in those latitudes. Desmond was to keep the first watch, with one man at the helm and another on the look-out; while Archie lay down just inside the door of the cabin, with Jerry near him, the other two men going forward.

"I'll sleep with one eye open, sir," said Jerry, "and will be up in a moment if I'm wanted."

The Arab crew were sleeping about in groups on the deck, where they had lain for some time, none of them having offered to lend a hand to do anything. Desmond had been awake for the greater part of the previous night, and, having undergone a good deal of excitement during the day, it was no wonder that he found it difficult to keep his eyes open; still, he did his best to watch a light which Adair had hung over the stern of his prize, and, after looking for some time, he felt convinced that they were slowly gaining on her. Every now and then he turned to the man at the helm with some remark, and then shouted to the other forward to keep a bright look-out. At length, however, the light ahead began to flicker and dance, and now to grow larger, now to decrease, till it was scarcely visible. He was holding fast on to the side of the dhow, and found some support necessary. He looked up at the huge sail, which, bulging out, seemed to grow larger and larger till it towered up into the sky. Desmond was a very promising officer, but even the most promising are made of flesh and blood, and require sleep to restore exhausted nature. The most vigilant would not have found him nodding, for he would have promptly answered with perfect correctness had he been spoken to. Notwithstanding that, Gerald Desmond was certainly not broad awake—or rather, he was as fast asleep as a midshipman standing on his legs, with his eyes wide open, could be. His thoughts, too, were wandering, now to Ballymacree, now to Commander Murray's home in the Highlands, and now away to the West Indies, where he might still be for all he knew.

Just then, suddenly he felt a cloth thrown over his eyes, and before he could put up his hands to draw it away, he found his

6

arms pinioned behind him. The same instant he heard Archie and Jerry Bird sing out, and the man at the helm struggling desperately with a number of the Arabs, while from every part of the dhow arose shouts and cries. Then there came a splash, then another and another; the next instant he was hurled head-foremost overboard, happily his arms getting free as he struggled impulsively to save himself from his impending fate.

CHAPTER VI

Adair boards the third Dhow—Her Crew and Passengers—Pango discovers that the latter are Slaves—Adair returns with the Dhow to the Island—Green absent on an Expedition—Adair's Fears as to Desmond and Archie—Green returns with the Dhow left in charge of Desmond, but without the Midshipmen—Adair's Anxiety increases—Interrogation of the Arab Crew—A Sail in Sight—She proves to be the Opal—*Adair informs Murray of the Loss of the Midshipmen—The Commander's Grief—The Dhow blows up with all on Board, and saves the Hangman a Job—The* Opal *goes in search of the Midshipmen.*

ADAIR, after leaving the midshipmen on board the first dhow, eager to capture the second, urged his crew not to spare their arms, or the tough ash-sticks they handled. They, fully as eager as the lieutenant, were not the men to do that, and the boat made rapid progress through the calm water. They had every hope of catching her, unless a breeze should suddenly spring up, when they well knew that she would slip away from them at a speed which they had no chance of equalling. In case of such an occurrence, the gun mounted on the bow was reloaded, ready to send a shot after her.

The wind continued light, and at length, laying in their oars, they ranged up alongside, taking good care to make the boat fast; when, following their lieutenant, all hands leaped on board with cutlasses and pistols, ready to make short work of any who might oppose them—though, to their surprise, not the slightest resistance was offered. The deck appeared crowded with passengers, their skins black as jet, but dressed in every variety of Oriental costume. The numerous crew, a large proportion of whom were black, were collected forward; while the negoda stood aft, near the man at the helm. He advanced with a smiling countenance, and made a profound salaam to Adair, who, sheathing his sword, with his men at his back, stood ready to receive him; a couple only, one of whom was Pango, remained in the boat to look after her.

He was a wiry, daring-looking fellow, with a bold, piratical swagger, which gave an impression that he would not hesitate at the most audacious acts of atrocity which he might suppose would forward the object he happened to have in view. He put out his hand in the most cool and impudent manner to shake Adair's, and then stood calmly eyeing his uninvited visitors, as much as to say, "Now make the most of me you can."

"Well, amigo, where are you come from?" asked Adair. The negoda, who seemed to expect some such question, though he probably did not understand the words, pointed to the south, and then uttered a long string of sentences, in which Adair thought he could distinguish Zanzibar.

"Well, my friend, and who are all these people you have got on board?" continued Adair, pointing to the silent figures on deck.

The Arab poured forth a torrent of words, pointing in the same direction as before, and next putting a piece of coin from one hand into the other.

"Yes, I understand; they are travellers, going to see the world, and have paid their passage-money, all right and proper. And when they get to Zanzibar, what are they going to do?" asked Adair.

The last question the Arab evidently did not understand, and Adair saw that it would be useless to press the point, knowing that whatever the Arab might say, whether true or false, he should not be the wiser. "And now, as to those fellows tumbling about there, and butting against each other with their curly pates, and looking more like chimney-sweeps than sailors," said Adair, "what have they got to do here?"

The Arab, who guessed by the direction of Adair's eyes that he was asking questions about the men forward, made signs of pulling and hauling.

"Oh, they form part of your crew, do they? Well, I should like to see your papers, and how many hands you are licensed to carry," said Adair, making the usual signal of pretending to write, which the negoda clearly understanding, produced from his capacious pocket various documents scrawled all over with Arabic characters.

Adair took them, but of course did not understand a single one of the curious-shaped letters and papers. "Very ship-shape," he remarked, pretending to scan the papers. "If you have no slaves on board, nor fittings for slaves, we must let you proceed on your voyage," he added, returning the papers with a polite bow, on which the skipper appeared highly delighted. "You'll give me leave first, however, to search the hold and take a look into your cabin." The negoda's countenance fell, as Adair, followed by two of his men, made their way into the space under the high poop. "Hallo! who are all these?" he exclaimed, as he saw seated round the sides some thirty sable damsels, bundled up in silks and cottons, with a variety of ornaments on their curly heads, most of them with children in their arms, or seated by their side, little and big.

The skipper looked somewhat nonplussed; but presently, pointing out three of the best-looking, he tried to make his visitor understand that they were his wives.

"Oh! very well," said Adair, who comprehended his meaning; "but to whom do all those others belong?"

To this the negoda, without replying directly, shouted to his Arab crew, who came aft, each man taking the hands of a couple of negresses, and declaring that they were his better halves. Thus all the people who had hitherto been seen were accounted for, and the hold alone remained to be examined. Above the cargo, which was stowed in no very regular fashion, was a bamboo deck; but that of course would be necessary for the numerous male and female passengers and their offspring, and was not sufficient in itself to condemn the vessel. Still Adair was not altogether satisfied.

On returning on deck, he determined to interrogate some of the silent negro passengers, who did not look as if they were accustomed to the fine clothes they wore. Without an interpreter, this was a difficult undertaking. When he addressed the blacks, men or women, they put on the most stolid looks, showing him that it would be vain to hope to get any information out of them; but it was a wonder that such stupid-looking people should have any desire to see the world, or could be travelling either on business or pleasure. At last he had to give it up, and to turn to the black sailors. Going forward, he addressed one after the other; but as he spoke, their countenances also changed, and they stood before him with downcast looks, pictures of stolidity. Suddenly he at last bethought him of calling up Pango from the pinnace, to try if he could elicit any information from his sable countrymen. Pango, on being summoned, immediately sprang on board. No sooner had he done so than his eye fell on one of the blacks, from whom Adair was vainly endeavouring to extract information. The two negroes stared at each other for an instant. "Ki!" exclaimed Pango. "Ki!" answered the other, scanning Pango's nautical costume. "Ki!" cried Pango, in a higher key; and then, both making a spring, they seized each other's hands and began shouting at the top of their voices, now laughing, now crying, and again looking in each other's faces.

A rapid conversation then took place between them, the seeming Arab seaman asking Pango all sorts of questions, which he as quickly answered.

"What's it all about?" asked Adair, pointing to the former.

"Brudder! brudder!" answered Pango.

"Where does he come from?" inquired Adair.

Pango gave the incomprehensible name of a village in the interior, adding, "Make slavey, make slavey."

"And who are all those others?" asked Adair.

"All slavey, all slavey," cried Pango eagerly.

"Ah! I thought so," exclaimed Adair. "Tell them that they shall be set free, and that they need no longer sham being sailors, which one can tell with half an eye that they are not."

Pango understood enough of what Adair said to make his fellow-countrymen understand that they would be liberated very soon, as they had the British flag hoisted over their heads. Although a few believed what Pango told them, the rest did not appear altogether convinced of the fact. Adair, however, had now sufficiently ascertained the character of the vessel to warrant him in keeping possession of her.

The negoda, on discovering the resolution which the English officer had formed, looked very much taken aback. In vain he stormed and swore in the choicest Arabic, and cast vindictive glances at Pango, threatening him with condign punishment should he ever catch him on shore. Pango, caring very little for his threats, talked away eagerly with his countrymen, and soon the greatest number went over to the side of the English tars.

Their first care was to disarm the Arabs, and to throw their weapons overboard, while the dhow was searched fore and aft for any others which might be concealed. The negoda, finding he was discovered, very quickly stripped the blacks of their fine garments, and reduced them to the primitive appearance of veritable slaves, giving Adair to understand that the dresses were his private property, and that he expected to be allowed to carry them off. The poor women seemed very loth to part with their borrowed plumes; but the negoda treated them without ceremony, and, as evening approached, sent them and the children all down into the hold. The men were then made to follow them.

Adair had the satisfaction of feeling that he had caught a second slaver, but he saw that it would require all his vigilance to prevent the Arabs from playing him any trick. Looking out astern, he saw the first captured dhow following in his wake. "All right with the youngsters," he thought; "they and Bird have their wits about them, and will keep the slaver's crew under."

As the dhow appeared to be coming up with him, he saw no necessity for shortening sail, as he hoped that she would close with him before nightfall. By the time the sun went down she had got considerably nearer, and, satisfied that all was right, he stood on. The night came on much darker than usual, but he made out the peak of her triangular sail rising against the sky, and therefore still felt perfectly at ease about her. With so many doubtful characters on board, he would not lie down even for a moment, or allow any of his crew to do so, but kept them together, ready to defeat any attempt the Arabs might make to regain their vessel. As they hoped to reach the island the next day, they might then take a long snooze to make up for their want of sleep. Several times he looked astern, when he saw the other prize still about the same distance as before. Suddenly there came a squall and a downpour of rain, but the wind being right aft, the dhow flew on before it. He, however, thought it prudent to send his men to the halyards, so as to be ready, should the wind increase, to lower the sail, the Arabs showing no inclination to assist in working the vessel.

The darkness was greater than ever. The rain indeed, even by itself, was thick enough to hide any objects except close to. In about an hour it cleared off again, when, on looking out for number one prize, he could nowhere distinguish her. "I suppose Gordon and Desmond judged it prudent to lower their sail; they will be hoisting it again presently," he said to himself. Soon afterwards he thought he made her out, rather more over the port quarter than she had been before. Yes, he was certain of it, though she seemed to him farther off than she had hitherto been; still, if the midshipmen had lowered their sail that was to be expected.

Adair, still believing that all was right, continued his course, eager to reach the island, and to arrange for despatching the two dhows to the port of adjudication; though he had no doubt that they both would prove lawful prizes. When morning at length broke, dhow number two was nowhere in sight. This made him somewhat anxious, and he regretted that he had not shortened sail at first to allow her to come up. Still the midshipmen had their wits so completely about them, and Bird was so trustworthy a fellow, and fully alive to the importance of keeping an eye on the Arabs, that he had no very serious apprehensions about their safety.

A clump of trees rising in the centre of the island at length, to his infinite satisfaction, came in sight. He dropped his anchor in the small harbour formed by the coral reef which circled round the southern portion. He was seen coming in, and one of the boats pulled off to welcome him. He was informed that a vast number of dhows had been boarded, but none as yet captured, all being, as far as could be ascertained, lawful traders; though several had, like his prize, no small number of black passengers on board.

"Depend upon it, then, you have been deceived," said Adair, "as I should, had I not the fortunate chance, by means of Pango, to discover the trick the rascally Arabs are playing us. All those black passengers were really slaves, dressed up by their masters. However, we'll take care in future that their trick doesn't avail them, and they must take to some other dodge if they wish to escape us."

Jos Green, he found, had gone over towards the mainland, to watch for any vessels running in or out of Angoxa, or slipping by up the coast, and as he had been away for several days, it was expected that he would soon be back. Several times before going on shore Adair swept the horizon with his glass in search of the missing dhow, expecting every instant to see her sail, like the dark fin of a shark, rising above the waters. He looked, however, in vain. The other officers climbed, one after the other, to the look-out place, but came back with the report that no sail was in sight.

He at once, therefore, made up his mind to send the pinnace, with a fresh crew, in search of the dhow. The wind, though contrary, was slight, and she might reach the spot where the dhow had last been seen before nightfall, and, if any accident had happened to her, render assistance. His only dread was that she might have been leaky, as he knew to be the case with many such craft, and perhaps have gone down.

He and his men were pretty well worn-out from want of sleep and hard work. Having seen the slaves landed, and fresh hands placed in charge of the dhow and the Arab crew, he therefore lay down in his tent to obtain the rest he so much required. Completely exhausted, he slept on till morning.

His first inquiry on awaking was for the pinnace. She had not returned, nor had Green made his appearance. He naturally became more anxious than ever; something serious, he feared, must have happened to the midshipmen, or they would not have failed to have reached the island by that time.

He was on the point of despatching another boat, when the look-out man from the signal-station reported that a dhow was in sight coming across from the mainland. Her arrival was eagerly looked for. There could be no doubt that she was a prize made by Green. This was ascertained positively to be the case, and in about an hour she came to an anchor off the island, having Green's boat astern. The two remaining boats at once put off, Adair going in one of them, accompanied by Pango (Bango had gone with Green to act as his interpreter).

"Why," exclaimed Adair, as he drew near the dhow, "she's the very vessel we captured! and has, I hope, the midshipmen and the rest of the boat's crew on board."

Green hailed them from the deck as they approached. "Glad of your assistance," he said, "for I've got a pretty shipload of scoundrels, who gave us a tough job to take them."

These words made Adair feel more anxious than ever. He recognised the Arab skipper and Mustapha Longchops on deck, but neither of the midshipmen nor any of the men. He was quickly on deck and shaking hands with Green, though the dreadful feeling which oppressed him prevented him for some moments from speaking.

"Where are the midshipmen, Desmond and Gordon," he asked, "and the men I left on board this vessel?"

"You left?" exclaimed Green; "why, I only captured her last night, and had no notion that she had ever been in our hands before, except, by the bye, that Bango has tried to make me understand something which he had heard, though I confess I couldn't exactly comprehend his meaning."

"The night before last I left the midshipmen safe and sound, with four hands and a canoe towing astern," said Adair; "the canoe, I see, is gone, but they would certainly not have deserted the vessel. We must seize these scoundrels, the skipper and that black fellow, with the rest of the Arabs, at once, for I very much fear they have been guilty of some foul play."

Calling more of his men on board, Adair ordered them to handcuff the whole of the party. The Arabs looked somewhat alarmed, their skipper very much so. "What have you done with my officers and men?" asked Adair. The negoda, recovering himself, with the coolest effrontery made the action of shaking hands, then pointed astern, as if to signify that those whom Adair was asking after had parted good friends and gone off in the canoe.

"A very likely tale," said Adair sadly; "let's try what Pango and his brother can make out of the old black chief." On this Green told them to hear what the old man had to say. They evidently spoke the same language. At last Pango, turning round to Adair, tried hard to give the information he had obtained. What with the numerous signs, and the few words of English uttered by the black, Adair understood that the old chief grieved for what had happened, but that he himself had nothing to do with it; that the Arabs had set upon the Englishmen, two of whom were below, had blindfolded them and thrown them overboard.

Adair and Green both interrogated their black friends, and each time came to the same sad conclusion. There could be no doubt that the two lads, Jerry Bird, and the other men had been foully murdered. Adair felt very much inclined to hang all the fellows at once, but of course this could not be thought of; they must first be tried, and there could be no doubt that they would be convicted. What satisfaction would it be to hang the scoundrels? Putting them to death would not probably prevent others from committing similar deeds, nor would it bring those who were lost to life.

It was necessary, however, to land the slaves at once, for the sake of preserving their health; for even during the last few hours several of the grown-up people had died, and nearly a dozen of the children; and others, it was clear, would not survive unless carried on shore, and supplied with better food and fresh water. Superintending this work occupied Adair, and prevented him from mourning over the loss of his young nephew and Archie. The party on shore had been occupied for some time in putting up huts for housing any slaves who might be brought to the island. These were soon filled with the women and children and the sick men. The others not so greatly requiring immediate shelter were set to work to put up some huts for themselves, an operation most of them seemed to understand very well.

In the meantime, the Arab crew were kept on board, under charge of an officer and a party of seamen. Towards evening the boat was seen returning, and Adair had some faint hopes that she might have obtained some information of the midshipmen, in case the skipper's version of the affair was true. Adair hurried down to meet her.

"We bring you no news of the missing ones," said the officer in charge; "we went as far as you directed, and then swept round inshore, but no dhow could we see."

Adair, more out of spirits than he had ever been in his life before, got back to the camp. One of the men came running in with the information that a ship was in sight to the northward. Adair and several others hurried to the nearest point from which they could see her, and he and Green were both of opinion that she was the *Opal*. This was confirmed when she got near enough to make her number. Hopes were entertained that she was coming to take them off; for, though not exactly tired of the life they had been leading, they would gladly have gone to some other locality, where they would be likely to meet with better success than they could boast of hitherto. Adair, however, found himself wishing that Murray had not come back. How could he face him with the account of the loss of the two midshipmen? Murray might blame him, and not unjustly, for want of judgment in leaving them in charge of a vessel manned by desperate ruffians, who would, of course, be glad of the opportunity to revenge themselves on their enemies. "Why did not I think of that before?" exclaimed poor Terence more than once.

However, he ordered the gig to be manned, and as soon as the corvette approached the anchorage, he pulled away for her. She had just brought up, and the hands were aloft furling sails, when his boat got alongside. Murray was, of course, well pleased to see him, though struck by his grave looks.

"All hands are well, I hope? and the youngsters, have they managed to keep themselves out of mischief?" asked Murray.

Adair, a very unwonted thing, felt inclined to hang down his head, as, with a faltering voice, he told the story of their loss.

"You don't mean to say you left those two lads, with only four careless men, to manage a set of cut-throats!" exclaimed Murray.

"I am sorry to say I did, not supposing that the said cut-throats would venture to turn upon them," answered Adair.

"That's it, Adair, that's it," exclaimed Murray, more testily than he was accustomed to speak; "you are too apt not to consider the consequences of what you do, and, from want of judgment, the lives of those boys have been thrown away."

"Really, you are hard upon me," cried Adair. "I acted as well as the circumstances would allow, and it was my duty to try and get hold of the other dhow."

"You should have left a stronger force to keep in check a set of ruffians, with whom only a few minutes before you had been engaged in a struggle for life and death," said Murray; "they acted according to their instincts, and murdered the poor boys."

"I had no time to think of that or anything else," said Adair, about to turn away; "it was my duty to take the other dhow, and I succeeded in doing so."

Murray, observing how much Adair was moved, felt that he was speaking too harshly. "Well, well, I am sure you did as you considered best," said he. "It is a very sad affair, but I don't know that we ought to give them up as lost. You may have misunderstood the two blacks, though circumstances are strongly against the Arab captain. However, I will examine him and his crew and the old black chief, with the aid of Hamed, whom he can understand; and perhaps we may elicit something which will give us ground for hoping that they after all escaped."

"I wish I could think so," said Adair; "I shall blame myself as long as I live for their loss. I am certain they would not willingly have deserted their charge."

Murray, having ordered Hamed to accompany him, pulled off in his gig with Adair. He found the rest of the officers standing on the beach ready to receive him, and he at once issued orders to have the slave captain and his companions brought on shore. Two boats were on the point of putting off to bring them, when a loud report was heard, and thick wreaths of smoke were seen issuing from the dhow, followed almost directly by flames bursting out from all parts. The boats dashed on to rescue those on board; as they did so, they saw a number of men, whom they recognised as their shipmates, swimming towards them, but not the dark face of an Arab among them.

The boats quickly picked them up one after the other, none, happily, of the party left on board being missing. Neither the officer nor any of the men could account for the accident. They were all on deck, the sentry near the hold in which the prisoners were confined; suddenly an explosion occurred which lifted up a portion of the deck, and sent the sentry and two other men standing near him overboard. Flames instantly afterwards burst out both fore and aft, and the natural impulse of the rest was to leap into the water to save their lives. The master's assistant, who commanded the party, seeing that any attempt to rescue the prisoners would be utterly hopeless, to save his own life was compelled to follow his men.

Just as the last English seaman was picked up, the dhow's stern, already a mass of flames, lifted, and she glided down, bow foremost, beneath the surface; a few pieces of charred wood and bamboo marking the spot where she had lately floated.

"Serve the fellows right," observed several of the men who were watching the occurrence; "the hangman has been saved a job, and stout rope left for a better purpose."

Murray and Adair, although acknowledging that the murderers, as they deemed them, had met with a just fate, could not help regretting that all means of obtaining information as to what had become of the midshipmen and their companions had thus been lost.

"All I can now do," said Murray, "is to cruise over the ground the dhow must have traversed after you left her, and look out for the canoe, in case any of the party may have succeeded in getting into her. It is possible that some of them may have done so, although in this long interval they must have suffered fearfully for want of food."

As no time was to be lost, Murray returned on board, leaving Adair with his party still on the island. The corvette, immediately weighing anchor, stood away close-hauled to the eastward, that she might on another tack fetch the spot where her search was to begin. Murray's remarks had slightly raised Adair's hopes that one if not both of the midshipmen might have been saved, had they been hove overboard alive; but it was too probable that the Arabs would have knocked them on the head first, and then thrown them into the water. He expressed his thoughts to Green.

"I don't altogether give them up," answered Jos. "Midshipmen have a wonderful way of keeping in existence, and by some means or other they may have escaped, though I can't say how it may have happened."

Adair's anxiety prevented him from sitting quiet in his tent, and, in spite of the hot sun, he continued walking about, now visiting the look-out man, now seeing how the unfortunate slaves were getting on. Pango and Bango were of great assistance in communicating with them and dissipating their fears, though their captors had taken good care to instil into their minds the belief that the Englishmen wished only to catch them for the sake of salting them down for food, or disposing of them in some other horrible manner. Poor creatures! what their future lot was to be no one could tell. One thing was certain: they had been torn from their homes and families, many of those dearest to them had been killed by the savage men-hunters, and they themselves had been treated with horrible cruelty.

The boats, as usual, were kept in readiness to start off at a moment's notice, while the look-out men had their eyes about them in search of any dhows running up the coast. "A sail in sight to the southward," shouted the man up the tree.

"What is she like?" asked Adair.

"Square-rigged vessel, sir, with a broad spread of white canvas."

Here was likely to be work. She might prove a Spanish or American vessel, or carrying the flag of one of the other powers which still permitted the slave-trade. If a slaver, she was not likely to yield tamely if she had a chance of escape. Many such vessels were known to be strongly armed, and to be commanded by daring fellows, who would be perfectly ready to fight if they saw a chance of success. All the boats, therefore, were manned, to be ready to attack her should she stand near the island; which, from the course she was steering, there was every probability she would do. Everyone looked forward to the work with satisfaction. The only fear was that she might be empty, and might simply be coming north to take in her slaves at Angoxa, or some other place farther north. Cutlasses were buckled on, pistols freshly capped, and other usual preparations made when fighting was in hand.

The wind was somewhat light; but at length the stranger's courses rose above the horizon, when Jos Green, who had mounted to the signal-station, shouted out, "She's an English brig-of-war, and is making her number." Adair sent for the signal-book, and, inquiring the flag seen, quickly made her out as the *Romp*.

"Why, she's been on the East India station," he observed. "We shall soon know all about her, for she's evidently steering for the island, and the breeze seems to be freshening. She'll come to an anchor before long."

CHAPTER VII

The Midshipmen swim for their Lives—Find the Canoe—Adrift on the Ocean—Their Sufferings—Picked up by the *Romp*, Commander Jack Rogers—Tom's Meeting with Desmond and Archie—Adair's Joy on seeing them—The Banquet on the Island—"Music hath Charms"—Burning of a Native Village—The *Opal* and *Romp* sail for Zanzibar.

WHEN Gerald Desmond, surprised by the Arabs, was tumbled overboard, he happily managed to get his head clear of the cloth which had been thrown round it, and, striking out, he endeavoured to keep himself afloat, though he had little hopes of saving his life. Though the night was dark, he made out two or three objects floating near him. "Who's there?" he shouted out.

"Is that you?" asked a voice which he knew to be that of Archie Gordon. "Help me, Gerald, to get this thing off my head, or I shall be drowned. Where are we? What has happened?"

A few strokes brought Gerald up to his messmate, and he quickly tore off the cloth which the Arabs had bound round his head.

"Praise Heaven that you've escaped, young gentlemen!" exclaimed another person, who proved to be Jerry Bird; "we've a long swim before us, but we must try to keep afloat somehow."

While these remarks were being made, the dhow was gliding rapidly away, leaving them astern. "I'm afraid it's more than mortals can do to swim all that distance," said Desmond; "but hallo! what's that? a huge fish coming to seize us?"

"No, sir," cried Jerry Bird, "it's the canoe. Someone has cut her adrift, and we've a better chance for our lives than I thought for."

While they were speaking, a fourth head was seen, which Jerry hailed, and found that it was that of the man who had been at the helm Urging him to keep up his spirits, the midshipmen and Jerry swam towards the canoe. It was no easy matter to get in without capsizing her; but they managed it, Desmond climbing over the bow and Jerry holding on to the stern. As soon as the two were in, Archie followed Desmond, and then Jerry himself got in. Their first impulse was to go to the assistance of the man who was swimming some little way off; but what was their disappointment on feeling about for the paddles to discover that none were on board. They managed, however, with their hands to work up to the poor fellow, who, being a bad swimmer, was almost exhausted, and on the point of sinking. Jerry caught him by the collar just as he was going down, and sang out to him to catch hold of the stern; but the difficulty was to get him in without the greatest possible risk of filling or capsizing the canoe, her gunwale being almost flush with the water.

"You must manage, Sam, to get in of yourself," said Jerry at length; "I'll go more for'ard. But take your time about it; there's nothing to gain by being in a hurry, and all to lose."

Sam Potts, having recovered his presence of mind, did as he was advised, and, the rest nicely trimming the canoe, he was enabled to crawl in directly over the stern, though not without causing a considerable amount of water to flow in over the gunwale. The midshipmen with their caps, and the two men with their hands, quickly baled it out; but so low was the canoe with their weight, that it was very evident, should any sea get up, that they would run a great risk of being swamped.

In vain they looked out for the other men, but no sign of them could they discover. They hailed, on the chance of their having been thrown overboard when the dhow had got more ahead, but no reply came to their shouts. They must either have been kept on board, or sunk immediately. Their own situation was, however, too precarious to allow them to trouble themselves much about the fate of their companions—without food or water, or the means of propelling their canoe, they might too probably, even if not drowned, die of hunger and thirst. Still, they had reason to be thankful that the canoe had been cast adrift at that very moment, and that they had been enabled to get on board her. The circumstance appeared providential, and why should they, therefore, fancy that they were to be allowed to perish?

The sea continued calm, and a downpour of rain gave them a sufficient amount of fresh water, which they caught in their hats and caps, to quench their thirst. They dared not move, so Sam Potts remained aft, Jerry amidships, Desmond next to him, and Archie forward, all of them sitting with their legs stretched out at the bottom of the canoe. The rain made them feel somewhat cold, notwithstanding that after some time Desmond went off to sleep, to finish the snooze so fatally indulged in while trying to keep his watch on the deck of the dhow. Before long Archie followed his example, as did Sam Potts, leaving Jerry alone awake.

Thus the night passed away. The two midshipmen were both awoke at the same moment by finding the rays of the sun shining in their eyes. "Where are we?" exclaimed Desmond. "Faith, I fancied that I was away snug at home at Ballymacree, and little did I think that I was floating about in a canoe out in the Mozambique Channel."

"We may be very thankful that we are not at the bottom of the said channel," remarked Archie.

"Faith, you may say that, my boy," said Desmond; "small thanks to the rascally Arabs that we are not there. I only hope another of those slaving dhows won't come by and run us down. They're not likely to treat us with much courtesy if they guess what has happened."

"If a dhow does come by, we must try to board her and take her," exclaimed Jerry Bird.

"But we've got no arms," said Archie; "how are we to manage without them?"

"Take them from the rascals, to be sure, if they show fight," said Jerry. "As to running us down, we'll show them that they've made a mistake if they attempt it. If a dhow comes near us, we must make the canoe fast alongside, jump on board all together, seize the arms of the fellows nearest us, and then lay about us with right goodwill till we've driven the crew below or overboard."

Although Jerry's plan seemed a somewhat desperate one, its discussion served to keep up the spirits of the party, who entered into it cordially; and all agreed that it should be attempted, should they have the opportunity. The sun now rose and beat down on their heads with fearful force, while around them the calm sea shone like burnished gold. Their hunger increased, while already they began to feel the want of water. The midshipmen suffered most.

"I say, Archie, I'm getting mighty ravenous," whispered Desmond; "I shall be turned into a living skeleton pretty soon, with no more flesh on my bones than some of the unfortunate slaves."

"I've taken in a couple of reefs in my belt, and somewhat stopped the gnawing I was feeling just now," answered Archie; "you'd better do the same."

"Faith, I should be after cutting myself in two," said Desmond, "before I could stop this abominable biting in my inside."

Still the two midshipmen kept up their spirits, and talked away in a cheerful strain, in spite of the heat and their consequently increasing thirst. The sea continued calm and the wind so light that it would be long before a dhow or any other vessel could reach them. As their thirst increased, their inclination to converse lessened; and at length they and the two men continued, often for half an hour together, without uttering a word.

"I wonder what's become of Harry and Bill," said Sam Potts. "I've been thinking of them. Maybe they're worse off than we are."

"Too likely," said Jerry. "The slaver's crew wouldn't have left them alive to bear evidence that we were hove overboard; so, depend upon it, if they didn't send them after us, they knocked them on the head, or cut their throats whenever they found them. Bad as we are off, they, poor fellows, are much worse. We may be thankful, Sam, that we are where we are. This isn't the first time that I've been in a boat out in mid-ocean, without a drop of water, and with nothing to eat except maybe a flying-fish and a brace of noddies we caught, and a dead bird we picked up, till we came across a whale floating, and fed on the blubber for a week or more, though we had to hold our noses as we put it into our mouths, till we were at length picked up. So you see, bad off as we may be, we've no business to give way to despair; help will come from one side or the other."

These remarks contributed to keep up the spirits of all the party, which had naturally begun to flag. As the day advanced the heat became greater and greater. They did what they could to keep themselves cool; they wetted their shirts and their clothes, but they very speedily became dry again. The evening of another day was approaching; nearly four-and-twenty hours had passed since they had taken any food, and not a biscuit had anyone by chance in his pocket. At length, after rummaging in his pocket for some time, Sam Potts drew out a black-looking lump of about the size of the end joint of his thumb. "Hurrah!" he exclaimed; "here's a treasure! Jerry, ask the young gentlemen if they'd like to have a chaw. I suppose they won't take it amiss, seeing we're all in the same boat."

The midshipmen thanked Sam, but declined his offer, feeling that it was more likely to increase their thirst than to lessen it. Jerry, however, expressed his gratitude to his mate, who generously gave him half his precious quid, which he immediately stuffed into his cheek. "Ah, this is something like!" he exclaimed; "bless my heart, it's like meat and drink. Them as never was out at sea in an open boat, without as much food as would cover a sixpence, they shouldn't cry out and abuse us poor fellows for taking a chaw, or enjoying a blow of baccy when we've a chance."

"You're right, mate," said Sam; "I'd have given my last golden guinea for a quid, and I believe it will help to keep our bodies and souls together better nor anything else we was likely to find out here."

The midshipmen, who had heard Jerry's remarks about noddies and flying-fish, kept looking out in the hopes that they might get hold of some denizens of the sea or air. Though occasionally the fin of a shark appeared above the surface, or some huge monster was seen gambolling at a distance, no living thing, however, came near to enable them to satisfy their craving hunger. Thus the day passed away, and night once more threw her sable mantle over the ocean. The sky was clear. Archie thought it was his duty to try and sit up and keep watch, but it was more than he could do, and in a short time both he and Desmond dropped off into a sound slumber. Hour after hour they continued in a half-waking, half-sleeping state, their strength decreasing for want of food, and even when awake their minds wandering in a strange fashion, from which they were only aroused when Jerry or Sam spoke to them. Their case was becoming, they could not help feeling, serious indeed, and they were conscious that, should relief not arrive, they must, ere many hours were passed over their heads, succumb to hunger and thirst. The night seemed interminable, and they could only pray that the daylight might bring them assistance. Towards morning they were somewhat aroused by feeling the canoe tossing about far more than she had hitherto done, while every now and then the top of a sea washed over her gunwale, just sufficiently to show them that they had a new danger to apprehend. By this time, however, they felt almost indifferent to anything that might happen. They were, at length, aroused to action.

"It won't do, sirs, to let the canoe get swamped. We must turn to and try to get the water out of her as fast as it comes in," cried Jerry.

"Of course," answered Archie, throwing off the torpor which oppressed him; "we'll do our best." Gerald said the same, and at once they began baling away. They were thus employed, managing to keep the canoe pretty clear of water, when dawn again broke.

"A sail! a sail!" cried Jerry, as he was casting his eyes round the horizon, from which the shades of night were gradually rising; "she's coming up before the wind, but I'm much afraid that she's one of those slaving craft after all. Still, though her crew may be arrant cut-throats, they can't do us much harm, seeing we're bad enough off at present."

All the party now kept their eyes fixed on the approaching sail. On she came, steering apparently directly for them. As she drew nearer, she was seen to be a large dhow, and, there could be little doubt, a slaver. She was within a mile of them, when, just in her wake, rising above the horizon, appeared the loftier sails of a square-rigged vessel, also approaching directly before the wind. The crew of the dhow had in all probability seen her, and were endeavouring to escape.

"By the cut of her canvas," exclaimed Jerry, after watching for some moments, "she's an English man-o'-war." Sam was of the same opinion. The two midshipmen hoped they were right. The question, however, was how the dhow would treat them. They were certainly less anxious than they had been before to get on board her. Would her crew, from mere revenge, on recognising the midshipmen's uniforms, give them her stem? If she did, they must do their best to scramble on board; but then, with their strength so diminished, they would scarcely be able to clamber up, much less to fight, as Jerry had proposed.

A few minutes more must settle the question. As the ship was standing directly after the dhow, they might, at all events, be picked up by her; and they, therefore, earnestly hoped that the latter might pass without observing them, or, if she did, without molesting them. On she came.

"She's steering somewhat wide of us, sir," exclaimed Jerry, "and I don't think we've been seen as yet."

What the Arabs might have done had they not been chased, it was difficult to say. The canoe was apparently not discovered till the dhow was within a few cables' length of her. The dhow would have had to deviate slightly from her course to run down the canoe; as it was, she passed scarcely twenty fathoms off, her dark-skinned crew casting savage looks at the Englishmen. While the dhow was gliding by, the two midshipmen and their companions sat up watching her.

"They've made out who we are, sir," cried Jerry; "and the villains, if they're not pointing their matchlocks at us! Lie flat down, and we shall have a better chance of escaping." Scarcely had he spoken than several shots came flying by the canoe, one close over her; but happily, as Jerry's advice had been followed, no one was hit, and the dhow, impelled by the fresh breeze, went rapidly ahead, leaving the canoe far astern, before the slavers could fire another volley.

"You arrant scoundrels!" shouted Jerry; "we'll pay you off one of these days."

After this excitement the whole party would have sunk back into their former state of apathy, had not the approaching vessel given them matter to keep them aroused. Her topsails were now above the horizon, and soon her courses appeared; by which time, however, the sails of the swift dhow had already begun to disappear on the other side. Indeed, it was evident that she was gaining rapidly on her pursuer, which would have very little chance of catching her.

"That craft is an English brig-of-war," exclaimed Jerry, at length. "Though she hasn't a chance of catching the slaver, she'll see us, I've a hope, and before long we shall have some grub and water on board."

"There's no chance, I trust, of their passing us?" said Archie.

"No fear of that, sir," replied Jerry; "they keep too bright a look-out on board. Depend on't, they've made us out before now."

The wind was again failing, and should it become calm, the brig might not come up before dark. Still, if the canoe, as Jerry supposed, was already seen, of course a look-out would be kept for her. For half an hour or more, hopes and fears alternately predominated. "They've made us out—no fear on that score," cried Jerry; "I saw the people on the foc'sle waving to us." As he spoke, the brig shortened sail; a boat was lowered, and, ere a minute had passed, she sheered alongside the canoe. A midshipman and warrant-officer, with four hands, were in her.

"Bear a hand; lift the poor fellows on board carefully—sharp about it," cried the former. "We must not lose a moment;

they seem very far gone." Desmond and Archie were placed in the sternsheets, while even Jerry and Sam could not, without the help of others, manage to crawl into the boat.

The canoe was dropped astern, while the boat pulled back to the brig; the whole manœuvre, being properly executed, occupying but a very few minutes. The midshipman, attending simply to the work in hand, had not looked at the countenances of the people he had rescued. Just, however, as the boat had hooked on, he cast his eyes at the face of one of his companions, and then at the other. "Why, gunner," he exclaimed, "I do believe that they are Gerald Desmond and Archie Gordon!"

"You're right, Tom," cried Gerald, who was not so far gone as to be unable to speak; "and mighty glad I am to see you—only, as you love us, get us some grub, or we shall be after hopping the twig."

"No fear about that, young gentleman," said Dick Needham, who was the warrant-officer in the boat; "we'll have you on board in a quarter less no time, and under care of the doctor; he'll soon bring you round, though you mustn't be eating too much at first."

The midshipmen and their companions were speedily hoisted on board, when Tom Rogers announced to the commander who they were, and the condition in which he had found them. Broth and other restoratives being quickly prepared, and duly administered, in a very short time they were able to use their tongues sufficiently to give an account of themselves.

"Well, I'm glad we fell in with you," cried Tom, "and so is my brother Jack—if not for your sake, on account of his old shipmates, Murray and Adair. They would have been precious sorry to lose you, and so should I. And now we've fallen in with each other, we shall have the chance of some good fun together, for the brig is to be employed, during the remainder of her commission, in slave-hunting. My brother Jack is only acting-commander of the *Romp*, but he's sure to be confirmed before long. He got no end of credit in the work we've been engaged in up the Irrawaddy, of which I'll tell you by and by. I often wished that you fellows were with us. It beat all the service we saw out in South America."

"And Archie and I have often, of late, said how we longed to have you with us, Tom," answered Desmond; "not that we've had the same sort of fun we enjoyed in our first cruise. It has been much rougher work, on the whole, and I haven't fallen in with any Irish cousins, or the lots of nice girls we met in the West Indies; but, after all, the life we lead when boat-cruising is as much to my taste as anything I can fancy."

Tom, of course, replied that he hoped to have some of it, and that he should try to get his brother to send him away on an expedition.

Though but a short time had been lost in picking up the canoe, it was sufficient to allow the dhow to run out of sight. Jack, who was bound for Zanzibar, of course had now to bring up off Mafamale, for the sake of landing Archie and Gerald, and to set Adair's anxiety about them at rest. He was very glad also of the opportunity he should thus obtain of seeing his old shipmates.

The two midshipmen, though still somewhat weak, had greatly recovered by the time the island was sighted. Scarcely had the *Romp* dropped her anchor than Adair came on board. His surprise on seeing Jack was almost as great as his satisfaction at finding the midshipmen and the two other men safe and sound. Jack had some time before heard of the death of Kathleen. The recollection of her threw a shade of melancholy over the meeting of the two friends, but after a short time he managed to cast it off, and talked away eagerly of their past adventures and future prospects.

"I am glad to find, Jack, that you are so certain of your promotion," said Adair; "I wish that I could think the same of my own prospects. Lord Derrynane will do the best he can for me; but when he paid his last visit at the Admiralty, the First Lord told him that, though I was a remarkably promising young officer, he had so many promising young officers deserving of promotion that he should fill the service with commanders if he was to attend to the requests of all his friends. I can only hope for the chance of doing something which must compel their Lordships to promote me."

"I hope you may, Terence, with all my heart," exclaimed Jack; "and if not, we must get Admiral Triton to advocate your cause. I shouldn't feel comfortable getting my step unless you, who deserve it quite as much, obtained yours also."

As soon as Adair returned on shore, he found that Jos Green and the rest of the party had been arranging to invite the commander and officers of the *Romp* to a banquet on the island; and a note, couched in the usual formal style, was immediately despatched, a favourable answer being returned.

"But, as to provender—what have we got, Green?" asked Adair.

"Some of it isn't yet caught, to be sure," answered Green; "but we've sent the men out with the seine, and we shall have an ample supply, though there may be no great variety."

Shortly before the dinner-time arrived, a sail was seen standing up from the southward, and was soon pronounced to be the corvette. The proposed banquet was therefore postponed till her arrival; an additional haul of the seine was made, and a further supply of fish secured. The breeze was fresh, and, as she was under all sail, the *Opal* soon came to an anchor, and Murray and his officers at once accepted the invitation sent off to them. He had naturally become very anxious at discovering no traces of the midshipmen, and was proportionately thankful when he found that they were safe.

Thus the three old shipmates, after an absence of upwards of two years, once again met. At the appointed hour, the invited guests from the two men-of-war arrived on shore. Jos Green had undertaken to superintend the arrangements. All hands who could be spared from their culinary duties, rigged out in their cleanest, were marshalled to serve as a guard of honour. He had formed also a band, and though regular musical instruments were scarce, he had with much ingenuity contrived half a dozen drums made out of empty meat-tins, the same number of horns formed of conch shells, and a similar number of fifes and flutes, which had previously been manufactured on the island, during the leisure hours of some of the men who took delight in harmonious sounds.

Murray and Jack, as they walked up from the landing-place, laughed heartily at the preparations for their reception. Though the music was open to criticism, the banquet surpassed their expectations. Their seats were three-legged stools, but the table was bountifully spread. At one end was a huge bowl of pea-soup, at the other a similar one of fish; at the sides were several varieties of fried fish and boiled fish, roast and boiled fowls, obtained from a dhow—a legal trader, which had been overhauled; salt junk, of course, was not wanting, with preserved vegetables, and a liberal supply of yams; while bottles of beer, porter, and rum, constituted the chief beverages. Lastly, too, plum-puddings, somewhat resembling those stone-shot used by the Turks in days of yore, were placed before the carvers, and were pronounced excellent as to composition, but were declared to possess rather more consistency than was absolutely requisite. Indeed, few of the guests, with the exception of the midshipmen, made any great inroads on them.

The viands being removed, songs were sung and healths drunk; the most important of the latter being the success of Britain's arms by sea and land, a speedy end to the slave-trade, and health and prosperity to the Queen and all the royal family. Dinner being over, races were run, leap-frog indulged in, games of rounders played on a grand scale, and hits made such as only sailors could accomplish, and a variety of other sports which the nature of the ground and circumstances would allow.

Business, however, had to be attended to. Adair had left four men on board the dhow, and two only besides the midshipmen had been recovered. There could be no doubt, therefore, that two had been murdered, as would have been the case with the whole party, had not the canoe so providentially got adrift at the right moment. It was suspected that the old chief, Mustapha Longchops, had instigated the crime, and though he and the Arabs had been sent to their account, his people, who had so grossly insulted the British officers, were not to be allowed to escape unpunished. The corvette and brig, therefore, early the next morning, accompanied by the boats, proceeded off to the village, where they brought up. The sea being tolerably calm, and there being no surf, as they neared the shore six boats were at once manned and sent in to inflict condign punishment on the heads of the transgressors.

The party, headed by Rogers and Adams, formed on the beach. Their arrival had been observed by the natives, who, with tom-toms beating and horns sounding, were drawn up in large numbers on the side of the hill to defend their village. Jack gave the order to advance; the natives stood for a few seconds—then, even before a single shot had been fired, they turned tail and scampered off as fast as their legs could carry them. The only volley fired brought a few down, and hastened the flight of the rest, who were out of sight before the village was reached. Not a human being was found in any of the huts, which were speedily set on fire and burned to the ground, while a grove of trees growing near was cut down—a far more severe punishment than the burning of the miserable huts, which could be easily restored. This necessary though unsatisfactory work being accomplished, the party returned on board, and the corvette and brig, having received the captured slaves, made sail for Zanzibar.

CHAPTER VIII

Another Dhow chased—Slaves thrown Overboard—Dhow captured—Her Hold—Zanzibar—"Spicy Odours"—A Trip on Shore—The Slave-Market—Horrors of the Slave-Trade in the Interior—A Store in Zanzibar—Murray and Adair pay a Visit to the Sultan—Summary Justice.

UPWARDS of a fortnight had gone by since the corvette and brig last weighed anchor. Neither of them had been idle; numerous dhows had been chased, some of them overtaken and boarded. A large proportion of them had been of necessity let go, from want of sufficient evidence to warrant their condemnation. The corvette had captured two with slaves on board, and continued her course with them; while the *Romp* had parted company, chasing a suspicious sail which made every effort to escape. On being turned from the shore by the *Opal*, whose boats had been sent after her, she had stood to the eastward.

She was a large craft, with an enormous spread of canvas, and the little *Romp* had to put her best foot foremost to keep her in sight. Jack Rogers, however, was not to be disappointed of his prey. Setting every stitch of canvas the brig could carry, he steered after her, hoping that by some fortunate chance he might at length get her under his guns.

Dick Needham and Tom were standing on the forecastle, with their glances directed towards the chase, on which it was evident they were at length gaining. "It seems to me, Mr. Needham," observed Tom, who had been taking a long, steady look at the chase, "they're heaving something overboard; what it is I can't make out,—scarcely a cargo of ballast,—but we shall soon discover when we get up to her, as we shall, I hope, before long."

Needham took another steady look. "As true as I'm an Englishman, it is her cargo though," he exclaimed; "a living cargo, or what was living not long ago. They're heaving overboard the black slaves; not one at a time, as I've seen down on the West Coast, just to induce the cruiser in chase to heave-to for the purpose of picking them up, but dozens at a time, so it seems to me. Yes, I am sure of it, the outrageous villains! they've no notion of the power of our glasses. I wish our guns would carry as far; we'd soon make them understand that we'd our eyes upon them."

"I'll go and tell the commander," exclaimed Tom. "Can nothing be done to stop them?"

"We're doing all we can, for we can't make the brig walk faster than she's going," answered Needham.

Tom hurried aft with the information, and Jack and most of his officers were soon directing their glasses on the dhow. Although some doubted that the black objects they saw thrown over the side could really be human beings, the majority were of opinion that such was the case. Little had Jack thought, when going in chase of the slaver, that he was to be the unintentional cause of the death of numbers of his fellow-creatures; yet he was convinced that such really was the case.

Eager as all were to stop the butchery they believed going forward, it was impossible to set more sail or to do anything else to make the brig move along faster. They could only wish that they had steam-power, when, if a dead calm should come on, they might quickly have got up with the dhow. As it was, all they could do was to steer steadily after her, and as soon as they could get her within range of their bow-chasers, to fire away, and compel her to heave-to. The best of the day was before them, so that, should the wind hold, they must ultimately come up with her. This was their only consolation. Since she was first sighted they had gained a couple of miles on her, and should they continue to gain on her at the same rate, they might soon be throwing shot and shell through her canvas.

The men, when they heard what was taking place, entered fully into the feelings of their officers. Many a sincere prayer was offered up that the dhow might be taken and the murderers punished. Anxiously the course of the sun was watched as it sank towards the distant coast; for should night come on before the dhow was captured, the murderous Arabs might escape from the avenger of blood in hot pursuit after them.

"If they have been guilty of the horrible deed we suspect, I don't think that they will escape," said Jack. "Even if they do get free of us, Heaven will inflict on them the punishment they deserve, by some other means."

Two more hours passed, when, the brig having gained another mile, the hopes of all on board rose proportionately. At length Needham came aft. "I think, sir, we might reach her with our long six-pounder, and a shot or two through her sails would take the speed out of her." Already the sun's lower limb was touching the horizon.

"The experiment is worth trying," answered Rogers.

The gun was mounted on the forecastle, and charged with a shell. The first shell burst astern of the dhow, which still continued standing on. Needham was quickly ready, and fired another. "Hurrah!" he exclaimed; "I thought so." It touched her large sail, and, exploding at the same moment, rent it in all directions. Still she did not heave-to. A third and fourth shell were thrown, the sail being again torn by the latter. The brig now gained fast on the chase; still, so rapidly does darkness come on after sunset in that latitude, that the Arabs possibly still hoped to effect their escape. Their courage, however, at length gave way, as one shot after another struck them, and both sails were seen to come down together. The brig now quickly got up with the chase, and, heaving-to to leeward, two boats were lowered, Tom accompanying the second lieutenant in one, with the interpreter, while Needham had charge of the other.

As they got up alongside, about thirty piratical-looking ruffians, headed by their skipper, stood prepared to receive them. They appeared in no way disconcerted as the English leaped on board.

"Ask the negoda what has become of the slaves with which he lately sailed, Hamed," said the lieutenant.

The Arab answered at some length: "He says they have had no slaves on board, and the dhow was becoming leaky, and they had to throw the cargo into the sea," said Hamed.

"Then inquire why he ran away from us," said the lieutenant.

Again Hamed and the skipper had a long talk. "The negoda says he was in a hurry, and thought the brig was a pirate," said Hamed.

"Very likely. You don't think he speaks the truth?" observed the lieutenant.

"He speakee lie," said Hamed.

"Tell him we, at all events, intend to search his vessel," said the lieutenant, "and we shall judge whether she's leaky or not, or whether there's any foundation for his statement."

Lanterns had been brought in the boat. While one-half of the English kept watch over the villains on deck, the others descended with Tom and Needham into the horribly-smelling hold. A large quantity of bamboos were found, the remains of slave-decks, with a larger supply of rice, millet, and water than the Arabs were likely to carry for themselves. There was a miscellaneous cargo below under the slave-deck, which had certainly not been interfered with. There was evidence sufficient to condemn the vessel, but not a proof that the slaves had been murdered, though there could be no doubt that, if not lately landed, they must have been disposed of by foul means.

"I fancied I heard a groan," said Tom, as he was groping about. Needham came to the spot, and eager hands were soon engaged in removing some of the cargo; when, from beneath it, in a hollow space, they drew forth a human being, a boy ten or twelve years of age, fearfully emaciated. One of the seamen carried him on deck, his appearance causing a considerable agitation among the Arab crew. Hamed addressed the lad, who replied to him in a faint voice. Even the interpreter's unattractive countenance expressed horror.

"He say he got loose, and hide away because he hear the cries of the rest of the slaves. The Arabs cut their throats, and tumble them into the sea. He sure they were two hundred or more this morning, men and women and children, and now he alone remain," said Hamed. No further evidence than this was necessary to condemn the Arab crew, and the lieutenant immediately ordered them into the boats, and sent them on board the brig, leaving Tom with four hands to take charge of the dhow.

On their arrival Jack immediately held a court to try the accused, with himself as judge, and his two lieutenants as assistants. The evidence of the slave boy was considered conclusive; the prisoners were called up one by one for their defence, but as they had no time to concoct a story, they each of them told a different tale. Jack felt very much inclined to run them all together up to his yard-arm, but as this might be looked upon as too summary a way of proceeding, he ordered them to be placed in irons, to undergo a regular trial as soon as he could fall in with the commodore. He arrived, however, at the conclusion that the dhow was a lawful prize, and to prevent the risk of her ever carrying more slaves, he issued an order that she should immediately be set on fire. Tom, who had been anticipating the result, was very much pleased when the gunner returned with Jack's orders for her destruction. Light was set to her fore and aft, and as the boats pulled away, flames burst out from all directions, the glare, as they rose higher, extending to a far distance across the ocean.

The Arabs were kept on deck to witness the burning of their vessel. For a few minutes the fire raged furiously, the flames rising in one huge pyramid, till on a sudden they disappeared as she sunk beneath the surface, to which so many of her hapless passengers had lately been consigned.

"It would have served the villains right if they'd been left on board," observed Needham; "and I say, Hamed, just tell them so, and it is to be hoped they will get their due before long."

Meantime, the *Opal*, with her prizes, sighted the southern end of Zanzibar. As she ran along the western shore, the flat-roofed buildings, like palaces with numerous windows, gave the place an appearance of considerable opulence and magnificence. On either side of the city stretched away a low coast-line of glittering sand, above which could be seen cocoa-nut palms, raising their lofty heads at intervals, while the country, gradually rising towards the centre, appeared covered with bright green plantations of cloves, pineapples, and sweetly blossoming mangoes, the perfume of which Mildmay declared he could inhale even from that distance.

"Wait till you visit the town, and then you may talk of inhaling perfumes, though they're not of the sweetest," observed Jos Green. "If the wind comes off shore we may get a sniff of spicy odours, but I never found them quite strong enough to swear to, whatever the poets may say on the subject."

"Your olfactory powers are too coarse to enjoy them, that's the fact," observed Mildmay.

Here and there valleys opened up covered with orange-groves, sugar-cane, cassava, and other valuable productions of the soil. The harbour was full of dhows of all sizes, some at anchor full of slaves bound northward, but which, having licences from the Sultan, the English cruisers could not touch; others close to the wharves, landing or trans-shipping ivory, brought across from the African coast, gum, copal, spices, cocoa-nuts, rice, mats, and other produce of the island, besides several German, American, French, and other foreign vessels. Here also lay the Sultan's fleet, with blood-red ensigns floating from their mastheads, the ships being remarkable. if for nothing else, for their weather-beaten, sunburned appearance.

"They put me in mind of scarecrows in a garden, which the birds have learned to look at with contempt; and so, I doubt not, do the Arab slavers or piratical gentry who cruise in these seas laugh at these useless ships," observed Green.

In the afternoon, Murray, accompanied by his second lieutenant and the two midshipmen, went on shore. "We shall be after smelling the spicy odours in full vigour," observed Desmond to Mr. Mildmay, he having overheard the conversation of the morning. They had not, however, set foot on the shore many seconds, and commenced their walk through the narrow streets, before the lieutenant had his handkerchief to his nose. "Horrible! detestable!" he muttered; "never was in so vile a place in my life."

The whitewashed houses, too, which appeared handsome palaces in the distance, were now discovered, with few exceptions, to be sadly dilapidated; while the streets were thronged by an ill-favoured mob of all hues, from jet black to a sickly parchment-like yellow. There were shops in the dirty-looking town, filled with all sorts of goods from Birmingham and Sheffield. Their owners were chiefly Banians, who were seen sitting cross-legged among their wares, the men dressed in turbans of many folds, reaching to a point, with long robes and collars of gold or silver round their necks; the women profusely decorated with ornaments, with rings on their fingers and toes, and golden nose-ornaments and ear-ornaments studded with precious stones; while many had massive silver bracelets and anklets.

In an open court under the verandah was seated a schoolmaster, with long white beard, his pupils sprawling about on not over-clean mats, studying a huge Koran placed on a stand before them, mumbling in monotonous tones their lessons; the teacher more asleep than awake, the pupils imitating his example, and looking as lazy and indifferent as possible.

Inside and out of many of the shops were heaps of ivory-tusks, collected by the traders in the interior of Africa, and brought down to the coast; and in others food of the most disgusting appearance—sharks' flesh, rancid ghee, and other unsavoury articles, the vendors of which were hideous negresses, rolling in fat, scarcely bearing any resemblance to the female sex. The commander and his followers, glad to get out of the narrow streets, found themselves in a square, where in a semicircle they saw collected a number of slaves, some standing up, others sitting down, incapable of supporting themselves on their feet; most of them miserably emaciated skeletons, looking as if they had not many hours to live. Within the semicircle were a number of Arabs of high and low degree, a few of them well-dressed and armed to the teeth, others dirty and shabby; but all intent on business. They were either slave-dealers, or purchasers of slaves for their private establishments. In one part of the square were five or six female slaves for sale, their ages ranging from twelve to sixteen, gorgeously dressed in coloured garments. One of the gentlemen Arabs approached to make a purchase. The slave-dealer vaunted the qualifications of his merchandise, much as an auctioneer does the goods of which he has to dispose. The purchaser felt the poor girls' limbs, looked into their mouths, and trotted them out to see their paces; then, after haggling for some time, walked off with two which he had selected. The others were purchased much in the same manner; the remainder of the lots were disposed of with much less ceremony. On one side was a row of little boys from four to six years old, who were valued, so Hamed said, at about three dollars apiece. The girls, who were of a somewhat maturer age, went at from six to twelve dollars, while stout young fellows, out of whom plenty of work might be got, went for much higher prices.

The rest were wretched old men, broken down by the hardships they had endured during the fearful overland journey, and the not less miserable voyage. Many fetched not more than a dollar apiece. The old women, all of whom were either hideously tattooed, or had their lips extended with large holes, showing their teeth, went for very little more than the men. There they had been sitting since the morning, exposed to the fierce rays of the sun, their brutal owners having given them no food, or even a cup of water to quench their thirst. So worn out were several, that even when told to get up, they, as if not understanding the order, stared in stolid apathy. Had they exhibited the same obstinacy on the mainland, they would, in all probability, have been knocked on the head, and left to die on the roadside. Perhaps the most melancholy sight was the group of little children, all infantine life and animation crushed out of them. There they silently sat, without attempting to move, till ordered by their owners to rise. Poor little creatures! long ago they had been torn from their parents, and those parents probably murdered, or, if captured, disposed of to some other slave-dealers, while the persons around were in most instances utter strangers, perhaps from distant parts of the country, and unable to understand their language. They had been brought in legal traders under the sanction of the Sultan, and were intended either for domestic service, or to labour in the various plantations on the island.

Murray was glad to quit the scene, but it was important that he should have seen it. He was satisfied that his midshipmen should have done so likewise, that they might the better understand the horrors and abominations of the slave-trade.

"Faith, I'll never complain of any hard work we may have to go through, provided we can catch more of those slavers," exclaimed Desmond; "it would be a glorious thing to put a stop to the traffic altogether."

"We'll do our best, Desmond," said the commander; "though it may take us long before we can teach the Arabs that it is more profitable to them to deal in the produce of the country than in their black-skinned fellow-creatures."

Every seaport town abroad has its general store, kept by some noted individual, at which articles of every possible description, from a chain cable to a paper of needles, can be purchased, at more or less exorbitant prices; where masters and mates of merchantmen, and ofttimes their crews, as well as traders of high and low degree, congregate to discuss their business affairs, and to renovate the inner man with beverages more or less potent. Zanzibar, albeit not one of the most civilised cities, boasted such an establishment, kept by a personage yclept French Charlie. Although he possessed a Gallic appellation, he had nothing French besides his name about him; he being a mongrel of mongrels, with a large dash of Portuguese, and perhaps some African and Arab blood. Whatever his other qualifications, he had his eye open to the main chance.

Murray having now to order some stores, directed Hamed to lead him to the house. With pocket-handkerchiefs at their noses, the party proceeded along one of the narrowest and most dirty of the streets till they arrived before a stone edifice in a most dilapidated condition—such, indeed, is the normal state of all the buildings in the city. The main door opening into the street, they immediately entered the store, having to pick their way amid casks and huge coarse sacks filled to bursting, piled up to the ceiling; the dirty earthen floor full of holes more or less deep, while countless ants, cockroaches, spiders, centipedes, and other reptiles, crawled in all directions. On one side through an archway was seen a second apartment, in which, round a large table covered with tumblers, jugs, and flat round bottles, were seen seated a dozen or more merchant seamen of various nations, those from Yankee-land predominating, with an equal number of half-caste females gaudily dressed in Oriental costume, the whole party by their attitudes and looks already more than half-seas-over; some shouting and singing at the top of their voices, others attempting to sing, but uttering only spasmodic sounds, as the fumes of the liquor they were pouring down their throats mounted to such brains as they might possess.

Murray turned from the disgusting scene, and, passing on, was met by Monsieur Charlie, who, order-book in hand, with his dark-skinned, woolly-covered cranium and squat figure, resembled more a toad than a human being. "Anything, Señor Captain, you vant?—me got in my store, all so cheap and so excellent," he said, making an attempt to bow, his keen, twinkling eyes fixed on his visitors, while he waited eagerly to note down the orders he might receive. "You will take vun glass, sare, of something cool? I have Bordeaux just arrived; and de young gentlemen, dey surely like something—and my goot friend Hamed, we know each oder, and surely de Prophet not object to him to take just a little vine for him tummuck."

Murray, who had no wish to inhale longer than necessary the ill odours of the place, declined his liberal offers for himself and his companions, and, examining his list, gave an order for the articles he required, which Señor Charlie promised should be on board punctually the first thing next morning.

On their way back to the landing-place they caught sight of several of the *Opal's* crew, who had been allowed to come on shore, surrounded by a group of ill-looking Arabs, all with arms in their hands, by their gestures showing that they were endeavouring to incite the Englishmen to quarrel, as they kept stalking round them, clutching their daggers. The sailors, each of whom carried a thick stick, regarded the Arabs with the utmost contempt, as they rolled onward along the streets, every now and then only turning round and advising them to keep at a respectful distance. As they caught sight of their commander, touching their hats, they came to a standstill, while the Arabs, scowling fiercely at them, hung back. Murray was thankful that he had fallen in with them, for it was evident that the Arabs would have taken the earliest opportunity of attacking them, in revenge for the loss of the slaving dhows which they had assisted to capture. He ordered them, much to their disappointment, to return with him to the boat, thereby saving them from the Arab daggers, or an almost equally dangerous visit to French Charlie's store.

As he got down to the harbour, much to his satisfaction, he saw the *Romp* standing in, and before returning to his own ship he went on board her. Jack gave him an account of his capture of the slaver, and, having Hamed with him, they were at once able to interrogate the slave boy who had been saved, and to examine some of the prisoners. The boy, who had lately recovered by a few days' good food and kind treatment, showed more than the ordinary intelligence exhibited by captured slaves. He had been taken while away from his native village, with several other boys, watching their cattle. The men of their tribe, hearing of their capture, attempted to rescue them, but were driven back with the loss of several killed and a considerable number taken alive. They were all, he and his friends, dragged away, till they joined the main body, who were forced along, secured two and two by a heavy pole with a fork at each end, into which their necks were fixed. He saw several drop from fatigue, whom the Arabs endeavoured to compel to rise with the points of their spears; if they refused to do so, the masters either killed them with their axes, or, driving their spears into their bodies, left them weltering in their blood, either to die of their wounds or to be devoured by wild beasts. After travelling for upwards of twenty days, the coast was reached, and they were embarked on board the dhow, which ran in to receive them, taking many more at other places, till her hold was filled. Having been detained by calms, they had been badly fed, with a limited amount of water; and, an epidemic breaking out among them, several had died, and not only they but others who appeared in a dying state were hove overboard. He, being strong and active, had been employed in assisting to carry food to the other slaves. He had, moreover, learned a little Arabic.

When chased by the brig-of-war, he had overheard the Arabs talking about what they would do should it become likely that they would be captured. He understood that they intended to throw all the slaves overboard, so as to pass for a legal trader. On finding this, he managed to creep below, and to stow himself away in the place where he had been found. Scarcely had he concealed himself when he knew, by the cries and shrieks of his own countrymen, that the work of butchery had begun. He had little hopes of escaping, but life even to him was dear, and he kept in his hiding-place, hoping, at all events, to prolong it. His evidence was clear and circumstantial.

Several of the Arabs were next examined, and had no valid excuse to offer, except that the slaves were their own property, and they had a right to do with them as they thought fit. As many had already died, and as, probably, the greater number would have been carried off by disease before they could reach their destination, this was probably their real opinion, and accounted for their determination to murder the whole of their captives in the hopes of saving their vessel from condemnation.

Murray and Jack at once resolved to call on the Sultan, and to state the case to him, on the possibility of its opening his eyes to the horrors of the slave-trade, and inducing him the more willingly to assist in its suppression.

As it was still daylight, and Hamed informed them that the evening was the best time to see the Sultan, they at once pulled on shore. Going through the dirty streets, they reached the Sultan's tumbledown-looking palace, where His Majesty was seen seated in a half-open apartment facing the street, furnished with divans and piles of mats. He was surrounded by Arabs of rank, many of them dressed in rich costumes, talking familiarly with him, while his bodyguard of Beloch soldiers, cut-throat-looking individuals, lounged outside.

Murray and Jack, accompanied by the midshipmen, entering the hall, made their salaams, Hamed following them to act as interpreter. The universal pipes and coffee having been produced, they sat smoking, with intervals of dignified silence, while Hamed did the talking. The Sultan inquired whether the English commanders had made many captures, to which Murray replied that they had condemned only such vessels as were without legal permits; and Jack then introduced the subject of his capture, and described the murder of the slaves by the Arab crew.

The Sultan did not look quite as horrified as they expected he would.

"Surely the villains deserve condign punishment," observed

Jack; "if they are your Highness's subjects, you will, of course, at once have them all hung up."

His Highness shrugged his shoulders. "If I had to hang all the cut-throats in my dominions, there would be more work than a dozen executioners could get through," he answered. "If they are my subjects, I give you full leave to treat them as you think fit; and if they are not, you are the best judges as to what should be done with them."

Jack, who was convinced that all the Arabs on board the dhow, taken red-handed as they were, deserved hanging, would gladly have left the task of putting them out of this world to the Sultan. The difficulty was to prove that they were his subjects; and they were not likely to acknowledge this to be so, unless they thought that he would pardon them. After some further conversation, the two officers, with their companions, took their leave, feeling that they had taken very small change out of His Highness.

Jack accompanied Murray on board to dinner, and Adair, of course, was asked to join them. It was the first time for several years that they had been together with time to talk over old days. Though now and then a shade of melancholy came over Jack's honest face, a joke of Adair's, or some pleasant recollection conjured up by Murray, quickly banished it, and a very pleasant evening they had.

"Here's to your speedy promotion, Terence," said Jack; "the last letter I had from Admiral Triton, he told me that he had seen Lord Derrynane, who had promised that he would stir heaven and earth, and such bowels of compassion as the Lords of the Admiralty might possess, to obtain it, so that I've little doubt that you will ere long hear that you've got your step."

"Faith, I've a great deal of doubt about the matter," answered Terence. "To tell you the truth, I would rather get it in consequence of some dashing deed which would give me a claim to it than through family influence, by which any dolt may be pushed forward in the service."

"Well, for my part, I hold that we should be thankful for favours on whatever account they may be granted," said Jack; "you have seen as much service as any officer nowadays, and have twice been highly spoken of, and no one who knows you doubts that you will do any work which may fall in your way as well as it can be done."

The three old shipmates were laughing and talking right

merrily, when they were interrupted by a loud cry. Murray sprang on deck, followed by the rest of the party. Just as he reached it, an uproar of voices arose from forward, amid which those of Pango and Bango were the loudest, shrieking for help, while Ben Snatchblock was calling out, "Seize the rascals! tumble them overboard! knock them on the head! they've no business here!" while other voices in Arabic and negro language were uttering various incomprehensible cries, betokening either anger or alarm.

On going forward, Murray saw a confused mass of his own men, with three or four turbaned strangers and several blacks in their midst, among whom he distinguished Bango and Pango by their nautical costume. The strangers were quickly mastered by the seamen. Among the crowd he perceived the old pilot, who was forthwith dragged up to him.

"What's all this disturbance about. You seem to have something to do with it," said Murray.

"Me know nothing except that man come to take away him slaves," was the answer.

"Who are the men who dared to venture on board with any such intent?" asked Murray; "and as to slaves, none remain such under our flag."

"Me know nothing," answered the pilot, in a dogged tone, which showed that he did not intend any more information should be got out of him. Hamed, who had turned in, was summoned on deck, and the strangers were speedily examined. One of them, with considerable hesitation, believing that he should be put to the torture if he did not, answered that he and his companions had come by the express orders of the pilot, for the purpose of seizing his former slave Bango; that while the boat was alongside, Bango having been enticed on deck to come and hear about some of his old friends on shore, he had been suddenly gagged and nearly tumbled over the side, when Pango, who, suspecting mischief, had drawn near, shouted out and called some of the watch to their assistance, who had seized the Arabs before they could make their escape.

Murray was much inclined to have the fellows who had attempted so daring an outrage triced up and thoroughly flogged; but, not wishing to create more ill-feeling among the Arab population of the island than already existed, he merely ordered them and the pilot to be trundled forthwith into the boat and dismissed, with a warning not again to attempt a similar undertaking. The pilot, to whom some pay was due, was mulcted of it—a punishment which he would consider pretty severe; besides which, he was warned that he would never again be employed on board one of Her Majesty's ships.

It was some time before poor Bango could recover from his alarm, and the thoughts of the narrow escape he had had. "If him me get, he sure kill, after floggee," he exclaimed; "oh! him poor black feel de whip even now," and he wriggled and rubbed his shoulders about, as if undergoing the torture he believed his late master would have inflicted.

"Never fear, my man," said Snatchblock, to whom he spoke; "we'll take care the Arabs don't get hold of you, and as long as you do your duty aboard here, and don't get drunk, there's no fear of the cat and your back becoming acquainted."

The next morning Jack again examined his Arab prisoners, when one and all declared themselves to be the subjects of the Sultan of Zanzibar. As there was no proof to the contrary, Jack handed them over to the authorities to be tried and punished for the murder of the slaves. They, having numerous friends in the island, fully believed that through their influence they would escape. No one appeared to assist them, and the Sultan, wishing to prove his zealous desire to put down the slave-trade, ordered them to be taken out and shot; and as they had lost the means of bribing their guards to assist them in effecting their escape, they met the fate they so richly deserved.

CHAPTER IX

Tom Rogers spins a Yarn—Adventures in Burmah—Up the Irrawaddy—Capture of Martaban—Tom's Whiskers—Capture of Prome—Expedition on Shore—General Bundoolah thinks Discretion the Better Part of Valour—Camping out in the Jungle—Attack on the Guerilla's Fortress—Death of Captain Loch—Archie corrects Tom's Latin—The *Opal* ordered to Seychelles—Disembarkation of the Slaves.

THE corvette did not sail so soon as Murray had at first intended, it being necessary to allow the captured slaves a longer time in harbour to recruit their exhausted strength, glad as all hands would have been to get them out of the ship. Poor wretches! their unclean habits made them far from pleasant visitors. They were housed under awnings rigged over the deck, which it was necessary to wash down frequently with abundance of water; but even then the sickly odour which pervaded the ship was not only unpleasant, but calculated to produce sickness among the crew. Notwithstanding this, the officers made themselves as happy as circumstances would allow. The midshipmen of the corvette invited those of the brig to a dinner on board, and Tom Rogers, with several companions, arrived at the appointed hour.

"Satisfactory enough to capture slavers, but I don't envy you fellows having to look after the poor slaves now you've got them," observed Tom, as he glanced his eye over the long rows of negroes seated on the deck, the men on one side, the women and young children on the other, all looking pictures of stolid misery, and scarcely yet comprehending that they were free. All they could think of was that they had been torn from their homes and families, and were to be carried to a strange land, where they must of necessity toil hard to support themselves. They could not yet understand the real benefit they were to derive from the change, that from henceforth they would live in peace, able to enjoy the proceeds of their labour without any further expectation of attacks from foes, and having their dwellings plundered and burned, and themselves murdered; and, above all things, that they would be instructed in Christianity and civilisation.

Archie had been looking into the subject. "You see, Tom," he observed, "until the slave-trade can be altogether abolished on shore, we do all we can to put a stop to it afloat. The atrocious Arabs are the cause of all the misery and suffering the slaves endure. It is impossible to return them to their homes; indeed, in most instances, those homes have been utterly destroyed; but if they were not, the poor creatures would run the risk of being again captured; so we do our best to place them in a far better position than they before enjoyed; and though I'm afraid that a large number are carried into perpetual slavery, and that many more perish miserably, still that's not our fault."

"You're right," answered Tom; "I only wish that we had twenty times as many cruisers out in these seas as we have at present, and that it was lawful to hang up every skipper, if not the whole of the crews, of all the dhows with slaves on board whom we could catch. If people in England knew all the horrors the poor Africans endure, which seem to me twice as bad as those of the West Coast traffic, I believe they would rise to a man, and insist on its being put down at whatever cost."

The rest of the midshipmen responded to Tom's generous sentiments, and the young ones, at all events, agreed that they should be ready to devote their lives to the service.

A wind-sail brought sufficient air down below to enable the midshipmen to sit with comparative comfort in their berth—comparative, for the thermometer stood at not less than 85 degrees; but they were by this time well accustomed to heat, and endured it with stoical indifference. Archie and Desmond were especially eager to hear an account of Tom's adventures since they parted, and he, having no objection to spin a long yarn, was willing enough to recount them.

"I little thought, when Jack and I went out, that we should see so much service in a short time," he began. "On our arrival in the Hooghly river, we found that an expedition had been despatched to teach the King of Ava better manners than he had lately been exhibiting towards the British. You will understand that a large river, the Irrawaddy, flows from north to south through the country. It has several mouths. On the shores of one of them is situated the town of Rangoon, a biggish place, with a good deal of trade. Higher up is Prome; while there is another place, Martaban, on the shore of the gulf of that name. Ava, the capital, where the king lives, is situated in the interior.

"The governor of Rangoon had been playing all sorts of tricks, imprisoning several merchant skippers, and insulting and fining others. They laid their complaints before the authorities at Calcutta, who resolved to make the governor of Rangoon apologise and recompense the sufferers. We were, therefore, immediately ordered off to the Irrawaddy, as soon as we could get in a supply of fresh provisions and stores. We found the squadron, with a considerable number of troops on board, anchored off Rangoon. It is a pretty strong place, fortified by stockades, with heavy batteries of guns. The commodore had sent on shore to demand an apology of the viceroy, and, as it was supposed he would at once give it, we had very little expectation of fighting. However, in the evening, instead of an apology, came a message, declaring that, if the British ships should attempt to pass the stockades erected along the banks of the river, they would be fired on. We had heard that a large number of troops, some said five thousand, were collected within the fortifications; and each of the boats which had been sent out reconnoitring brought word that, during the night and day, they had seen no end of war-boats, full of men, coming down the Pegu river, evidently to assist in the defence of the place. Instructions were at once sent to the merchant-vessels to get under way, and drop down out of the line of fire, while a steamer towed the commodore's frigate within four hundred yards of the stockade. Here she anchored to protect the merchant-vessels as they dropped down.

"We had heard, meantime, of a large Burmese war-vessel, of which one of our steamers was sent in search, while the company's steamers proceeded up the river to meet a fleet of war-boats, pouring in a tremendous fire on the stockades on their way. The war-boats, in spite of their gay flags, and the row their crews kicked up to frighten us barbarians, were speedily sunk or sent to the right-about; while the batteries on shore, having soon had enough of it, ceased firing. In a short time we saw our steamer, the *Hermes*, come puffing up, with the huge Burmese war-vessel, which she had captured, in tow. After this we did nothing for some time, except blockading the mouths of the river, completely putting a stop to the enemy's trade. It was thought by this that the King of Ava would knock under, but he held out, till at length Admiral Austin arrived in the *Rattler*, and some days afterwards General Godwin, as commander-in-chief, with twelve of the company's steamers, which had nearly six thousand troops on board.

"Our first work was to take Martaban. The steamers, running close into the city, discharged broadside after broadside, our fire being returned with considerable spirit; but the enemy's guns being silenced, the troops were landed, and the Burmese, not liking the glitter of their bayonets, took to their heels in all directions, we having completely knocked to pieces all their defences. Leaving a garrison at Martaban, we proceeded to Rangoon, which had not given in. The fleet, therefore, took up a position before it, and began in earnest firing away shot and shell into the batteries for the best part of the day. We soon knocked the enemy's outer stockades to pieces, and set them on fire; but to do the Burmese justice, they fought as obstinately as bull-dogs; so we sent the naval brigade on shore to help the troops. For three days the fighting continued; stockade after stockade was stormed and taken in gallant style. Still the enemy retained possession of the city and the great pagoda.

"On the third day a grand attack was made on it by all the troops and the naval brigade, and, after some pretty sharp fighting, it fell into our hands, though we lost several officers killed and wounded.

"We next attacked Basein, where the Burmese fought with a good deal of bravery, defending themselves in the great pagoda of the city. Again the naval brigade showed what they were made of. Having landed with a party of troops, they stormed the great pagoda, into which a large body of the enemy had thrown themselves; but the place was gallantly taken, though not without some loss on our side. Meantime, we heard that Martaban, which had been left with a very small garrison, had been attacked by the Burmese. We were hurrying back to the assistance of our friends, when we received intelligence that Major Hall, who had been left there in command, had driven off the enemy. We had made pretty sharp work of it already, but there were other and more important places up the river to be taken. Orders were, therefore, received to send a squadron of man-of-war's boats to accompany the *Phlegethon*, carrying between two and three hundred soldiers and about a hundred bluejackets; and I had the luck to go with them.

"Leaving Rangoon, the *Phlegethon* steamed away with the boats in tow, like a comet with its tail out. We came near Pegu, when we found ourselves under a hot fire from the Burmese on the top of the high banks. As we were unable to fire in return from the boats, a strong party was landed under the command of Captain Tarleton. The Burmese were driven from point to point, till they took shelter within the walls of the city, when they began firing away pretty warmly with their jingalls and muskets. As the enemy's shot were flying somewhat thickly about us, it would never have done to halt. Captain Tarleton, therefore, having found a native, who, for a bribe, undertook to show the way, pushed on along the causeway till the city ditch was reached. Here it was seen that, on one side of the gateway, part of the wall had tumbled down. Halting for an instant to gain breath, Captain Tarleton singing out, 'On, my lads!' away all hands dashed right up to the wall, and, scrambling over it like cats, jumped down inside, to the great astonishment of the enemy, who, not liking their looks, fled for shelter within their great pagoda; for these fellows always seemed to think that their temples were the safest places.

"The boats had, in the meantime, been attacked, but were bravely defended; and the troops, pushing on, soon made their way unexpectedly into the city. Before the Burmese were aware what we were about, we stormed the great pagoda, which we soon carried, and the city was ours, with the loss of one man killed and three wounded. After blowing up the fortifications, as we had not troops enough to hold the place, we returned to Rangoon.

"After this we had a good deal of boat-work, cruising along the banks of the rivers, and dislodging the enemy, who often appeared in some force, for the purpose of trying to stop the provision-boats which came down to supply the fleet with grub. Sometimes we landed and drove the fellows far away into the country. Although they were ready enough to fire at us from a distance, they never liked the look of our whiskers," whereat there was a general laugh.

"Whose whiskers, Tom?" asked Archie.

"Well, those of the sogers and bluejackets, of course," said Tom; "how could they tell that I hadn't a pair too?"

"Well, go on, Rogers," cried several voices; "what did you do next?"

"There was another large place," he resumed, "called Prome, high up the river, which it was considered important to take, as it formed the chief defence of the capital. Captain Tarleton was, therefore, ordered to proceed up the Irrawaddy in the *Medusa*, with three other steamers, of one of which my brother Jack had the command. Away we steamed for some distance, without any of the enemy daring to show their faces. We had, as you will understand, already put them all to flight. At length, at a place with a precious hard name, Kononghee, about twenty-five miles below Prome, we came in sight of a large body of men collected on the banks. We threw a shell into their midst, as a hint to them to be off, instead of which they began firing away at us with musketry and several heavy guns. We returned the compliment pretty briskly, till they, getting the worst of it, as usual, showed their discretion by scampering off, and not stopping till they thought our shot would not reach them.

"As we were in a hurry to be at Prome, we didn't stop till they came back, but steamed on till sunset, when we anchored off the town of Meaoung. We found that the river divided just ahead of us into two streams, the western and deepest being the only navigable channel for the greater part of the year. We had arrived, however, at a time when the eastern channel had plenty of water in it, as we learned from the pilots. This was a fortunate circumstance, as you shall hear. When we got near the western channel, we found an immensely strong fort at the end of a range of hills which completely overlooked the river, garrisoned by a force of not less than ten thousand men, under a certain General Bundoolah, the most celebrated warrior in the Burmese army, so the pilots told us. Though his troops were only armed with matchlocks, and might have been bad shots, they would have committed a good deal of mischief by peppering down on our decks; not to speak of what the heavy guns might have done, placed in a position to rake us as we steamed up. Had it been necessary, I have no doubt Captain Tarleton would have stood on; but as there was no object in running the risk if it could be avoided, just as we came close to the works, and the enemy had begun to pepper us, he put his helm to port, and, greatly to their disappointment, steered away up the eastern channel, where not one of their shot could reach us. We kept the lead going, every moment fearing that we might get aground, when we should have been somewhat in a mess. We never had less than two fathoms of water, and sometimes more, so that we got through without accident; and by steaming on all night, the next morning at daylight came off Prome.

"At the south end of the city we made out four heavy guns, but the troops, every man Jack of them, had gone off with General Bundoolah, and left not one behind to fight them. We therefore brought up abreast of the spot, and hove them off, spiking the iron guns, and carrying the brass ones on board, twenty-three in all. Higher up we found between twenty and thirty more.

"This done, we again got up steam, and paddled ten miles higher. We were now within four days' steaming of Ava, with a broad, deep river, easy of navigation, before us. We all hoped that the commodore would push on and capture the capital. As far as we saw, there was nothing to prevent him, but the orders he had received were simply to survey the river as high as Prome, and then to return; so of course he had to obey them. Why he had not been given discretionary powers to proceed farther, I don't know. A golden opportunity was lost of catching the King of Ava by the nose, for we had so nimbly doubled on old Bundoolah that the chances were we should not have met with the slightest opposition. You may fancy, therefore, our disappointment when the order was received to ''bout ship,' and run down the stream again. But it couldn't be helped—orders are orders—it wasn't the fault of our gallant commodore.

"After holding Prome four-and-twenty hours, we evacuated the town, and soon got back into the shallow channel up which we had come. On getting into the main stream, we caught sight of General Bundoolah's army, some of the troops on shore, some in boats crossing the river, evidently with the intention of following us along the banks. I don't suppose they much liked our looks, for they evidently didn't expect to see us so soon. Steaming on, we quickly got up to them, and opened with shot and shell, both on the boats and on the dark-skinned troops which, crowded together, covered the shore. You may fancy what fearful havoc and confusion our shells created among the masses of human beings. Many of the boats were sunk, and the people in the others, finding escape impossible, hauled down their flags, and made signs that they surrendered. It was calculated that we captured or sunk forty or fifty boats. Among them was the old general's state barge and several large war canoes. On board them were found loot of all sorts, with two gold umbrellas and a standard. It was some consolation to have these trophies to exhibit; and as soon as we got back, the commander-in-chief, who, I daresay, was somewhat vexed at not having beforehand told our commodore that he was to do as he thought best, ordered us to go back again with a large body of troops and to take possession of Prome.

"As soon as we got ready, away we steamed, and, the river being still full, quickly reached our destination. There was not much fight in old General Bundoolah, after all; one reason was that we had carried off all his heavy guns. After battering the city, the troops were thrown on shore, and though the Burmese stood their ground for a short time, they quickly turned tail, and we entered the city in triumph, without a single man killed, and only four wounded. As we left Pegu without any defenders, though the inhabitants had taken a strong liking to us, while we were away a pretty large Burmese army marched into the place and began fortifying it. We had therefore to attack it again. Perhaps our chiefs thought that there wouldn't otherwise be work enough, and so left the cities we took unguarded.

"We proceeded up the river, and during the night came off the place. At daybreak, during a thick fog, with as little noise as possible, a body of troops and another of bluejackets were landed, and we making a dash on the town, the Burmese, who had no notion we were at hand, were completely taken by surprise, and away they scampered as hard as their legs could carry them, as usual to the pagoda, just as rats do to their holes; whether from being a sort of sacred place they fancied that it was safer than any other spot, I don't know; at all events, it was more easily defended. We, however, did not allow them to hold it long, though they fought desperately. Our troops, making a rush, dashed into the place and drove them out, not, however, without some considerable loss, half a dozen of our men being killed, and more than thirty wounded.

"We had now got hold of all their chief cities except Ava, and why that was not taken is more than I can say. We might certainly have captured it, with the king, his white elephant, and all his lords and ladies together, not to speak of his treasure, which would have given us something handsome in the way of prize-money. Perhaps it was thought best not to drive him to desperation, as we had already punished him, or rather. his unfortunate subjects, pretty severely.

"We had still no end of expeditions on shore; one especially turned out most disastrously. The Government of Burmah, fancying that we had now become pretty quiet, and that they could drive us into the sea, allowed a number of guerilla bands to be organised, which scoured the country in all directions, and mercilessly robbed the unfortunate people. Among the most noted of the leaders was a fellow called Mya Toon. After burning down a number of villages, and committing all sorts of mischief, he threw himself into a stronghold about twenty-five miles inland from Rangoon, or rather from a place called Donabew, on the river. A force of about six hundred men was ordered to get ready to attack the daring chieftain; about half were soldiers, the remainder seamen and marines, with their officers. Jack and I had the luck to be chosen, and we expected to see something of a new style of fighting, and to enjoy a tramp of twenty miles or more through the country. The expedition was placed under the command of Captain Loch, whom we all knew to be as good an officer as any in the service. We carried with us two three-pound field guns, and on reaching Donabew landed, and began our march without encountering an enemy. We were fortunate enough to get hold of some natives who were willing to act as our guides; for you will understand that the natives everywhere were friendly to the English, and the troops only were our enemies.

"We started early on the 3rd of February, the natives drawing our guns along the pathway, which lay through a thick jungle of tall trees and brushwood. It was not the pleasantest style of country to traverse, seeing that a tiger might spring out and carry off a fellow, and that the enemy, if they had had the wits to do it, might have placed an ambush, and shot us down without our being able to see one of them. However, after marching about fifteen miles, we arrived at an open valley, where we bivouacked. We could hear the enemy all night long popping away ahead of us pretty smartly. I suppose it was under the idea they should frighten us barbarians, and prevent our advancing. However, in that they were mistaken. We lighted our fires and cooked our suppers, and pretty hungry we were. We then lay down to sleep, thinking of the work before us on the morrow, and we were of course all very jolly, expecting to get hold of Mr. Mya Toon, and to carry him back with us in triumph. Little did many of the poor fellows who lay down that night suppose that it was to be their last on earth.

"The bugle sounded at daybreak, and, springing up, we breakfasted and recommenced our march, moving along the same sort of path as before, till it suddenly terminated on the side of a broad nullah, a sort of natural ditch. The bank on the opposite side was much higher than the ground we stood on, and we soon saw that it was strongly fortified, after the Burmese fashion, with sharp-pointed bamboos, over which it was as difficult to leap as it was to force our way through. The path, too, was here narrowed by an abattis of the same sharp-pointed bamboos, which made it impossible to deploy the whole strength of our column; indeed, our advance guard, consisting of seamen and marines, could only march two abreast, while our two guns, hauled along by the natives, were in the rear. Suddenly, as we were looking about us, and thinking what a nasty sort of place it was, we found ourselves exposed to a tremendous fire from a horde of banditti, who had hitherto been concealed behind a breastwork on the opposite bank.

"A gallant officer of the *Fox*, Lieutenant Candy, who commanded the advanced guard of the bluejackets, and Captain Price, of the Bengal infantry, led on their men in the most dashing style, intending to force their way across the nullah and to storm the breastworks. Before they had gone many paces they were both shot dead, as were many of their followers. Captain Loch now hurried to the front, and led another party to the attack. It got some way across, when so murderous was the fire that he was compelled to retreat, leaving a number of men behind who had been killed close to him. Still undaunted, he again made the attempt, and a second time was driven back.

"'We must take the place!' he shouted out; and a third time, rallying the seamen and marines, he rushed forward, sword in hand, determined to capture the fort. The Burmese must have had their marksmen, for one after the other our officers were struck. This time everybody thought he would succeed, when, as he was advancing, a fellow who had climbed up a tree overlooking the nullah fired at him, and wounded him desperately, driving his watch right into his body. Though he suspected that the wound was mortal, he had strength sufficient to fall back to the rear, when Commander Lambert, the son of the commodore, took his place. Though our men were falling thickly around, two more attempts were made to get across that horrible nullah. Commander Lambert, who had himself received four shots through his clothes, though he had escaped unhurt, seeing that success was impossible, as more than half our party had been killed and wounded, at length ordered us to fall back. I had not thought about myself, but I thought about my brother Jack a great deal, and I was thankful to see him get off clear without a wound.

"The enemy kept firing at us as we retreated, but their shot did not commit much damage, after we got to a little distance. One bad part of the business was that we were obliged to leave the dead on the field, for our rascally dhoolie bearers and guides had treacherously decamped, and we had scarcely men enough remaining to carry the wounded. The seamen undertook this duty, while the Bengal infantry, in a very gallant way, for which we were heartily obliged to them, covered our retreat. The only road that we could possibly take was the one we had come by. The jungle on each side was so thick that we could not force our way through it. Happily, for the same reason, I suppose, the enemy did not get round and meet us in front. They followed, but were afraid to advance near enough to molest us, the soldiers' rifles reaching farther than their jingalls or Birmingham muskets.

"We all felt very downcast at the loss we had sustained, but more especially for that of our brave leader, Captain Loch. He was still alive, but the surgeon gave us no hopes that he would recover. The heat was tremendous, the sun burning down on our heads, while we hadn't a drop of water, and the men had to carry our leader and the rest of the wounded for nearly twenty miles. Still, all hands did their best to keep up their courage and discipline, the strongest helping, as far as they could, the weakest; four or five of our officers, who were themselves wounded, setting the rest an example. Thankful enough were we when we caught sight of the river, after a march of twelve hours, and found ourselves at length seated in the boats, the troops being embarked on board the *Phlegethon*. Shoving off, we made our way back to Rangoon, and the next day we heard that Captain Loch had expired within two days after he had received his wound. We agreed that it was a very sad affair, and it would have been better had we tried to catch the robber and his band while they were out foraging.

"We buried Captain Loch on shore, near the great pagoda, at Rangoon, and I am sure I never joined in a sadder procession than we formed, as, shoving off, we followed the coffin of our late gallant chief on shore, and marched to the neighbourhood of the great pagoda. He was buried with all the honour we could show.

"The robber, Mya Toon, held out for some time longer, till a considerable force, under Sir John Cheape, was sent against his stronghold. Even then he showed much pluck, and was not dislodged till several officers and men on our side had fallen. This was just before the King of Ava knocked under and sued for peace, giving up the province of Pegu, which was accordingly attached to the British dominions. The soldiers had most of the fighting, but we had a good share of it, *quorum pars magna fui*, and so ends my yarn."

"Bravo, Rogers! an excellent yarn, and capitally told," said several voices.

"Ye dinna pit your light under a bushel, laddie," remarked Archie.

"Why should I?" exclaimed Tom; "it was for your sakes more than for mine; you wouldn't have been half as interested if I'd only told you what I'd heard, whereas I've enabled you, in imagination, to take part in all the scenes in which my brother Jack and I were engaged."

"Then you should have said *quorum pars magna* fuit *frater Jackus meus*," said Archie; "but I suspect that he was the principal actor."

"Of course he was," said Tom; "there's not another fellow in the world like my brother Jack; I always said so before I came to sea, and now I have been with him so long, I can say it from my own observation. I might have said a great deal more about him, only my object was to be brief." Others of the *Romp's* youngsters who had been in the expedition corroborated all that had been said, and made Tom's hearers wish to have the chance of sailing with Jack Rogers, who was sure, they agreed, wherever he might be, to cut out work of some sort or other.

More yarns were spun, and many a song sung, before Tom and his shipmates returned to the brig.

Next morning, as the corvette was weighing anchor, the frigate was seen coming in from the southward. The *Opal* accordingly again brought up, and waited for her arrival. As she came to an anchor, the flags run up to her masthead summoned Murray on board. The commodore, on hearing of the number of slaves he had taken, ordered him, instead of going on to Aden, to proceed to Seychelles, where arrangements had been made for the reception of liberated Africans, and, as soon as he had landed them and refreshed his ship's company, to return to the coast, and prosecute his search for slavers.

"We must strike a blow at this abominable traffic, and put it down at all cost," exclaimed the commodore; "we have done nothing effectual as yet—for one vessel captured, fifty have escaped."

The commodore, having come on board the *Opal* to inspect the slaves, ordered Murray to get under way immediately. The corvette, running out round the north end of the island, hauled her wind, and stood eastward till she reached Seychelles. A look-out was still kept for slavers which, having hugged the Madagascar shore, might be steering for the Gulf of Persia. All hands, from the commander downwards, were eager to arrive at their destination, and to land their cargo of blacks. Everything possible was done to keep the poor creatures in health, but notwithstanding this, several died on the voyage every day. Part of the deck was cleared, and they were encouraged to dance and sing, and amuse themselves after their own fashion. At first, when they stood up, they appeared scarcely able to move, but in a short time, their spirits rising, they began to snap their fingers, bend their bodies, and shuffle round and round; then to clap their hands and shout and laugh as if all thoughts of the miseries they had suffered had vanished. To the intense satisfaction of all on board, the corvette at length, just as the sun was setting, came in sight across the purple ocean of the green, foliage-clad islands, in a setting of white sand, surrounded by coral reefs, amid which she had carefully to pick her way. At some distance rose the lofty mountains of the principal island of Mahé, while on either hand were tree-fringed islets, backed by others far off, blue and indistinct.

The pilot, coming off, brought the ship to an anchorage a considerable distance from the town. Anxious as Murray was to get the slaves on shore, it was impossible to do so that night. Next morning the disembarkation commenced. Those who wished it were allowed to engage themselves either as domestic or agricultural servants to the inhabitants, while the rest were placed on a island where they might erect huts and cultivate the ground for their own advantage. Pango and Bango had their choice of landing or remaining on board, but they preferred continuing in the ship among the crew, whose goodwill they had secured by their good-humour and willingness to oblige.

All hands luxuriated in the endless variety of fruits brought off by the boats which were quickly alongside; oranges, plantains, bananas, alligator-pears, limes, pineapples, and numberless others, including the bread-fruit; and on going on shore, as some compensation for the horrible odours they had lately inhaled, they enjoyed the scent of the countless beautiful flowers which grew not only in every garden, but lined the roadside and covered the slopes of the hills.

Though the islands belong to England, nearly all the inhabitants appeared to be French, and French was everywhere spoken. Mr. Mildmay, the only officer who professed to care much for society, was sadly disappointed on finding that there were no ladies in the place. He, therefore, in some stanzas which he wrote, described it as a "Paradise without an Eve."

The great drawback to the place was the heat; for behind the town rises a precipice upwards of seven thousand feet in height, which effectually shuts out the breeze, except from one quarter. The summit, however, being covered by luxuriant vegetation, adds another beautiful feature to the scenery of the island.

CHAPTER X

News from England—Jack Rogers appointed to the *Gauntlet*—Adair promoted, and succeeds him in command of the *Romp*—The Three Midshipmen transferred to the *Gauntlet*—A Trip on Shore—Sailors in the Slave-Market—The Sultan appears—*Gauntlet* on the Northern Station—Tom Kettle and Bill Saucepan, the Kroomen—A Trap for Slavers—Mr. Large's Expedition in search of Wildfowl—Finds more than he bargained for—Is the Island bewitched?

THE corvette was within a hundred miles of the African coast, when a sail was sighted on the port-bow coming down before the wind. She was soon seen to be a large ship, and little doubt was entertained that she was the *Radiant*. That she was so was in a short time proved, when she got near enough to allow her number to be seen. The corvette accordingly hove-to, to await her coming. As she drew near, she shortened sail, and hoisted a signal to send a boat for mail-bag. No summons could be more willingly attended to. The boat was soon alongside, when a large letter-bag was lowered into her, and Adair was summoned to give an account of the trip to Seychelles. He of course inquired the news. There were some changes in the station.

"Commander Rogers has been confirmed in his rank," said the commodore; "and I have appointed him to succeed poor Danvers, the late commander of the *Gauntlet* steamer, which arrived out on the station after you sailed. I hope that he'll have gained some experience in the *Romp*, for I mean to do something in putting down the slave-trade. I am determined to strike a blow at the traffic before I return to the Cape, where the doctor tells me I ought to go for the sake of the health of the ship's company and my own; and so I will, as soon as I hear that a few more captures have been made. By the bye, you've been pretty successful, and I'll give you an acting order to command the *Romp* till someone is appointed from home. I expect you to show your zeal in the service, and I have no doubt that you will be able to give a satisfactory account of your proceedings."

Adair, highly pleased, thanked the commodore, and hastened back with the letter-bag to the corvette. He longed to see its contents, for he felt sure that he should hear from Mrs. Murray, if not from Lucy herself. The contents of the bag were quickly distributed, and every officer, and not a few of the men, were soon deeply immersed in perusing their various epistles. It was a wonder the corvette did not run away with them; fortunately Jos Green was the officer of the watch, and, shoving his letters into his pocket, he issued the order to brace round the foreyard, and the corvette once more stood close-hauled to the westward, while the commodore ran on for the island of Pemba.

Murray, of course, had a letter from his wife, containing a smaller missive, which he held in his hand while he read the contents of the former. Adair had just received a long official-looking epistle, at which his eyes sparkled with more than usual animation. "Good luck has come at last!" he exclaimed; "I've got my promotion, thanks to Admiral Triton and Lord Derrynane."

"I congratulate you heartily," said Murray; "and here's a little billet which I hope may add to your satisfaction. I suppose Stella thinks it all right, or she wouldn't have undertaken to forward it." Adair took the note, and, eagerly opening it, ran his eyes rapidly over the delicately-formed characters.

"Hurrah, my boy, I'm the happiest fellow alive!" he said, with difficulty restraining an inclination to throw his cap into the air and give an Irish caper. "That capital fellow, Jack, has been taking my part; and Lucy says that Sir John and Lady Rogers are inclined to relent, and she's certain would not withhold their consent provided I obtain what I've just got; and so I may conclude that it will all be settled, and that I may make my appearance at Halliburton as soon as I return to England."

"I'm truly glad to hear it," said Murray; "from what my wife says, I thought you would be satisfied with her friend's letter. The only drawback, as far as I am concerned, is that I shall lose you as my first lieutenant. However, I mustn't complain, and I might have a much worse one than Mildmay, who will, I am sure, turn to with a will when he finds himself once in the position, and I only hope I may get an efficient officer in his place."

Adair was sorely tempted to go home by the first opportunity, instead of taking command of the *Romp*; but two motives prevented him—first, he had been appointed commander; and, secondly, hoped by capturing a number of dhows to be able to pick up some prize-money, which might assist him in setting up house when he got back to England.

"I say, Uncle Terence, am I to follow you on board the brig or to remain here?" asked Desmond, when he heard of Adair's appointment and promotion.

"If the commander can spare you, I think, Desmond, I will take you with me," answered Adair, "but it must depend upon him. He may be unwilling to lose the services of so valuable an officer."

"Arrah now, Uncle Terence, you're poking fun at me," exclaimed Desmond; "but I'm after thinking how Archie Gordon will get on without me. We've been together ever since he came to sea, and it will seem strange to him and to me if we're separated."

"I've a notion that each of you will get along very well by yourselves, and neither of you will be able to lead the other into mischief," said Adair.

"Mischief d'ye mane, Uncle Terence," cried Desmond; "sure it's what neither of us are capable of."

"No, of course you are both of you wonderfully well-conducted young gentlemen," replied Adair; "and, besides, you are getting rather too old for playing monkey tricks; but still I'd rather keep my eye upon you, and so I intend to ask Commander Murray to lend you to the *Romp* till she's ordered home."

The next day the corvette reached Zanzibar, where the first object which greeted the eyes of those on board was a fast-looking screw-steamer such as had never before appeared in those waters. The first person who stepped on board was Jack Rogers, looking as fresh and jolly as if he had just come from England, instead of having been roasting in the East for the last two years or more. Following him came Tom, who dived down into the midshipmen's berth to have a talk with his old friends.

Jack expressed himself well pleased with the steamer, though he had never belonged to one before. "The only bother is that I don't understand the engineer's reports; and when he tells me that so much steam has been blown off, all I can reply is, 'Make it so,'" he observed, laughing; "however, I suppose I shall know all about it by and by, as I go down as often as I can into the engine-room and inspect the machinery, with as knowing a look as I can assume. I've a notion that the engineer has found me out, but he is a discreet man, and doesn't take advantage of my ignorance; so I expect to get on very well, and hope that we shall catch no end of dhows, which will be unprepared for our mode of making our way through the water."

Adair at once went on board the *Romp*, accompanied by Desmond, who took Tom's berth. Thus the three young commanders found themselves all together, each captain of his respective ship. Their great object was the suppression of the slave-trade; for this purpose they laid their heads together to concoct a scheme to carry it effectually out. Their plan was to proceed along the coast, each taking up a position a couple of hundred miles or so apart, and to send their respective boats' crews north and south, thus keeping up the chain of communication, imparting information, and the one aiding the other.

Jack was glad to find his old friend Higson first lieutenant of the *Gauntlet*. He had become, if not a temperance man, at all events as sober as a judge, and devoted to the duties of his position. His old shipmates were glad to meet him. He dined with Murray and Adair the two days they remained at Zanzibar, "the only times," he declared, "that he had been out of the ship since she left England."

The three commanders had a consultation regarding the disposal of their three young relatives. They agreed that as they were all well up in seamanship, and knew nothing about steam, that it would be to their advantage to remain for some time on board the steamer. "There's no doubt that steam is making great progress, and for the sort of work on which we are engaged, at all events, steamers will be universally employed," observed Murray, with his usual forethought. "I should not be surprised if we were to have all our larger as well as the smaller vessels fitted with the auxiliary screw, and it is, of course, very important that an officer should be well acquainted with its management, as well as with the working of steam-engines in general."

"Faith, I believe you are right," answered Adair; "though I'm mighty afraid that if steamers come into vogue, they will do away with all the romance once upon a time supposed to belong to a naval life."

"I shall not make myself very unhappy on that account," said Murray, laughing; "it will be a great thing not to have to depend on the fickle wind for making a passage, and still more to know that we may pounce down upon those rascally fast-sailing dhows whenever we can sight them in a calm, and be sure of overtaking them."

"I agree with you," said Jack; "I only wish that I knew a little more about a steamer. However, I shall pick up some knowledge of the matter before long, and hope to make good use of it. My engineer appears to be a sensible man, and I shall be glad to have Gordon and Desmond on board, and to place them under his instruction. I will, of course, look after them as carefully as I do my young brother Tom."

So it was arranged that Archie and Desmond should be lent to the *Gauntlet*, she having only one other midshipman and two old mates on board. They, of course, were highly delighted to hear the decision to which their elders had come, not so much perhaps on account of the advantage it was expected they would derive, as from the thoughts of the fun they would have together. As the ship was not to sail till the next day, they all three forthwith asked leave to go on shore for the purpose of getting a ride into the country, in company with the master of the *Opal* and some of the midshipmen of the other vessels. As Jos Green undertook to look after them, Jack gave them leave, charging them to be on board before dark. A party of the men from each ship had likewise obtained leave to go on shore to purchase curiosities for their sweethearts and wives.

The Sultan had lately made it known that his stud, consisting of a hundred horses and more, was at the disposal of the British naval officers who might wish to take a ride into the country; and the midshipmen were therefore directing their course to the palace, when Desmond proposed that they should take a stroll first through the town.

"It isn't the sweetest of places, I'll allow, but we may come upon something worth seeing, and have some fun or other," he exclaimed. All hands agreed to the proposal, and two and two they made their way through the narrow streets, not exactly knowing where they were going. They agreed, however, that except the crowds of savage, dirty-looking Arabs, and still more hideous blacks, tumbledown houses, and bazaars full of trumpery goods, there was nothing to be seen in Zanzibar. Suddenly they found themselves in a square, which Desmond recognised as the slave-market. It was far more crowded than when Archie and he had been there before. As they looked round, they calculated that there were three or four hundred slaves of all degrees; some, mostly women, gaudily, if not gorgeously dressed, looking plump and well; and others, who had apparently lately been imported, in a most miserable state of starvation. The sight was sufficient to excite the feelings of the most callous observers. Many were little more than skeletons, with their skins, often covered with sores, drawn tight over their distorted bones; their eyeballs protruding hideously, evidently in consequence of the falling away of the flesh on their faces; their chests sunk, and their joints swelled and knotty, contrasted with their withered limbs.

Several such groups were seen in different parts of the square. In another part, seated under the shade of a projecting roof, were a group differing greatly from the last described. They were women-slaves, considered of high value. On their heads they wore dark veils, covered with glittering spangles, and various ornaments, though the way in which their faces were painted with black and yellow detracted from any natural beauty they might have possessed, according to the taste of the English officers. Another similar group of ten or a dozen negro girls were still further decorated with mantles of a blue muslin thrown over their shoulders, of which they appeared to be not a little proud, though, from the expression of their faces, it was impossible to say what feelings animated them. Although some few of the poor girls might have been considered attractive but for the daubs of paint on their faces, the greater number were fearfully scarified, not from cruelty, but in order to increase their beauty according to the taste of their countrymen.

There were numerous groups also of men and boys, such as have before been described. Each of the groups was in charge of an Arab auctioneer, who put them up to sale, much in the way that ordinary goods and chattels are disposed of at auction marts in England. A dozen or more auctioneers were busily at work together, trying to attract purchasers, pulling at the sleeve of one as he passed by, then at the skirt of another; somewhat after the fashion of old-clothes sellers in London. The Arab purchasers showed no eagerness, however, but turned away from the tempting offers, however much they might have desired to possess them. Business was going on in a tolerably quiet way, the appearance of the midshipmen in no way interrupting matters, till a large party of bluejackets arrived on the scene. Just then, some of the least interesting lots having been disposed of, an old Arab, with a long white beard, was putting up for sale one of the highly-adorned female lots, his example being followed by several of his rivals in trade. A stout female, with a face deeply scarred and hideously painted, and an arm strong enough to fell an ox, was speedily disposed of. As she seemed to take kindly to her new master, no sympathy was raised in her behalf. The case, however, was different with regard to a group of young girls, many of whom could not fail to excite interest. Two, especially, who were apparently sisters, were seated together, with their hands clasped, and their arms round each other's necks, their countenances exhibiting a greater expression of shame and grief than did those of most of their companions.

Notwithstanding the horrors innumerable they might have gone through, they seemed to be aware that a still greater trial was in store for them. Several of the number had been knocked down, not literally, but to buyers, after a considerable amount of bidding, and all, it seemed, had gone off at high prices. The sailors had been looking on, making remarks, which it was as well neither auctioneers nor purchasers understood. Their feelings of sympathy, already excited by the sales they had witnessed of the other groups, were rapidly becoming less and less controllable. They eyed with no very friendly glances the ill-favoured Arabs who, grasping the poor girls by their arms, claimed them henceforth as their chattels. At length the turn of the two sisters came. Several bidders stood by, each offering an increase on the price last named by the auctioneer. Jerry Bird, who was among the seamen, could not make out whether they were to be sold together or singly. "It will be a shame if they're parted; but the whole thing is a shame, and there's nothing I'd like so much as to send the rascally buyers and sellers to the right-about, and to set the poor creatures free," he exclaimed.

Just then a wizen-faced, one-eyed old Arab, his rich dress showing that he was a man of wealth and importance, came up and fixed his single blinker upon one of the negro girls. He quickly outbid all competitors. The auctioneer offered him the other sister, but he only wanted one, and nothing could induce him to offer for the other. At length, losing patience, he grasped the negro girl by the arm, and was about to drag her off by the wrist, when her sister, not yet sold, threw her arms about her neck, both uttering a wail of despair which might have gone to the hearts of the most obdurate. It had an electrical effect on the sensitive seamen. "Well, that's more than I can stand," cried Jerry. "Down with the brutal Arabs, and let's set the whole lot of the poor creatures free!"

He gave but expression to the feelings which were animating the breasts of his companions. Dealing blows right and left, they simultaneously set upon the surrounding Arabs, the old fellow who had bought the girl being the first knocked over, and the auctioneer with the glib tongue the second, the others, who drew their daggers, having their weapons whirled from their hands; while the greater number, astonished by the suddenness of the attack, took to flight in all directions, pursued by the now infuriated seamen. The girls crowded together, more alarmed, probably, than delighted at the efforts made by the gallant tars in their favour.

Having succeeded, as they believed, in rescuing one of the party, the seamen, without an instant's hesitation, set upon the other auctioneers in their immediate neighbourhood, whom they quickly put to flight; and sweeping on, flourishing their cudgels and shouting at the top of their voices, they in a short time cleared the square of every trafficker in human flesh. Jos Green and the midshipmen, who had been at the farther end of the square, did not understand what was happening till they saw the Arabs scampering off, turbans trailing behind them, daggers whirled through the air, slippers left on the ground, sword-blades shivered into fragments, while not a few long-robed rascals lay sprawling in the dust; the rest flying at sight of the enraged bluejackets at their heels. However much Jos and his party might have sympathised with the men, they at once saw that their proceedings might lead to serious consequences. In vain, however, he shouted out to them to hold fast; the sailors were too eager to be stopped, and continued the pursuit of the Arabs towards every avenue opening into the square. Whenever a party halted, they immediately, with loud shouts, made at them, compelling them again to take to their heels.

The midshipmen, indeed, who thought the matter very good fun, encouraged the men by their shouts and laughter, instead of abetting Green in his efforts to stop the fray. They were now undoubted masters of the field, but what to do with the liberated blacks was a question which had not entered their heads. Had they been allowed, they would have liked amazingly to have followed up their victory till they had driven the Sultan and all his subjects out of the city, or burned it down over their heads; but before they proceeded to extremities, His Highness himself, with a body of his troops, happening to be passing through the neighbourhood, encountered some of the flying populace, and, ascertaining the cause of the uproar, rode into the square.

Instead of charging the British and cutting them down, he wisely, by means of an interpreter who happened to be with him, shouted to them to keep together, and let him hear what they had to say for themselves. On this Green and the midshipmen hurried after those who were still pursuing the Arabs in different directions, and succeeded in calling them back. They quickly collected in a body, and, not dreaming that they had done anything especially out of the way, but rather had fought bravely and in a laudable cause, without hesitation, still grasping their cudgels, boldly faced the Sultan and his party.

"Tell His Royal Majesty that we found them rascally Arabs knocking down these here unfortunate blackies, just like so many hogs at Smithfield market," answered Jerry to the interpreter's interrogations.

The latter was sorely puzzled to explain the sailor's reply to the Sultan. "Neither the auctioneers nor the others would do anything to knock down the slaves or do anything to hurt them," he answered. "Inshallah! His Majesty allows no violence in his dominions."

This was a broad assertion on the part of the interpreter, considerably remote from the truth. However, the Sultan, who was extremely anxious not to get embroiled with the English, at once accepted their excuses, and either believed, or pretended to believe, that the slave-dealers had been using violence towards the blacks. Catching sight of Green and the other officers, he sent to request their attendance, and desired them to collect their men and march them down to the water, undertaking to protect them from the violence of the inhabitants, who would have otherwise undoubtedly set upon them in overwhelming numbers, and cut them to pieces. He observed, however, that they must on no account again venture on shore, as it would be impossible to guard them from the violence of the Arabs, who would certainly attack them if they had the opportunity.

Green, thankful to get the men out of the scrape, ordered them to keep close together, and follow the Sultan's advice.

"But what are we to do with the poor nigger gals, sir?" asked Jerry, who seemed in no way conscious that he and his companions had illegally transgressed the bounds of propriety.

"I'm afraid we must leave them to their fate," answered

Green; "if you'd carried them off, you wouldn't have known how to dispose of them; and, when we get to sea, we must do our best to put a stop to the traffic by catching as many slave-dhows as possible."

"Ay, ay, sir," shouted the men. The affair, which, at first, appeared likely to be very serious, was thus terminated satisfactorily; and the scene they had witnessed certainly contributed to make both men and officers more eager than ever to catch the slavers, independent of any secret hopes they might have entertained of collecting a good quantity of prize-money.

Jos Green and his companions, though deprived of their ride, resolved not to bring the matter before their officers, who might look upon it in a different light to the seamen, unless complaints were made by the authorities. In that case they determined to defend them as far as they had the power. The consul, however, was likely to hear of the matter, and it would, they suspected, prevent any man-of-war's men being allowed on shore at Zanzibar.

The three vessels sailed together for the northward, when the *Gauntlet*, with her screw lifted, was found to make as good way as her full-rigged consorts. She was destined to take the most northern station, the corvette to cruise next to her, and the brig to remain in the south, to watch Pemba and the adjacent coast. The brig was the first to haul her wind, the corvette next; and Jack then, parting from her, stood for his station in the north. Higson had been out on the coast before, as had the gunner and boatswain, and Jack was therefore glad to consult them. The boatswain, Mr. Large, was very unlike his brother officer of the corvette, his appearance answering to his name. Although not unusually tall, he required an unusually wide cot in which to stow himself away. His countenance was stained red by hot suns and air, rather than by any excess in drinking, though he took his grog, as he used to observe, "like an honest man, whenever it came in his way, either afloat or ashore." He was sufficiently active, and remarkably strong.

On her outward voyage the *Gauntlet* had touched at Sierra Leone, and shipped a gang of Kroomen, who proved as efficient as any part of the ship's company. The head Krooman, a fine-looking fellow, rejoiced among his shipmates in the name of Tom Kettle, while his mate was christened Bill Saucepan,—names to which they willingly answered,—while on the rest of the gang similar names were bestowed. The men of the tribe to which they belonged are infinitely superior to all others of the West Coast, and every man-of-war employed on the station has been for long accustomed to receive a party of them on board to perform the severer labours of the ship, under which English seamen, in that climate, would not fail to suffer. Their dress is that of ordinary seamen, and they are particularly clean and neat in their persons, while they receive the same rations as the other seamen; indeed, they are treated in all respects like the rest of the crew, except that they mess by themselves, and are under the immediate command of their head man and his mate. They are good-natured, merry fellows, as brave as lions, active and intelligent, and always ready to perform the most dangerous and fatiguing duties without grumbling. Tom Kettle and his men were therefore great favourites on board. Black Tom, as he was generally called by the midshipmen, soon became great friends with his namesake and his companions, who treated him with the respect which was his due, and consequently won his affections.

He had nothing of Captain Marryatt's Mesty about him. He did not pretend to be the son of a prince, or to have any wrongs to avenge; on the contrary, his boast was that his father and grandfather were seamen before him, who had ever proved true to their colours; and he was prouder of that than he would have been of being allied to the greatest potentate under the line.

Jack was on the alert himself, and kept everybody else on board on the alert, in the hopes, by some means or other, of inflicting a heavy blow on the abominable slave-trade, for he felt as much interest in the matter as did the old commodore himself. It reconciled him completely to being compelled to command a steamer, which formerly, with the feelings of the old school, he had looked upon as a somewhat derogatory employment. Night and day the brightest look-out was kept, and every suspicious dhow chased and boarded. For some time, however, only legal traders were fallen in with.

It was natural to suppose that as Jack was fresh on the station he would require the most efficient interpreter, and Hamed was therefore transferred to the *Gauntlet*, Murray taking another provided by the consul in his stead. Jack began to feel vexed at his want of success, but Hamed assured him that only the first part of the trade had begun to move northward, and that the slavers would soon be coming, fast and thick.

"I hope so," said Jack, "for this is fearfully dull work."

"Well, captain, I tinkee you gettee more prize if you hide

ship under lee of some island, and den pounce out on de dhows like wasps," said Hamed.

Jack, accordingly, examining the chart with Higson, looked out for the most suitable island for their purpose. The first on which they fixed, a short way to the northward, was low and sandy. It had some tall trees in the centre, of a height to hide a ship's masts. The *Gauntlet* accordingly proceeded on to the northern end, off which she brought up, thus concealed from any dhows coming from the southward. A mile and a half or so to the north was another much smaller island, towards which numerous birds were seen wending their way; and it was evidently, from some peculiarity of the soil, a favourite resort of the feathered tribe.

The ship had been at anchor for several hours, and as no dhows had as yet been seen, and it was thought probable none would make their appearance for a day or two, the time hung heavily on the hands of all on board. Desmond and Tom, having been at work all the morning studying the steam-engine, took it into their heads that they merited some little relaxation, and set to work to persuade Mr. Large to accompany them on a shooting expedition to the island. "You see, Mr. Large," observed Tom, "we're certain to make a good bag, and you like roast goose as much as any man; though we shall have to do without apple sauce, I'm afraid. I'm certain that the birds I saw must have been geese, from their size; we can even now make them out, hovering over the island. We shall very likely get enough to dine the whole ship's company."

Mr. Large's mouth watered as Tom expatiated on the dainty dish he hoped to provide. "If we can't get any of the boats, we can at all events have our canoe," Gerald Desmond observed. It was the same canoe in which they had been picked up and saved by the *Romp*, and which Adair and Murray, who both claimed the ownership, had presented to Jack.

Mr. Large, in an evil hour, yielded to the midshipmen's representations, and consented to accompany them. They, without difficulty, obtained leave from the first lieutenant, promising to be back before dark with the canoe loaded with birds. Mr. Large, who considered himself a first-rate shot, was the happy possessor of a fowling-piece, which he boasted was superior to the best owned by any officer in Her Majesty's Service. The midshipmen contented themselves with two ship's muskets, which, as they carried a large amount of shot, would, they conceived, kill no end of birds every time they were fired.

Having dined, they had no need of provisions; so, taking plenty of powder and shot, with their three weapons, they shoved off, Mr. Large sitting in the after-end, while the two midshipmen paddled well forward, in order in some degree to counteract his weight, which, as it was, brought the canoe considerably down by the stern, and lifted the bows almost out of the water. Tom Kettle, who was unaware of their intention, did not see them till they had got some distance from the ship. "They had better take care," he observed, "or sea come over de stern and swamp de canoe."

The water, however, was smooth, and neither Mr. Large nor his companions had any apprehensions on the subject. Away they went, intending to land on the nearest point. As they approached the point, they were not disappointed in their expectations of finding it crowded with sea-birds, many of large size, which Tom averred were the geese he had seen; while there were various species of ducks, which appeared to be living in harmony with the other inhabitants.

The wind had got up a little, and as they drew near they saw that there was some surf on the shore; but Mr. Large declared that it was nothing to hurt the canoe, and that they might pass easily through it without shipping a thimbleful. He hesitated, however, as he drew nearer. "Don't quite like the look of it," he observed. "If we'd had the large boat we might have got on shore easy enough, but if a sea was to catch us we might be rolled over before we could tell where we were."

"Arrah, but it won't do to turn back," cried Desmond; "those geese now will be after roasting us instead of our roasting them, not to speak of the laugh that there'd be on board when we got back without a feather to show, except the white feather which they'd be after talking about."

Thus incited by Desmond's wit, the boatswain determined to attempt landing. "Now, young gentlemen, paddle away with a right good will," he shouted out, moving farther from the stern. The midshipmen pulling away with all their might, on flew the canoe, with every chance, apparently, of reaching the beach, when the boatswain, turning his head over his shoulder, saw a huge foam-topped sea come rolling up with unusual speed. He shouted to his companions to paddle on. In half a minute more the stern of the canoe would have touched the beach, but before it got there, down thundered the sea upon them, deluging the boatswain, washing the two midshipmen high up on the beach, and capsizing the canoe, which it rolled up with Mr. Large under it close after them. Picking themselves up, without losing their presence of mind, they turned round to see what had become of their companion, and were happily in time to catch hold of him and drag him up before the following sea carried him off.

"Thank you, young gentlemen; you've saved my life, and I've saved my fowling-piece. But I'm afraid the muskets are lost, and, what's as bad, so are the powder-horns and shot," said Mr. Large.

"No, there's one of the muskets," cried Tom, as he caught sight of the butt lifted above the surface amid the creamy water, and, rushing in, he seized it, though the next sea nearly carried him off his legs.

"And there's the other," exclaimed Desmond; and, notwithstanding Tom's narrow escape, he plunged in and secured it. The canoe was thrown up on the beach, not much the worse, and the two paddles were saved. "I'm afraid there's little chance of our finding our ammunition," said Tom in a melancholy voice, not a bit minding the wetting, "and unless we can manage to knock down the birds with our firearms, we shall have to go back after all without any game to show."

"But we must manage by hook or by crook to catch some of them," exclaimed Desmond. "Sure we may catch them by the legs, if we lie quiet, as they come flying by. There seems to be no end of young ones; we may get hold of them, at all events."

While Tom and Desmond were discussing the subject, Mr. Large was watching the breakers, which came tumbling in every instant with increased violence. "I am sorry to say, young gentlemen, that we've no chance of getting off till the sea goes down," he remarked, "unless we drag the canoe across the island, or a boat is sent from the ship to our assistance; and I'm afraid that that mayn't be thought of till night comes on."

"Well, perhaps we may find some eggs," observed Desmond; "they will afford us a supper, and we can manage to get back in the morning."

"They may chance to be over-savoury, considering that so many young ones have already been hatched," said Tom. "However, if we get hungry we shan't be particular."

The boatswain continued looking with a dissatisfied glance at the tumbling waters. "I doubt, even should the boat be sent, whether she would be able to take us off," he observed. "The commander won't be very well pleased when he finds what's happened. Instead of sleeping comfortably on board, we shall have to spend the night out on the bare sand."

"No very great hardship in that, is there, Mr. Large?" observed Tom, trying to console the boatswain. "If we light a fire and roast a goose, we may be pretty jolly after all."

"We must catch the goose first, Mr. Rogers; and then, as to lighting a fire without a match-box or gunpowder, how is that to be done?" asked the boatswain.

Tom had forgotten, and had to acknowledge that they might have to go without the fire. It was agreed, however, that they should search for eggs, which, although they might be somewhat high, might assist in keeping body and soul together.

"Roast goose would have been very pleasant, and a drop of grog to wash it down," observed the boatswain, who could not forget the loss of his creature comforts.

Having hauled the canoe high up on the beach, the boatswain set off in one direction, and the two midshipmen in the other, in search of eggs. They discovered here and there a few broken egg-shells and a few young birds. At length Tom came upon two or three eggs, which he eagerly seized. "Here's a supper for us," he exclaimed, breaking open one of them; but he threw it down with intense disgust.

"Faith, a fellow must be hard up before he could eat that," said Desmond; "try another."

"No, thank you," answered Tom; "one is enough to satisfy me. But we'll keep them for Mr. Large; he may not be so particular. Only we must take care not to break them in our pockets, or we shan't be able to wear our jackets again."

They went on some way farther, the birds shrieking and pecking at their legs as they passed, but showing no further sign of anger, as they had not time to seize the young ones. As they got farther round the island, they saw, from its peculiar conformation, that the sea swept round it, and broke almost with as much violence on the one side as on the other; though still it might be possible, could they get the canoe across, to launch her. However, they were very unwilling to return without having something to show, and agreed that it would be better to wait till the following morning.

They had got more than half-way round when loud cries reached them, and, looking ahead, they caught sight of the boatswain scampering away over the sand faster than he had run for many a year, with a vast flight of birds hovering about his head, and uttering loud shrieks and cries of anger; some darting down and attacking him from behind, and others wheeling round and flying at his face, which he had the greatest difficulty in defending. The midshipmen, seeing the predicament that he was in, hurried forward to his assistance; when the birds, undaunted by their appearance, commenced an assault on them, and they too had to beat a retreat, pursued by their persevering foes. In vain they struck about them with their muskets, which, being heavy, the birds easily evaded, only to return to the assault with greater vigour, caring neither for their aimless blows nor their loud cries.

The midshipmen could easily have outstripped the boatswain, who, already blown, rushed on puffing and panting like an asthmatic steam-engine; but they, like young heroes, refused to desert him, although Desmond, as he flourished his musket, very nearly brought the muzzle down on his companion's nose. The faster they ran, the more determined the birds became, till matters were really growing serious; and the poor boatswain, unable any longer to continue his flight, suddenly came down with a run on his face in the sand.

The midshipmen now making a stand in order to defend him, the birds retreated, croaking and shrieking louder than ever. "We must lift Mr. Large up, or he'll be suffocated," said Tom, and, aided by Desmond, they rolled him round till his face was out of the sand. He was breathing very heavily, and they became greatly alarmed. "I'm afraid he's got a fit of apoplexy, or something dreadful," cried Tom. "I say, Gerald, go and fetch a cap full of water,—there's no other way of getting it,—and we'll try and bring him to."

Gerald, as desired, ran off to the beach, and hurried back with his cap, from which the water was of course rapidly streaming out. They managed, however, to clear the boatswain's nostrils and mouth of sand, and at length had the satisfaction of seeing him open his eyes, his first impulse being to try and get up. He could not as yet speak, and gazed about him wondering what had happened. The shrieks of the birds still hovering near reminded him, and he soon came to.

"Thank you, young gentlemen; if it hadn't been for you, I don't know what would have happened," he said, in a faint voice. He had reason, indeed, to thank the midshipmen; for had they not stayed by him, he would, to a certainty, have been suffocated. Some time had thus been spent. They had been longer making the passage than they had expected, and night was fast approaching. They were wet and hungry, and not very well satisfied with their performances; knowing also that, whether a boat was sent for them or not, they would all be severely reprimanded on their return on board.

After sitting for some time, the boatswain declared that he should catch his death of cold if he remained quiet much longer; so, getting up, they all three set off running to try and restore circulation. No sooner did the winged inhabitants of the island see them on the move than, perhaps supposing that they were again about to invade their nests, with loud shrieks they darted once more to the attack, flying round and round them, and every now and then threatening to pounce down and attack their faces. Even when they did stop, the enraged creatures hovered round them, giving them no rest, and keeping them constantly on the watch to ward off their threatening beaks. At last Tom thought of the paddles, which had been left in the canoe, and, making their way back to her, he and Desmond armed themselves each with one, which were likely to prove more serviceable weapons than the heavy muskets. The birds seemed to be of this opinion, for no sooner did the midshipmen boldly assault them than they flew off to their nests. The boatswain, between his fear of catching cold should he lie down in his wet clothes, and his weariness, was in a sad perplexity. At length, however, he threw himself on the sand, declaring that he could no longer move about, and must submit to his fate, whatever that might be. The midshipmen themselves were getting somewhat tired, but tried to amuse themselves by talking of old times, every now and then taking an anxious look in the direction of the ship, in the hopes of seeing a boat coming to their assistance.

No boat, however, was discernible; nor indeed could they see the ship. They began to grow somewhat uneasy. What could have become of her? Had she steamed away and left them to their fate? but that was not at all likely to be the case. The boatswain had been for some time quiet, and a loud snore showed them that he had fallen fast asleep. Desmond was the first to speak. "I say, Tom, what do you think of our trying to knock some of the birds on the head while they're asleep on their nests; we might in a little time kill as many as we should have shot; and if we could return with a boatful, we should, at all events, not be laughed at, as we shall be if we go back empty handed."

Tom was perfectly ready, and, armed with their paddles, they set off along the beach, creeping quietly forward, in the hopes of coming suddenly upon a colony of the birds. On and on they went, but no birds could they find, the fact being that the tide was low, and they had kept close down to the water instead of making their way over the dry sand. This they did not find out till they had got to a considerable distance. Turning off inland, they, however, quickly found themselves in the midst of hundreds of birds, when they began to lay about them right and left, knocking over vast numbers; those they missed only poking out their long necks, and quacking and screeching at them.

"I thought we should have good sport," cried Desmond, highly delighted; "we shall surprise the old boatswain when he wakes by and by and finds a pile of birds close to him."

On they went for some time, till they found themselves among a colony of a different species, who, instead of tamely submitting to be knocked on the head, flew up with loud screams, and attacked them with the greatest desperation. The midshipmen, of course, fought bravely, wielding their paddles with some effect, while they retreated to the beach. Their assailants then took to flight, and they set to work to collect the birds they had knocked over. Some had partially recovered, and showed fight with their beaks when they attempted to catch hold of them, so that they had to give a good many the *coup de grâce* before they could throw them over their backs. Having each collected as large a load as they could carry, they set out to return to the canoe along the line of hard sand. The road seemed much longer, as they were now heavily laden, and it was some time before they came near the canoe.

As they approached, the shouts of the boatswain and the shrieks of a multitude of birds reached their ears. Hurrying on, they saw dimly through the gloom numberless wings flapping in the air, circling in the darkness, now advancing, now rising, while the figure of the stout boatswain appeared in their midst whirling round his fowling-piece, with which he every now and then caught a bird more daring than its companions, and brought it to the ground or sent it shrieking away.

"Help, young gentlemen, help!" he shouted out, though almost breathless with his exertions, "or these imps of Satan will be too much for me."

Tom and Desmond rushed to the rescue, and, laying about them, at length succeeded in again driving off the birds to a respectful distance. "Glad you came when you did, young gentlemen," said the boatswain, after he had recovered his breath. "Thinking you were keeping watch by my side, I was enjoying my first sleep, when I was awoke by a sharp tweak of my nose, and such a shrieking in my ears as I hope never to hear again. It was a mercy I hadn't both my eyes pecked out; I started up, thinking that a whole horde of niggers were upon me, or might be a party of these beastly slave-catching, murderous Arabs had landed, when I discovered that they were those savage birds again; and finding my fowling-piece in my hand, I began to lay about me, as you saw, with right goodwill, though I own they were almost too much for me. I can't help thinking that the island is bewitched, for such birds as these I never met in my life before, and hope never to meet again. Maybe an empty stomach makes matters worse, for I feel all nohow—more like a sucking baby than the boatswain of Her Majesty's steamer *Gauntlet*."

"You'll get all right in the morning, Mr. Large," said Tom; "I believe you've hit the right nail on the head; but we shan't starve; see, we've brought plenty of food, and we left fifty times as many behind us, waiting till we go and get them."

"If we had a fire it would be very well," sighed the boatswain; "though I suspect they're somewhat of a fishy flavour—not that we should be particular when sharp set."

"Faith, I forgot, Mr. Large," said Desmond, "that we've found some eggs, and we've brought you a couple, knowing that your constitution requires nourishment."

"It does, young gentlemen, it does," said Mr. Large, in a grateful tone; "I feel a gnawing in my inside which quite unmans me."

"Here they are," said Desmond, producing the eggs from his pocket; "they may perhaps have a strong flavour, but, as you say, one shouldn't be particular."

"If we'd but a fire we might make an omelette of them," observed the boatswain, holding one of the eggs in his hand, and preparing to crack it, so that he might gulp off its contents. Scarcely, however, had he done so, than he threw it from him, exclaiming, "Faugh! it's as bad as the essence of a slave-hold."

"We thought it might be pretty strong, Mr. Large," said Desmond, stuffing his wet handkerchief into his mouth to prevent himself from laughing; "but try the other, perhaps that is sweeter."

As Mr. Large was not a man to be knocked down by an egg, he did as he was advised, but the odour which issued from the second was even worse than that of the first, and, throwing it to a distance, he declared that it would be long before he would try another duck's egg.

Gerald asked Mr. Large if he had any tobacco and a pipe. "I have the first, young gentlemen, and thank you for reminding me of it; but how is the pipe to be lighted without a match?" he replied; "but I'll take a quid, though I've given up chawing since I became a warrant-officer; I used once to indulge in it. I wouldn't advise you, though, to do so, for it's very likely to turn your insides out."

Mr. Large had his reasons for giving this advice to the midshipmen, seeing that he had only tobacco sufficient to form a decent-sized quid for himself. It comforted his heart, and, advising his companions to follow his example, he once more lay down to sleep. They tried to do so, but they had not been quiet for many minutes before the birds found them out, and, with loud screeches came flying above them, quickly awakening the boatswain, who declared that he believed they were imps in the form of birds, and would to a certainty attack them again if they had the chance. Tom said he thought so too, and that he remembered reading at school about some harpies who lived on an island, and played all sorts of tricks—that was in the Mediterranean, but he saw no reason why the same sort of creatures should not be found in the Indian Ocean; perhaps they had flown to this very island, as they certainly were no longer to be found in their old locality.

This information did not much comfort poor Mr. Large. At last a bright idea struck Gerald. "Let's turn the canoe bottom upwards, and creep under her; the beasts can't find us there, at all events," he exclaimed.

"I wonder we didn't think of that before," said Tom, and they immediately carried out Gerald's suggestion. Mr. Large had some difficulty in creeping under it, and very nearly brought the canoe down upon himself, but by choosing the broadest part he found sufficient room to lie on his back; while Tom took one end and Gerald the other. Though the birds screamed as loudly as ever, the canoe-wrecked party knew that they were perfectly safe, and could afford to laugh at them. However, they soon went to sleep and forgot all about the matter. They might have slept on till the middle of the next day, as there was no one to call them, had not Tom been awakened by the pangs of hunger; when, starting up, forgetting where he was, he gave his head such a thundering knock against the bottom of the canoe that the noise awakened Desmond, who did precisely the same thing. When the boatswain, giving a heave with his body, turned over the canoe, they discovered that the sun had already risen several degrees above the horizon.

"Here's a pretty kettle of fish to fry, as my missus would say," exclaimed Mr. Large, as he sat up rubbing his eyes; "we ought to have been on board by daybreak, and here we are as if we were upon leave for a month."

"I only wish we'd something for breakfast," exclaimed Desmond, as he got on his legs; "we shall have to breakfast on the raw birds after all."

"Look out there, young gentlemen, where we left the ship—what's become of her?" cried Mr. Large.

The midshipmen looked round with dismay; the ship was certainly not where she had been. "I can't make it out," he exclaimed; "if she's gone I ought to have gone with her, and a pretty scrape I am in. It won't matter so much for you young gentlemen, as, of course, it will all be laid to my door; and here we are now without a drop of rum, or a drop of water to mix with it, or anything more eatable than raw, fishy geese. We shouldn't starve if we were left here for a week, but we should suffer pretty severely from want of water."

"I hope that we shall not have to wait here for a week," said Tom; "and as it seems to me that the surf has gone down, I think the sooner we load the canoe and go in search of the ship the better, since she doesn't come in search of us."

Tom's proposal was at once agreed to, it being evident that the surf had considerably gone down. The only objection to shoving off was the want of the third paddle; greatly, however, to the boatswain's satisfaction, they espied it washed on shore. The only difficulty now remaining was to know where to pull to. The boatswain suggested that they should make the best of their way to the other island, as the ship was certain to return to her former anchorage. They accordingly loaded the canoe with as many birds as she could carry, and while the two midshipmen ran her off, Mr. Large sat aft ready to use his paddles directly they jumped on board. This they nimbly did, and seized their paddles. Mr. Large would have certainly upset the canoe, had he made the attempt to get in after she was afloat. Desmond and Tom managed it, however, very cleverly; and away she dashed. They were soon amid the breakers; the canoe, however, rode buoyantly over them, and was quickly skimming across the placid water to the southward.

They had not gone far, when a wreath of smoke was seen rising above the island, and presently the *Gauntlet* herself appeared towing a dhow, which they had little doubt she must have captured.

"My luck!" cried the boatswain; "I'd have given a week's pay rather than to have missed being on board while she was catching her first prize; however, it can't be helped. There's one good thing; as the ship must have gone away early in the night, for what the commander and everybody else knows, we may have been waiting out here for them ever since. Don't talk about the way I was treated by the birds, young gentlemen, if you please; my brother officers, the gunner and carpenter, would never cease chaffing me about it."

Of course Tom and Gerald promised to be discreet; and they were now only anxious to get over the interview with the commander, hoping that they would not be asked any questions difficult to answer. "At all events, it was not our fault that we were not on board earlier," said Tom; "he can't say that; and as we bring a good supply of birds, both he and everyone else ought to be thankful to us."

The canoe was alongside directly the steamer came to an anchor. They took good care to hand up the birds first; and Jack, on hearing their story, took very little notice of their prolonged stay, only expressing his satisfaction that they had got off safe. Before the ship was under way, blue lights had been burned and guns fired to recall them; but it had been at the time when they were having their first skirmish with the birds, and the signals had not been observed. What those birds were none of them could ever discover; and the boatswain was fully persuaded that they were the harpies of whom Tom had told him.

Tom was tolerably discreet, but Gerald, before long, let out the whole story, greatly to the amusement of the other warrant-officers, who were continually reminding poor Mr. Large of his night on "Harpy Island."

"Harpy it might have been, but *happy* it was not," he

answered with a groan. "I only wish that you two had been there; you wouldn't be so fond of talking about it as you seem to be now."

As the boatswain had supposed, a dhow had been made out by the party which had landed on the larger island, and as soon as steam could be got up, the ship had gone in chase of her. She had managed, however, to run up a somewhat narrow creek, into which the boats had been sent to bring her out, and had succeeded in doing so; though all the slaves had been taken out of her, with the exception of two who had been found in her hold in an almost dying state. The Arab crew had escaped; the examination of the poor slaves the next morning left no doubt of her character. She was accordingly scuttled, and being then set on fire, went to the bottom.

CHAPTER XI

The Look-out Party on the Island—A Slave Caravan—Unwelcome Visitors—Three Dhows chased—Wreck of the Dhows—Rescuing the Slaves—Dangerous Position of the Party on Shore—The Kroomen cross the Surf with Supplies—Tenderness of the Sailors to the Slaves—"Washing a Blackamoor white."

AS Jack was not perfectly satisfied with the anchorage near Harpy Island, he proceeded farther north, to a spot which answered all his requirements, off a lofty headland with a deep bay. On the northern side of it lay a rocky island of considerable height, with trees covering the larger portion. Here a line-of-battle ship might have remained concealed from any vessels coming from the southward, till they were within range of the ship's guns; so that she might, if necessary, compel them to strike, without even getting under way. Farther north the island assumed the low and barren appearance of that part of the African coast, a region as inhospitable and unattractive as could well be conceived. Within the bay was a smooth beach; farther on, the coast was lined for some miles with threatening rocks, against which should any unfortunate vessel be driven, she must quickly be dashed to pieces.

The *Gauntlet*, carefully feeling her way, came to an anchorage in the bay. The second lieutenant was at once sent on shore, with a party of men, to climb to the summit of the peak; no very easy task, as it turned out. However, they got up at last, and the lieutenant on his return reported that from the summit of the headland he had enjoyed a view over fully thirty miles out to sea, and up and down the coast, so that in the daytime no vessel could pass within that distance without being sighted.

Several dhows had been chased and boarded, but the evidence for their condemnation had been insufficient, and with much reluctance Jack had to let them go. Both he and all under his command would have liked to be allowed to burn every dhow with a black man on board, but as such a proceeding would have been illegal, they were compelled to restrain their zeal. The *Gauntlet* had again come to an anchor; an hour before daybreak Tom and Desmond, with a party of men, had been despatched to make their way to the top of the headland, that they might obtain as extensive a view as possible over the ocean. As soon as the sun rose above the horizon a ruddy glow suffused the sky. On reaching the rocky height at which they were aiming, the rocks they saw around appeared as if ready to topple down into the plain on the one side. On the other were deep crevices, sufficient to contain a number of men; thus forming a natural fortress which might be held by a small party against greatly superior odds, while here and there shrubs jutted out from the hollows in which soil, in the course of ages, had been deposited.

As, however, it did not appear likely that any foe would take the trouble of climbing up to molest them, the midshipmen did not bother themselves about the advantages of their position. They valued the hollows rather as affording them at some period of the sun's course a shelter from his rays, and enabling them to take a quiet snooze while off watch. The summit of the cliff, however, on which they had to make their signals to the ship, was perfectly exposed on all sides, and from it they could take a view, not only over the ocean, but across a considerable part of the country to the eastward.

"There's a sail," cried Tom, as he swept the wide expanse of water with his telescope; "and there's another, and another. They're coming up with a spanking breeze, and will try the old kettle's powers to get up with them. Make the signal, Desmond; she must stir up her fires and get under way pretty smartly, or they will have slipped by before she can pounce down on them."

The signal was made, and in a short time a column of black smoke was seen ascending from the funnel of the ship. Two of the boats were at the island, with armed crews ready to pull off towards any dhows which might come near enough to be overtaken. The boats had already seen the signal from the headland, and were pulling out from under the lee of the island. The dhows had not as yet, apparently, discovered that foes were at hand. Out glided the steamer, her black smoke clearly indicating what she was. Two of the inshore dhows quickly disappeared behind an intervening point, almost as high as that on which Tom and his party were posted. The boats, each selecting her prey, pulled away towards two dhows nearest the island, while the ship steered towards three others which were somewhat farther out and ahead of the rest.

The wind was strong; they were all carrying moderate sail, and as they made no apparent effort to escape, it was supposed that they were legal traders. Such for some time, apparently, was the commander's opinion, as the ship's head was seen to be turning more to the southward towards one of the other dhows. Just then a sail of one of the leading dhows was seen to come down.

"She's carried something away," exclaimed Tom; "and the ship can easily overhaul her."

"No, she hasn't," exclaimed Desmond; "see, she's only been shifting her canvas;" and presently, in spite of the fresh breeze, an enormous sail was spread in lieu of the smaller one. The other dhows followed her example, and the ship was quickly in chase of them, setting, as she went along, sail after sail; and as the broad sheets of white canvas were expanded to the breeze, her speed was evidently increased.

"She's not got her full steam up yet," observed Desmond; "when she has, she'll be after them like a shot."

"The shot must fly pretty fast then; see how they bowl along," cried Tom; "look, two of them are edging in for the land, while the third holds her course. The ship seems doubtful which she will follow. They may be all rogues together; or the last may be honest, and only wishes to lead her a wild-goose chase for the sake of favouring the others. No; the commander has made up his mind that the last is no better than the rest. See, he's determined to make her heave-to, at all events."

As Tom spoke, a puff of white smoke was seen to fly out from the bow of the *Gauntlet*, and the faint sound of a gun reached their ears. Another and another followed, forming curves in the air; the ship was throwing shells over and around the nearest dhow to frighten her into submission. For some time she stood on, when she too altered her course to the westward; this was probably what Jack desired, because he might thus hope to capture two or three vessels instead of one. Two other guns were now discharging shot and shell from the port bow.

"I wish I was on board," cried Tom; "surely one or other of the rascals must be caught." It was doubtful, however, whether this would be the case. One thing alone was clear, that all the three vessels had slaves on board, or, rather than run the risk of being struck, they would immediately have hauled down their sails. Tom now turned his attention to the boats, which were still at some distance from the southernmost dhows, and seemed likely to cut them both off. The other two had not reappeared, but had probably found anchorage in a bay to the southward, not supposing perhaps that they had been seen.

"Hurrah!" exclaimed Desmond, who had been watching the ship; "she's brought down the sail of one of the rascals, and is firing away sharply to prevent her rehoisting it."

Some few more minutes passed. "She's up to her," he cried; "see, she's shortening sail, which will help to give the other fellows a better chance of escaping; but she'll not be long about it."

Once more the sails were sheeted home, and the ship rushed forward after her prey, the boat she had lowered appearing like a small speck on the ocean, close to the dhow about to be boarded. The steamer was now in hot chase after the other two dhows, still considerably ahead of her, and making, apparently, for the shore, from which she was endeavouring to turn them by a rapid discharge of shot and shell. The boat's crew she had left behind were quickly in possession of the dhow, the Arabs, as far as could be seen, having made no resistance.

"I thought the coast was rocky all the way to the north," observed Tom; "if those dhows run on shore they will be knocked to pieces in no time, and every human being on board them drowned."

"I heard the master say only yesterday that there were one or two sandy beaches of no great extent some miles on, and I suppose the dhows are making for them, though I shouldn't have thought they had got so far," answered Desmond; "I only hope the ship won't be knocking her nose on the rocks in her eagerness to get hold of the fellows."

"No fear of that," said Tom; "my brother Jack is too careful to do so bungling a thing; though he's ready enough to run every risk when necessary. He wouldn't esteem your remark as a compliment."

"I don't doubt his judgment," said Desmond; "though if you are not on board to give him the benefit of your advice, he may be after getting into a scrape. But, I say, what are the other two boats about? I had almost forgotten them."

Tom turned his telescope to the south-east, in which direction the white bulging sails of the dhows could be seen shining brightly, as they floated above the blue ocean; while the boats lay ahead of them, like two crouching savage animals waiting for their prey. They were more than a mile apart, so that they could render no assistance to each other; but, apparently, they considered that would not be necessary, as the Arabs, even if they had slaves on board, were not likely to offer any resistance with a man-of-war in sight. There was no escape for either of the dhows, for the surf broke upon every part of the coast visible to the southward with a fury which must preclude all hope of escape to any human being on board; and thus, if they intended to fight, they must be prepared to conquer and run ahead of the ship while she was engaged with her companions nearer the shore. Still, there was sufficient probability of their doing so to make Desmond and Tom, with all the men on the rock, watch the proceedings with intense interest.

On flew the dhows, their bulging sails swelling in the breeze, and the white foam flying up under their low bows. Matson, the second lieutenant, commanded one of the boats, and the senior mate the other. The object of the dhows, since they could not avoid the boats, was to try and give them the stem, but the English officers were not to be caught so at a disadvantage. The second lieutenant's boat was nearest in; as the dhow came dashing on, the lieutenant ran his boat alongside, and he and his men, like ants, could be seen scrambling up over the bulwarks. Some small tiny puffs showed that fighting was going on. Then came a pretty considerable number, though the reports which reached them sounded no louder than those of pop-guns. Tom declared that he could see the flash of steel as the cutlasses glittered in the sunshine. One thing was certain, that the British crew had gained the slaver's deck—for that a slaver she was there could be no doubt.

Again puffs of smoke were seen, and the cutlasses flashed once more; and then all was quiet. The midshipmen would have given anything to have distinguished what was going forward on deck, but they could only make out that the boat was alongside, and they could have little doubt that their friends were victorious. Still the sail continued set, which was a suspicious circumstance, but the dhow was scarcely yet sufficiently to the northward to run in under the island. In the meantime the second dhow had got up to the mate's boat; but she being still farther off, it was difficult to see what was taking place. She had a gun in her bows, which, as soon as the fighting began on board the first dhow, was fired into her antagonist; then there came puffs of smoke from the latter, and she was presently alongside; whether or not the English had got on board, it was impossible for some time to ascertain. Desmond thought that they were firing from the boat, while the Arabs were returning their fire from the dhow. Whether or not such was the case, it ceased on both sides.

"Our fellows have got on board, depend upon it," cried Tom; "and they're making short work of it; the Arabs can never stand our fellows' cutlasses."

The second dhow, like the first, continued her course; in about a minute, down came her huge sail, making it evident that she was captured, as the Arabs, if they had been successful, would have been in a hurry to get away. The first dhow had now got sufficiently to the northward to haul in for the anchorage, her helm was put down, and, heeling fearfully over, she made her way towards it.

"Good heavens!" cried Tom; "what's happening to the other dhow?" He had turned his glass but for a minute to look at the first, when, on again glancing at the latter, her bows had disappeared, and her high stern was just sinking beneath the surface. The boat was there, but it was impossible to see who was on board. The party on the cliff were therefore left in a state of intense anxiety as to the fate of their shipmates. They could only picture to themselves numberless human beings struggling for their lives, those in the boat employed in endeavouring to pick them up. The lieutenant's party had too much to do in keeping the Arabs under to go to their assistance; by the time they could have arrived, indeed, all who had not been picked up by the boat must have sunk for ever.

The first dhow was rapidly approaching the anchorage, and the boat, hoisting her sail, soon afterwards followed her. At all events, it was evident that their shipmates had been successful. The two midshipmen were eager to go down and meet them, to hear what had happened, but they had been ordered to remain on the cliff, and could not—without being guilty of disobedience—leave their post; they had, therefore, to sit quiet and curb their impatience, while they continued to keep a look-out over the ocean.

Tom and Desmond now turned their glasses towards the

ship. The dhow she had captured lay with her sails lowered, waiting for her return, to be towed up to the anchorage, while she herself was still seen afar off, though at too remote a distance for her proceedings to be understood. Against the wind, however, the dhow could do nothing, and was drifting away to the northward. They were for the present, indeed, more interested with the dhows taken by the lieutenant and the other boat. Both appeared crowded with people, Arabs and blacks, besides the seamen of the *Gauntlet*. The boat which had carried Tom and Gerald's party on shore had returned to the ship, so that even could they have ventured to leave their post, they would not have been able to get off to satisfy their curiosity. According to the directions given, they continued looking out to the southward for the approach of any other dhows, although there was but little chance of their being stopped; as it was very evident that neither of the boats were in a condition to put off in chase of them. In a short time they saw that the boats were employed in carrying the people from the dhow to the shore, but even before they landed they were hidden from sight by the intervening rocks and trees. From the frequent trips the boats had to make, they judged that the dhow had contained a large number of slaves.

By the time the blacks had been landed, three of the dhows they had at first seen had got almost up to the southern end of the island. "Why, I do believe they are coming to bring up at our anchorage," observed Tom. He was right; the headmost dhow, hauling her wind, stood close round to the north of the point, as if well acquainted with the locality; and although the dhow at anchor must have been seen by those on board, she stood on past her without lowering her sail. She rounded to at some distance farther in; as near, indeed, to the shore as it was safe to go. The inside dhow followed her example, as did the third, and all three lay close together, as if no enemy existed near them.

"They seem pretty bold fellows," observed Tom; "or else they confide in their numbers. Supposing each carries thirty men, and I think I can count as many on their decks, there must be ninety in all—rather heavy odds against our boats' crews, who have, besides, their prisoners to look after. I say, Desmond, suppose they land? we should be feeling rather foolish."

"I don't think the lazy rascals would take the trouble to climb up here," answered Desmond; "and if they do, we've got our revolvers, and the men have their muskets and cutlasses, and we shall easily be able to defend ourselves; but they probably are not unprovided with long guns; though they may be only matchlocks or old muskets, they may contrive to pick us off while they keep at a safe distance."

The state of affairs had indeed become serious. The midshipmen and their party were completely cut off from receiving any assistance from their shipmates on the island, who might indeed also not be in a condition to afford it. In all probability, with the pretty severe fights both boats had had, some of the men had suffered; still, if one whole boat's crew could be mustered, Lieutenant Matson would scarcely fail to try and capture the three dhows which had so audaciously entered the lion's den. That he had not done so already made Tom and Desmond not a little anxious; although the Arabs on board the dhows might not have seen the boats or the people on shore when they first entered the bay, they could not fail to do so where they now lay; yet, instead of again weighing and standing on, which would have been their wisest course, they remained as quiet as if no enemy was near.

The midshipmen's chief hope now was that the ship would quickly come back and catch the three dhows before they again stood out to sea. They expected every instant to catch sight of the boats pulling off to attack the dhows. Neither appeared, and they at length began to fear that either Lieutenant Matson or Collins the mate, or perhaps both of them, had been killed or wounded; and that so many of the men had been hurt that they were unable to make the attempt.

The day was drawing on. They had brought up a small keg of water and some provisions, or they would by this time have been almost starved, as under ordinary circumstances they would have been relieved at noon. However, as Desmond observed, they had to "grin and bear it." Still, not forgetful of their duty, they were keeping a look-out over the ocean, when one of the men exclaimed, "We shall have more visitors than we bargained for; see, Mr. Rogers, here come a whole tribe of the rascally Arabs; and if they find us out, we shall have a squeak for it."

Tom turned his glass in the direction to which the man pointed. "There are Arabs, and not a few, but the greater number of the people are blacks," he observed; "by the way they are walking, they must be slaves. That accounts for the dhows bringing up here; I've no doubt it is a caravan from the interior, and the poor wretches are being brought down to be embarked. Had the ship remained here, all three would have been set free as local traders. I fancy Mr. Matson suspects something of the sort, and is just waiting till they get their slaves on board to capture them. Now I think of it, I heard him yesterday say that he had discovered a deep bight at that end of the island, into which the boats could be hauled and remain perfectly concealed. If that is the case, the dhows have not seen them, and fancy that the people on shore, whom they can't have failed to discover, have no means of getting off."

"Faith, I hope that's the case," observed Desmond; "for if those Arabs who are coming this way were to find us out, they'd be after shooting at us in a somewhat unpleasant manner."

Tom and the rest of the party could not help feeling that Desmond was right. However, they determined to make the best of a bad case; and, as they were tolerably well posted, to defend themselves against all odds. In their exposed position there could be no doubt that they had already been seen, so that they could not hope to conceal themselves, which might have been their wisest course. Tom, therefore, ordered his men to fire off two muskets to attract the attention of the party on the island, trusting that they would, as soon as they saw the Arabs, push off to their assistance.

No answering signal, however, being made, the midshipmen began to have serious misgivings as to what had happened. "Well, my lads," cried Tom, addressing the four seamen who had accompanied him and Desmond, "we'll make the best of a bad case, and hold out as long as our ammunition lasts and we've got strength to hold our swords and cutlasses."

"Ay, ay, sir—no fear about that," was the answer; "the brown-skinned beggars won't be in a hurry to climb up here; and if they do, we'll tumble them back again faster than they came."

That their men would prove staunch, the midshipmen had no fear; still it would be very provoking to see the Arabs embarking the slaves, and not be able to stop them. It would, however, be the height of madness to venture down from their post; for the slave-traders, being all well armed, would, to a certainty, over-power them with numbers, and, however they might have acted alone, were not likely to abandon their prey when on the point of receiving payment from the purchasers in the dhows. The Arabs, who had just approached cautiously, on discovering how small was their party, looked up at them, making threatening gestures, and uttering loud shouts and cries. The poor slaves, apparently, could not understand the matter, and marched on with their heads cast down, many of them pictures of wretchedness and despair. There were women, some with infants in their arms, others leading little children by the hand; a large number appeared to be girls of all ages, who walked together, with scanty garments, but unencumbered by the loads which were carried by most of the rest. Then came a gang of boys, many of whom limped sadly, as their drivers compelled them to move forward at the point of their spears.

Some few old men were among them, who were tottering under loads too heavy for their frail limbs to bear; and then came a numerous body of men, secured two and two by heavy poles, with their necks bolted into forks, one at either end of the pole. Some trod the earth boldly; others tottered at every step, trying to exert themselves to avoid prods from the points of the spears with which their drivers were constantly threatening them. Such had, too probably, been their mode of journeying for many weary miles of desert, since they had fallen into the hands of their persecutors.

"I wonder how many of those poor wretches have sunk down and died on the road?" observed Tom; "or been knocked on the head by those wretched Arabs?"

"Faith, it makes one's blood boil!" cried Desmond; "in spite of all odds, I should like to pounce down upon them, and set the poor negroes free." The men expressed themselves much in the same strain, and would very willingly have followed the midshipmen, had they acted according to their wishes; but both knew that they had no business to leave their post, even had there been any probability of success.

Boats now came off from the dhows, and the business of transporting the slaves on board commenced; while an armed party of Arabs was drawn up near the foot of the cape, to prevent any attempt which might be made by the British seamen to interfere with their proceedings. Nearly all the slaves had been got on board, when the Arabs, no longer being engaged in guarding them, began to show evident signs that their intentions were hostile. Presently a personage of more importance, probably the chief slave-dealer, arrived, with several additional armed attendants. The midshipmen saw the other Arabs pointing them out to him. A consultation which was then held resulted, apparently, in a resolution to attack them. Shouts and cries of hatred arose from the assembled Arabs, who, flourishing their weapons, advanced towards the hill, evidently with the intention of climbing it.

We must leave the midshipmen in their perilous predicament, and follow the *Gauntlet*, which, having captured one of the dhows, of which she was in chase as has been described, stood after the other two. They were both fleet vessels, and, with their enormous sails filled to bursting, seemed to glide over the surface like those winged creatures which may be seen in summer skimming across the surface of a pool. The boilers were heated to the utmost, and with sail and screw the ship dashed forward in chase.

The nearest dhow was the first to haul in for the shore, while the other continued her course, hoping to escape. "The first bird is already ours," observed Jack to Higson; "she'll not venture to run her stem on the rocks, and if we attempt further to interfere with her, we shall lose the second. If she ventures to run out to sea, we shall have time to settle with the one ahead, and catch her into the bargain."

The dhow spoken of was continuing her course towards the shore, with the intention, it was supposed, of anchoring, and waiting till she could again make sail, and run out to sea before the ship had settled with her consort. The *Gauntlet* stood on as before, though she was gaining little, if anything, on the fast-sailing dhow; still, one of the shot or shell she was firing might carry away a mast or tear the sail in pieces; and Jack, trusting to that chance, hoped to capture her at last.

A stern chase is a long chase, under most circumstances, and the Arabs probably thought that they might possibly keep ahead till nightfall, and escape during the darkness. She was a large vessel, and she might have three or four hundred slaves on board, and was on every account, therefore, worth catching. On she went for several miles, the *Gauntlet* inch by inch at length gaining on her. Two shot had already passed through her sail, and a shell had burst so near that possibly some of her crew might have been hit. Gradually she was edging towards the shore, where a sandy beach could be discovered from the ship. It was of no great extent, as there were rocks at either end; but if the dhow could reach it, she might be run on shore, and the blacks landed before the boats could reach her to prevent them. To stop her from doing this was impossible, unless a happy shot should carry away her mast or yard.

Nearer and nearer she drew to the beach, on which a heavy surf was breaking. "The fellows will drown themselves if they attempt to land there," said Jack.

"I'm not so certain of that," answered Higson; "a certain percentage may be lost, but the Arabs will care nothing about that, provided they can get the greater number on shore; and as they themselves swim like fishes, they have no fear of losing their own lives."

The dhow heeled over to the breeze, but still kept her large sail standing; there was no longer any doubt that the Arabs had resolved to beach her. "Give her a shot," cried Jack, "right over her; it may show them that even if they do reach the shore, they have no chance of escaping from us." A shot was fired; another and another followed, flying over the dhow's sail and pitching into the beach, towards which she was rushing to her destruction. Should she strike it, could any of the human beings on board escape? The surf was rolling in heavily, and breaking with continued roar on the sand; rushing far up, and then receding with still greater rapidity. Notwithstanding this, the Arabs, maddened at the thoughts of capture, stood desperately on; they themselves might escape, and what mattered to them the lives of their wretched captives? should a few be rescued, it would be better than letting the whole fall into the hands of the hated white men. The miserable blacks had no choice between a speedy death or a lingering captivity. The foam-topped breakers were dancing up on either side of the devoted vessel; through them she rushed, and the next instant, by the fearful heave she gave, it was seen that she had struck.

Every glass was turned towards her as the ship stood on, keeping the lead going, till, the water shallowing, she must come to an anchor. A minute scarcely had elapsed after the dhow struck, when a black stream was seen issuing from beneath her, some moving figures on shore in coloured dresses showing that the Arabs had first escaped. But of what does that string consist? Of hundreds of human beings, men, women, and children, who had, when the vessel struck, been set free by their owners.

Now one breaker, now another, burst down upon them, and carried some of the dark string away. Their ranks were quickly filled up, and on the string went. It seemed never-ending, as the blacks in the hold, scrambling up on deck, threw themselves overboard to join those who had already reached the shore.

"They must be stopped, at all events," cried Jack; "if they attempt to cross the desert they will be starved to death, or fall into the hands of the murderous Saumalis."

Notwithstanding the heaviness of the surf, it was soon seen that a large number of blacks had reached the shore. At first they assembled in groups; but now, as they looked towards the ship, terrified by the tales their Arab captors had told them of the white men's cannibal propensities, they began to fly, as fast as their cramped limbs would allow them, in parties towards the interior.

"They will escape to their certain destruction, if they are not frightened back," said Jack; "keep the guns playing; fire another shot ahead of them, it will stop them from going off in the direction they are taking."

Several shot were fired over the heads of the fugitives, each column being turned as the wretched beings saw the sand thrown up just before them, and believed that destruction would await them if they took that direction; it was, however, only to try and escape in another. In the meantime, the instant the steamer had stopped her way, three boats had been lowered, and, impelled by their hardy crews, regardless of the danger run, were making their way towards the dhow. Two boldly pushed through the surf, while the third brought up just outside the breakers, ready to receive any of the slaves who might be caught. Archie Gordon was in one, with the second master; the boatswain was in another, with Hamed, the interpreter; while Higson took command of the large boat.

Jack watched them with no little anxiety, for the expedition was a hazardous one. The guns continued firing away, now by their shot or shell checking the advance of the fugitives in one direction, now in another. Still, in spite of the shot, the Arabs kept urging on the slaves, and, making them scatter far and wide, induced them to continue their flight. The two boats, at some little distance apart, entered the breakers, and almost immediately were seen to have reached the shore, while Mr. Large remained by the boats with three hands to look after them.

The rest of the party, led by Archie and Hamed, set off in pursuit of the fugitives. Strong and active, they quickly overtook a large party of the blacks; and Hamed, as was seen by his gestures, was addressing them, probably telling them of their folly in being alarmed, and advising them to return to the shore.

As the crews had landed, the boats had been hauled off by their crews from the beach. Presently Mr. Large was seen hauling one of them up on the beach, and, having done so, he hastened away towards the second; but before he arrived, she was observed in the midst of the breakers, the next instant to be cast a shattered wreck on the beach. He and the two men with him twice rushed down into the surf, the second time with another man who had joined them; again and again they made the same desperate rush into the boiling waters—the life of a fellow-creature depended upon their success. The last rush they made they were successful, and a human form was soon dragged out of the water; but he did not rise to his feet. Carrying him up some little distance, they laid him on the sand, bending over him; then, rising and casting a lingering glance behind them, hurried on to meet a party of blacks who, escorted by some of their shipmates, were approaching the beach.

The Arabs and fugitive slaves had, in the meantime, disappeared over the sandhills, with the seamen still in hot pursuit, enjoying the chase, shouting to each other, and turning here and there as they caught sight of the larger party of blacks ahead, whom they were striving desperately to overtake. Sometimes one, in his his eagerness, would tumble over on his nose, but quickly picked himself up again. Now an unfortunate black was overtaken, and seized by the arm,—for collar he had none to catch hold of, —down he would fall on his knees, imploring his captor not to murder him, when the sailor would pat him on the head and try to make him understand that his intentions were friendly.

Hamed, with his robes girded round him, was as active as anyone, shouting to the blacks that no harm was meant them, and that the sailors only wished to prevent them from being carried off into the desert to perish miserably. His exhortations, and the seamen's activity, resulted in the capture of fifty or sixty blacks, who were brought in from all directions; but still some of the seamen continued the pursuit, and Jack, fearing that they might be carried by their ardour too far, fired a gun and hoisted a signal for their return to the beach. Fortunately the signal was seen by Archie, and the stragglers returned, most of them leading one or more blacks, some with children in their arms, one or two trotting along with a child under each arm, generally squalling and crying like a couple of sucking pigs.

It took some time before the whole of the party were collected on the beach. It was then seen that they were making arrangements for coming off. Jack felt considerable anxiety about the matter; the surf had greatly increased since they went on shore, and even then one of the boats had been lost. Now all depended upon one boat, which must of necessity be heavily laden. He was not quite at his ease, however, with regard to the ship; she was much closer inshore than any sailing vessel would have ventured. Though he knew that the screw would enable him quickly to gain an offing, he had not as yet that thorough confidence in its powers which long experience could give. Nearly all his officers, and a large portion of his crew also, were away; indeed, he had never before been so short-handed. However, nothing could be gained by delay. He made a signal for the boat to come off as soon as possible, a line being carried from the first lieutenant's boat outside the surf to the shore, and by its means the small boat was to be hauled through the breakers.

First a portion of the blacks were placed in her, when, the boatswain taking his seat in the stern, with four hands to pull, she, with her living freight, was shoved off. Now she rose to the top of a sea which rolled in, and now she sank into the hollow between that and the following sea, which so completely hid her from sight, that it appeared as if she had gone down. Jack heard one of the youngsters crying out, "She's lost, she's lost!"—but no; once more her bow emerged amidst the foaming waters, and on she came towards Higson's boat, his crew hauling away manfully at the tow-line.

Jack breathed more freely when he saw her alongside, and the blacks being transferred to the large boat. The instant they were out of her, she made her way once more to the shore. A second cargo was now embarked, and the process was repeated, happily without any accident. "She must make two more trips before they are all off," said Jack to the surgeon, who was standing near him.

The third was accomplished as safely as the other two. "The rest will have no difficulty in embarking, I hope," observed the surgeon.

"The sea has been rapidly getting up," replied Jack; "I wish that they were all safe on board." The fourth and last trip was about to be made; even the ship was much less steady than at first. As he took a glance to the eastward, he observed that the foam-crested seas which rolled in had increased in height. Every man on shore had embarked, and Higson's crew now began to haul in on the line. As they were doing so, a huge sea which came rushing on struck the boat, sending many a bucketful into her, and then, with a thundering roar, hissing as it went rolling on, caught the smaller boat, which had by that time performed half of her passage. Down it came upon her; the next instant the men at the warp were seen to come toppling down backwards—the rope had parted.

For an instant the boat had disappeared; the next, she was seen rolled over in the surf, while those who had been in her were struggling desperately to regain the shore. Jack felt more anxious than he had ever before been in his life; fortunately, four of the Kroomen had gone away in the boats. Numerous heads were seen amid the seething waters; now one emerged, and now another, as the beach was gained, while the gallant Kroomen, with the best swimmers of the party, went darting here and there to assist their shipmates or the drowning blacks.

All eyes in the ship were fixed on them. By degrees they emerged from the breakers, and Jack was in hopes that all had escaped, when he observed three of the Kroomen and two of the sailors plunge once more into the foaming waters. They returned dragging a body with them; then they went in and brought out another and another. One of these, by his dress, was seen to be a seamen, and the rest were blacks.

Then the party rushed down to save their boat, which was hurled on the beach; but their efforts to preserve her were in vain. Down she came with a thundering crash, those in the water narrowly escaping being crushed by her. Getting hold of her they dragged her up, and were seen standing round her It was, however, very evident that her bow had been crushed in, so as to render her unfit again to be launched.

Higson, on coming on deck, expressed his fears that some of their shipmates had lost their lives in addition to the poor fellow who was first drowned. Fifty blacks had been rescued; as many more possibly had been drowned, with numerous children whose bodies had been seen floating about, while many had been dragged off, to undergo fearful sufferings, if not a cruel death, by the slaver's crew.

How to rescue the party on shore was now the question; two boats having now been lost, and three others being away, only the dingy and a canoe remained for use. Their situation on shore seemed dangerous in the extreme; all the arms they had carried had been lost, and should the Arabs discover their defenceless condition, they would certainly not lose the opportunity of avenging themselves. Still, by no ordinary means could they be got off. Jack bethought him of consulting Tom Kettle, who, coming aft, touched his hat.

"Billy Saucepan and I, we do it, sir. We go on shore in the canoe, and carry whatever you wish to send," answered Tom.

"I am sure you will," said Jack; "we must send them some arms and ammunition, a keg of water and some provisions, though it will not do to overload the canoe."

"We take four muskets and whatever you order to send, they not sink the canoe," replied Tom Kettle.

Jack directed that the arms should be wrapped in oil-cloth, and that they, with the keg and a small cask containing a few eatables for the party, should be secured in the bottom of the canoe; so that, should she be capsized, they might not get washed out or be damaged. Going below, he also wrote a letter to Archie, directing him to fire off three muskets should the Kroomen reach the shore in safety.

"All ready, sir," said the head Krooman; "we get there, never fear." The canoe was lowered, and Tom and his companion shoved off. Away they dashed, energetically working their paddles. The canoe was seen to enter the surf. Jack was too anxious to speak.

"They'll do it," cried the doctor; but he was mistaken. The canoe dashed into the surf, and the next instant appeared bottom uppermost, rolling over and over. "The fine fellows are lost!" he exclaimed. A time of anxious suspense passed by; now the canoe could be seen in the surf, now she disappeared; but the gallant Kroomen could not be discovered, though many an eye was looking out for them.

Jack took a hurried turn on deck, considering what was next to be done. Higson proposed once more going in the large boat, and sending a line on shore, so as to tow the people singly off. "They would be drowned before they got half-way," said Jack.

"I fear they would," answered Higson; "and the dingy would never live in such a sea, even with only one man in her."

Jack feared that he should have to remain till the next morning, but in the meantime he would certainly lose the other dhow which had been seen close inshore, while it was important to get hold of the first captured before dark, and to carry her to an anchorage. While he and Higson were discussing the subject, their ears were saluted by the report of three muskets, fired in rapid succession. "Tom and his mate are safe, at all events," he exclaimed; "and the best thing the party can do is now to make their way overland to the bay. Having got arms, they will be able to beat off any Arabs who may venture to attack them."

The proper signal was accordingly made to Archie, who showed that he understood it by waving a handkerchief; and the whole party were seen at once to put themselves into marching order, when they began moving to the southward along the shore. The anchor was then weighed, and the ship stood towards the spot where the dhow she had before chased was last seen. The slaver, which had some time before hoisted her sail, was seen standing to the eastward; but suddenly down came the sail.

"She's given in, finding it useless to attempt escaping," remarked the doctor.

"I'm not so sure of that," said Higson. "See, up goes her canvas again; there, she's standing for the shore on the other tack."

All hopes of cutting her off were vain; the ship dashed on, head to wind, while the dhow bounded towards the rocky coast. "The madmen!" cried Jack; "she'll be dashed to pieces in a few minutes. Throw a shell ahead of her, it may induce the Arabs to haul down their sail."

The missile flew over the doomed vessel, but still she held on towards the coast. "Try and hit her," he cried out; "it may be better to sink her where our boats can pick up some of the poor wretches, than allow them to be dashed to pieces on those cruel rocks—fire shot." Gun after gun sent their shot at the dhow; but the range was a long one, and tossed as she was from sea to sea, while the ship herself was far from steady, they flew ahead of their mark. Jack had a hard matter not to stamp on the deck from rage at the conduct of the Arabs, and pity for the poor creatures they were thus carrying to destruction. Nothing he could do would make the ship steam faster, nor could he blame the gunners for not taking better aim.

"Cease firing," he cried at last; "it is of no use now, as the dhow is within a cable's length of the breakers." The dhow flew on with her huge sail stretched to the utmost, and already heeling over fearfully. It seemed that the water must be rushing into her hold.

"There is a narrow opening between the rocks," exclaimed Higson; "the dhow has been making for that." Scarcely had he spoken when she was in the midst of the breakers. They roared around her, and the next moment she was hurled up towards the beach, her huge sail flying away to leeward, and flapping wildly in the wind. It seemed impossible that any human being could escape from amid that furious mass of foam, except the strongest of swimmers; but notwithstanding this, ere another minute had passed, a black line was seen here and there, like some enormous serpent, crawling over the yellow sand from the dark wreck, the Arabs being distinguished by their coloured dresses as they made their way on shore. Onward went the miserable blacks, the line becoming thinner and thinner; still the headmost were flying, when an enormous sea, dashing on the shore, enfolded the stranded dhow in its embrace. Even the escaping blacks halted to gaze at the spectacle, as the despairing shrieks of their wretched countrymen reached their ears; while the dhow, shattered to fragments, was carried off with all those remaining on board by the receding billows.

The blacks stopped but a few moments, and then, terror-stricken, fled on into the desert, there in all probability to perish miserably. "This is terrible work!" exclaimed Jack. "Had we allowed the dhow to pass, though those poor creatures might have been kept for ever as slaves, they might have retained their lives, it may be, and bettered their condition; but it was our duty to destroy the dhow at all events. Do you think it possible that any can have escaped, Higson?"

This question was put as the ship neared the scene of the catastrophe. "Not likely," answered the first lieutenant; "but we can but look for them." The ship's way was stopped, and a boat being lowered pulled towards the shore. Here and there a few fragments of the wreck were seen, but not a human being could be distinguished. After examining the rocks on either side of the spot where the dhow went on shore, Higson returned to the ship; the boat was hoisted up, and a course steered for the dhow which had at first been captured.

Jack had been looking out for the shore party; he saw them, as he believed, still farther to the northward, making their way over the sand. "A dreary march they'll have of it," he observed to Higson; "but with the firearms they possess they will be able, I hope, to keep the Arabs at bay, should any of the rascals take it into their heads to attack them."

"It is fortunate that Hamed is with them, as he may be able to communicate with any natives they may fall in with, and obtain them as guides over the hills," said Higson.

"I would rather they should not fall in with any natives, who are more likely to prove treacherous than to afford them assistance," answered Jack. The attention of the officers was now, however, engaged in looking out for the dhow; evening was approaching, and it was important that they should pick her up before dark.

"There she is, right ahead," cried the look-out from aloft. With her sail lowered she presented but a small object on the water.

The ship soon neared her; the officer in charge replied to Jack's hail, "All's right, sir; but I hope that the blacks may be received on board; for if you take us in tow, I doubt if the craft will hold together."

"The sooner they are out of her the better," answered Jack. The dhow was accordingly brought alongside, and now began the task of removing the unhappy beings to the ship. The men eagerly came forward to assist in carrying the weak and helpless creatures up from the hold of the slaver, the horrible odour from which was sufficient to overcome the most hardy. So weak and emaciated from their long confinement, and their still more dreadful overland journey, were most of the negroes, that the greater number could not walk without assistance, and were carried on deck in the strong arms of the seamen. With the greatest tenderness and care did those gallant fellows carry their helpless burdens, notwithstanding the mass of filth with which they were covered, in consequence of their long imprisonment in the pestilential hold.

There were nearly a dozen infants on board; the mothers of some of them being too weak to carry them, they were lifted up by the seamen, who tenderly bore them along the deck, chirruping and talking to them as they would have done to their own offspring. Though two or three were sickly, and one was found dead in its mother's arms, yet they had suffered less than the somewhat older children, who had been unable to obtain their share in the scramble for food, which, from the mode the Arabs had of distributing it, must have taken place; the more helpless ones went without it, while the stronger got a double portion.

There were nearly a hundred and fifty children under ten years of age. Some were in the very last stage of suffering, and were mere skeletons. There were comparatively few middle-aged men, showing that they must have either fallen in battle, or escaped the raids made on their villages by the slave-procurers. Some, again, were old women, who would, it might be supposed, from their very worthlessness, have been allowed to remain behind by their barbarous captors.

"The poor old crones would not have fetched half a dollar

apiece," observed Higson; "had these rascals any bowels of compassion, they would have spared them all the sufferings they've had to endure; but for the sake of the few dollars they may pocket, they would not mind what amount of torture they inflict. I wish we had liberty to string up the whole lot of them at our yard-arms, they would only get their proper deserts."

Some time was spent before the dhow was cleared. Her Arab skipper and crew were then placed on the poop, as they came, sulkily enough, on board. They were received by the ship's corporal and corporal of marines with no very friendly looks, and were compelled pretty roughly to strip, in order that they might be searched for arms and money. While they took charge of the former articles, the latter commodity was handed to the paymaster. On their clothes being returned, they were sent on to the poop under charge of a sentry, to await their fate, whatever that might be.

"Are all out of the dhow?" asked Higson of the carpenter and his crew, who had been sent on board her.

"I'll take one look more round," was the answer; and a lantern being handed to him, he descended with some of his men into the hold. They presently returned carrying three human beings, but what they were it was difficult to say, till they were handed up on board. One proved to be an old woman, who could scarcely open her eyes; the other two were lads, who had been found almost buried in the sand which served as ballast for the vessel. They were placed among the other worst cases, of whom the doctor expressed his belief that several were past recovery. The younger and best-looking young women, as being the most profitable part of the cargo, had been better cared for than any of the rest, while the men and boys had been almost starved, the object of the Arabs being to expend as little on food for them as possible.

"The dhow is clear, sir," reported the carpenter.

"Scuttle her," said Jack, "and set her on fire. The Arabs shall see that we don't take them for the sake of their craft; it may serve as a slight punishment for them to see her burning."

With infinite satisfaction the carpenter and his crew distributed some bundles of oakum and shavings in different parts of the vessel, and, setting them on fire, quickly climbed out of her, when Jack shouted, "Turn ahead!" and the *Gauntlet* steamed on, leaving the dhow enveloped in flames. The whole operation was so speedily performed that the Arabs opened their eyes with astonishment. Most of them took it, however, quietly enough; but the negoda, to whom the vessel belonged, plucked his beard with rage as he saw his property destroyed.

"Serve him right," was the remark made by not a few of those on board, though the greater number were too actively employed to notice what had occurred. Their first business was to clear the unfortunate creatures from the filth with which they were literally covered from head to foot. Warm water and sponges and towels were brought from below to perform the operation on those who were too weak to bear any more severe process; while the larger number were placed under the steam hose, which was set to work pumping water over them, the seamen turning them round, and exposing those parts of their bodies to which the dirt clung the thickest.

"Well, if we can't make a blackamoor white, we can wash him clean, at all events," remarked Nat Bolus, the wag of the crew; "though I don't think as how we could have done it without the help of this here steam."

Even the stronger ones were handled kindly, but the poor weak creatures, who could scarcely lift their arms, were treated with such gentleness by the rough seamen as any trained hospital nurses could have used. Their dirty rags, on being removed, were immediately thrown overboard as utterly unfit for further use. In the meantime, the cook had been busy in the galley boiling beans and rice, some of which had been found in the dhow, though the ship had a quantity for such emergencies. The next operation was to clothe the poor blacks, for which purpose both officers and men ransacked their wardrobes. Sheets, tablecloths, towels, bed-curtains, shirts, and flannels, were willingly brought forth and put over their naked bodies as they came out from under the hose.

By the time they were all washed, the cook announced that the food was ready, and they were made to sit down in circles of twenty on the deck, when the men told off for the purpose carried round the bowls, which were placed in the centre of each ring. The degraded state to which they had been reduced was now more fully exhibited, for, instead of gratefully receiving the food, they rushed at it much as a pack of hungry dogs would have done, scratching, crying, and striking at each other, for fear that their neighbours might get a larger share than themselves. It was humiliating to the lookers-on to see beings with immortal souls thus acting the part of wild beasts; and yet these very beings were capable of receiving the truths of the gospel, and it might be hoped that even now many might have the opportunity of being raised to a state much superior to that from which they had fallen.

In spite of the exhortations of the seamen to the poor creatures to be quiet, they continued their shrieks and cries, each thrusting his or her hand into the dish to seize as large a portion as it would hold, and then to cram it into the mouth much after the fashion of a monkey. Indeed, as Nat Bolus remarked, "they looked for all the world like an assemblage of huge baboons."

The smaller children, who were too weak to feed themselves, were committed to the care of the seamen; and a dozen or more hardy tars were to be seen with basins and spoons in their hands, and little children on their knees, ladling the food down their throats, till the doctor had to interfere to save the infants from being killed from repletion. The worst cases had been removed to the sick bay, where every care was bestowed on them both by the surgeon and officers, who produced preserved milk, wine and spirits, and various delicacies which might assist in restoring almost exhausted nature. Many were too far gone to exhibit any feeling, their only desire apparently being to be allowed to die in peace; but others endeavoured to express their gratitude by all the means in their power, though, as Hamed was on shore, they had no means of doing so in words.

The great difficulty was to stow away so large a number of persons on the deck of the ship. Of course they could not be allowed to go below, where the crew were already somewhat closely packed for that hot climate. The poor creatures were made to lie down side by side, and sails being got up were spread over them, while screens were rigged to keep off the wind, and an awning stretched over all. Here, at all events, they had fresh air, and were tolerably protected from the weather. Even now many, it appeared, did not understand that all was being done for their benefit; while a large number, their limbs aching with pain, gave utterance to the most lamentable groans and shrieks, which were heard all night long throughout the ship, as she made her way to her former anchorage.

This was only one of many similar scenes which Jack witnessed while engaged in the suppression of the slave-trade.

CHAPTER XII

The Look-out Party attacked—Repulse and Flight of the Arabs—Securing the Prisoners—A Night on the Beach—Rejoin the Ship—Burning of the Dhow—Arabs attempt to escape to the Mainland, but fall Victims to Sharks—Encounter with another Slave Caravan—Return to the Ship.

TOM ROGERS and Gerald had watched the approach of the Arab slave-dealers to the foot of the hill. "You may howl as you like, my boys," cried Gerald, "but if you attempt to climb up here, you will be sent tumbling down again faster than you came up." Tom, meantime, was keeping an eye on the movements of the Arabs, and the moment he saw them lift their matchlocks, he shouted to his men to jump down into one of the hollows, he himself setting the example; so that the bullets either flew over their heads, or struck the rocks behind which they were concealed.

"The rascals think they've blown us off the face of the earth," said Tom, who had found a spot with a bush through which he could thrust his telescope and yet remain perfectly sheltered behind the rock; "they're looking about them, wondering where we've gone to. If we had but a few more muskets, we could pick off every one of them."

Still the Arabs showed no inclination to climb the face of the hill. Had the midshipmen and their party remained concealed, possibly the slave-dealers might have taken their departure inland; but Gerald, forgetting the danger they were in, could not resist jumping up on the top of the rock, and shouting out in a tone of derision at their foes. Tom, seeing the Arabs about to take aim at him, pulled him down just at the moment that a whole volley of shot came whizzing through the air.

"You may fire away as much as you like," cried Desmond, "but you won't hurt us."

Though it would have given the Arabs infinite satisfaction to cut the throats of the whole of the party, they still hesitated to run the risk of being shot themselves at close quarters, probably supposing that the English were better armed than was the case. Tom watched all their movements through his glass. At length the chief of the slave-dealers, who had gone off to the dhows, returned on shore with several companions. Tom saw the others apparently telling him what had occurred. He appeared to be addressing them and working them up to mount the hill, then, waving his crooked sword, he led them on towards the only path by which they could ascend, they following, shouting and shrieking out vows of defiance.

"They're coming," cried Gerald; "there's no mistake about it this time."

"Well, then, you take one pistol and I'll take another," said Tom, "and as they get near enough we must pick off the leaders. Tim Nolan and the other fellows must manage the rest, after they have fired their muskets, with their cutlasses; and I've no fear but we shall give a very good account of the whole party." Tom directed the men where to post themselves, so that they could remain concealed behind the rocks till it was time to spring out and meet the enemy hand to hand.

"That chief, or whatever he calls himself, seems a bold fellow," observed Tom, "for he keeps ahead and seems to be encouraging his followers, who wouldn't, without him, have had any stomach for the fight. We must do our best to try and pick him off, and if we can manage to give him his quietus, the rest will very quickly run away."

The path made by the signal party was so narrow that there was not room for two people abreast; some little way down, however, there was a sort of platform, on which a considerable number could collect together. "If we could stop them before they get up there," observed Tom, "we should have only one at a time to handle, whereas if they manage to assemble at that place, they might pepper us in an unpleasant manner."

"I'm ready," cried Desmond; "if you'll give the word, we'll all spring out together and stop them before they reach it." Desmond told the men what Rogers proposed doing; they, of course, were ready to obey him, though it might have been safer to remain where they were. Still it was important that they should conceal themselves till the last moment. The leading Arab, with his sword in his teeth, was only about a couple of yards or so below the platform.

"Let fly at the fellows," cried Tom. The men fired their

muskets. "Now, lads, we'll be at them," shouted their young leader, and, springing up, he bounded over the rock, followed by Desmond and the four men, just in time to catch the leading Arab as his band was on the edge of the platform. With a downhanded cut of his sword, Tom sent the Arab falling headlong down the cliff. The next met with the same fate, but the chief, who had allowed the other two to precede him, shouted to his followers to fire at the Englishmen. The order was obeyed, and a shower of bullets came whizzing by them. Tom, in return, fired at their leader, and, without stopping to see the effect of his shot, shouted to his men to fall back under cover before a second volley could reach them. Scarcely had they got under shelter when the Arabs again fired. He saw that his former manœuvre would not be again executed with the same success.

The death of two of their companions appeared to have damped the ardour of the Arabs, who remained perched about the rocks, waiting for an opportunity to pick off any of the defenders of the height who might venture to show themselves. This, however, neither Tom nor his companions intended doing. Tom had recovered his glass, which he had left behind, and had taken a glance over the ocean to the northward in the hopes of seeing the ship, believing that her appearance would very quickly induce the Arabs to hurry off. She was nowhere to be seen, though he caught sight of several dhows running to the northward.

While thus engaged, the voice of the old chief was again heard, and though they could not understand his language, yet they judged from his tones that he was endeavouring to induce his countrymen to renew the attack. "It can't be helped," observed Tom calmly; "if they attempt to storm our position we must drive them back. Our wisest plan will be to keep under shelter as long as we can, and then to spring out on them as soon as they get their noses near enough."

"Ay, ay, sir!" cried the men in cheerful tones; "we'll soon give them a taste of our cutlasses, and they'll not wish to have a second bite."

Tom's suspicions were confirmed, when in another minute a hot fire was again opened, the bullets just clearing the edge of the platform; and directly afterwards the chief and several of his followers sprang up upon it. Once having gained possession of the ground, it was easy enough for the rest. Matters were now becoming far more serious than before. From another opening in the rock, Tom, although still concealed from the

Arabs, was able to look down upon the anchorage. "Hurrah!" he exclaimed; "Mr. Matson has not been asleep; there comes the boat from the island, and if the slavers are not sharp about getting under way, she'll have the whole of them; but one or two are pretty sure to be caught."

As he spoke, the report of a gun was heard, and it was seen that the boat, as she pulled towards the slavers, was firing at them from her bow. The Arabs on the hillside, startled by the sound, looked round; those who were in a position to see what was happening below, shouted to their companions, who speedily began to leap down the rocks; most of those on the platform, in their hurry and fright, springing down a distance by which they ran an imminent risk of breaking their necks; others bounded down the pathway in a mode terror alone could have prompted them to venture on.

"Now's our time!" exclaimed Desmond, seizing several large stones which lay in the hollow; "if our bullets can't reach them, these will;" and he and Tom, leaping from under cover on to the platform, while their men kept up a brisk fire, began to pelt the retreating Arabs, three of whom were knocked over, several others having broken their legs or necks in their flight, till the hillside presented the appearance of a battlefield. All this time the midshipmen and sailors were shouting and hallooing at their flying foes. The larger number of the Arabs, however, reached the bottom of the hill unhurt, and were seen hurrying down to the shore, apparently with the intention of shoving off to the dhows to assist their countrymen. They were all collected together, engaged in launching a boat, when a shell plunged right in among them, killing and wounding several. The rest, fearing the visit of another missile, took to flight. The desire, however, of preventing the slaves being captured, either by bringing them on shore or beating off the English, induced them to go back and make a second attempt; but scarcely had they collected when another shell pitched right into the boat, shattering her to pieces, and laying low two more of their number.

This was more than their greed of gain could stand; again they took to flight, following their chief, who made towards the only shady spot in the neighbourhood, where a horse was left tethered. Mounting, he galloped off, followed by the rest of his gang on foot.

The party on the hill were at first doubtful whether they ought to follow the fugitives, as Desmond had suggested. Tom, however, thought that they decidedly ought to prevent any slaves who might be landed from escaping. One of the dhows was seen hoisting her sail. Having cut her cable, she stood out to sea, while the other two, in order to give her a better chance of escaping, commenced firing at the boat, expecting that she would at once attack them. The lieutenant, however, had made up his mind to have all three, and, disregarding their shots, he pulled away after the first, at the same time firing his bow-gun at her rigging. She was a fast vessel, and was leading the boat out of harbour. The other two dhows, seeing this, began to hoist their sails for the purpose of slipping out astern of her. As he might possibly lose all three, the lieutenant now put back, and managed to run on board one of the dhows.

The Arabs fought desperately, and it seemed doubtful who would gain the victory. "I wish we were on board to help them!" exclaimed Desmond; "if I thought we could swim as far, I should propose going off to her."

"Better stay where we are," said Tom; "we shall have work enough to do. See, the other dhow is coming round with the intention of running on shore; probably those on board don't see their friends scampering off, and they hope to re-land their slaves. It is fortunate we are here to prevent them escaping; perhaps they have been so busily engaged that they may not have seen us, and I propose that we hide ourselves behind those rocks out there, and, if the slaves land, we can rush out and surprise them."

The plan suggested by Tom was instantly put into execution. Notwithstanding the opposition of the crew, the dhow attacked by the lieutenant was quickly captured, and again brought to an anchor; when, leaving some of his people on board, he made sail after the first dhow, which there was still a possibility he might overtake The midshipmen could hear his gun rapidly fired, showing that he was trying to bring down her sail.

The last of the three dhows had now stranded, and the cries and shrieks which arose showed that the Arabs were throwing the unfortunate blacks into the water, and compelling them to make their way on shore. Tom and Desmond agreed that it would be no easy matter to stop the blacks and to fight the Arabs at the same time, as they would be certain to try and make off with as many of the negroes as they could. Looking out from their hiding-place, they saw the beach covered with blacks, who had swum and waded on shore; but the Arabs themselves were waiting on board till all were out of the vessel, intending to come on shore in their boat. Probably they expected that their friends would hurry down and assist them in securing their captives.

Just as the boat left the side of the dhow, the midshipmen, uttering loud shouts, rushed out of their hiding-place; while the blacks, seeing them, ran on either side like a flock of scared sheep. The sailors in vain tried to reassure them; as they had not much time to do it, it was necessary to attack the boat before the Arabs reached the shore. The latter were evidently taken by surprise, and, cramped in the boat, which was tossing about, were unable to use their firearms to any effect. A few shots were fired wildly, and the next instant, as she was thrown on the beach, the midshipmen and their followers, rushing into the water, attacked the crew so vigorously with their cutlasses that half their number were killed or wounded before they could defend themselves; while the rest, as they were dragged out, were made prisoners. The wounded were allowed to lie on the shore, while the rest were secured by ropes, which had been brought on shore to bind any refractory slaves.

No victory could have been more complete. The next business was to stop the blacks, who were hurrying away in different directions. In vain the sailors shouted to them, some persisted in running off into the wilderness; but a considerable number were at length turned back to the seashore, where they all stood crowded together, too much alarmed to know what to do, and gazing at their late masters with astonishment. Still, should they attempt to break loose, it would be no easy task to stop them. Every now and then Tom kept looking out for Mr. Matson's boat, and was not sorry to see her returning, though one of the dhows had escaped.

"There is a chance still that the ship will pick her up," observed Tom. "We want his help to take care of the poor blacks, and to look after these Arabs. How to feed them all will be a puzzle."

"I suppose there's food on board the dhow?" observed Desmond.

"Yes, but how are we to get it? If we pull off to her, the blacks will run away, or the wounded Arabs will get up and release their companions," said Tom.

"Faith, then, the best way will be to take them on board with us," said Desmond; "it's somewhat like the story of the fox and the goose and the peas."

The day was wearing on, and the lieutenant's boat had been led a long way out to sea, so that it would be almost dark before she could reach the shore. The midshipmen themselves were becoming very hungry and thirsty, for they had left their provisions on the top of the cliff, and could not venture back to procure them. They had not a moment's rest; every now and then they were compelled to start off, now in one direction, now in another, to turn back the negroes, who were constantly making attempts to run off.

While Tom was watching the boat, two shots were heard in rapid succession from the island, towards which he at once saw her alter her course.

"She'll not be coming here, after all!" he exclaimed; "something has happened on the island, and that was a signal to her to put in."

"We must make the best of a bad case, then," said Desmond. "I propose that we compel all the blacks to sit down in a ring; they will be better off than they were in the hold of the dhow, and will have no reason to complain. We must make them understand that if any of them attempt to get up they will be shot. As for the wounded Arabs, we must place a sentry over them, and tell them the same; while we must see that the prisoners' arms and legs are securely lashed. If the other fellows don't come back, I see no reason why, provided we keep our eyes open, we shouldn't get on very well. It won't be very pleasant to walk about all night, but it will be better than allowing the Arabs to cut our throats, or letting the blacks escape, for their sakes and our own."

"A very good proposal, Desmond," said Tom; "I couldn't have thought of a better myself, and we will at once carry out your plan." Tom explained to the men what they wished to have done, who, choosing a spot just above high-water mark, made the blacks understand that they were to go and sit down there. They put the women and children in the centre, then the weaker-looking people and lads, and the stronger men outside of all. They could thus better keep an eye on those most likely to try to escape; and they managed to impress on their minds pretty clearly what they intended doing, should they make the attempt. These arrangements being made, they hoped to get through the night without losing any of their prisoners, even should Mr. Matson not arrive to their assistance. They were, however, suffering considerably from hunger and thirst, and at last

Tim Nolan, touching his hat, offered to go off to the dhow and bring on shore something to eat.

As there was still some daylight, Tom thought that he could manage to keep the blacks in order, and agreed that Desmond should go, accompanied by Tim, while he and the other two men kept a strict watch over their charges. As the tide had already run out, the boat had but a short distance to traverse. In a short time Desmond came to the bow of the dhow, and shouted out that he had found plenty of food, and would bring some kettles on shore to cook it.

"By all means," answered Tom. After a little time the boat returned with several casks and bags, two large cooking-pots, and a quantity of wood. These things were indeed welcome. Being carried up to a spot somewhat inland, where the blacks sat, a fire was kindled, the pots put on to boil; and a cask of water having been brought from the vessel, with some bamboo cups, it was served round to the prisoners, after they themselves had first drunk. It was difficult, however, to help them, as the first who seized the mug would not pass it on, in spite of all the seamen could do, until he had drained it to the bottom. The seamen would not allow those who had already drunk to have any more till the whole of the party had been supplied.

By the time the water had been served out, the contents of the pots were sufficiently boiled. Now came the most difficult task—to divide the food fairly among so many people. They would gladly have fed the children and women first, but, placed as they were, that was impossible. However, they were afraid to let them shift their positions; the moment a basin was handed to one of the men, he would not give it up until he had emptied it. Even when the men had been fed, they would scarcely allow their weaker companions to receive their portion, but tried to snatch it from the hands of the seamen.

Night found them thus employed. The fire they had kindled was now of the greatest assistance in enabling them to continue serving out the food, and, at the same time, to watch their prisoners. Though some figs and other delicacies were found on board, the midshipmen would not give them to the Arabs, but properly allowed them only such food as they had laid in for their captives. The fellows grumbled, but hunger made them accept it. At last, by using kind tones and by gentle treatment, the seamen quieted the fears of the blacks, who now seemed perfectly resigned to their lot, and showed no inclination to run away. Still the midshipmen did not relax in their vigilance; so busily employed were they that the night passed away more rapidly than they had expected.

Their chief anxiety was regarding the events which had happened on the island, and which had induced Mr. Matson to land there instead of coming to their assistance. They feared that the Arabs taken in the dhows had given more trouble than those they had captured; possibly the lieutenant, confiding in the strength of his party, had not thought it necessary to bind them, and they had consequently attempted to regain their liberty. However, this was only conjecture, and they were compelled to wait patiently to ascertain the truth, hoping that nothing very serious had happened.

Notwithstanding the general quiet observed by the prisoners, now and then a black got up and looked about him as if contemplating a start, but was detected almost immediately by Tom and Desmond, or one of the seamen, and compelled to sit down again in a good-humoured manner. "You mustn't be after giving leg-bail to us, old fellow!" exclaimed Tim Nolan, patting the black on his back; "you'll have plenty of grub to-morrow, and we'll be taking you to a pleasanter country than this. Ah, there's another of them!" and away he would start farther round the circle.

There was evidently no combination among the blacks, or by a number rising together they might have made their escape. They had all, probably, been brought from different districts, and scarcely understood each other's language, many of them having come from the neighbourhood of Lake Nyassa, and others purchased from the Portuguese much farther south. A still stricter watch was kept over the Arabs, who growled and cursed at their captors, but were unable to cast off the well-secured lashings by which they were bound. Thus the night passed on; tired as all hands were, no one sat down even for a moment, and six people, armed only with pistols and cutlasses and a couple of muskets, were able to keep three hundred in subjection.

"I'd give a good deal to be able to turn into my hammock!" exclaimed Desmond.

"We may have the chance before long, then," said Tom. "See, there are the first streaks of dawn; and, hurrah! there comes the ship. I thought I saw her a minute ago, and now I I am certain of it," he added, looking through his telescope. "She'll be here in less than an hour."

As daylight increased, some of the blacks caught sight of the ship, which, steaming on, head to wind, seemed to create no little astonishment, and still more alarm, in their minds. The seamen did their best to quiet them, going round and round the circle, and talking in cheerful tones, which had their due effect, although the words they spoke were not understood. Desmond proposed getting some more wood and provisions from the dhow. They were quickly brought on shore, when the fires, which had almost burned out, were again made up and another supply of food cooked. The same scene took place as before. The poor negroes scrambled and screamed over it, though the seamen did their best to serve it out impartially. Then the Arabs had their share of food, and the wounded men were looked to. One of them had died during the night, it having been impossible to attend to him—indeed, they were not aware how badly he had been hurt.

With infinite satisfaction the two midshipmen at length saw their ship come to an anchor. A couple of musket-shots attracted the attention of those on the look-out on board, and a boat was seen to put off from her. In a short time Higson, with a party of men well armed, stepped on shore. "I can heartily compliment you both," he said, after he had heard the account Tom and Gerald gave of their proceedings. "Now, the sooner we get these poor fellows on board the better. We have a good number already, and there must be as many more, from what I saw on the island; but they stow pretty closely, and we must make the best of our way to the Seychelles or some other place to dispose of them. The Arabs deserve to be left behind, but, as they would certainly die in this inhospitable region, we must in charity carry them off and leave them to be disposed of by the Sultan of Zanzibar as he may think fit."

Although the women and children under some circumstances would have been the first to be removed, as the men would be likely to give most trouble if left on shore, fifty of them were embarked and carried on board the ship, the boat then returning for another cargo. Thus, in the course of time, all were transferred on board. Tom and Gerald, who had gone in the second trip, received their due praise for their conduct. The prisoners from the second dhow, captured by Mr. Matson, at length arrived, with a large number of slaves and the Arab crews. He had a sad account to give, but Tom and Gerald, though they had been eager to hear it, were by that time fast asleep in the berth, thoroughly done up with their exertions.

Both the dhows were set on fire, that they might not fall into the hands of the Arabs. On the sinking of the dhow by the senior mate, in his attempt to save some of the women and children, he himself had lost his life; but the Arab crew, from swimming well, had been picked up. Two seamen had been killed, and only forty blacks had been rescued; and the boat herself had been so damaged that it was with difficulty she reached the island, when the Arabs, who had not been secured, leaping on shore, made off among the rocks. The dhow captured by Mr. Matson was in so leaky a state that he had been compelled to land all the blacks, as well as the Arabs, who entreated not to be left on board. Trusting to their gratitude, he allowed them, when landed, to remain at liberty, without having examined them to ascertain whether they had concealed any arms about their persons. His boat also had suffered considerably; he was thus prevented from attacking the three dhows when they first came to an anchor. He had, indeed, enough to do to look after the numerous liberated blacks; while several of his crew, who had been badly wounded, required to be attended to.

So occupied had he been that not till the dhows appeared did he think of sending the carpenter's mate and two men to repair the boat. In the meantime, several of the Arabs had stolen off and joined their countrymen who had before made their escape. Leaving a small party only to guard the blacks and protect the wounded, as soon as the boat was repaired he set off, as has been described, to attack the three dhows. After his unsuccessful chase of the one which escaped, he was returning to help Tom and Gerald when he was summoned to the island by a prearranged signal. On landing, he found that the Arabs had rushed down on the camp, liberated the remainder of the prisoners, and, having attacked the party left in charge, were inciting the blacks to escape. His speedy return compelled the Arabs to fly, but not till they had induced thirty of the blacks to run off with them.

As they could not get over to the mainland, Jack sent a large party on shore to sweep the island from one end to the other, and to capture every Arab and black who could be found. Tom and Gerald, who, after their snooze, awoke, as they declared, perfectly fresh, begged leave to join it, as they were as eager as any to rescue the poor blacks who had so quickly again been brought into slavery by the Arabs, while they wished to recapture the latter, and to stop their slave-dealing for the future.

The party had proceeded half-way along the island, Tom and Gerald being on the right or the western side, when he caught sight of a black object in the water moving away from the shore. Directly afterwards he saw several others in the same direction. "Those must be Arabs attempting to swim to the mainland," he shouted; "on, lads, and stop them! Pass the word along the line."

He and the men accompanying him hurried on, and were soon joined by Gerald and his party, when they caught sight of a dozen Arabs in the water, while many more were on the beach, endeavouring to induce the blacks to accompany them. Tom shouted to those in the water to return. The nearest obeyed on seeing the seamen present their muskets, but the others still held on their course.

"Stop the fellows!" cried Tom; when the seamen fired several shots. One of the nearest was hit, but the rest continued striking out. Another volley had the effect of making two more turn back. Six or seven still held desperately on. Shot after shot was fired at them; but the wretches had other foes besides the British seamen. Soon after the leading swimmer had got out of gun-shot he was seen to throw up his arms, a piercing shriek was heard, and the next instant he disappeared beneath the surface. The rest still held on, as it was as hazardous to turn back as to go forward. Another shortly afterwards shared the fate of the first. What horror must have filled their minds as they made their way through the water, knowing that at any instant a ravenous shark might seize their legs and drag them under!

Two or three, however, reached the shore. Tom, who was watching them through his glass, saw them throw themselves, utterly exhausted, on the beach. "Without food or water, their fate will be as terrible as that of those who have just lost their lives. They deserve it richly, however; there will be so many slave-traders less in the world," he observed coolly. He, like many others acquainted with the atrocities committed by the Arabs, could no longer feel the slightest compassion for any sufferings to which they were subjected.

The whole of the blacks were secured, as were the surviving Arabs, and marched back to be carried on board the ship. Jack, meantime, had been very anxious about the party who had to proceed overland; and he determined to send some men, well armed, with provisions and water, to meet them. Tom and Gerald begged leave to go, in company with the doctor, who carried restoratives and medicines. The day was far advanced when they landed. They at once struck off to the north, keeping a bright look-out for the Arabs on one side and their friends on the other.

It was near evening when they saw some figures wending their way over a rocky hill to the northward. They were at first doubtful whether or not they were Arabs; if such was the case, they were fully prepared for them. "No, they are our fellows!" exclaimed Tom. Just as he spoke, another much larger party were seen on the left, making their way towards the first. Tom's glass was at his eye in a moment. "Those are Arabs; no doubt about it," he said. "They have muskets, too, and it's very evident that they are intending to cut off our friends. We shall disappoint them, though, I hope."

The officer in command of the party, having ascertained that Tom was right, gave the order to push forward as rapidly as possible. The Arabs had apparently not yet discovered them, and were still advancing, with their gaze fixed only on those whom they hoped to make their prey. Besides the Arabs, there were numerous blacks, secured together, in the ordinary barbarous fashion, with forked sticks. There could be little doubt that they were slaves who had escaped from the wrecked dhow, and were being taken back to the coast, to be embarked on board another slaver.

The seamen, descending into the valley, soon lost sight of both parties. In spite of the burning sun, which made the air in the valley like that of a hothouse, they pushed rapidly on. Presently they heard some shots fired, which seemed to come from the heights above them. Those heights must be scaled before they could reach their friends. The firing became more and more rapid as they climbed up; they at last caught sight of Archie and his party, who, posted on some rocks, were defending themselves against overwhelming numbers of Arabs. Tom and Gerald uttered a loud cheer, which was taken up by the men, and then, without waiting an instant to gain breath, first firing a volley, they rushed with their cutlasses at the Arabs, who, turning and throwing down their arms, scampered off with the activity of cats, leaving five or six of their number dead or wounded behind them.

The seamen pursued them along the ridge of the hill, cutting down all they overtook; but the larger number saved themselves by the fleetness of their feet. A party of them kept together, however, and made their way towards the group of slaves, in the hope, as it seemed, of carrying them off. The seamen were, however, at their heels before they could accomplish their object; and they were glad to make their escape into the desert, leaving their captives in the hands of the victors.

Hamed, who had followed them, was soon able to calm the fears of the blacks, whose bonds were speedily loosed, and their necks relieved from the forked sticks. A spot which could be easily defended, should the Arabs venture to attack them, was selected for their night encampment. The ground being too uneven to allow them to travel in the dark, it was necessary to remain till the next morning to return to the ship. They had brought an ample supply of provisions, and the Arabs had compelled the slaves to carry food for themselves. The low shrubs growing on the hillside afforded an abundance of fuel; camp-fires were soon lighted, and pots set boiling. Altogether, the midshipmen made themselves perfectly happy. The other officers sat round the fire, recounting their various adventures; Archie's party had met two or three wild beasts, and been threatened on their road by the Arabs who had escaped from the wrecked dhow, but they kept them at a distance with their firearms; and the fellows had not dared to attack them till, joined by other parties proceeding to the coast, they gained confidence from superior numbers.

"They must be remarkably bad shots," observed Archie; "for though they had thirty muskets among them, at the least, not one of us has been hit."

In the morning they returned to the ship, having seen nothing more of the Arabs, who thought it prudent to keep at a distance from the hated Feringhees.

CHAPTER XIII

Six Months pass away—The *Gauntlet* goes in Search of the *Romp*—Jack stands by her—"Breakers Ahead"—Anxious Suspense—Probable Fate of the *Romp*—Jack proceeds to Zanzibar—Search for Adair—Desmond and Hamed captured by Arabs—Adair and his Companions rescued—*Opal* and *Gauntlet* at the Cape—A Ball on Shore—Jack meets an old Friend—Falls in Love—Return to England—Prospect of War with Russia—Massacre of Sinope—The Three Commanders appointed to Ships.

SIX months had passed away, and Jack Rogers had disposed of the liberated blacks, and had since been the means of setting many others free, though unhappily also the innocent cause of sending not a few to destruction, who might have otherwise drawn out a weary existence in abject slavery. Often had he to console himself with the reflection that their death truly lay at the door of the accursed slave-dealing Arabs. "It is the only way of putting down slavery that I can see, though a rough one," said Jack to himself, "till English missionaries and English merchants take possession of the country, and we can drive the Arabs and Portuguese out of it, and induce the natives themselves to rise and aid us in the glorious work; however, I shall not see those days, I fear; and in the meantime we must do what we can to catch the villains at sea."

The *Gauntlet* was slowly proceeding southward when she fell in with the commodore. Jack, going on board to receive orders, was directed to look out for the *Opal* and *Romp*, which were to proceed to Zanzibar, and thence to the Cape of Good Hope. "That means that they are to be sent home, I suspect," observed Jack to Higson, when he returned on board; "the commodore ought to be going there too—he looks very ill; and the ship's company have suffered much from sickness."

"I hope that we shall soon follow," observed Higson; "this slave-hunting is all very well in its way, but it's a style of work one might get easily tired of." Jack agreed with him; but as the ship had not yet been her full time on the station, there was every probability of her having to remain some months longer.

She had proceeded some way down the coast, when she fell in with one of the *Opal's* boats, of which Jos Green had the command. He had captured one full slaver, but said that the ship had taken none. "Nor will she," he added; "steamers or boats are the only craft suited for this sort of work." He was very thankful to have his boat hoisted on board; and the next day the *Opal* was fallen in with. The news that there was a prospect of her returning to England was received on board the *Opal* with immense satisfaction, by no one more than by her commander.

Jack paid Murray a short visit, but, having a cargo of liberated slaves on board, he had to continue his voyage to Zanzibar. The *Opal*, meantime, sailed in search of her missing boats. Two days afterwards, as Jack was running down the coast, a bright look-out being kept for the *Romp*, the weather, which had been threatening for some days, became rapidly worse; the wind shifted to the south-east, then to the eastward, blowing furiously on the coast. A headland had just been doubled, forming the northern side of a deep bay, and Jack was about to put the ship's head to the eastward to gain a safe offing, when a sail was sighted on the quarter, some way up the bay. He turned his glass towards her; "What do you make of her?" he asked of Higson.

"I have little doubt that she is the *Romp*, and, if so, I wish that she were well out of her present position," he answered. "See, she has just gone about, she's carrying on in the hopes of beating out of the bay, but it's as much, I fear, as she will do; and, as far as I know, there isn't a place in which she can anchor—while the shore all round the bay is as wild and rocky as can be."

"We must stand in and help her!" exclaimed Jack.

"We should only run the risk of losing the ship if we attempt it," said Higson, "for it will be as much as we can do to hold our own in the teeth of this gale; and as to towing her off, that will be impossible."

Jack took a turn on deck. "I cannot bear the thoughts of leaving you, Terence, to your fate," he said to himself. He knew, as well as Higson, the danger that would be run, for even a steamer embayed in such a place, with the full force of the gale blowing into it, would have hard work to get out. He took another turn on deck. "We must try it, notwithstanding!" he exclaimed; "should the wind moderate ever so little, we may carry her out; and if we are compelled to cast her off, she may still have a chance of escaping by bringing up and riding out the gale."

Higson was not convinced, though almost as anxious as his commander to assist the brig, which was heeling over to the blast, rushing at headlong speed towards the southern side of the bay. She appeared already close upon the rocks, when about she came, and, her sails flattened in, she began racing back through a mass of foam towards the point from which she had come. Again she went about; but the slightest change of wind at the moment, or any want of seamanship, might allow her in a few seconds to be sent, by the furious seas rolling in, on to the black rocks under her lee.

"She's gaining nothing, I fear," observed Jack, as he watched her.

"She's rather losing ground, I suspect," answered Higson. Presently the brig fired a gun; another and another gun followed, at the interval of a minute. "It is as I feared," observed Higson, "she's driving farther and farther up the bay, and Commander Adair knows that there is no holding-ground which can be trusted to."

"We must go in and help her, at all risks!" cried Jack; and the helm being put up, the steamer, under her head-sails, went rushing forward towards her small consort. In the meantime, the engineers were also ordered to get up as much steam as possible. Again the guns were heard. "Adair would not make those signals unless he were in great distress," observed Jack; "tow her out we must; though I fear that unless we're very brisk about it, we shall lose much ground in doing so."

Two stout hawsers had been ranged aft and well secured, ready to carry on board the brig. Her movements were eagerly watched by all eyes on board. Desmond felt more anxious than he had ever before been in his life, for he loved his uncle heartily, and clearly saw the danger he was in. All round the shores of the bay appeared a broad line of snowy foam, contrasting with the dark shore. Not a break was there to be seen, not a spot where the brig could be beached with any prospect of affording escape to her crew. As she stood across the bay, she appeared to be not more than a couple of miles from the deepest part— and in how few minutes would she be driven that distance!

She had again reached the northern shore; once more her head-sails shivered in the gale, and the hearts of the bravest on board the *Gauntlet* trembled, lest, missing stays, her fate might be sealed. "She's about all right!" shouted several voices; and like a gallant steed galloping across the course to the winning-post, she came plunging on through the troubled waters. Though Adair saw his friend coming to his assistance, he must not for a moment, he knew, relax his own efforts. By this time the *Gauntlet* had reached the centre of the bay, and her head being put to the wind, she waited at a spot which the brig must pass on her next tack to cross the bay.

The *Romp* was nearing the southern shore; again she came about. Adair gave proof that he was a good seaman, and his crew in prime order, or it could never have been done. He was seen standing aft conning the brig; the topmen were in the rigging, ready to swarm aloft to shorten sail; a party of the hands stood on the forecastle with the second lieutenant and boatswain, ready to secure the hawsers. The rest of the hands were at their stations on deck. The work, to be done successfully, must be done smartly; everyone knew that. Rapidly the brig approached. Two of the strongest and most active seamen were on the poop ready to heave the lines on board. Adair's voice was heard above the gale, shouting, "Down with the helm—shorten sail!" In an instant the topmen were on the yards, the staysails were hauled down, and, the brig luffing up, the *Gauntlet* moved slowly ahead, while the hawsers were rapidly hauled on board.

Some flags were run up to the foremast and head of the brig. "He thanks you, sir," said Desmond, who had the signal-book in his hand; and Adair was seen pointing significantly at the fierce breakers dashing over the rocks astern.

Short as had been the time occupied in the operation, the vessels had drifted farther into the bay. Now came the tug of war. The hawsers being secured, the *Gauntlet*, with all her boilers at full pressure, steamed ahead. Jack kept his eye on the shore, anxiously watching what way was made; both hawsers were at full stretch; though the screw was exerting all its power, yet the vessels scarcely seemed to move onwards. Higson, who was looking out at the other side, was unusually grave; anxious as he was to assist Adair, he thought that Jack had no business to venture into his present position.

"If anything goes, we are done for," he muttered to himself; "she doesn't move an inch ahead." Jack thought the same; he sent for the chief engineer to ascertain if more pressure could be put on the engines.

"They will not stand it—they are doing their utmost, sir," was the answer. Still, Jack was determined not to abandon Adair. On board the brig the hands were still aloft sending down topgallant-masts. Jack hoped against hope that the gale would decrease, and that he should then be able to tow Adair out of the bay; if he once weathered the headland, the brig might stand away on a bowline and gain the offing—but within the bay she lost, each time she tacked, more ground than she had gained.

Clouds were gathering thickly in the sky; down came a deluge of rain, such as is only known in the tropics, like a thick veil of mist obscuring the brig astern. The water lay deep on the decks before it had time to run off; all sight of the shore was completely shut out. As the steamer plunged into the sea, tugging away at the tow-ropes, Jack could not help believing that she must be going ahead; on and on she went—the rain showed no sign of ceasing.

"It must come to an end, at last!" exclaimed Jack, trying to peer through it at the shore, the dim outline alone of which he could distinguish.

The lead was of course kept going, but as it reached the bottom, it scarcely ran out of the lead-man's hands. "She's going more astern than ahead!" he shouted at length.

"Provided she doesn't go much astern, we must keep at it in the hopes of a lull," observed Jack to Higson.

Another ten minutes passed. Various were the expressions of opinion on board; the midshipmen were sanguine that they would succeed. "My brother Jack has determined to do it, and he will do it," said Tom.

"Suppose the hawsers were to carry away?" said Archie.

"There are two of them; if one doesn't hold, the other may," answered Desmond.

Jack paced the deck; at length the rain passed by. The marks on shore showed that they had not changed their position; still the destruction of the brig had been delayed, for by this time she would have been on the rocks. Thus far something was gained; still the appearance of the sky indicated no improvement in the weather. "Hoist the signal—'Prepare to anchor and strike topmasts,'" cried Jack at length. The brig made the answering signal. Preparations had already been going forward on board her, the topmasts were at length struck; still no effect was produced. Nobly the steamer tugged and tugged away. Higson did not offer any advice, but he was ready to give it as soon as his commander should ask for it. "There's a lull!" cried Jack; "thank heaven, we may do it!"

Now the vessels moved ahead; had the water been smoother, by a steady pull the work might have been done; but, as it was, having to plunge into the heavy seas, the *Gauntlet* was in the trough of one while the brig was on the summit, or sometimes on the other side, of the one which had just passed astern of the leading vessel. "Here comes a lull—Heaven be praised! Surely she's going ahead, Higson?" said Jack.

"It may be, though slowly," was the answer. The occasion was a trying one to the young commander. "She's doing it now, sir!" exclaimed Higson, with more hope in his tone than he had yet shown. There could be no doubt about it—the vessels were drawing out from the bay, but still the headlands appeared over the bows on either side.

"If the weather continues to be moderate, all may be right!" cried Jack, taking a turn with more elastic step. All on board were looking forward to saving the brig, when suddenly down came the tempest with renewed force, and a report like thunder was heard; one of the stout hawsers had parted. Still the other held, and might possibly hold. It was watched as anxiously by Jack and those in the ship as by all on board the brig, whose lives, in all probability, depended upon it. To replace it was impossible, as no line had been retained for the purpose; should the ship's speed be slackened, and thus take off the strain, both vessels must drift back, and perhaps share a common fate. All now depended upon the single hawser. Hope was not abandoned; the day was drawing on; for more than three hours the steamer had been tugging away at the brig, and if the hawser would hold, Jack determined to tug on till the storm should abate. In that he was following the instincts of his nature—every British officer worth his salt would have done the same. He was impelled also by his faithful friendship for Adair, and he would have been ready to risk his own life to save that of his old shipmate.

Again there was a lull, and the hopes of all revived; but it was only for a time. A squall, heavier than any of its predecessors, struck the vessels, accompanied by a tremendous downfall of rain. Every fibre of the hawser was stretched to its utmost; a fearful sea came rolling in, deluging the deck; two poor fellows on the forecastle were washed off, but no help could be given them. Not a sound was heard as they were borne into their ocean graves. Shrieks and cries arose from the unhappy blacks on the maindeck, who believed that their last moments had come. Just then another loud report was heard, the hawser flying like a huge snake in the air; and many a voice exclaimed, "She's parted! she's parted!"

As they looked astern, the brig was seen broadside to the sea, driving helplessly before the gale; while the ship, relieved from her task, seemed to bound forward. With a heavy heart Jack ordered her to be kept on her course; stern duty demanded that he should abandon his friend; nothing that he could do could save the brig. Painful as it was to watch her, he could not help looking out aft to try and ascertain her fate. She might have been about two miles from the shore when she broke adrift, driving before the furious gale, but a few brief minutes must elapse ere she would be hurled on the iron-bound coast. On and on she drove, growing dimmer and dimmer to view, shrouded by the spray which filled the air.

"She's scarcely a mile now from the shore," observed Higson; "she's making head-sail; they must be looking out for the least dangerous spot on which to run her." Just as he spoke there came another furious downpour, forming a thick veil round the ship, which shut out every distant object, so that scarcely the outline of either lofty cliff could be seen.

"She may bring up and cut away her masts," said Jack, with a deep sigh; "it is her only chance."

"The holding-ground may be better than we suppose," observed Higson, wishing to console him; "or there may be some opening up the bay which we could not discern; he has probably surveyed it."

"I hope so," said Jack. "Who are the men who are lost overboard?" he asked, turning his mind to his own ship's company. The crew was mustered, and on the names of John Jackson and William Davis being called, no reply was made. The paymaster struck them off the ship's books, and the next day their effects were sold, and the proceeds placed to the credit of their heirs, and all matters concerning them were brought to a conclusion, though now and then their shipmates might mention them with an expression of regret at their untimely fate.

The gale continued blowing as fiercely as ever, while the ship was still forcing her way ahead, and Jack could not help confessing that the steamer was a finer craft to command than he had ever supposed. His own ship in safety, his thoughts again recurred to Adair. He was acquainted with Lucy's feelings for him, and, should he have lost his life, he thought of all the sorrow it would cost his sister. Desmond was very unhappy, though Tom and Archie did their best to console him. The general opinion on board was that the brig would go on shore, and that few or none on board her would escape with their lives.

Not only provisions for the blacks, but coals were running short, and it was therefore important that the ship should get to Zanzibar as soon as possible, when Jack intended to return and ascertain what had become of the *Romp* and her crew. If she had gone on shore, and the crew had escaped, they would be exposed to many dangers, either from want of food or from attacks by the natives.

On the arrival of the *Gauntlet* at Zanzibar, the slaves were handed over, by the directions of the consul, to another vessel, which was to take them to their future home. The *Gauntlet*, having then, with all possible despatch, obtained a supply of coals, steamed away northward to ascertain the fate of the *Romp* and to rescue any of her crew who might have escaped on shore.

Nothing had been seen of the *Opal*, and Jack began to fear that she might have suffered in the gale, which had blown with unusual violence all along the coast. The *Gauntlet* had got nearly up to the bay she was to visit, when, much to Jack's satisfaction, the *Opal* was sighted, steering for Zanzibar. Jack immediately signalised that he wished to speak her. In a short time the two vessels hove-to, and lay within a few cables' lengths of each other, when Jack immediately went on board. Murray heard, with great concern, of the too probable fate of their old shipmate, and, having no liberated slaves on board, willingly agreed to assist in the search, as his boats' crews would be of service should an armed force be required to obtain the liberation of any of her crew who might have been made prisoners.

The wind being favourable, he followed Jack into the bay, where he brought up at a respectful distance from the shore; while Jack steamed farther in to look out for the wreck. All eyes were turned towards the shore, where, instead of the belt of surf, there now appeared a broad fringe of rocks, some rising to a considerable height out of the water.

"A cruel place that for the ship to go on shore," observed Jack, with a sigh, "there would not have been much left of her by the morning."

"There she is! there she is!" cried several voices from forward; in another minute or so the wreck of a vessel, with her masts gone, could clearly be discerned jammed in between two rocks.

"She has held together better than I could have supposed," said Higson.

"Put the ship's head off shore; we will bring up," said Jack.

As soon as the ship came to an anchor, two of the boats were lowered, Jack himself going in one, with Hamed and Tom and Desmond, Jack knowing that the latter was eager to gain the first tidings of his uncle. They pulled in with some faint hopes of finding the people still on board, or encamped on the shore; but no signal was seen, and their hopes grew less and less.

Jack now looked out for a place suitable for landing, and as he approached, he saw several small sandy beaches, where a boat could land without danger. He chose one nearest the wreck, and both boats steered in for it; still not a sign of human beings could be seen. He at once landed, with Matson, who was in the second boat, and accompanied by him and the two midshipmen, and a party of his crew, well armed, proceeded at once to the wreck. It being now low water, they could almost reach her by clambering along the rocks. On getting close to her, it was seen that she had suffered more severely than had been supposed; her whole stern frame was knocked in, and the sea must have made a clean breach through her, so that no one could have remained on board. Her masts and guns were gone, and the whole of her stores had either been washed out of her, or had since been carried away. There were signs, indeed, that she had been plundered by a large party, as the marks of numerous feet were discerned on the sand above high-water mark.

While Jack and most of the party had been examining the rock, Hamed, with Desmond and Tim Nolan, had gone on towards a height some distance from the shore, under the expectation of being able to obtain from its summit an extensive view inland. After leaving the rock, Jack sent the party, two or three together, to examine the rocks, to ascertain if the bodies of any of the crew had been washed up upon them,

Jack still had hopes that the crew had been able to hold on to the wreck, till the falling tide should have allowed them to reach the shore. Still he could discover nothing to settle the point; it was only evident that the guns must have been thrown overboard, and the masts cut away, before she reached the shore. Perhaps Adair might afterwards have set off overland to try and reach one of the Arab towns belonging to the Sultan of Zanzibar, where he could obtain provisions, and from whence he could send notice to the consul where he was, so that a ship of war might be despatched to render him assistance.

Jack was looking out for Hamed, when he caught sight of a figure running along at full speed from the direction of the hill, and every now and then casting a look behind him indicative of alarm. Jack immediately summoned the men from the rocks, and, as he hurried forward, he recognised Tim Nolan.

"Yer honour, it's bad news I bring!" he exclaimed, panting for breath, though he did not forget to touch his hat to his commander; "the spalpeens of Arabs have been and taken Mr. Desmond, and our 'terpreter Hamed, and they'll be after cutting their throats if we don't look sharp and carry them help. As they were hurrying them down the hill, and looking thunder and lightning at them, Hamed cried out to me, 'Run for your life and tell the captain!' and shure, run I did, for they'd have been after cutting my throat if I hadn't."

On receiving this intelligence, Jack immediately despatched Mr. Matson's boat to the ship with directions to signalise Murray to send his boats, well armed, on shore, desiring his own lieutenant to return with two more from the ship. He immediately, with his boat's crew, pushed on in the direction Tim believed Desmond and Hamed had been carried. Instead, however, of going over the hill, he led his men round it at a turn, hoping by this to cut off the Arabs as they descended into the plain. Tim, one of the most active of the party, kept well ahead. He had just rounded the rocky point, when he caught sight of a party of Arabs, twenty or more in number, with Desmond and Hamed in their midst. Hamed, by the gesticulations he was employing, was apparently expostulating with his captors; while Desmond was using strenuous means to show them that he was disinclined to move forward.

The Arabs were so engaged with their prisoners, that they did not observe the approach of the English till they were close upon them. Jack and his companions redoubled their speed.

"Hurrah!" shouted Tim. "Knock the blackamoors down right and left, and we'll be up soon."

Desmond was perfectly ready to follow this advice, and two or three well-directed blows enabled him to spring out from among the astonished Arabs and join his friends. Hamed made a similar attempt, but, being tripped up, was caught by the Arabs, two of whom held their daggers at his breast.

"They stickee into me, they stickee into me!" shouted poor Hamed, "if you not doee what they ask."

"What is it?" inquired Jack, who continued advancing towards the Arabs.

"Dey let goee if not shootee," answered Hamed.

"Tell them that, though they deserve to be punished for daring to capture Her Majesty's officers, I will not injure them if they will inform me in what direction our friends have gone," said Jack.

Hamed on this appeared greatly relieved, and a long parley ensued between him and the Arabs. Their chief, a ragged old fellow, with somewhat tattered, though once rich, garments, stepped forward, and, making a profound salaam, uttered a long address, which Hamed briefly interpreted. "He say you pay him a hundred dollars, he takee where English stop, and fightee black fellows." The Arab himself and his followers were as black as negroes, by the bye, having probably more African than Asiatic blood in their veins.

"The rascals!" exclaimed Jack; "why, we are sparing their lives, and they have the impudence to name their own terms. Tell them we'll shoot every one of them if they refuse to guide us to our friends."

Hamed had another talk with the chief. "He say very well, you shootee his people, and be no wiser than at first."

"The old fellow's got sense in his brains," observed Jack, "and as we can't pay him the dollars till we get back to the ship, the bribe may prevent him from acting treacherously and leading us into an ambush. Tell him that if through his means we recover our friends, I promise him the hundred dollars, though he must come on board my ship to receive them."

The old slave-dealer again salaamed, and, through Hamed, expressed his perfect satisfaction with the arrangements. Jack would gladly have set off at once, for he suspected, from what Hamed had learned from the chief, that Adair and his crew must be very hard pressed, and destitute both of provisions and water.

The Arabs looked greatly astonished at the strong force which landed, and became very humble and submissive. Perhaps Jack might have saved the hundred dollars, which were certain to be employed in the slave-trade, had he waited the arrival of the other boats. He had, however, promised them, and there was no help for it; he could only hope that the old fellow and his crew might be caught with a full cargo of slaves on board their dhow.

To Jack's surprise, instead of proceeding south, their guides led the way to the northward. Hamed explained that so large a force had appeared in the south, that the shipwrecked crew had been compelled to retire northward; and Jack concluded that they had done so in the hopes of being able to communicate with the corvette, which Adair knew to be in that direction, or perhaps with some of the *Romp's* boats which might be cruising in the same quarter.

Sailors are always in high spirits when tramping overland, in the hopes either of having a fight, or succouring those in distress. If the chief was to be believed, there was a fair probability of both these events occurring. Murray, as senior officer, of course took command of the expedition. He and Jack marched on together. Not entirely trusting their guides, they sent out scouts on either hand to feel the way, while the men were ordered to keep well together, and to be in readiness at any moment, in case of a surprise.

"Arrah, now," exclaimed Desmond, who with Tom and Archie were in the rear, "I hope we may get a scrimmage with these blackamoors; the spalpeens, to be attacking my uncle and his shipwrecked crew instead of lending them a hand, as any decent people would, when we want to help them and to put a stop to slavery."

"That's the very thing they don't want to have stopped," observed Archie; "as long as they can make more money by selling their fellow-creatures, though no blacker than themselves, they'll do it."

"If we had a fleet of merchantmen on the coast," said Desmond, "ready to give good prices for their ivory and ostrich feathers, and anything else their country produces, while all and every slave-trader knew that if caught he was to be hung up, I fancy that the slave-trade would soon be knocked on the head."

"A very good idea of yours, Desmond, but it may be a difficult matter to induce merchants to send their vessels out.

It will be done in time if they find out that it is to their advantage," said Archie.

"If I had the management of affairs, I'd make them do it!" cried Desmond. "When a thing ought to be done, the sooner it is done the better; and if, as you say, it is the only way to stop this abominable slave-trade, and the misery and death of tens of thousands of Africans, we Englishmen shouldn't stop haggling about the cost, but do it at once."

"That's my notion," said Tom; "and when my eldest brother gets into Parliament, I'll give him no rest till he gets the thing done, somehow or other."

The other midshipmen were all of accord on the matter, but their conversation was interrupted by one of the scouts coming in with the information that he had seen a large party of men at the foot of a rocky height in the distance ahead, very busy about something or other, but what it was he could not make out. Hamed, after questioning the old chief, informed Murray and Jack that the people seen were undoubtedly those who had followed Adair and his crew, who were in all probability not far off.

The force therefore pushed on, and, passing over some very rough ground, reached a spot whence they could make out three or four hundred people on the low ground, and a small party on a rocky height. Two or three tiny jets of smoke, sent forth every now and then by the latter, showed that they had firearms, though very few; and, from the intervals which elapsed between each shot, it was evident that they were husbanding their ammunition, and only firing when necessity compelled them to keep their assailants in check.

On observing this, Murray ordered his party at once to fire a volley, which would inspirit their friends, and intimidate the enemy. "Forward!" cried their commanders; and they pushed on at a rate which quickly brought them close to the scene of action. As they advanced, leaping over rocks and all impediments, towards the mongrel army, the leaders of the latter were seen to be moving about in evident alarm. At the instant a shower of bullets was sent rattling among them, they, to a man, faced about, and scampered off as fast as their legs could carry them. The relieving force quickly surmounted the height, where they found Adair with six or seven of his officers, and little more than half his crew. Jack and Murray were soon shaking him warmly by the hand; his and his companions' appearance showed, before a word had been spoken, that succour had come most opportunely. Their emaciated looks and hollow eyes told too plainly how they had suffered from hunger; not a particle of food remained in the camp, or a drop of water; and not more than three rounds of ammunition for the six muskets which had been saved from the wreck.

"If you hadn't come, my dear fellows, it would have been all up with us, I fear," said Adair; "we'd made up our minds to rush down on the enemy and try to put them to flight; but without food, and no chance of getting any, we should only have gained the advantage of being allowed to die in peace, unless one of our boats had appeared, for which we came here to look out. It is the saddest thing which has ever happened to me; twenty poor fellows drowned, besides the loss of the brig; and as we have seen nothing of our boats, I am afraid some harm must have happened to them."

Jack and Murray did their best to comfort him, while all hands were employed in serving out the provisions and water which had so thoughtfully been brought. As the *Romp's* crew were too weak to march, the party bivouacked on the hill, with plenty of camp-fires, for which the blacks collected abundance of fuel.

Just as they were about to start at daylight, two boats were seen rounding a point, and Adair had the satisfaction of finding that they were those which had been despatched from the brig some weeks before, and which had since been cruising in search of her. The more sickly men were at once placed on board them, and they were sent round to join the *Gauntlet*; while the rest of the party set off overland, accompanied by their Arab guide, who kept close to them for fear of losing his dollars.

On getting on board, Jack paid him punctually, with a warning, imparted through Hamed, that if they were employed in the slave-trade he would lose them again, and get himself into further trouble. Whether or not the old fellow followed the advice he received, Jack had no means of ascertaining.

On their return to Zanzibar, the *Opal* and *Gauntlet* received orders to proceed to the Cape. Loud cheers rose from the decks of both ships as the news was announced on board; and even poor Adair, though he had the unpleasant anticipation of a court-martial for the loss of the brig, felt his spirits rise considerably. Jack comforted him with the assurance that the evidence his officers had to give must acquit him of all blame, and that he himself had done everything possible to save the brig.

"But I had no business to have been caught in the bay," sighed Adair. "My prospects in the service are ruined, and I shall never get another ship."

"Never fear," answered Jack; "we shall have perhaps a war before long, and, depend upon it, you will not be overlooked when ships are fitting out. Officers of dash and determination will be wanted, and you possess the required qualities."

The packet from England had come in the day before they arrived at the Cape, and Jack found a letter from Admiral Triton. "We shall have some of the old work again before long, my boy, depend upon that," he wrote. "I have it from the best authority that the Russians have made up their minds to quarrel with the Turks, and take possession of Constantinople. They have been for some time past badgering them about the Holy Places, and insisting that their co-religionists are ill-treated by the Moslems,—not that they really care about the matter,—and that is sufficient to convince anyone who has got his weather-eye open that they only want a pretext for war, decent or indecent. The news has just arrived, though it has not yet been made public, that we should be suspicious of the designs of Louis Napoleon, who has so wonderfully been transmogrified into an emperor—though for my part, I believe that no ruler of France has ever been more friendly disposed towards us, and the Russians will find that they are mistaken in wishing to set us by the ears. That Prince Menzikoff, their ambassador to the Porte, has presented the ultimatum of the Russian Government, which means war, for the Turks are certain not to knock under; and we and the French would not let them, if they thought of doing so. The Russians intend to invade Turkey with all possible despatch; indeed, they have an army all ready to throw across the frontier. Menzikoff will be away from Constantinople in the course of a day or two, and then the business will begin. Our Government intends to send a fleet through the Dardanelles without delay, and as the Russians have no small number of ships in the Black Sea, we may hope to have a brush with them. I wish you were here, Jack, to take a part in whatever goes on; and I am glad to find that your ship is ordered home, so that there is a chance of your being in time; you will not let the grass grow under your feet; and as you can steam through the calm latitudes, we may hope to see you here before long. I never liked steamers, but they have their advantages, there's no doubt about that. In the meantime, I'll use all the influence I possess to get you a craft you'll like; and as I fancy that more work is to be done in a steam-vessel than in a sailing-ship, I'll try and get one for you."

The admiral's letter contained a good deal more in his usual style of chit-chat; Mrs. Murray had gone to stay with her friend Lucy at Halliburton Hall, though he expected both of them back again, and hoped that they would be with him when Jack arrived. Jack showed the letter to Terence, who sighed when he read it.

"What's the matter?" asked Jack.

"I'm only thinking that an unlucky dog like myself, who has lost his ship, has very little chance of getting another," said Adair; "and that the bright hopes I entertained of soon getting my post-rank must be abandoned for ever."

Jack, of course, did his best to console him. "Come along," he said; "there's a grand ball to-night at the governor's, and we're asked; we'll take the youngsters—it is a good thing to let them enjoy a little society, and will help to polish them up before they return home."

Adair was unwilling to appear in public, but he yielded to Jack's wishes. The three midshipmen were of course delighted, and busily employed themselves, with the aid of their marines, in burnishing up their long unused uniforms; so that when they entered the ballroom they presented a very respectable appearance following in the wake of their commanders.

Adair soon recovered his spirits, and Jack laughed as he watched him whirling round and round in the valse, or prancing away in the galop with true Hibernian vehemence. The midshipmen had entered into a compact to introduce each other to their partners. They did not fail to admire the blue eyes, light hair, and fair complexions of the Dutch damsels.

"Never saw so many pretty girls under one roof in my life!" exclaimed Tom; "I'm over head and ears in love with every one of them."

"'There's luck in odd numbers, cried Rory O'More,'" answered Desmond; "to my fancy, the girl I last danced with is handsomer than any of them. She was asking me all sorts of questions about our ship and the commander and my uncle, and seemed very sorry about the loss of the brig, of which she had evidently heard. I'll introduce you, Tom,—she was engaged for the next dance, but said that she should be happy if I would bring you up for the following one,—so come along. She's only been here for a short time on her way home from India, so I gathered from what she said; but I daresay she'll tell you if you ask her, for there's evidently no nonsense about her."

"That's just the sort of girl I like," said Tom, as Desmond led him across the room to a young lady who was seated far back in an alcove, from whence she could watch the crowd without being observed. Tom, as he made his bow, and was received with a sweet smile, thought that she fully came up to Desmond's description, though she was certainly older than most of his previous partners. He willingly, in answer to her inquiries, told her all about the ship, his brother Jack, and Adair. She then got him to talk about Halliburton, and he was surprised to find that she was well acquainted with the country. At last she said, "I wonder you do not remember me, Tom;" on which, looking into her face, he exclaimed, "Why, you are Julia Giffard!"

She acknowledged that such was the case, and that she had gone out to India with her father, Colonel Giffard, who had been compelled, on account of ill-health, to visit the Cape, and had been advised to return home without going back.

"Jack will be delighted to see you," said Tom; "I'll go and find him and bring him to you, if you will allow me."

Julia replied that she should be very happy to talk about old times with Captain Rogers, and Tom, after the dance was over, leaving her in her former seat, hurried off to find his brother.

"I thought it must be her," said Jack; "but yet, as I fancied she was at home, I concluded that she was only remarkably like herself. She doesn't look a day older than when I last saw her."

Miss Giffard held out her hand as Jack approached, and they were soon engaged in an interesting conversation. Jack did not dance with anyone else during the evening. He promised to call the next morning on Colonel Giffard, who had not been well enough to come to the ball. The result of the visit was that Jack offered to convey him and his daughter to England. As the *Gauntlet* was to sail immediately, and might hope to make a quick passage, and the colonel being anxious to arrive at home as soon as possible, he gladly availed himself of Jack's offer. Julia seemed very well pleased at the arrangement, and the midshipmen were delighted when they heard that they were to have a lady on board.

The *Gauntlet* and *Opal* sailed the same day. It was to be a race between steam and wind; at first the trim corvette, with a fair breeze, distanced her consort, and Archie, who, though still on board the steamer, retained a natural feeling of pride in his own ship, declared that she would win.

"Stay a bit, till the wind falls, and we get our fires alight," answered Tom; "the old kettle will then show how she can go along."

Miss Giffard had not been on board long before the commander's attentions to her were remarked, and in the midshipmen's berth it was decided that it was a gone case. Miss Giffard had heard of Jack's engagement to the beautiful Irish girl, and of his bereavement; and the sympathy she exhibited quickly melted any ice which might have existed round his heart. His sisters would have been highly pleased could they have known the turn affairs were taking. Long before the ship reached Spithead, Jack was engaged to Julia Giffard, with the colonel's full consent.

The *Gauntlet* received orders immediately to go into harbour, and scarcely had she picked up her moorings, than a note from Admiral Triton came on board, begging Jack to come to Southsea as soon as possible, as his sister and Mrs. Murray were anxious to see him. Jack and Adair escorted Colonel Giffard and his daughter to The George, where leaving them, they hurried on to the admiral's house. Stella was anxious to receive news of her husband, while Lucy's happiness at seeing Jack and Adair was somewhat marred at being told of the loss of the brig. When, however, the admiral heard all the particulars, he assured Adair that he would be honourably acquitted, and that it would not stand in the way of his getting another ship.

"I've good news for you, whatever others may think of it," he added; "the Russians have already invaded the Principalities, and, at the Sultan's request, the British and French fleets have passed through the Dardanelles, and taken up an anchorage before Constantinople. They were there when news arrived—which reached me only this morning—that the Turks had a squadron of eight frigates and a few smaller vessels lying at anchor in the harbour of Sinope, according to Turkish custom, totally unprepared for battle. Instead of remaining where they were, they would have acted more wisely had they got out of the Black Sea and run for safety to the British fleet. As it was, there they lay, not dreaming of danger, when, during a thick fog, the Russian admiral, Natchimoff, sailed out of Sebastopol with six line-of-battle ships, two frigates, and several small vessels, and suddenly appeared off the port, when the Turks, not liking his appearance, fired a few shots at him. Unfortunately for themselves, he immediately, without giving them the chance of striking their flags, opened upon them a tremendous fire from the broadsides of his line-of-battle ships. Though they could not have had the slightest hope of victory, they fought on with the utmost desperation, either refusing to strike their colours, or, if they were hauled down, the Russian admiral was too blind to see it. With barbarous resolution, he continued blazing away, till frigate after frigate sunk or was blown up; and four thousand of the brave fellows who had manned them were killed. One steamer only managed to get away and carry the news to Constantinople. Scarcely four hundred Turks, all of those more or less wounded, escaped on shore. The town was also dreadfully knocked about, and many people were killed. Natchimoff, having waited till the next day, returned to the harbour of Sebastopol. I only hope the next time he sails out of it, whether or not he has the whole of the Russian fleet to back him, that he will fall in with a British squadron. Depend upon it, England will not allow this outrage to go unavenged. The allied fleets are by this time in the Black Sea, looking out for the enemy. I wish you were there, but we shall be reinforcing the fleet in the Black Sea, as well as sending another up the Baltic to attack the Russians on their northern shores."

This was not a time that Adair could press his suit with Sir John, though Colonel Giffard promised to use his influence as soon as he returned home. Meantime the colonel and Julia accepted the admiral's and Mrs. Deborah's invitation to remain at Southsea till Jack had paid off the *Gauntlet*. She was to be immediately recommissioned as soon as she had undergone the necessary repairs.

The court-martial to try Adair for the loss of the *Romp* immediately took place; when not only was he honourably acquitted, but next day he was appointed to the command of the *Gauntlet*, ordered to proceed with the squadron under Sir Charles Napier to the Baltic. Jack, taking it into his head that he was to be placed on the shelf, proposed to marry at once; but the very next day he was appointed to a new steamer ordered to be brought forward with all despatch for the Mediterranean squadron. He had time, therefore, only to run home for a few days, and to return immediately to Portsmouth.

The *Opal* meantime had arrived, and, being paid off, her

crew were turned over to Jack's new ship, the *Tornado*. Murray, once more with his dear Stella, very naturally had no wish to leave her, and they were on the point of setting off for Scotland, when he received a flattering note from Captain Hemming, which completely altered his plans. "I have been appointed to the *Briton*, seventy-four, and, having to select my commander, I beg that you will allow me to name you, as I am very sure that you will get her well manned and quickly fit for sea, and that you will ably second me in any work we have to perform. I consider you, my dear Murray, as efficient an officer as any with whom I am acquainted. I do not know yet whether we are to be sent to the Baltic or the Mediterranean, but we are certain to go to one or the other."

Alick placed the matter before Stella, who looked very pale, but answered heroically, "You must do what you conceive to be your duty. I have before advised you not to give up the service, and I must therefore say, accept Captain Hemming's flattering offer."

"I knew that you would decide rightly," answered Murray.

"I heartily congratulate you!" exclaimed the admiral. "Deb and I will take good care of your wife while you're away; it won't be for a long period, I hope; and it won't be Hemming's fault if you have not some opportunity of distinguishing yourself and gaining your post-rank. I should like to see you all three captains before I slip my cable, which I must expect to do before many years are over; and it will give me more pleasure than I can well express to see you all whom I knew as youngsters gain your well-earned promotion. You've always done your duty, and will, I am sure, prove ornaments to our profession as long as you remain afloat."

CHAPTER XIV

Review at Spithead—Admiral Triton's Opinion of Steam-vessels—The Allied Fleets in Cavarna Bay—Jack visits Murray on board the *Briton*—Bombardment of Odessa—Loss of the *Tiger*—Jack in Command of the *Tornado* runs into the Harbour of Sebastopol—A Visit to the Guards' Camp.

A MAGNIFICENT sight! What would Nelson have done with such a fleet?" exclaimed the admiral, as, with his eye at a telescope turned towards Spithead, at an early hour on the morning of the 11th of March 1854, he gazed at the fleet collected there under Sir Charles Napier. "We must have a nearer look at them, ladies; the *Gauntlet* goes out of harbour, and Adair has sent his coxswain to say that his gig is waiting at the pier. Come, Deborah; come, Mrs. Murray; get on your wraps. Lucy, my dear, you mustn't mind appearances; though the sun is bright, the wind is still keen, and you will find it cold enough coming on shore again."

The ladies, who had already finished breakfast, were soon equipped; and the admiral, helped by Miss Rogers and his sister, had got into his pea-jacket, and, Lucy having tucked the ends of the comforter which surrounded his throat well into it, he was ready, stick in hand, to tramp across the common. Lucy's well-fitting yachting-dress, with an overcoat calculated to withstand all weathers, became her well. The gig was soon alongside the *Gauntlet*, at whose gangway Adair stood ready to receive his guests. It was the first time Lucy had come on board, and with no little pride and happiness he helped her up the accommodation ladder.

The next instant, casting off from her moorings, the *Gauntlet* steamed out of the harbour towards Spithead. "Well, after all, there is something to be said in favour of steam," observed the admiral; "and though I did once think it would never come to much, I must confess I was wrong; though, had it never been invented, we should not have felt the want of it."

"At all events, admiral, it enables us to get out to Spithead, which we otherwise should have found it a difficult job to do," auswered Adair, laughing. "Look at the magnificent *Duke of Wellington*, with her 131 guns; see the *Royal George*, and *St. Jean d'Acre*, with what ease they can now manœuvre, by the aid of their screws. I suspect Nelson would have been willing to exchange the whole of his fleet for three such ships at Trafalgar, and not only would have gained the victory, but would not have allowed one of the enemy to escape."

"It might have been so," said the admiral; "but I suspect, had the chance been given him, he would have preferred having his tough little *Victory* and the other stout ships of his fleet, to all the new-fangled contrivances." The admiral, it was evident, had still a hankering for the good old days when he first went to sea.

The *Gauntlet* was able to steam through a considerable portion of the fleet before she took up her destined station; thus passing in succession the *Duke of Wellington*, Sir Charles Napier's flagship, the *Neptune*, *St. George*, and *Royal George*, 120-gun ships, the *St. Jean d'Acre*, 101 guns; fourteen other ships carrying from 60 to 91 guns, most of them fitted with screws; five frigates, each able to compete with an old line-of-battle ship; and eighteen paddle-wheel and screw steamers, any-one of which would speedily have sunk the largest ship of ancient days.

In a short time the Queen appeared in the *Fairy* yacht, passing through this superb fleet, when, the yards being manned, the crews greeted her with hearty cheers, and such a salute broke forth from their guns as had never before been heard.

"Well, admiral, I hope when we come back we shall be able to give a good account of our proceedings, if the Czar ventures to go to war," observed Adair; "we may at least expect to take Sweaborg, Helsingfors, and Cronstadt, and perhaps lay St. Petersburg itself under contribution."

"If Sir Charles is at all like what he was a few years ago, I hope you may," answered the admiral; "but though Charley is some years my junior, I should have declined ten years ago accepting such a command. He may be tough enough, but the sort of work he has to do wants nerve, and that, as a man advances in life, is apt to slacken."

Still, notwithstanding Admiral Triton, the prognostications of Adair were shared in by all in the fleet, as well as by the nation at large, and grand results were expected. The admiral had engaged one of the steamers plying between Ryde and Portsmouth to come alongside and take his party on shore. Poor Lucy, it was very trying to her, though Mrs. Murray from experience could give her heartfelt sympathy. Alick had already sailed for the Black Sea, and Jack some weeks previously had proceeded in the same direction.

We will make our way on board the *Tornado*. She had a quick passage under sail and steam to Malta, where she lay taking in a fresh supply of coals, and thence proceeded on through the Ægean Sea up the Bosphorus. Jack recognised with no small amount of pleasure many of the islands he had visited as a youngster; he had then thought them very beautiful, and he acknowledged that they were so still, though the proportions of the scenery appeared lessened in his eyes after the grander features of the West Indies and South America.

Tom and Desmond were inclined to turn up their noses at them, not having any great respect for the surrounding classical associations. "Very pretty hills to adorn the surface of a moderate-sized lake," observed Tom, "but Trinidad and Jamaica completely take the shine out of them." Higson, whom Jack had obtained as his first lieutenant, was much of the same opinion. Mildmay, who had been appointed by the Admiralty, not having seen the West Indies, was in raptures, and, with notebook in hand, stood dotting down the lines inspired by his muse. Jos Green, the master, suggested that he would be better employed in making outlines of the headlands and other prominent features of the land.

"Very well for you, master, who have to navigate the ship, but we are above such grovelling notions," answered Mildmay; "you have nothing Byronic in your composition."

"Just take care when it's your watch that you don't run the ship ashore in a fit of poetical abstraction," said Green, laughing; "your Byronic enthusiasm would not be received as a valid excuse at a court-martial."

Besides the officers named, Jack had several of his own and Murray's old shipmates—Dick Needham as gunner, Ben Snatchblock as boatswain, with the two midshipmen, Dicky Duff and Billy Blueblazes; Jerry Bird; the Irishman, Tim Nolan; and several others, all good men and true.

With patriotic pride Jack saw the magnificent fleet under Admiral Dundas lying at anchor in Cavarna Bay as the *Tornado* steamed into that roadstead. It lies on the western side of the Black Sea, a little to the north of Varna. There lay the *Britannia* and *Trafalgar*, of 120 guns, the admiral's flag flying at the masthead of the first; the *Queen*, of 116 guns; the *Agamemnon*, a name renowned in naval story, of 101 guns, carrying the flag of Rear-Admiral Sir Edmund Lyons; the *Albion*, of 91 guns; the *Rodney* and *London*, of 90; the *Vengeance*, *Bellerophon*, and *Sanspareil*, of 84, 80, and 70 guns respectively; the *Arethusa*, of 50 guns, twice the size of her predecessor, known in song as the "gallant *Arethusa*"; and numerous other frigates and steamers, the smallest equal in power to any frigate of the olden times. There too lay the French fleet, fifty sail of the line and twenty-one frigates and smaller vessels, with the flag of Admiral Hamelin flying on board the *Ville-de-Paris*, of 120 guns, and that of the second in command, Admiral Bruat, on board the *Montebello*, of the same force. What might not these fleets accomplish if only the Russians would dare to sail out from amid their stone walls and fight? There was the rub.

Jack, having paid his respects to the admiral, made his way on board the *Briton*, accompanied by Archie, whom he knew Murray would be glad to see. Jack, of course, brought despatches from Stella. "Now, Alick," he said, after the first greetings were over, "you read those quietly, while Gordon and I look up some of our old shipmates whom you have on board."

Jack was not disappointed, for though he could not boast of having as many friends as Jos Green, he seldom went anywhere without finding some former shipmates. All were in high spirits at the thoughts of active service, though as yet nothing of importance had been done. A very gallant act, however, had been performed, of which Jack now heard. It was very important to gain exact information as to the present state of the harbour of Sebastopol and the forts protecting it, for there was every reason to believe considerable alterations had of late been made. As soon as the news of the massacre of Sinope had reached England, the Government sent out orders to the admirals to enter the Black Sea, to stop every Russian ship they met, and to prevent by force, if necessary, any fresh aggression on the Turkish flag, that no repetition of such atrocity might occur. As war had not yet been formally declared, it was necessary to inform the Cabinet of St. Petersburg and the Governor of Sebastopol of this resolution. Captain Drummond, commanding the *Retribution*, a steamer of twenty-eight guns, was accordingly ordered to proceed to Sebastopol, and to deliver the despatches to the governor. In order to make the necessary survey, he was to remain there as long as he possibly could without allowing his design to be suspected by the Russians. It was the middle of winter; the weather, as is generally the case at that time of the year, was very thick. This was favourable to the design. As he had a good chart of the coast, he stood boldly on, keeping the lead going, till he made his way between the two outermost forts into the mouth of the harbour, when he came to an anchor before he was discovered by the Russians. Great must have been their astonishment at seeing an English frigate thus boldly bearding them.

The fires were kept banked up, so that she might, if necessary, make her way out again, should the Russians venture to fire at her, of which there was a very great probability; indeed, it was said that the guns in the forts were actually loaded, ready at a moment to sink the audacious intruder. The instant the anchor was dropped, the boats were sent out to take the necessary soundings, while an accurate survey was commenced of both shores of the harbour and the forts, with the number of their guns which guarded the entrance. The fortifications were indeed of a most formidable character. On two sides of the harbour eleven forts and batteries were counted; one, which appeared to be the key to the entire works of the place, had its guns concealed from view, but in the other ten no fewer than 722 guns, mostly thirty-two pounders, were counted, half of which pointed seaward, and commanded the approach to the harbour; and the other half commanded the harbour, in which lay the Russian fleet itself. In every direction men could be seen strengthening the works and erecting new ones. The town was surrounded by a wall fifteen feet in height, and loopholed for musketry, with a ditch in front. So narrow was the entrance that two line-of-battle ships could barely sail in abreast.

Having delayed as long as he could, Captain Drummond sent a boat with an officer to convey the despatches to the governor, who at first expressed himself very much astonished at the appearance of an English ship at such a juncture. Being assured, however, that the frigate had come to perform an act of courtesy, he was satisfied, and, salutes having been exchanged, the *Retribution* lifted her anchor and steamed again out of the harbour, with the important knowledge which had been obtained, and which was quickly conveyed to Admiral Dundas. Captain

Drummond was of opinion that the place was entirely unassailable by ships alone, but that it might easily be blockaded and harassed by shells thrown into it at night, though he was convinced that should a ship enter the harbour in order to destroy the Russian fleet lying there, it must be annihilated before it could get out again. He advised, therefore, that Sebastopol should be attacked by a combined naval and military force; and, as far as could be learned, the authorities had determined on this mode of proceeding.

Jack, having left Murray time to read his despatches, rejoined him, and heard more of what had taken place. "The army have suffered dreadfully," said Murray, as Jack was seated in his cabin; "not from the enemy, but from cholera and fever. It has also appeared on board the fleet, and nearly every ship has lost a good many men. Upwards of fifty have died on board the flagship, and we have had thirty or forty on the sick list at a time, many of whom have succumbed to the disease. The steamers have, I hope, a better chance of escaping, but it has not left them entirely alone."

"Well, I trust we shall keep free," said Jack. "The best thing we can hope for is that the commander-in-chief will give us something to do before long."

After describing the halt of the British forces at Scutari, and various incidents which had occurred, Murray went on with an account of what had since taken place: "After remaining for some time at Scutari, the greater part of the English force was moved on to the neighbourhood of Varna, where they have been distributed on the heights south of Varna Bay, and at various other points," he continued. "The first division, consisting of the Guards and Highlanders, with two field-batteries, are encamped at Gevreckler, a dreary common covered with a short, wiry grass, one of the most desolate-looking plains I ever visited."

"I am sorry to hear that," said Jack, "for my brother Sidney is out there. I must try if I can get the chance of paying him a visit. Poor fellow! he was very anxious to come out, but he will find campaigning very different sort of work from a review in Hyde Park."

"The chances are you are sent there on duty," observed Murray; "if you go, remember me to Mackenzie, Gordon, and Douglas, of the —— Highlanders. Heaven knows whether we shall meet again, for the cholera, I am sorry to say, has got among them, and it is expected that the allied army before long will have some hot work with the Russians, who are now besieging Silistria. The place is holding out nobly, the Turks being aided by those two gallant fellows, Captain Butler and Lieutenant Nasmyth. The Russians have already lost several thousand men before the place, but everybody believes that it must fall ere long, and that the Russians will then march on Constantinople. We shall do our best to stop them; and though we, of course, shall win, it will not be without heavy loss."

"The fortune of war," said Jack. "I only hope that the Russian fleet will soon sail out of Sebastopol and give us something to do. I have no fear but that we shall lick them."

"Of course we shall," answered Murray; "and if Charley Napier can meet their fleet in the Baltic and give them a drubbing too, they will have had enough of it, and we shall shake hands and be friends."

Little did the young commanders, who thus easily settled the campaign, dream of the prolonged and sanguinary struggle which was about to take place. Jack and Archie remained on board to dine. The latter went back to the *Tornado* full of the news he had picked up, which he was as ready to impart to Tom and his shipmates as they were anxious to hear it.

"Look here," said Archie, as he sat on one side of the berth, with Tom opposite to him, and most of the midshipmen surrounding the table, "I've been studying the chart, and I think I've a pretty correct notion of the position of the different places. Here's the Black Sea, which we'll call an irregular oval running east and west, and at the north side is the Crimea, something like a shoulder of mutton in shape, hanging on by the Isthmus of Perekop to the mainland. Sebastopol, the fortress we hear so much of, is at the southern end of a broad bay on its western side. Going back to the mainland, we find on the southern side of the Danube, which as it approaches the sea runs north, and then again to the east, at a considerable distance from the sea, the fortress of Silistria, where the Turks are bravely holding out against a numerous Russian army. South of Silistria are Varna and Schumla, between which places our troops are encamped, to be ready to intercept the Russians whenever they have captured Silistria, and thus to prevent them from getting to Constantinople. Some way north of the Danube, on the seashore, is Odessa, not far from the mouth of the Dnieper. To the north-east of the Crimea, with a narrow passage between it and the mainland, is the Sea of Azov. Near the entrance to that sea is the mouth of the river Kouban, where the gallant Circassians have long held out against the Russians. Here we have the Bosphorus at the south-west corner of the Black Sea, with Constantinople on the one side, and Scutari on the other; and rather more than half-way along the southern coast is Sinope, where the Russians so barbarously massacred the unfortunate Turks. Thus Russia possesses the northern shore of the sea, Turkey the western and southern, and Circassia the eastern. Still, with a tremendously strong place like Sebastopol almost in its centre, Russia may be said to command the whole of its waters; and that's the reason, I suppose, that we shall try to destroy Sebastopol and the fleet, which at present lies snugly under the batteries."

All hands agreed that they understood Archie's account. He forgot to mention that several fortresses had been erected by the Russians on the Circassian coast. Their garrisons were, however, seldom able to venture far beyond their walls, the brave mountaineers being continually on the watch to attack them. Among other pieces of news that Archie had heard, was that the *Furious*, Captain Loring, had been sent to Odessa with a flag of truce, to bring off the British consul and any British residents who might be in the town. The day after Jack had joined the fleet, the *Furious* was seen coming in from the northward, and, soon after she anchored, it was reported that, notwithstanding her flag of truce, the Russians had fired at her, and also at the people she was bringing off.

This, of course, made the admirals very indignant, and several steamers were sent to the north to blockade the port; and, on the 17th of April, the combined fleets weighed and proceeded in the same direction, arriving off Odessa on the 28th.

"I thought it wouldn't be long before we had something to do," said Archie, as he and Tom stood on the deck, watching the coast along which the *Tornado* was steaming.

The city stands on the southern shore of a bay, with the houses built on the slopes, with moderately high hills rising up from it. In the centre of the bay was a citadel armed with heavy guns, overlooking the whole of the bay, with strong batteries placed at different points, so as to sweep it with a cross-fire; while the ends of three piers were heavily armed with batteries.

As soon as the ships came off the place, the admiral sent in a summons to the governor, demanding, as an atonement for the insult offered to the flag of truce, that all English and French ships should be sent out, and the Russian ships surrendered; and threatening, should this demand not be complied with, that the combined squadron would open fire on the place. The officers and men on board the ships waited eagerly for the governor's answer, whether he would yield to their demands and send out the vessels, or would try the chances of war. All hands hoped that he would prove obstinate, and give them the chance of trying their shot and shell against his stone batteries.

By the evening of the 21st no answer had been given, and Jack, with the other captains and commanders, having been summoned on board the flagship, returned in high spirits with the announcement that the place was to be attacked.

The next morning, Ben Snatchblock's shrill pipe sounding along the decks roused up the watch below, who sprang on deck with even more than their usual alacrity. The midshipmen, turning out of their hammocks, quickly dressed. Everybody by this time knew that work was to be done. The grey light of morning was just breaking in the eastern horizon, beyond the combined fleets of England and France, which lay outside of the steamers. On the west was the city of Odessa, rising to a considerable height above the calm surface of the water, green fields and woods on either side, while in front could be seen the citadel and its numerous forts armed with heavy guns, ready to pour showers of shot and shell on the ships which might dare to oppose them.

The English and French admirals threw out the signal for the steam-squadron to weigh. It was answered with alacrity—the vessels, urged rapidly through the water by their paddles, stood in towards the shore. As they approached, the silence of the morning was broken by the loud roar of the Russian guns from the citadel and lower forts, responded to by those of the allies fired from the decks of the steamers; which, having delivered their broadsides with excellent aim, stood off again to give place to their successors in the line. Having made a semicircle and reloaded, they again came into action; this manœuvre being repeated without cessation, so that not a moment of breathing-time was allowed to the Russians in the batteries. Most ably were the guns of the latter served, many of them firing red-hot shot as well as round-shot. At length, several of the former striking one of the French steam frigates, flames were seen to burst out from her, and she was compelled to stand out of action while her crew, not without difficulty, extinguished the fire.

A breeze springing up, the gallant *Arethusa* was seen standing in under sail, and as she closed with the batteries, she opened her fire with tremendous effect; then, putting down her helm, she came about and stood off once more, amid showers of shot and shell which came sweeping over and about her; though, close as she was, not a shot touched her. Greatly to the disappointment of her gallant captain, he saw the signal made from the flagship for his return. Thinking that he might shut one eye, as Nelson did at Copenhagen, he however once more stood in, delivering a fire from his eight-inch-shell guns, standing in even closer than before. This manœuvre he repeated several times; but again the admiral, fearing that he would receive more damage than would be compensated for by the injury inflicted on the enemy, finally recalled him, and, sending for him on board the flagship, complimented him upon his gallantry and the skilful way in which he had manœuvred his ship.

The attacking squadron was now strengthened by several other steamers and gunboats. The *Tornado* had been playing her part. "We shall make our fire tell before long," observed Jack to Higson, who stood by his side, just as the ship had delivered her broadside and was standing out of action. "See, flames are bursting out from the fort at the end of the mole,—that won't trouble us again,—look there on the other side, there must be numerous works and storehouses on fire. If we keep on in this fashion the Russians will have the whole place burnt about their ears."

The men were at their quarters, with shirt-sleeves tucked up, their heads bound by handkerchiefs, and belts round their waists. Another circle was made, when, just as the *Tornado* had delivered her fire, a terrific sound was heard; the fort in front of her seemed to rise in the air, the flames shot upwards, and huge blocks of stone came hurtling down on either side. Loud cheers burst from the British crew. "Hurrah!" cried Tom, "I hope that won't be the only fort blown up before long." As he spoke, it was seen that several other forts were in flames. Soon after the squadron was brought closer in to attack the shipping within the mole. The shot and shell poured upon them rapidly did its work. Some of the vessels were sunk; others, with the rest of the storehouses, were set on fire. No efforts made by the

Russians could quench the flames, which continued burning all night.

The work was most complete; all the Government vessels, barracks, storehouses full of ammunition and military stores, were completely destroyed. Next day the Russians were, however, seen attempting to rebuild their earthworks; but a few shells from the *Arethusa* dispersed them. Several Russian vessels having been captured at sea, the admiral sent in to propose to exchange their crews for those on board the vessels which had been detained in the harbour. The governor, however, replied that he had no authority to make an exchange of prisoners, which personally he much regretted. Admiral Dundas, on hearing this, sent his prisoners, who were all merchant seamen, on shore, observing that he was at war only with the Government of the country, and did not wish to inflict annoyance on the peaceable inhabitants. Some time after the return of the fleet to Baljik, the English merchant seamen who had been detained at Odessa made their appearance, having been released by order of the Czar, who would not be outdone in generosity by the English.

Several vessels had been left in the north to cruise up and down the coast. Among them were the *Tornado*, *Tiger*, and two others. Several prizes had been made when the *Tiger* parted company in a thick fog. Jack had been for some time looking out for her, when the sound of heavy guns was heard inshore. The *Tornado*, in company with another steamer, stood on in the direction from whence the sounds proceeded; in a short time a rapid firing of musketry was heard.

"One of our cruisers is being engaged with the enemy," observed Higson.

"I suspect so," said Jack; "but I very much fear that she must be on shore. At all events, we must stand in and drive away the enemy, while we try to get her off."

Jack hailed his consort, and, putting on all steam, the two vessels stood towards the land. Just then the firing ceased, and directly afterwards, the fog lifting, Cape Fortan, a headland about four miles to the south of Odessa, appeared in sight. Every glass on board was turned in the direction of the land.

"There is a vessel on shore close to the cape," observed Higson.

"She must, I fear, be the *Tiger*," said Jack; "we may still be in time to help her. Perhaps she has driven off the Russians."

"I am afraid not," said Higson, "for I can make out several boats surrounding her. I fear that Captain Giffard has been compelled to strike his flag, and that the Russians are removing the prisoners."

"He would not have done that as long as he had the slightest hope of saving his ship," said Jack; "still we may be in time to prevent her from falling into the enemy's hands."

While all on board were watching the ship on shore, flames were seen to burst out from her fore and aft.

"She's done for; and all her crew, I fear, will be made prisoners," said Jack.

Deep sympathy was felt on board for the unfortunate ship's company, and vexation that so fine a vessel should be lost. Little hope remained of their being able to extinguish the flames. Still Jack determined to try what could be done. In a few minutes, however, the matter was set at rest—the fire increased, the masts and spars of the doomed ship were enveloped in flames; and then there came a thundering report, her deck lifted, the masts shot upwards, and an instant afterwards, as they came down hissing into the water, a few blackened timbers alone remained of the stout ship which had lately floated buoyantly on the ocean with her gallant crew.

Jack and his consort opened their fire on the Russian troops, who still remained in sight; but they, knowing that their field-pieces could produce no effect upon the ships, quickly retired out of harm's way, and the steamers again stood off the shore.

It was not till some time afterwards, on the release of the crew, that Jack heard of the circumstances connected with the loss of the *Tiger*. She had gone on shore during a fog, when her situation was perceived by a body of Russian troops, who at once brought a battery of field-guns to bear upon her, assailing her incessantly also with a fire of musketry. Her captain was suffering from a severe fever at the time, but, immediately going on deck, was giving directions for hauling her off when he fell mortally wounded, both his thighs broken by a round shot. Several of his men were struck down at the same time; and at length the first lieutenant, finding it impossible to get the ship off, hauled down his flag. Directly the Russians ceased firing, boats came off, and the officers and crew, with their wounded captain, were carried on shore. Instead, however, of receiving the rough usage they expected, all the prisoners, especially the wounded, were treated by the Russians with the most considerate humanity; and they acknowledged that, had they been wrecked on their own coast, they could not have received greater attention and kindness than was bestowed on them by their enemies. Nothing, however, could save the life of Captain Giffard, who quickly sank from the effects of his terrible wound.

Jack, as well as several of his brother commanders, had long been wishing to take a look at Sebastopol, knowing that the information they might gain would be acceptable to the admirals. The Russian fleet, supposed to be numerous and powerful, had not yet shown itself outside the harbour since its cowardly attack on the Turks at Sinope. Jack talked the subject over with Mildmay; the latter was ready for anything. He especially wished to take a sketch of the renowned fortress, and purposed making some lines on the subject. Jos Green was delighted with the idea; but how was it to be accomplished? They might run in at night, but then, as he observed, as they should see nothing, they would not be much the wiser. They were discussing the matter, when the look-out shouted, "A sail on the weather-bow."

The vessel's head was turned in the direction of the stranger, and, the wind being light, she had no more chance of escaping than a mouse has from a cat in open ground. She proved to be a brig under Russian colours, though the master and several of the crew were Austrians. They took their fate very quietly, and were ready to give all the information they possessed. The master had frequently been at Sebastopol in former days; he stated that an Austrian steam-packet, about the size of the *Tornado*, occasionally called off the port. Jack got a full description of the vessel from his informant, and he and his lieutenants agreed that they could give the *Tornado* much the same appearance.

"I have often read in the old war of the way vessels were disguised to deceive the enemy. It is quite a lawful proceeding," Jack observed.

Sail-makers and painters were fully employed in shaping and painting old sails to conceal the heavy guns and figure-head, and to alter the general appearance of the ship. When all was done, Jack, with his first lieutenant and Needham, pulled off to a distance to have a look at her, and were fully satisfied that the keenest of eyes on shore would not discover her real character. The crew were also ordered to rig in their working-day clothes, and it was arranged that one watch should go below, while only a few officers in undress uniform were to appear on deck.

Highly delighted, Jack steered towards the lion's den. The Austrian skipper was in a state of great trepidation. "If discovered, the ship will be inevitably sunk!" he exclaimed.

"No fear," said Jack; "we'll see what's to be seen, and then steam out again at a rate which will give the Russian gunners no little trouble to hit us."

The midshipmen were of course in high glee; Tom was only sorry that Desmond was not with them. "How he would have enjoyed the fun!" he exclaimed; "only perhaps he's finding some still better in the Baltic."

That night, few slept out the morning watch, all being so eager to have an early look at the fortress, as Jack had determined to enter the harbour soon after daybreak, when, as might be supposed, the garrison would not have got the sleep out of their eyes. As morning broke, the high cliffs on either side Sebastopol appeared in sight. The Austrian colours were hoisted, the greater portion of the crew were sent below, the remainder being ordered to lounge about in merchantman fashion; while Jack and Jos Green and the two lieutenants, with the Austrian skipper, walked the deck with the perfect composure of men who were well acquainted with the place. Keen eyes were, however, looking out from many a port at the rocky shores ahead, as the *Tornado* drew in to the land. Two brigs-of-war were discovered at anchor on either side of the harbour's mouth, and as of course they would be on the alert, there was a great probability of their discovering the character of the stranger. A few shot might, however, quickly send them to the bottom, in case they should attempt to stop her. The crew were ordered to be in readiness to spring on deck at a moment's notice, and every man below hoped that that notice would be given. On stood the *Tornado*, no sign being given on board the brigs that her character was suspected. Jack and his officers, as the steamer ran in, had time to count the guns which frowned down upon them from the four forts on either side of the harbour, each with three tiers of batteries; and, what was of more importance still, to make out the number of ships in the harbour.

"I can see three three-deckers and several two-deckers," said Jack.

"There are at least four frigates," added Higson, "and fully half a dozen smaller craft; and see, over the point, those mastheads; there are four of them, and evidently ships of the line. That makes not much fewer than our fleet; if they've any pluck in them, they'll come out and fight us; and our admirals are the men to give them every chance of doing so."

The *Tornado* had now got as far up the harbour as Jack considered prudent, and she was gradually brought round as if about to come to an anchor, with her head turned towards the harbour's mouth. It had required no small amount of resolution to bring her into that position; at any moment twelve hundred pieces of artillery in those frowning forts above their heads might open their fire, and send their shot, which, plunging down upon the ship's deck, would turn her into a sieve in a few seconds. Jack and his officers were equal to the occasion. He and Higson calmly lighted their cigars, and, as they walked backwards and forwards on deck, puffed away with might and main; both of them, however, keeping an eye on the forts, waiting for the moment when they might open fire. The ship, having been brought round, glided slowly on for some distance; then Jack gave the order to turn ahead at full speed, and out she shot between the two brigs, their crews even then wondering what had induced her so suddenly to take her departure. Not till she was well outside them did they begin to suspect the character of the stranger which had paid them a visit that morning, when their signal-flags were seen run up to the mastheads, answered by two or three of the outermost frigates.

Just then a schooner was seen entering under Russian colours. "We must take her," cried Jack; "the impudence of the act will have a good effect, and show the Russians what Englishmen can dare and do. Haul down those colours—hoist our ensign," he added. The change was rapidly effected; the signalising between the brigs and frigates went on still more vehemently, while the former sent a few ineffectual shot at their audacious visitor.

"Keep her for the schooner," cried Jack. The skipper of the Russian merchantman was evidently much astonished at perceiving the Austrian steamer suddenly turned into an English man-of-war. Finding that he could by no possibility escape, he hauled down not only his colours, but his sails, when the steamer, running alongside his vessel, took her in tow, having first removed him and his crew to her deck. He proved, like the first, to be an Austrian; the two skippers mutually condoled each other on their misfortunes.

Away the *Tornado* steamed out to sea, but a sharp eye

was kept on the proceedings of the Russian fleet. The two brigs were seen getting under way; presently afterwards three of the outside frigates slipped from their moorings, and stood out under all the canvas they could spread in chase of the daring intruder. The officers and crew had now mustered on deck, and, the painted canvas being got rid of, the ship was quickly made ready for action.

"Only let two of them come on at a time, and we shall have them in tow before long," observed Dick Needham, a sentiment which was heartily responded to. The breeze, however, increased, and the frigates came dashing on, keeping pretty close together, at a rate which made it more than possible that they would overtake him. Jack heartily wished that he could have carried off the schooner as a prize, but it was not worth while to risk the loss of his ship in making the attempt. He could not hope to capture even one of the enemy, unless he could separate them, and this, as they were favoured by the wind, he saw that he should be unable to do. Prudence, therefore, compelled him very unwillingly to cast off the prize, upon which the Russians speedily pounced, but only to find her empty.

The crew cheered heartily, while many a laugh resounded through the ship, as they witnessed the Russians' disappointment, and saw the squadron sail back again into port. Jack communicated the information he had received to the admiral. Soon afterwards the fleet of the allies appeared before Sebastopol, two or three of their ships having been sent out of sight in order to make their forces equal, and to induce the Russians to come out and fight them. The latter, however, knew too well what would be the result to make the attempt. Admiral Lyons sailed away with a small squadron to reconnoitre the shores of Georgia and Circassia. During the trip, he endeavoured to persuade Schamyl, the far-famed Circassian chief, to co-operate with him in taking the fortresses of Soujak and Anapa, two of the only three fortresses still held by the Russians; but the old warrior was not in a condition to undertake the enterprise. Redoubt Kaleh was however attacked, and the garrison, after setting fire to it, retreated. The number of prizes captured by the squadron, which sailed throughout the Black Sea, sweeping it of every vessel except those of the allies, was very great. Jack was elsewhere, he having been employed in running several times to Constantinople, and back to Cavarna.

He at length obtained the wished-for opportunity of visiting his brother at Gevreckler. Taking Tom with him, they landed at the nearest village on the shore, where they obtained horses. The scenery was picturesque, and sometimes exceedingly beautiful. They passed through a Turkish village at the base of some low hills. The village consisted of mud-walled and thatched houses built on either side of green lanes bordered by trees, with farmyards attached, and enormous whitewashed, dome-shaped clay ovens. The streets all led to a common centre, like a village green in England; here and there were wells, from which girls in Oriental costume were drawing water. They were perfectly ready to chat with the strangers had they understood each other's language, but, as that was not the case, they laughed and smiled in friendly fashion. On the level ground vast cornfields appeared spread out, already yellow with ripeness, and here and there patches of tall guinea-grass of deepest green, the fields being intersected by low copses, and occasionally rows of trees of greater height, while to the west appeared numerous hills of graceful form covered by waving woods. Far in the south could be seen the blue outline of the Balkan range.

At length, mounting the last height, Jack and his companions reached the plateau of Gevreckler, when the white tents of the Guards and Highlanders appeared, extending far and wide before them. Here lay encamped the flower of England's warriors; but, alas! Jack, as he rode through the camp, was struck by the pallid countenances and feeble gait of many of those he met, while from the canvas walls of a large tent came the cries of strong men in mortal agony. He inquired of a soldier near the cause of the cries.

"Some more fellows down with the cholera," was the answer; "they've got the cramps, and they are precious hard to bear, I know; had them myself last night, but they passed off." As the man spoke, his countenance was overspread by a deadly pallor; he sank on the ground, shrieking out. His cries attracted several of his comrades, who, lifting him up, carried him into the nearest hospital tent.

A little farther on Jack came upon an open space, where groups were collected round a person acting as an auctioneer, who was disposing of uniforms, clothes, camp equipage, and even horses and various other articles which had belonged to officers and men just carried off by cholera. It could not fail to have a depressing effect; he almost dreaded to ask about his brother Sidney. Regaining his composure, he inquired the direction of his tent, and was relieved to hear that he had been seen a short time before alive and well.

In a few minutes he found him, seated in front of his tent, in a washing-tub, which served as an arm-chair, with a book on his knee, and a cigar in his mouth. "What! Jack! Tom!" he exclaimed in a more animated tone than was his wont in England; "I am very glad to see you, for I little expected that you would be able to make your way out here. I can't give you a very hospitable reception; but here's a camp-stool for you, Jack; and bring yourself to an anchor on the top of my hat-box, Tom. Things don't look as bright as we should wish, but we can keep up our spirits with the hopes of a change for the better. The Turks are tremendously hard pressed in Silistria, and we are expecting every hour to hear of the fall of the place; when we shall have the Russians down upon us. I turn out every morning in the belief that before the day is over we shall be ordered to march and meet the enemy; when the wind's from the north we can hear their guns and those of the fortress thundering away at each other; and any day we can hear the sounds of mines exploding, and other music of glorious war," and he smiled faintly; "I painted the pleasures of fighting in a very different light, and cannot say that the reality comes up to them. However, you must have some luncheon, and then we'll ride towards the Schumla, where we can hear, though we can't see, what is going forward."

As soon as luncheon was over, Sidney ordered his horse, a sorry steed, not quite suitable for Rotten Row. He, with his two brothers, set out for the position of the second division. They had got but a short distance from the camp, when they passed a party of men carrying stretchers, on each of which was laid a human form, the rigid outline of the features and feet showing through the blanket shroud. The chaplain followed to read the funeral service; but few, except those required officially to attend, followed their comrades to their last resting-place. Farther on were two groups of men, six or eight in each, shovelling out the earth from some oblong holes. Silently they laboured; no smiles were on their countenances, no jokes passed between them; they themselves might soon be the occupants of similar resting-places. Tom shuddered. "I have been too much accustomed to scenes like these to take notice of them," said Sidney; "we seldom pass a day without the loss of two or three men, and sometimes many more."

They at length reached the height towards which they were riding, and, on dismounting from their steeds, they could hear the rolling thunder which came from far-off Silistria, one continued roar, as the garrison poured the fire of their guns on the persevering hosts of Russia.

"It seems to me as if every man in the Russian army must be blown to pieces by this time," observed Tom.

"So they would if they were above ground," answered Jack, "but they are in their trenches, and only occasionally do those iron missiles carry death in their track, except when an assault is being made, and then they sweep them down by hundreds."

The despatches Jack had to convey not being ready, he was compelled to remain on shore till the following morning. All night long the low thunder of the siege was heard even more continuously than before. He awoke just at dawn, and listened; the wind came from the same quarter, but no longer was the booming sound of the cannon heard. "It is all over with the brave garrison of Silistria, I am afraid," he observed to Sidney, who had joined him outside the tent.

"If it is, we shall soon have a brush with the Russians," was the answer; "I heartily hope so, for active service will help to stop the fearful ravages of the cholera. Half a dozen of our poor fellows have died during the night, and the army will be decimated unless something is done to arrest the disease." Just then the réveille sounded, and the camp was quickly astir. The news spread that Silistria had fallen. The hope that the time of inaction was over was expressed by everyone in the camp. The event detained Jack on shore much longer than he had expected. At length a Turkish horseman was seen spurring towards the camp of the allies. Officers and men hurried out to meet him, fully expecting to hear that the enemy were advancing. He pointed to the north, however, and an interpreter explained what had happened. He brought glorious news, of which his countrymen might well be proud. Prince Paskiewitch, with his shattered hordes, had raised the siege, and was in full retreat from before the brave city he had in vain assailed for so many long weeks; but one of its gallant defenders, Butler, after exhibiting the most heroic bravery and skill, had fallen.

Soon afterwards another important victory was gained over the Russians by the Turks, led by General Cannon and several other English officers, in which also Lieutenant Glynn and Prince Leiningen, of the *Britannia*, commanding some gunboats, took an active part. This compelled the enemy to abandon the Principalities. Jack after this had to return to Constantinople, where Sir Edmund Lyons and Sir George Brown were busy in preparing rafts and chartering steamers for the embarkation of the artillery and cavalry.

On Jack's return he again paid a visit to Murray on board the *Briton*. The cholera had been making sad ravages among her crew, as well as on board other ships of the fleet, but, strange to say, not an officer had been attacked. Hearing that Murray was below in the sick-bay, he sought him there, and found him, with two lieutenants, assisting the surgeons in attending to the sufferers, of whom there were at least thirty in various stages of the disease. Murray was standing by the hammock, and holding the hands of a poor fellow—a stout, thick-bearded man, whose countenance was of a livid hue.

"It's hard to bear, sir, it's hard to bear!" cried the sufferer, writhing in agony. "Shall I get over it, do you think, sir?" looking up in the commander's face with an inquiring glance, such as a child might cast at its mother.

"I hope you may," answered Alick; "but cheer up—many have been as bad as you are, and have recovered; hold on bravely." The man seemed to grow calmer; again, however, there came over him a fearful paroxysm of pain. "Don't leave me, sir, don't leave me!" he exclaimed, as soon as he could speak. Alick, who was about to go on to another man, again held his hands, pouring some cordial down his mouth, which the doctor handed him. He was soon quiet, but it was the quiet of death; and the commander passed on to others who required his aid.

Thus he and the other officers went from hammock to hammock, endeavouring to soothe the pain of those to whom their services could be of any avail. The dead man was lifted out and quickly sewn up in his blanket, with a shot at his feet, to be launched overboard. Three were committed to the deep at the same time.

Such were the scenes going forward on board most of the ships in the squadron; the *Britannia* alone was destined to lose upwards of a hundred men. On board other ships the officers devoted themselves in the same way, and in many cases succeeded, where the medical men might have failed, in arresting the malady. It was now known that a descent on the Crimea was to be made; as, however, in the suffering state of the ships' crews, it would be impossible to embark the troops, the admirals put to sea, in the hopes of arresting the progress of the cholera. It appeared not to have the desired effect, and many more lost the number of their mess; and fears began to be entertained that the enterprise must be abandoned, when suddenly the disease stopped; not a man more was attacked.

The ships sailed back into Cavarna Bay, and soon the operation of embarking the army commenced. The duty was under the charge of Sir Edmund Lyons. By the aid of the rafts he had constructed, which consisted of two boats lashed together with a platform on the top, he got on board the ships destined to carry them sixty pieces of field artillery and the complement of horses belonging to every gun. He then commenced embarking the cavalry, to the number of a thousand horses, and twenty-two thousand infantry, on board the numerous large transports waiting for their conveyance.

The officers of the fleet were engaged under him in superintending the operation. During some days a heavy swell set in, which put a stop to the business of embarking the cavalry. The weather again changing, however, the whole of the force was got on board without the loss of a man. Never before had so large a fleet anchored in those waters. There were hundreds of sailing transports, steamers innumerable, both men-of-war and merchantmen, while above all towered the tall masts of the line-of-battle ships. The French, having only their own infantry to embark, most of whom were taken on board their men-of-war, got through the process more rapidly than the English.

Men-of-war's boats were pulling backwards and forwards, some carrying messages, others towing-off the rafts; while smaller craft of all sorts were moving about in every direction, bringing stores and provisions. It was hard work for all hands, but it was cheerfully and willingly performed.

Jack, having to pass near the French fleet, observed a boatful of Zouaves pulling off to a transport; the French steamer was approaching her; the crew of the Zouaves' boat attempted to pass her bows, while those on board her were keeping a bad look-out. The consequences was that the steamer ran right into the Zouaves' boat. The poor fellows, encumbered with their knapsacks and greatcoats, being utterly unable to swim, the larger number, uttering shrieks of despair, sank like shots before help, so near at hand, could be afforded them.

Unhappily the cholera lingered among the troops on board

the transports, and every day several were launched into their ocean graves, as it was impossible to carry them on shore for burial. Under such circumstances it is usual to secure shot to the foot of the corpse in order to sink it rapidly to the bottom. In some instances shot of insufficient weight were used; for though the body at first sank, yet when decomposition set in and gases were generated, it again rose to the surface; and those on board the ships, as they looked over the side, were horrified at seeing the bodies of their late comrades floating about, bowing to them as if in mockery, moved by the undulations of the water.

One evening Billy Blueblazes was on duty at the gangway, with orders to report any boats coming alongside; as he was looking out in the dusk, he saw, as he thought, a man swimming and approaching the ship. He hailed, but there was no answer; still the figure came nearer and nearer, and presently touched the foot of the accommodation ladder. "What is it you want?" asked Billy; no answer was returned. As in duty bound, he went up to report the circumstance to the first lieutenant.

"There's a Turk, or some fellow of that sort, has swum off to the ship, sir; but he won't give his name, or say what he wants."

Higson ordered Tim Nolan, who was acting as quartermaster, to go down and ascertain who the man was.

"Arrah, sir, it's not a living being at all!" shouted Tim; "he's one of the poor fellows who slipped his cable in the cholera on board the transports, and the sooner he's made to go back where he come from the better, seeing he isn't altogether pleasant company to living men."

Higson was of Tim's opinion, and, ordering a shot to be securely slung, he directed Tim to make it fast round the neck of the corpse; this was quickly done, and the unwelcome visitor disappeared beneath the surface.

Many other similar occurrences took place, to the great annoyance of the seamen, as well as of the soldiers, and made them all the more anxious to get away from the spot beneath which lay so many of their unhappy countrymen. The English fleet having an ample supply of transports, no troops were taken on board the men-of-war, which were thus left free for action; but the French having secured only small vessels, their men-of-war were so encumbered with troops that they were ill prepared to go into action should the Russian fleet come out to attack them. The information was received with unmitigated satisfaction on board the British men-of-war, and all hoped that the Russians, gaining courage, would venture from beneath their fortifications, as on the English fleet would devolve the honour of engaging them.

To every English sailing ship-of-war a steamer was attached. The English army was under the command of Lord Raglan; Admiral Dundas had his flag flying on board the *Britannia*; while Admiral Sir Edmund Lyons, in the *Agamemnon*, had charge of the transports. To each vessel was assigned her particular place, so that there might be no confusion. It was generally believed that the Russian fleet would sail out of Sebastopol and intercept the flotilla, and that they would have to bear the brunt of the fight. The masters of the transports were accordingly called on board the *Emperor*, the largest of their squadron, where the admiral's instructions were read to them, and they were asked whether they would willingly take a part in the naval engagement, should one be brought on. Having satisfied themselves that their widows would receive compensation should they fall, they replied to the question with three hearty British cheers. Thus were the preparations made for the contemplated descent on the unknown shores of the Crimea.

CHAPTER XV

Descent on the Crimea—Landing Troops—Towing Rafts—Battle of the Alma—Tom and Archie on the Battlefield—The Horrors of War—Bringing off the Wounded—Bombardment of Sebastopol—Jack and Murray in Action.

"JUST gone seven bells, sir," said Billy Blueblazes, as he entered Jack's cabin, sent according to orders by Mr. Mildmay, who had the morning watch on the 7th of September 1854. Jack was speedily on deck, for there was plenty of work to be done that day. A gentle breeze blew off the shore; not a cloud dimmed the sky, from which the moon cast her beams over the calm surface of the ocean. By her pale light the sailing-ships in all directions could be seen loosing their canvas, while from numberless funnels wreaths of smoke were ascending, showing that the steamers were preparing to move. All the officers were quickly assembled on deck; many an eye was cast eastward to watch for the first signs of coming day. The men were ordered to their stations. At length a ruddy glow above the eastern horizon announced the approach of day; shortly afterwards the loud roar of a gun from the lofty side of the *Britannia* gave the signal to weigh. The sails hanging from the yards were let fall and sheeted home, the steamers sent forth denser columns of smoke, which, rising in thick wreaths, floated in all directions round the ships' funnels, obscuring the view.

The order had been given to rendezvous forty miles due west of Cape Tarkand. Instantly the outer ships began to move; Sir Edmund Lyons' ship, the *Agamemnon*, with signals flying at her masthead, proudly gliding through their midst. The English transports, in five columns of thirty each, obeying his orders, moved slowly eastward; then came the ships of war, the guardians of the fleet, in single column. The French, more numerous, but with much smaller vessels, sailed out in less compact order, with their warships crowded with troops; the Turkish fleet, similarly encumbered, followed. Among the English perfect order was maintained, tor every captain could thoroughly trust, and well knew that he must obey, his gallant leader.

The French soon became scattered; their general, with some of their line-of-battle ships, had sailed several days before, and what had become of them was not known.

By the morning of the ninth the whole English fleet was anchored at the appointed rendezvous, but as yet the point at which the troops were to land had not been selected. Next morning Lord Raglan accompanied Sir Edmund Lyons, with several English and French engineer officers, on board the *Caradoc*, which, after passing the mouth of Sebastopol harbour, steered round Cape Chersonesus and looked into Balaclava, surveying those heights ere long to become the scene of many a bloody conflict. Returning northward, she steered close into the shore, the generals looking eagerly out for a fitting spot on which their legions might land. A low, sandy beach was at length perceived near Kalametra, with two lakes beyond it. It was exactly the spot Lord Raglan desired. Late in the evening the *Caradoc* returned.

During the two following days the French and Turkish vessels, which could be seen scattered in the far distance, came slowly in; and now it became known that the long looked-for enterprise was at once to be commenced.

Early on the 13th the fleet came off Eupatoria. A small party, with an interpreter, were sent on shore to summon the town to yield at discretion. The *Tornado*, with other steamers, being close inshore, Jack sent Jos Green, with Tom and Archie, to obtain some fresh provisions. They found the old governor a strict disciplinarian, protesting against the strangers landing without having performed quarantine, and he insisted on fumigating the missive sent him before reading it. They might capture the town, to that he had nothing to say—he was not there in a military capacity, but what he had to do he intended to do in strict accordance with his orders. As all the military authorities had run away, and only a few invalid soldiers remained, no resistance was made, and Eupatoria became the first place occupied by the British troops in the Crimea.

Jack, having obtained some Russian coin at Constantinople, was able to purchase provisions. The Tartar inhabitants, finding that they could bring their produce to a good market, were perfectly ready to part with whatever provisions they possessed.

The fleet, now proceeding southward, came to an anchor in a line parallel with the shore, the English to the north, the French and Turks to the south, about five or six miles to the north of the Balaclava River. During the night of the 13th it was arranged that a buoy should be placed, to divide the English and the French fleets, in the centre of the bay. When morning dawned it was found to be afloat almost at the northern end of the bay, having been placed in that position, either from ignorance or treachery, by the French. There was no time for expostulation, the French were found already to have occupied the whole ground. To avoid the risk of a dispute, Sir Edmund Lyons, like a wise man, knowing that a similar landing-place existed a little farther to the north, also with a lake inside it, at once ordered the transports to proceed there and take up their proper places.

The day was fine and the water smooth, and early in the morning the landing commenced. So admirably were the arrangements made that the troops landed in the order they were to take on the march, while the line-of-battle ships remained outside, thus keeping up the communication with a steamer stationed off the mouth of Sebastopol harbour, so that, should the Russian fleet sail out, they might at once proceed to meet it, and prevent it from interfering with the transports. Jack's ship, and other disengaged steamers, were in the meantime sent to cruise up and down the coast and annoy the enemy. Jack ran down to the south, and communicated with the vessel off the mouth of the harbour. Greatly to his disappointment, no signs were to be perceived among the Russian fleet that they were likely to come out and give battle. Now was their opportunity, if they intended to do so, for their scouts on shore must have informed them that the French and Turkish men-of-war were employed in landing their troops, and for what they could tell the English were similarly occupied.

"You may depend on it," observed Jack, "by some means or other they know that our ships are ready to meet them, and they feel pretty sure that they would get the worst of it."

The *Tornado*, keeping clear of the formidable batteries which frowned defiance from the northern side of the harbour, now stood close inshore. Above her rose a series of cliffs, with a broad plateau on the summit, extending as far as the mouth of the Alma River. A group of tents were near the edge of the cliff.

"Where there are tents there are men," observed Higson; "are we to fire at them?"

"It is our business to do so," answered Jack, "though it is not much to my fancy to fire at men who cannot return the compliment. Elevate the guns so as to clear the top of the cliff." The engines being stopped, the *Tornado* opened her fire. Presently one tent went down, then another and another, showing that she had got the exact range. The figures of men could be discerned scampering off, leaving their tents to their fate. The engines being put in motion, the ship steamed on till a body of horsemen were discerned, who had apparently come down to ascertain the cause of the firing. Several shot were sent flying close to them, making them wheel about; but before they had got out of sight two other guns were fired, and a horseman was seen to drop from his saddle. The rapid movement of the rest showed that they were wisely anxious to avoid a similar fate.

Near the mouth of the Alma a considerable body of infantry were observed; not being aware of the long range of the stranger's guns, they stood watching her approach. Suddenly stopping her engines, she opened on them with her whole broadside; two or three were seen to fall, but still they stood their ground.

"They are waiting for orders to march," observed Higson; "they would be wiser if they took ours." With considerable reluctance, Jack gave the order to fire another broadside; he did not like shooting down men in cold blood, but yet he must obey his superiors. Scarcely had the smoke of the guns cleared away than the Russians were seen beating a rapid retreat, though they still kept together. Three more shot had the effect of making them increase their speed, and they disappeared behind some rocky ground which afforded them shelter. Here and there some tents were seen, as well as cavalry and infantry, who, however, moved off as the warship approached, well aware, small as she looked, of the mischief she could do them.

Returning to the fleet, where the landing was taking place, Jack found that the greater part of the English infantry were already on shore. From what he had seen, he made his report that the enemy was not likely to make any immediate attack on the invading forces. Still a considerable portion of the cavalry had to be landed; the weather changed for the worse, and rain came down heavily, wetting the troops on shore, who had no tents or protection of any sort, to the skin. Jack received orders to send two of his boats to assist in towing one of the rafts now alongside the transport to the shore. Green had charge of one of them, and Tom and Archie the other. They found two heavy guns already on the raft, with several horses. The detachment of artillerymen belonging to the guns now came down the ship's side and took their places on board, forming altogether a pretty heavy cargo.

The raft was one of those built at Constantinople, and consisted of two clumsy boats lashed together side by side and boarded over; very well suited for smooth water, but extremely dangerous with a heavy sea running. However, as it was important to get the guns on shore, Green determined to make the attempt. Two of the artillery officers were invited into the men-of-war's boats, and all being ready, they shoved off, taking the huge raft in tow. By this time it was perfectly dark, and the sea increasing made the operation of towing the raft very heavy work.

"Give way, my lads," cried Green; "we haven't far to go; and see, we shall have a warm welcome when we get there."

He pointed to the beach, which was lit up along its whole length by fires which had been kindled with the planks of several disabled boats and rafts.

The heavy swell tossed the raft about not a little, but the crews pulled away lustily as British seamen always do, and the raft at length approached the shore. The roar on the beach as the surf broke on it was not encouraging; still, orders were to be obeyed. Just then a snorting noise was heard, and a magnificent horse came swimming by, as he splashed the water with his forefeet, surrounding himself with a blaze of phosphorescent light. To catch him was impossible.

"He has probably escaped from a raft which has been capsized," observed Green; "his chances of being drowned are considerable, though he may have sense to swim back to the ship which brought him here."

"I hope that won't be the fate of our own raft," observed the artillery officer.

"I can't warrant its safety," said Green; "had I been asked, I should have advised waiting till the morning; however, we'll do our best, and it will be a much harder matter to pull back than it has been to reach the shore."

Just then the light of the fires falling on the raft, showed her to those on the beach, from whence a loud authoritative voice came ordering her to return to the ship.

"More easily said than done," observed Green.

However, he gave the order to Tom and the officer in command of the other boat to pull round and do their best. Every instant the swell was increasing; the boats' crews, though pretty well tired, pulled as before. The raft tossed fearfully about, threatening to heave her whole freight of guns, horses, and artillerymen overboard. The latter, with their arms in their hands, shouted out that the boat was about to sink; and sad would be the fate, Green saw, of most of them if it did so; while in the darkness, amid the struggling horses, it would be scarcely possible to pick them all up. The only thing to be done was to pull away with might and main; sometimes, in spite of all their efforts, the raft seemed drifting back to the shore; at others the waves sent it rushing forward, threatening to stave in the sterns of the boats.

"Here's a pretty piece of work!" observed Tom; "I only hope we shall be able to get hold of one of the transports before long."

"There's one ahead of us, if we can but reach her," said Archie; "there's nothing like trying."

Try they did, cheering on the men; and by dint of hard pulling they got within hail of the transport, and asked for help. "We cannot give it you," was the answer; "we have a boat-load of horses alongside." A second transport was neared, and then another and another, but all declared their inability to render assistance. Green was almost in despair; the artillerymen were shouting out more lustily than before, asserting that the raft was fast filling. At length the boats managed to tow her up alongside a transport, the master of which responded to their appeal, and assisted them in securing her. Fortunately the artillerymen she had brought out had not yet been landed, and, the officers turning them out of their berths, they assisted the crew in hoisting the horses and guns on board. The gun-carriages, however, being too heavy, were left on board the raft, and she was let drop astern. As, however, their loss made the guns useless, Tom and Archie were sent to the nearest ship to obtain assistance. As they got alongside, they found that she was the *Briton*, and, Archie having explained matters to his uncle, who was on deck, Commander Murray sent a boat with a fresh crew, by whose means the gun-carriages were at length hoisted on board.

Soon afterwards the sorely-battered raft went to pieces. Tom and Archie were still alongside, when they caught sight of the noble horse which they had seen coming off from the shore still struggling in the waves. Instinct had directed it to the very vessel from which it had been disembarked. Shouting to the crew on deck, they called for slings, which were sent down, and being secured—not without difficulty—round the body of the horse, the animal was lifted safely on board, to all appearance not much the worse for its swim of upwards of two hours.

The weary crews at length got back to their ship. The next day, the wind going down, more of the artillery and horses were landed, and by the evening of the 18th the whole army was on shore without a man being lost; the disembarkation having been superintended by Captain Dacres of the *Sanspareil*.

The French were posted on the right, close to the sea, the Turks somewhat in their rear, and the English on the left of the line; the duty of protecting the left flank of the army being confided to the British cavalry. The Turks, accustomed to this sort of work, were at once at home, with their tents well pitched, and surrounded by such luxuries as they deemed necessary; while the young troops of England and France, few of whom had seen active warfare, were sitting wet and comfortless round their camp-fires.

The natives, with their black lambskin caps and long pelisses, came to the camp in considerable numbers, bringing provisions, and, what was of more consequence, camels, and carts drawn by oxen for the conveyance of stores.

On the morning of the 19th of September the bugles sounding through the camp aroused all sleepers, and in a short time the army began its march to the southward. The transports, having performed their duty, sailed away for the Bosphorus, while the ships-of-war moved slowly on abreast of the army down the coast, coming to an anchor when it halted, and again weighing when it recommenced its march; the larger ones, for want of water, being obliged to keep at some distance out, while the steamers stood in with the lead going as close as possible, somewhat in advance of the army, throwing in their shot and shells whenever they caught sight of any troops at which to fire.

Towards evening the armies reached the first river in their march, the Bulganak, on the banks of which they bivouacked for the night, in order of battle, as it was thought possible that at dawn they would be attacked by the Russians. The night closed in with rain—bad preparation for the work which all knew would take place on the morrow. The morning dawned more brightly; it was to be the last day many of those brave men in the allied hosts were to see, but few expected to be among the slain. A glorious victory was to be gained by their prowess, they believed, though victory was not to be won without hard fighting. As the sun glanced over the hilltops the steamers got up their steam, and the line-of-battle ships loosed their sails.

Tom and Archie climbed to the masthead, where they determined to remain with telescopes in hand till called down to attend to their duty on deck. In front of them was a line of cliffs extending to the mouth of the Alma, bordering a wide extent of undulating ground. Beyond the Alma rose broken cliffs with a broad plateau on their summit, on which the enormous army of Russia was posted, their lines extending from the coast far away out of sight. In front of the steep hillsides were numerous heavy batteries, capable of sweeping the invading force back into the stream of the Alma, till its waters should run dark with blood. More to the left the French forces could be seen forming in order of battle, with the Turks in the rear, while only for a short distance could the red-coated soldiers of England be distinguished. Now and then a party of horsemen could be made out. When the sun rose, its rays glittered for a moment on the helmets and breastplates of the heavy cavalry as they moved off to protect the left flank of the invading forces.

The hours went slowly by; they were of intense interest to the spectators, and much more so must they have been to those who had to take an active part in the coming strife. Not, however, till eleven o'clock were the armies seen to be advancing. The ships near the cliffs began the action by throwing shot and shell among the Russians posted on the heights. The light infantry regiments could be seen moving in advance, throwing out skirmishers; then came the heavy infantry battalions, with firm tread pressing the ground. At length the blue coats of the French, who had crossed the Alma at its mouth, were observed climbing the rugged heights, the summit of which being gained, they rapidly formed, greatly to the astonishment, apparently, of the Russians, who had not perceived their approach. Now there burst forth from the whole hillside the roar of artillery and the rattle of musketry, so rapidly as to blend into one continuous sound, telling of death to many a brave heart.

"The British are advancing!" cried Tom; "see, they are pushing across the river, but they don't appear on the hill yet.

The Russian skirmishers are disputing the ground with them. What a rattling fire they are keeping up!"

Some time passed by: the redcoats were hotly engaged with the enemy near a large village, that of Bourliouk. In a short time the village burst out into flames, completely hiding the troops on its farther side; then the British were again caught sight of, after they had crossed the river beyond the village, fighting their way up the slope, encountering the fearful fire of the Russians, and small red spots could be discerned on the ground over which they had passed.

Here and there the British redcoats could be distinguished fighting their way up the hillside; but the broken nature of the ground hid the larger number from sight, and it was impossible to discover how the battle was going. Only at length it was seen that the banners of France occupied the ground where the Russians had before stood; still some time passed before they advanced. The Turks remained below, which was a good sign, as it showed that their aid was not required. Now, far away, the redcoats could be discerned scattered over the hillside. Could it be that they were defeated? No; just then a long thin line, like a scarlet thread, was seen amid the smoke, far, far away, moving up the slope, in one spot having a parti-coloured hue.

"Those must be the Guards and Highlanders," exclaimed Tom. "My brother Sidney will be in for it; I hope he'll escape, poor fellow. I wish I could be there to help him, if he gets wounded."

Onward advanced that thin unbroken line up the hill; the brow was reached, when there appeared in front of it a grey mass, which seemed like a square patch of withered grass on the greener herbage. Many such patches were seen sending forth wreaths of smoke from their midst. The midshipmen guessed rightly that it was a column of Russian infantry. From the red column issued a sheet of flame and smoke; not for one moment did it cease. Minutes went by; now that parti-coloured portion of the line reached the summit of the hill and moved on, smoke issuing from it as it moved. The dark mass of the enormous Russian column began to recede before it, at length breaking and scattering in all directions.

The French, meantime, had disappeared, sweeping the enemy before them over the hill, till they were lost to sight. The batteries, which had been pouring their shot down on their assailants, had ceased their fire, for those assailants had already stormed and captured them. The English attack in front had been successful, and more troops, which had been kept in reserve, went streaming up the hill. The whole British and French armies had not only gained the heights, but, as it seemed, were sweeping the Russians before them. The rattle of musketry was now only occasionally heard; then came a few salvoes of artillery, and the fierce uproar which had raged for the last two hours almost ceased.

The slopes which partly faced the sea were the most visible, and on these could be seen numerous red spots—some strewn thickly together, others scattered more apart, marking the places where the Russian fire had carried death and wounds into the British ranks. Still at that distance nothing clearly could be seen.

"It must be the case," cried Tom at length. "Hurrah! we've won, and the Russians are running away; you'll see that I'm right. Now, my brother will be as anxious as I am to learn how it has fared with Sidney; I hope he's all right, poor fellow; but I am terribly afraid, with all that firing which has been going on so long, an immense number must have been killed."

The midshipmen, who had been allowed to retain their seats, were at length called down. There was considerable excitement on board, everybody anxious to hear news from the shore, though no one doubted that a splendid victory had been gained. They had not long to wait; the signal staff set up on shore was soon at work. A complete victory had been gained, and it was requested that boats might be sent immediately on shore with hammocks on which to carry the wounded on board ship. The appeal was quickly responded to. Jack immediately ordered two of his boats to be got ready under the command of Higson, with whom he sent Tom and Archie, giving the two midshipmen permission to make their way on till they could find the Guards, to ascertain the fate of his brother.

Tom was delighted with the duty.

"Stay," said Jack; "you may find many poor fellows wounded, who will be the better for some brandy, and some may want water. Take as much as you can carry; you'll not have more than is wanted, I fear."

Search was made for flasks, and each midshipman carried three, and two bottles of water. Archie, with due forethought, also tore up two of his shirts, which he stuffed into his pockets.

Higson followed their example in carrying a supply of spirits and water.

Away the two boats pulled for the beach near the mouth of the Alma, where numerous others were already assembled. For the first half-mile or so, after landing, there were few signs of the conflict, but in a short time they met parties of English and French soldiers carrying wounded men, most of them looking more dead than alive from loss of blood; while, as they advanced, they found numerous tents set up, in which the surgeons were already at work amputating arms and legs, and dressing the more severe wounds. Where the conflict had raged the hottest, the surgeons, who had followed closely the advancing forces, were employed with tourniquets doing their utmost to stop the life-blood flowing from the veins of the wounded. Although the two midshipmen had seen a good deal of fighting, they both turned sick as they gazed at the fearful wounds inflicted by the round shot.

The road they took leading them some way to the north of the Alma, it was only after they had proceeded a considerable distance that they came to the part of the ground where the English had chiefly fought. On the eastern side was the burned village of Bourliouk; the hillside was covered with the corpses of the men of the infantry regiments, intermingled with the bodies of the grey-coated, helmeted Russians. The cries of the wounded soon attracted those who came to succour them, and the seamen under Higson were speedily laden with wounded men. After the wounded had been inspected by a surgeon, and pronounced fit to be removed, the party set off to return to the boats, while Tom and Archie made their way up the hill in the track the Guards had taken, Tom looking out anxiously on every side in search of his brother, whom he dreaded to find among the killed.

They met numerous parties of soldiers, with a few sailors, who had already landed, some carrying wounded men towards the village on the banks of the Alma, the houses of which had been turned into hospitals; others going in search of fresh burdens. The work of burying the dead, who thickly strewed the ground in those parts where the fight had raged the hottest, had not yet commenced; the living men had first to be cared for. Here and there surgeons of the army, as well as many of the navy, who had landed even before the battle was over, were attending to the more desperate cases requiring immediate aid.

The Russians received the same attention as the English, and were at once carried off to the hospitals. Some poor fellows lay under the walls and other shelter, where they had crawled after being wounded; the larger number were found where they fell.

Tom was in a hurry to push on, while he looked about on every side for the uniform of the Guards. From all quarters came groans and cries, and the midshipmen could not resist stopping to afford some relief to the sufferers. Several Russians lay with their heads placed on the corpses of their brother soldiers; some had their arms, others their legs, blown away by round shot. One poor fellow was still alive, though both his thighs had been thus broken. He had strength to point to his lips, and Tom, kneeling by his side, poured some water down his throat. The dying man cast a grateful look at the young officer, but before they left him he expired. Several had their heads blown off; others, who had their faces carried away, presented the most dreadful spectacle.

At length Tom exclaimed, "There are some Guardsmen!" Several high bearskin caps marked the spot to which he pointed; the first men they came to were dead, but higher up the hill they saw more. One of them was alive, with a bad wound in his side, and a shot through his arm; he was apparently bleeding to death. Archie produced his bandages, while Tom poured some brandy down his throat. It contributed to revive him; Tom inquired eagerly if he had seen Captain Rogers.

"Yes, sir," was the answer; "he was marching on with the regiment when I fell."

Having done their best to stop the blood flowing from the man's wound, Tom and Archie hurried forward. Farther to the right the ground was still more thickly covered with corpses. On examining them, Tom observed that though many were Guardsmen, they did not belong to his brother's regiment. Several officers lay dead, numerous Russians mingled with the British. The greater number appeared to have been shot by bullets, but several had been killed by the bayonet or sword, and exhibited ghastly wounds. Apparently, the wounded officers had been removed, for none were seen alive. Numerous helmets, knapsacks, and other accoutrements thrown away by the Russians, together with the greater number of their dead, showed that they had been put to flight by the victorious advance of the British.

"This is terrible," cried Tom; "I had often pictured a battlefield, but I had not fancied it anything like so horrible as this is."

"It must be worse to the poor fellows who lie scattered about us, suffering fearful tortures from their wounds," answered Archie, "with the prospect of dying from them; or even if they recover, being maimed for life."

"I hope poor Sidney is not among them," exclaimed Tom, for the twentieth time; "I can't help thinking more of him than of anyone else."

Making inquiry of some soldiers whom they at length met with stretchers carrying the wounded men they had picked up, Tom asked if they could tell him over what ground the —— Guards had passed.

"You must keep farther to the left," was the answer; "you will come upon some dead Highlanders, and they are just beyond them."

The bonnets of the Highlanders were soon discovered, and not far off the tall bearskins showed where the Guards had fought. The midshipmen, however, made but slow progress, for they could not help stopping to relieve those who required their aid, both friends and foes, till Archie had used up all his bandages, and their spirits and water were nearly expended. As Tom had not found Sidney, his spirits rose with the hope that, at all events, he might have escaped being killed. The enormous number of Russian dead, who were now seen covering the plain, showed the part of the ground where the last desperate conflict had taken place. Whole ranks of the enemy had fallen under the withering fire of the Guards and Highlanders. In one spot they came upon an entire line of Russians, every man of whom had been shot down apparently at the same moment; indeed, far as the eye could reach on either side, the plain was thickly strewn with the dead.

At length a long line of upright figures was seen arrayed on the left, with numerous banners waving above their heads, and horsemen moving to and fro; the red hue on the left showing where the victorious soldiers of England stood, halted on the battlefield, while on the right appeared the masses of the French army, with the Turkish troops who had marched forward to their support. They occupied the ground on which they were to bivouac before advancing again in pursuit of the flying foe.

The midshipmen made their way towards the troops on the left, and were able, by looking at the lofty bearskins of the Guards, to find out the regiment to which Sidney Rogers belonged. Almost breathless with eagerness, Tom inquired for his brother.

"He is there," said a sergeant, pointing to a spot where a group of officers stood together, eagerly discussing the events of the day.

Tom, unable to restrain his feelings, gave a shout of joy, in which Archie joined him. As they hurried forward, Sidney advanced to meet them, and they were soon shaking him heartily by the hand, and congratulating him on his escape and the victory he had contributed to win.

"I am thankful to have come out of it unhurt," said Sidney, "especially when I hear of the number of officers who have been killed; between twenty and thirty, at all events; and not far short of a hundred wounded."

Tom then gave Jack's message, and delivered a case containing a few luxuries brought from the ship. The midshipmen could not, however, remain long, as they had received orders to return at night, and the day was now rapidly closing. They were brave youngsters, but they had no wish to be compelled to make their way over the battlefield in the darkness, amid the dying and the dead. Wishing Sidney good-bye, they rapidly retraced their steps; as they once more descended the hill, their ears were assailed with cries and groans, but as they had no longer any means of assisting the unhappy sufferers, they hurried on. At the foot of the hill they reached the road which ran along the bank of the river, having to pass in their way close to the smouldering ruins of the village which had been set on fire at the commencement of the battle. Here it was supposed that several English as well as Russian riflemen had perished, while engaged with each other, the flames having spread round them before they had time to make their escape.

It was already dark when one of the *Tornado's* boats came to take them off. Neither of them were very much inclined to talk of what they had seen; and even Jack, when they got on board, had some difficulty in gaining more information from them than the fact that they had found Sidney safe and well. After a glass or two of wine, however, Jack drew forth an account of the scenes they had witnessed on the battlefield. Tom often shuddered as he described the fearful condition of the wounded, and the numbers of dead they had seen.

Next morning they were all to rights, and were ready to go in charge of a fresh party of seamen, who were sent on shore to bring off more of the wounded. All day long the seamen were engaged in collecting the wounded men and carrying them to the hospitals, or bringing them off to the ships; while parties, told off from the different regiments, were employed in burying the dead, generally in large pits, into which friends and foes were tumbled without much ceremony. All the time bodies of cavalry were kept patrolling on the left to guard the people employed in the service from the attacks of the Cossacks, who were seen hovering in the distance, ready to pounce down upon any unwary stragglers.

As soon as Jack had received on board as many wounded officers and men as he could accommodate, he proceeded to Constantinople to place them in the hospitals which had been got ready for their reception. Several died on the voyage, some of their wounds and some of cholera, which killed many officers and men after the battle. Jack was eager to get back again to see what was going forward. Hopes had been entertained that the allies would at once enter Sebastopol; but the news had reached Constantinople that, instead of doing so, they had marched round the city and had posted themselves on its southern side, the English having occupied the harbour of Balaclava, while their army had taken up a position on the ground above it, extending towards the fortifications of Sebastopol.

The *Tornado* was still steaming at full speed across the Bosphorus, when, soon after dawn, though still out of sight of land, a loud booming of guns came from the northward over the calm water. "There is another furious battle going forward," said the first lieutenant to the commander, who had just come on deck; "I wish we were there—can the fleet be engaged?"

"I very much doubt that the Russians will have ventured out of their harbour," answered Jack; "I suspect rather that the allies have commenced the bombardment of the city. The last account stated that they were busy preparing for it, and I think it probable that the admirals will take the fleet in to engage the sea-batteries."

"They will not do much against those stone walls, unless they are complete shams," observed Higson; "however, we shall be there before long, and if there is an honest battle at sea going on, I hope we shall be in time to take part in it."

Of course there was great excitement on board, everyone looking out eagerly for the land. Surmises of all sorts were made as to what was going forward. The engineers did their best to urge the steamer along, but the wind was so light that the sails were wholly useless. Billy Blueblazes and Dicky Duff, who were somewhat jealous of Tom and Archie having been on shore, were eager to be there to see the "fun," as they called it.

"I can tell you fellows that it is no fun at all," said Tom, who had become unusually grave since he had visited the battlefield of the Alma; "I have got a brother there, and in all probability he is in the midst of the fight."

"And if the fleets are engaged, I have got a cousin who is as dear to me as a brother," observed Archie, "and I don't want any harm to happen to him. You youngsters talk glibly of fighting; but let me hear what you have to say about it when you have seen the thing in reality. It is an necessary evil, but an evil notwithstanding."

The younger midshipmen laughed, and declared that it was just what they had come to sea for. "So did we too," said Tom; "but only because it's our duty to fight to protect our country—not that I can see that we forward that object by coming out here to attack the Russians."

Soon afterwards, "Land! land!" was heard from the masthead, adding to the excitement of all on board. At length the high cliffs of the Chersonese appeared in sight; the thunder of the guns, as the ship advanced, increasing in loudness. Now the fleet could be seen coming forward from the roads off the Katcha River to the north; no sails were set, as the ships had either their own steam-power, or were moved by steamers lashed alongside.

"The French fleet are leading," observed Jack to Higson; "it is evident then that their destined position is the southern end of the line, and that our ships are to attack Fort Constantine and the other forts on the north side of the harbour." Slowly the proud ships glided onwards, but not a shot was fired from them; they were still out of range of the forts. It was already near one o'clock in the afternoon. In the French division thirteen ships could be counted, two of them carrying the Turkish flag. Onward they glided in admirable order, still preserving perfect silence.

"To my mind," observed Higson, "they would be likely to do much more good if they were farther in, and my belief is that so they would be if they had English captains to fight them."

"Probably the French admiral is afraid of getting his ships on shore were he to stand in closer," observed Jack, who held the French in more respect than did his first lieutenant. At length, as the French ships came within range, the Russian forts opened their fire, but still no reply was made. The whole French squadron had now one by one anchored at exact distances from each other, extending more than half-way across the harbour; then the signal was given, and the roar of six hundred guns broke the silence which had hitherto prevailed, the dense clouds of smoke which arose almost concealing them from sight. At the same moment the English flagship was seen to throw out a signal, when three of the English steam-frigates, which had been standing inshore, commenced firing away at the northern forts. Another signal presently went up, and the *Agamemnon* was seen gliding on at more rapid speed than heretofore towards the shore, some little distance to the north of Fort Constantine, the nearest point which a shoal running off from the land would allow her to reach. A gallant little steamer, the *Circassian*, was observed leading the way, fearless of the shot which the guns of the fort threw at her. As the *Agamemnon* passed the *Sanspareil*, which had been ahead of her, hearty cheers resounded from their crews, and then both commenced firing, clouds of smoke quickly enveloping them and assisting to baffle the gunners of the two batteries on the high ground above them. Meantime the *Britannia*, *Trafalgar*, *Vengeance*, *Queen*, *Rodney*, and *Bellerophon*, were proceeding southward in order to complete the line across the harbour, while the *Sanspareil*, *London*, *Arethusa*, and *Albion* took up positions to the northward of the *Agamemnon*.

Not till afterwards, of course, did Jack hear of the gallant conduct of Mr. Ball, in command of the little steam-tender *Circassia*, which was seen ahead of the *Agamemnon*, taking soundings for her, and leading her close up to the shoal. Sir Edmund told him that his ship would probably be sunk, and undertook to have his boats in readiness to pick up him and his crew should such an event occur. As the tender moved ahead of the great ship, the lead-line was struck out of the leadsman's hands; but another line was immediately found, and the little vessel continued her course. Though she received nine shots in her hull, the leadsman was the only man wounded on board. Having performed her duty, she steamed off out of harm's way. The *Agamemnon* was, however, so well placed to the north-west, that the rear guns only of the fort could be brought to bear on her, and as she was much nearer in than the enemy expected, most of their shot struck her masts and rigging.

So close was the *Sanspareil* to her stern that that ship's foremost guns could not at first be fired. This made it necessary for her to haul off, but it was only to return to render her able support to the *Agamemnon*. The greater number of the ships were now hotly engaged, well-nigh twelve hundred guns firing rapidly away at the various forts, and crumbling the upper works of the nearest to pieces; but still all the time the iron shower sent by the Russians came crashing on board the ships of the allies, sending many a brave seaman to his account, and wounding a far greater number.

"The admiral is signalising us," exclaimed Higson; "we are to run alongside the *Briton*, and carry her into action."

No sooner had he uttered the words, than a loud cheer arose from the crew; in a short time, having obeyed the order she had received, they were where they had longed to be—in the line of battle, under the enemy's fire, the *Briton* having, as was the case with many of the other ships, landed a considerable number of her people to join the naval brigade on shore. A portion of the *Tornado's* crew were called on board to assist in working her guns; happy did those consider themselves who were thus employed. Among the officers were Mr. Mildmay and Tom and Archie. As they were stationed on the upper deck, they could occasionally see, when the dense wreaths which encircled the combatants blew by, what was going forward. Mr. Mildmay stood as cool as usual, every now and then pulling out his notebook and making notes in it.

"I really believe," said Tom to Archie, laughing, "that he's writing a poetical description of the battle. Perhaps it's a song, to be called 'The Battle of Sebastopol'—'There we lay, all that day, At stone walls a-blazing away!'"

"I wonder when the Russians intend to give in—it doesn't seem much like it at present," observed Archie; "I expected that we should sail up the harbour and sink their ships."

"They've done that already themselves, right across the

mouth. I heard the first lieutenant tell the master so," said Tom.

"I only wish that they were afloat, and that we were fighting them instead of these forts," observed Archie. "When we have knocked them to pieces, I don't see what good they will do us."

"Why, of course, to help the soldiers on shore to get into the place," answered Tom.

These remarks, which were made at intervals between the firing of their guns, were cut short by a shot killing two of the crew of one of the guns under Tom's command. He had to summon others to take their places; after this he felt very little inclination to talk, nor, indeed, had he much opportunity of doing so. The position of those who remained on board the steamer was very trying; they had nothing to do, but were tolerably secure from damage, while the enemy's shot went flying over their heads. Hour after hour the battle continued to rage, the troops on shore being hotly engaged with the batteries turned towards them, the thundering roar of their guns answering to those of the ships. Never, perhaps, in the same space of time had so many round shot and shells been flying through the air.

Little more could be seen of the ships in line across the harbour's mouth. The French remained stationary, but some of the English frequently moved their positions to the support of Sir Edmund Lyons and the inshore squadron, which were enduring the brunt of the battle, exposed as they were to the tremendous fire from Fort Constantine and other batteries. Now flames were seen to burst forth from the *Queen*, when, a steamer taking her in tow, she stood off to extinguish them. Some time afterwards the *Albion* was seen to be on fire, fearfully mauled and unable to fire a shot, with the risk of drifting on shore. She also stood off, helped by the steamer attending her.

The *Rodney* was now seen standing in to support the *Agamemnon* when she took the ground, and though exposed to a tremendous fire, she continued fighting her guns. It seemed almost impossible that she should escape destruction, but she still kept firing away till, two steamers going to her assistance, she at length got clear. Not till darkness came on did the battle cease, when the ships returned to their anchorage. Jack was thankful to find that Murray and the midshipmen had escaped, though five of his own crew and many more of the *Briton's* had been killed. The next morning the "butcher's bill," as Jos Green called it, was made out, when it was found out that forty-four British seamen had lost their lives, and that two hundred and sixty-six had been wounded, while the *Albion* and *Arethusa* had been so knocked about in their hulls and rigging that the admiral sent them off to Malta to be repaired.

The French ships presented a still more disabled appearance, and had lost altogether in killed and wounded under two hundred men. Then came the question, what had been done? and the opinion generally was that, although a good many of the Russians might have been killed, no essential damage had been done to the forts, and that it would be wiser in future for the ships to let them alone.

"I suppose the work of the fleet is pretty well over," said Murray to Jack, who had gone on board the *Briton*, "unless we have to attack other places along the coast. You will probably be sent on that service, and I confess I envy you."

"I hope we shall," was the answer; "though I am afraid that at present we shall be employed as a despatch-boat. I should like to see what is going forward on shore, and shall be glad if I can take a turn of duty with the naval brigade, but I have very little hopes of that."

CHAPTER XVI

The *Tornado* at Balaclava—The Allied Camps—Russian Cavalry and Highlanders—The Flying Turks and the Highland Wife—Charge of the Heavy Brigade—"Into the Valley of Death rode the Six Hundred!"—Death of Captain Nolan—After the Battle—Tom and Archie propose to leave the Navy for the Army, but think better of it—Their Visit to the Guards' Camp—The Stern Realities of War—Attacked by the Russians—The Midshipmen in the thick of the Fight.

THE *Tornado* had been ordered to proceed to Balaclava. She entered that landlocked harbour, on the southern end of the Crimea, on the evening of the 24th of October. As she was to remain there the whole of the next day, Jack resolved to take the opportunity of paying a visit to his brother Sidney, and seeing what was going forward before Sebastopol. There was no time to set off that evening; he, however, landed with his second lieutenant and some of his younger officers, including Tom and Archie, to have a look at the country, and to engage horses for the next day.

Steep hills rose on either side of the harbour, on the right of which the little town was situated, with steep, narrow streets leading down to the water's edge. Above it was a line of defences, garrisoned by the bluejackets forming the naval brigade, and the marines of the fleet. To the left, across the Chersonese, ran the road to Sebastopol; while directly in front, connected by a gorge with the harbour, was a broad valley, called the South Valley. Beyond this rose a ridge known as the Causeway Heights, on which were situated six redoubts, garrisoned by the Turks, to whom had been committed what formed the outward defences of Balaclava; along this causeway ran the Woronzoff Road. At the eastern extremity of the valley there was a knoll between five and six hundred feet in height, joining the Kamara Hills to the right by a neck of high ground, the knoll jutting out over the valley, as a promontory does over the sea. This knoll, on which No. 1 redoubt had been thrown up, was called by the allies Canrobert's Hill. On the western extremity of the valley was the Col, or gap through which the road passed to Sebastopol. Eastward of Canrobert's Hill were the village and heights of Kamara; completely overlooking it. On the farther side of the Causeway Heights was what was called the North Valley, with a range of heights rising out of it on the opposite side, denominated the Fedoukine Hills.

Jack and his party, having ascended from Balaclava to the height of St. Elias, could look down into the South Valley, at the left end of which they saw the tents of the heavy and light cavalry, with their horses picketed about them, while just below them were encamped Sir Colin Campbell's Highlanders. Horses, mules, carts, and vehicles of all sorts were making their way from the harbour along the well-beaten road to the allied camps. Not a foe was in sight; some of the officers in command of the marines and bluejackets, who garrisoned the lines extending from St. Elias to the sea, whom Jack met, told him, however, that there were rumours of the Russians not being far off, and that they should not be surprised if before long they were attacked.

"You'll lick them, of course," said Tom; "but I should think they had enough of fighting on the Alma."

"I am not so certain of that," was the answer; "the Russians are brave fellows, and they would like to drive us into the sea if they could."

After spending some time with his friends, Jack returned on board, having arranged to start at daybreak the next morning. Tom and Archie again accompanied their commander. They turned out before daylight, and Jack, who was anxious to see as much as he could of the operations before Sebastopol, was ready to go on shore directly day broke. Their horses were sorry steeds, but would save them fatigue, and enable them to get over the ground faster than they could on foot. Remembering how acceptable were the provisions they had before taken to Sidney, Tom and Archie each carried a couple of baskets full of different articles of provender, from which they might also supply themselves when they got hungry.

Jack had promised to call upon another officer who had been sleeping on shore in the marines' quarters, and who had undertaken to act as their guide. As they were mounting the hill, the loud thunder of guns broke on their ears. "I suppose those are the siege guns," observed Tom; "they begin work pretty early."

"No; they came from the direction of Canrobert's Hill, to the eastward," answered Jack; "away on our right. They must be the Turkish guns in the redoubts."

They hurried up the height, whence they could look down on the South Valley and across the line of redoubts held by the Turks. They were quickly joined by Jack's friend, who, riding up, exclaimed, "We shall have some warm work before the day is over. Look, look! there come the Russians in great force over those distant heights. They evidently intend to attack the redoubts. Yes, I was sure of it; see, their leading division has already commenced the assault on Canrobert's Hill."

One of the first objects which had caught the eyes of the naval officer was the English cavalry already mounted and drawn up in front of their camps. A general officer, accompanied by other horsemen, probably his staff, went galloping by from the direction of the harbour.

"There goes Lord Cardigan to join the cavalry," observed their friend; "he has been sleeping as usual on board his yacht; a pleasant way of campaigning, eh, Rogers? However, he is no carpet knight, and if the Russians come into the valley, we shall see what he and his cavalry can do."

As far as the eye could reach Jack saw masses of Russians, some advancing southward, others apparently turning off to the right along the North Valley, when they were hidden from sight by the intervening ridge. Besides the Turks, the only troops to oppose them were the cavalry at the west end of the valley, the 93rd Highlanders, under Sir Colin Campbell, and the marines and naval brigade on the heights above Balaclava, with a battery of field-guns. Some little way from the foot of the hills, and almost directly in front of the gorge leading to the harbour, in which stood the little village of Kadikoi, was a long, low hillock running east and west, and inside it—that is to say, to the south of it—was the Highland camp. On this hillock the gallant 93rd was drawn up.

An officer had been observed galloping at full speed towards Sebastopol, evidently to inform the commander-in-chief of the appearance of the foe. Jack at once abandoned all idea of visiting Sidney, as he was sure that the chief part of the fighting, if there was to be a battle, would not be far off. The Russians, who had for some minutes been assaulting the first Turkish battery, now pushed forward in overwhelming numbers. In vain the Turks fought to defend the post committed to them; the enemy swarmed over their entrenchments, while at the same time another equally large body assailed the second redoubt. For some time the fight raged fiercely, the Turks were defending themselves with their accustomed bravery—a few hundred men against the seemingly countless hordes led to the attack.

"If they can but hold out till the arrival of the succour Lord Raglan will certainly send them, it will be a great thing, but the odds are fearfully against them," observed Jack.

Scarcely had he made the remark when one or two figures were seen leaping over the trenches and descending the hill; more followed, "as fast,' Tom declared, "as sand runs out through the hole in the bottom of a bag"; and then came others, till all the survivors of those who had garrisoned the fort were in full flight. In a few minutes the Turks in No. 2 battery, also taking to flight, came scampering down the side of the hill, making their way across the valley. Jack could only hope that the remainder of the batteries might be held till relief could reach them. As it proved, he was disappointed; presently the Turks in all the other batteries, seeing the fate of their countrymen, broke away from their posts, and, rushing at headlong speed down the hillside, were seen crossing the valley to Balaclava, those who were escaping from the two first batteries being followed by Cossack cavalry spearing all they overtook. Had not the English light cavalry made a demonstration as if about to charge, many more would have been killed. Meanwhile the Russian artillery poured down upon them the fire of their guns. As they approached, a naval officer who had hurried to the ground did his best to rally them, but though he succeeded with some, nothing could stop the rest till they reached the neighbourhood of the harbour.

Jack and his party hurried down to assist the officer, who, with cheery voice and gestures, was endeavouring to rally the Turks and induce them to form up on the right of the Highlanders. Having done all they could, the party rode up to higher ground, whence they could better witness what was going forward. In the far distance, to the north of the Col, Jack could distinguish through his glass a group of officers whom he guessed must be Lord Raglan and his staff, who had hastened up to direct the coming battle, while the heads of French and English columns were observed marching from the direction of Sebastopol. Soon after this, Jack and his companions, who were watching the English cavalry, expecting to see some of them sent in pursuit of the

Cossacks, greatly to their surprise observed the whole of them moving away to the northward over the ridge till they were lost to sight, summoned, apparently, by one of Lord Raglan's aides-de-camp, thus leaving Balaclava without any other defence than the Highlanders and the battery of field-guns.

At this juncture a large body of Russian cavalry appeared in the direction of the third and fourth redoubts, having come thus far up the North Valley. Just then the English batteries on the edge of the Chersonese opened on them; this turned them, and they came moving over the causeway, as if about to descend into the South Valley, while the Russian artillery, which had advanced over the ridge, opened fire on the Highlanders and Turks, who were posted at the foot of Balaclava heights. Sir Colin, therefore, ordered them to move back to the foot of a hillock which they had before crowned, and to lie down under shelter. Directly afterwards four squadrons of the Russian cavalry, detached from the larger mass, came shaping their way across the southern valley towards the gorge which led to the harbour, the defence of which had been confided to the Highlanders, who were now supported by a hundred invalid soldiers, marched up from Balaclava. Directly the Russian cavalry were seen, the greater number of the Turks, thoroughly disorganised by their previous defeat, again took to flight, and rushed off towards the harbour, shrieking out, "Ship! ship! ship!" as if their only hope of escaping was to get on board the vessels in the harbour. The Highlanders, who were still lying down, watched them with contemptuous looks, and not a little merriment, as they observed the frightened expression of their countenances. Within sight, behind them, was the Highlanders' camp. As the terror-stricken Osmanlis were scampering away past it, some even attempting to find shelter within, there issued forth a tall figure with a thick stick in hand, who, by her dress, was seen to be a female of Amazonian proportions.

Shouting loudly in Gaelic, she ordered the fugitive Turks to return to their ranks, but her voice being unheeded, she placed herself before them and attempted to drive them back with her cudgel. Her efforts being still of no avail, after striking at several on either side, she rushed at a big, burly-looking Turk who was coming headlong towards her, and, seizing him by his jacket, began belabouring his back and head with a fury which was likely to prove as effective as the shot of the enemy, from whom he was trying to escape, in sending him to enjoy the bliss of Paradise.

Shouts of laughter burst from her friends in the distance as they witnessed her exploit. The Osmanli on whom she had seized roared out for mercy, till at length she let him go, giving him a shove towards the position he had deserted, while she kept flourishing her club behind him till he returned to his post. Whether or not she added materially to the strength of Sir Colin's force may be doubted, but the incident had a good effect upon her Highland countrymen; reminding them that they had not only their own lives to defend, but hers and others in the camp in their rear. In spite of the serious state of affairs, Jack and those around him could not help bursting into fits of laughter, though they themselves were not free from danger, for occasionally a round shot came flying towards them from the Russian guns, but with not sufficient frequency to make them shift the advantageous ground they occupied for witnessing what was going forward.

Sir Colin was now left, exclusive of a small body of Turks who still kept their ground, with scarcely six hundred men to defend the approach to Balaclava.

The veteran general felt the gravity of the occasion; but his stout heart did not quail, for he knew well that the brave men under him would stand firm. Riding down the line, he exclaimed to them, "Remember, there is no retreat from here, men; you must die where you stand."

"Ay, ay, Sir Colin, we'll do that," cried the Highlanders. The four squadrons of Russian cavalry, amounting to not less than six hundred men, now approached over the northern side of the valley, making direct for the gorge; apparently ignorant that a body of English troops were ready to bar their way, and evidently hoping to seize one of the batteries on the side of the passage. Sir Colin allowed them to come within long-musket range of the hillock, when he gave the word to his Highlanders, who, springing up, in an instant afterwards crowned the whole length of the ridge, forming a line only two deep; Sir Colin, confiding in their muscular power and the nature of the ground they occupied, not deeming it necessary to throw them into square. When they saw their enemy before them, they exhibited the greatest desire to rush down into the plain and charge the cavalry with their bayonets.

"Ninety-third! Ninety-third!" cried the old general fiercely; "none of that eagerness." Sir Colin's stern voice checked the men, who now opened their fire. The Russians, evidently taken by surprise, wheeled to the left and swept round, apparently intending to attack the Highlanders on the right flank. Immediately the Grenadier company of the 93rd brought its left shoulder forward to show a front to the north-east, and, pouring in a rattling fire, compelled the Russian squadron again to wheel to the left, and retreat much faster than they had come. On this the English battery opened fire, considerably scattering the horsemen, as they galloped back across the valley to the north to join the main body, which was seen coming over the ridge, increasing every moment in size. It looked, indeed, more as if the whole surface of the earth was moving, so compact was the dusky mass of the several thousand units which composed it.

Onward it advanced, as if about to descend into the South Valley. Now was the Russian general's opportunity. As far as he could then see, he had only a weak battery and six hundred infantry opposed to his enormous band of horsemen. By making a sudden dash across the valley he might annihilate the 93rd before the still distant infantry of the allies could come to Sir Colin's relief.

"Matters look serious," observed Jack. "We can scarcely dare to hope that the Highlanders will be able to withstand the charge of that prodigious body of cavalry; and if they give way, the Russians will quickly be into Balaclava. We ought to be on board to fight the ship or to get her out of the harbour, though I don't like to leave the ground while there is the chance of a turn in the state of affairs."

"They'll not venture on it," answered his friend. "See! see!"

As he spoke, the cavalry halted on the side of the hill to the east of No. 5 redoubt. The Russian commander had indeed some reason to hesitate, for, besides the English battery posted in his front on the side of Kadikoi, which would play upon him as he advanced, he might have seen the leading files of a French column appearing through the Col, and which might, before he could overthrow the little band of Highlanders, attack him on the flank.

Just then also Jack distinguished, coming round from the north end of the ridge, several squadrons of English dragoons, their burnished helmets and breastplates glittering brightly in the rays of the sun. These were the Scots Greys, the Inniskillings, and two regiments of Dragoon Guards. They moved along at some distance from each other, riding carelessly, as if not aware of the near vicinity of the enemy. The rough nature of the ground had hitherto hidden the Russians from their view, and prevented the latter from seeing them. Scarcely, however, had their leaders caught sight of the foe than their decision was made. While one party came between the two cavalry camps, the larger body formed up to the north of the light cavalry camp, directly in front of the head of the Russian squadron.

"I do believe our cavalry are going to attack the Russians!" exclaimed Jack.

"No doubt about it," answered his friend. "That is General Scarlett at their head, with his aide-de-camp—and see, that must be Lord Lucan who has ridden up to him."

What was to be done could only be judged by the movements of the squadrons. About three hundred British horsemen, composed of Inniskillings and Scots Greys, were forming in line with as much care as if they were on parade. Another body of cavalry, the Dragoon Guards, were moving to the right; while two others farther off, also Dragoon Guards and Royals, formed more to the north. The arrangements were speedily made. Lord Lucan came galloping back towards the Inniskillings; and General Scarlett, accompanied by three other persons on horseback, was seen to place himself at the head of the Scots Greys and a squadron of the Inniskillings. The enemy's cavalry had now halted on the slope of the hill. General Scarlett giving the order to advance, his sword glittering in the rays of the sun, he, with his three companions, dashed forward, followed by the gallant troop of cavalry, their horses' hoofs shaking the ground as they rushed towards the enormous body of Russians.

"They must be swallowed up and annihilated," exclaimed one of Jack's companions.

"They have no intention of letting the Russians do that to them," answered Jack; "though I fear the general and his comrades will be cut to pieces before the rest of the men overtake them."

There was but little time, however, for making many remarks. Onward at full gallop went that gallant band of horsemen, their leaders still fifty yards in advance, while a shower of bullets poured from the Russian ranks. Every moment it was expected that the Russians would charge, but still motionless they stood awaiting their foe. Now, like a thunderbolt, Scarlett and his three hundred horsemen hurled themselves on the Russian cavalry, he and his companions still keeping the lead, and appearing like a sharp point of the mighty wedge of red which was clearing its onward way amid the dark-grey mass of Russians, the swords of the British troopers flashing as they whirled them right and left, or pointed them at the foe; the clash of steel and the muttered roar of the combatants being heard far away across the valley. On and on went those daring horsemen, till the greater number seemed engulfed, though not overwhelmed; for still the red coats and those flashing blades could be seen ever surging onward amid the surrounding mass of grey.

The Russians had thrown out a wing on their left flank; and notwithstanding the prowess of the British horsemen in their midst, there were no signs of their giving way. The spectators on the heights watched the combatants with a burning anxiety, expressed by the broken ejaculations they now and anon uttered. Still the tall horsemen, towering above their dark-coated antagonists, moved here and there, cutting their way as best they could amid the mass, who yielded as they advanced, only to close again. Anxiety for the fate of those who had thus hurled themselves amid numberless foes continued to increase, when the regiment of Inniskilling Dragoons on the English right went thundering down on the Russian left flank, while the Dragoon Guards dashed forward to attack their front. The Royals next advanced at the gallop towards the squadron sent out on the Russian right flank, and another regiment of dragoons which had just appeared on the ground, keeping close under the hill, assailed the enemy on the same flank; while numerous other horsemen, among whom was a butcher in his shirt sleeves, and several without helmets or breastplates, were seen galloping up from the camp to join in the fight.

Scarcely had the last-arrived squadron of Inniskillings cast itself at headlong speed on the Russians than their deep-serried ranks began to relax. Many an eye was watching the gallant leader of the charge, who, fighting his way round to the right, with a portion of his troopers, at length emerged on the left flank of the Russians, shortly afterwards followed by the colonel of one of the regiments; who immediately ordered the trumpeter to sound the rally, the other officers also quickly re-forming their men.

The whole mass of Russians had by this time begun to heave upwards against the slope of the hill; the horsemen on the outside were first seen breaking away, and the next instant the whole of the vast body began to disperse, retreating, and endeavouring to save themselves by flight, followed by some of the victorious troopers; who were, however, as speedily as possible recalled, to save them from being exposed to the fire of the Russian artillery, which would have opened on them from the opposite heights. As the enemy were seen in flight, the 93rd, which had been among the most eager of the spectators, greeted them from afar by a loud cheer; while Sir Colin Campbell, his countenance beaming with delight, was seen to gallop forward, and, taking off his hat, to compliment the Greys on their gallantry. Long as the time had appeared during which this strange combat had taken place, Jack, on pulling out his watch, discovered that but eight minutes had passed from the time when General Scarlett at the head of his three hundred threw himself at his foes till they were in full flight up the hill.

Jack and his naval companions, who freely criticised all that occurred, had been watching with astonishment the Light Brigade, to the number of nearly seven hundred, who all this time, drawn up on the side of the hill, had been spectators of the fight without attempting to take the least part in it. "I suppose we shall hear all about it," said Jack, "but to me it seems one of the most surprising things; and I suspect that the fellows themselves must have chafed not a little at being thus kept back, when they would have done such good service by following the enemy, and rendering their overthrow even more complete than it has been."

As there appeared to be no more chance of seeing any fighting where they then were, the party of naval officers directed their course towards the high ground on the Chersonese, whence they could look up the North Valley, at the eastern end of which it was evident the greater part of the Russian army was posted. As they rode along, they passed two French brigades, which had hitherto been watching the South Valley. The French officers greeted them in a friendly way, one and all expressing their admiration at the gallant exploit just performed by the Heavy Brigade. They caught sight directly afterwards of an English brigade, which they learned was General Cathcart's, coming down from the Chersonese. Trotting on, they themselves were about to climb up the heights on their left, where Lord Raglan and his staff were stationed, when some of the party proposed that they should turn to the right along the Woronzoff Road, in the direction of the redoubts now occupied by the Russians.

"We shall be able to beat a timely retreat, if necessary," said

Jack; "and we shall, from one of the higher points, have a view of what is going forward in the North Valley as well as in the South."

Without further discussion as to the wisdom of their proceeding, they trotted on eastward along the Woronzoff Road, keeping a bright look-out ahead, in order that they might avoid getting under the fire of the Russian riflemen who might be advancing along the causeway. Before leaving the hills of Balaclava, they had observed that the Russians had not got farther west along the causeway than No. 3 redoubt, known as the Aratabia redoubt. On they went, till they reached a height a little to the west of No. 4 redoubt, whence they had an excellent view up and down the North Valley, as well as across it to the Fedoukine Hills, where they saw that the Russians were strongly posted.

The Light Brigade had by this time moved from its former position down into the western end of the North Valley, where also the heavy cavalry regiments were drawn up, as well as the magnificent body of French cavalry, under General Maurice. Far off, at the distance of a mile and a half, they could see a large battery of Russian guns, supported by enormous masses of cavalry. Jack and his companions continued their comments on all they saw.

"To my mind," observed Jack, "the first thing to be done would be to retake the redoubts and prevent the Russians from carrying off the guns they captured from the Turks. I suppose that is what General Cathcart will do when he reaches the causeway, though he is a long time coming; and if I were Lord Raglan, I should be in a considerable rage with him. I only wish we had a few hundred of our bluejackets; we should very soon, I suspect, be masters of one or more of the redoubts the Russians have got hold of."

"See, see!" cried Tom; "here comes an aide-de-camp from Lord Raglan; for my part, I believe that the cavalry will do the work if General Cathcart does not come up in time."

Just as this remark was made, the English infantry were seen descending along the Woronzoff Road. As they marched on they left some troops in the two western redoubts deserted by the Turks; and the naval officers had to move down the hill a little way to allow them to pass on to No. 4 redoubt, close to which General Cathcart halted his troops. As he did so, a cloud of skirmishers were seen advancing along the causeway towards the Russians in front of the Aratabia. Here the general appeared to have made up his mind to remain, instead of advancing and driving the Russians before him, as Jack thought he would do. Having got clear of the English infantry, the naval officers again took up their post on the top of the hill, whence they could look directly down on the Heavy and Light Cavalry Brigades, near which they distinguished Lord Lucan, the general commanding them.

"I wonder nothing is being done," exclaimed Jack at length; "if they don't look sharp about it, those Russians will carry off the Turkish guns in spite of them."

"Here comes an officer, at all events, from Lord Raglan, in hot haste; he must be a first-rate horseman," exclaimed one of the naval officers, "or he would break his neck coming down that steep hill."

As he spoke, he pointed to the side of the Chersonese, down which an aide-de-camp was seen galloping at a speed on which few horsemen over such ground would have ventured. Though every moment it seemed that his horse must come down and crush him as it fell, he continued his course in safety, and then came galloping up to Lord Lucan.

"He's saying something pretty strong, if we are to judge by his gestures," observed Jack; "see, he is pointing with his sword up the valley. No, it must be at the Russians on the causeway. He's ordering the cavalry to do just what those infantry fellows ought to have done long ago; and so they would have done it if they had had their will."

"I know that aide-de-camp," remarked one of the party; "he is Captain Nolan, he belongs to General Airey's staff."

Directly afterwards Lord Lucan was seen addressing Lord Cardigan, who immediately galloped forward towards where the light cavalry were drawn up.

"See, the regiments of light cavalry are forming line; they are going to attack the Russians near the redoubts, after all," exclaimed Jack. "The heavy cavalry is preparing to support them; they will drive away the Russians as chaff before the wind."

After this, few remarks were made by any of the group, so deeply interested were they in watching what was going forward. Lord Cardigan was seen to place himself at the head of the light cavalry, while Lord Lucan came closer to them. All eyes, however, were riveted on Lord Cardigan and the light cavalry; he could easily be distinguished by his commanding yet slight figure, as he sat upon his tall charger at a distance of some five horses' lengths in front of the line, which now began to advance. The spectators expected to see the light cavalry wheel with their left shoulders forward towards the Russians on their right front, whom it was supposed they were about to attack. Instead of doing so, Lord Cardigan, sitting in his saddle, with his face down the valley, galloped on straight before him. Scarcely had he gone a hundred paces, when a figure, recognised at once as that of Captain Nolan, was seen to dash out from the left of the line and to gallop diagonally across the front. The aide-de-camp was waving his sword, pointing eagerly towards the Russians on the right, who were engaged in endeavouring to carry off the guns captured from the Turks.

He had just passed Lord Cardigan when a shell burst close to him, and his horse, wheeling suddenly, dashed back towards the advancing ranks. At the same moment, his sword falling from his hand, while his arm remained extended, a fearful shriek, unlike anything human, burst from him, and his horse passing between the 13th Light Dragoons, he at length fell to the ground a lifeless corpse. If, as it seems certain, his object had been to point out the direction the cavalry were to charge, Lord Cardigan took no notice of it, but continued on right down the valley towards the Russian guns and masses of Russian horsemen at its eastern end.

"Good heavens! they will be annihilated!" exclaimed Jack. "Where are they going?"

Well might he have said that, for in a short time from the heights on either side the Russians began to pour down showers of shot and shell and rifle balls upon the devoted band. Many were seen to drop; riderless horses came galloping back, some falling in their course, others uttering cries of agony from the wounds they had received. Here and there human forms could be distinguished, some lying in the quiet of death, others writhing on the ground or endeavouring to drag themselves back up the valley.

Now the guns in front sent forth their deadly missiles, filling the air with dense clouds of smoke, into which the cavalry charged with headlong speed.

While the Light Brigade was thus rushing on apparently to utter destruction, the heavy cavalry was advancing, following Lord Lucan.

"Can he be going to lead them to the destruction to which he has consigned the light cavalry?" exclaimed one of the naval officers.

"Thank Heaven, no," observed Jack; "they have had a

taste already of what they would have to go through. See, they've halted; though why he does not lead them up to attack the Russians on his right I cannot make out."

The heavy cavalry had already lost several men under the withering fire to which they had been exposed during the few minutes their advance had lasted, and they were now compelled to remain inactive while the action was going forward, as their brethren of the light cavalry had been in the morning. It was pretty evident that Lord Lucan could not be aware of the enemy on his right, or he would at once have found ample work for his heavy horsemen. At this juncture a portion of the French cavalry, the famous regiment D'Allonville, was observed to be moving forward, sweeping round the western base of the Fedoukine Hills, up which they charged, rushing forward as fast as the uneven nature of the ground would allow them at the Russian infantry and artillery which had so long been posted there. As they approached, the artillery limbered up and galloped off to the eastward, while the infantry quickly retreated, though not till many of the gallant Frenchmen's saddles had been emptied.

Several minutes of awful suspense had passed away since the last of the red line of light cavalry had been seen rushing into the cloud of smoke. The guns which had dealt death into their ranks had ceased to roar; but what had become of them or of the brave horsemen it was impossible to say. At length here and there a single horseman was seen moving slowly back, he or his charger sorely wounded. Now more and more appeared, several, alas! being seen to drop as they retired; the whole centre of the valley, as far as the eye could reach, being strewed with the bodies of men and horses. As the cloud of smoke cleared off, a dark mass only could be discerned in the distance, the glitter of sword-blades and the confused murmur of voices which came up the valley alone indicating that the fight was still raging, sounds ever and anon of musketry being added to it.

At length the numbers of those who were coming up the valley increased; among them appeared the tall form of their leader, he and his horse uninjured. Then came larger parties, followed again by single horsemen and men on foot, still exposed to the fire from the causeway. Presently a number of Cossacks came galloping after the fugitives, spearing some and taking others prisoners; but just then the Russian guns on the Causeway Ridge again opened, and the Cossacks were compelled to abandon the pursuit, many of those whom they had surrounded making their escape. The naval officers now rode back to the slope at the foot of the Chersonese, on which considerable groups had assembled, and towards which the gallant men who had come out from amid that valley of death were now collecting. The officers were speaking eagerly together; surgeons who had hurried down were attending to the wounded; several parties were on their way into the valley to endeavour to bring in those who were on the ground still, unable to move.

Among the last to come in was an officer on a weary horse, which could scarcely drag itself up the valley; numerous persons went forward to meet him. "That is Lord George Paget," said one of the naval officers. He had, with Colonel Douglas, led out the remnant of the 4th Light Dragoons and a portion of the 11th Hussars; not only had the brigade, though separated into several bands, broken through the guns, but, driving the Russian horsemen before them, and finally breaking through all opposition, had made their way again up the valley, passing directly in front of a large body of Russian Lancers, and once more, under a fire of shot and shell, they returned to the foot of the Chersonese. The naval officers could not, naturally, tear themselves from the scene. For some time stragglers and riderless chargers were coming in, and then there was the numbering of horses, and afterwards the melancholy roll-call. Of the gallant brigade, which half an hour before had numbered nearly 700 horsemen, not 200 now remained fit for duty. A hundred and thirteen men had been killed, 134 wounded; while close upon 500 horses were killed or rendered unfit for service.

Now came the sad work of searching for the slain who could be reached and brought in for burial; but numbers still lay where the fire of the Russian batteries commanded the ground, as they could not be interred till a cessation of arms was agreed on for the purpose. Many a gallant trooper hurried forward notwithstanding to search for his wounded officers or comrades, and several were thus saved from perishing on the battlefield.

Another scene took place, trying to many a trooper who had managed to bring his wounded steed out of the fight. The farriers went round to examine those which had been rendered unserviceable by their hurts. Some of the men pleaded hard for those that were condemned, in the hopes that they might recover, but the farriers knew well that they would never again be fit to carry their riders in the fight.

"Shure, it's myself would rather have been wounded than the poor baste," exclaimed an Irish trooper, throwing his arm round his horse's neck; "you wouldn't have shot me, at all events. Just be after letting him live for a few days, at laste, and I'll see what I can do to doctor him."

"I'm obeying orders, Pat; I tell you, if he gets stiff he'll never carry you fifty yards, much less the mile and a half you galloped over this afternoon," was the answer.

Poor Pat, whose hacked blade showed the deadly work he had been doing, burst into tears, as the farrier led off his well-beloved horse to the spot appointed for its execution, where, with upwards of forty others, it was shot.

As it was too late by this time to go on to the Guards' camp, Jack considering it his duty to sleep on board, and having had the satisfaction to hear that Sidney was well, and of sending him a message, he and his party returned to Balaclava. Tom and Archie were full of the exploits they had witnessed, and so excited did they become in describing them to their messmates, that they declared they would give up the service, and try and get their friends to obtain them commissions in the cavalry.

"Which means that your friends are to buy you commissions, which will cost them some thousands to begin with, besides finding you five or six hundred a year to enable you to live like the rest of your brother officers," observed the assistant surgeon. "I should just like to have the fortune which is lost to his family by each of the poor fellows who bit the dust this afternoon in yonder valley of death. I'd quit the service, you may depend on that, and buy a good practice on shore, with enough to set up my carriage at once." The next morning Tom and Archie had changed their minds, and had resolved to continue serving their Queen and country afloat.

Jack, finding that he could not sail till the evening, went on shore, taking the two midshipmen with him, to make another attempt to visit Sidney. Having obtained the steeds they had ridden the previous day, they took the way to the Col, halting on the first high ground they reached. They saw that the Russians still retained in considerable force the redoubts they had won from the Turks.

"They seem unpleasantly close to our lines," observed Tom to Archie; "our fellows must keep pretty wide awake, or they will be taking us by surprise some fine morning."

"Trust Sir Colin Campbell for that," answered Archie; "we

Highlanders are not men to be found napping in the face of an enemy."

They had not gone far when they met Lord Raglan and some of his staff, and presently afterwards Sir Colin Campbell came up, when an earnest conversation took place between the two generals. Jack was moving on with his two midshipmen, when an aide-de-camp overtook him, from whom he heard that it was in contemplation to abandon Balaclava, that the ships' guns and stores not in use were to be embarked, and that all the vessels not required were to go out of the harbour, or to be moved lower down towards its mouth. Disappointed again, Jack had to return on board to carry out his orders. He, however, gave the midshipmen leave to go as far as the Guards' camp, with directions to return immediately they had communicated with Sidney.

In high glee they rode on, determined, if possible, not to be again stopped. Having passed through the Col, they skirted the edge of the Chersonese to the right, when a windmill, for which they were told to steer their course, appeared in sight. After going about two miles they reached the Guards' camp, on some level ground at the top of the plateau. Sidney was seated in his tent, unwashed and unshaven, wrapped in his greatcoat, looking very unlike the trim Guardsman Tom had hitherto seen him. He had just come in from the trenches. Having thanked the two midshipmen for the welcome provisions they brought him, he made them sit down, one on a portmanteau turned sideways, the other on his only spare camp-stool.

"So you have come to witness the glories of war, Tom," said Sidney, with a faint smile; "for my part, I confess I wish we could have another stand-up fight, and get over the work in the trenches. I can tell you it is not very pleasant to stand out in the cold for hours together, with the chance of being shot at any moment."

"Archie and I couldn't help wishing that we were dragoons, with the chance of charging the enemy in the magnificent way we saw General Scarlett and his heavy cavalry do yesterday," said Tom.

"Such a chance doesn't come more than once in a campaign, and you wouldn't exactly wish to perform the feat the unfortunate light cavalry had to go through yesterday, from what I hear," answered Sidney. "Stick to the navy, lads; you have the best of it."

Luncheon was scarcely over, when a rattling fire was heard, followed by the sound of heavy guns. "There's something going forward," cried Sidney, going out of the tent. In an instant the whole camp was astir. The bugles sounded, and the brigade of Guards fell in, orders having been received to march northward along the heights, in the direction of Inkerman. The midshipmen, forgetting the caution they had received to return immediately to Balaclava, hurried forward, taking their way somewhat to the left of the line on which the Guards had marched, who were thus on their right.

"Push along!" cried Tom; "we haven't much time to lose, and we must see some of the fun at all events."

The direction they had taken led them along a high spur of the hill, past a small body of soldiers, some of whom called to them; but, not hearing what they said, they went on; when, coming to the extreme end of the spur, they saw a deep glen before them. Plunging into it, they quickly climbed up on the other side, when they again found themselves on high ground. Just as they reached it, the loud rattle of musketry saluted their ears, and they caught sight of a large body of Russians making their way over another hill on their right, their advance opposed by some English light troops who were skirmishing in their front. On looking back, somewhat to their right, they caught sight of a brigade of English troops drawn up, and apparently standing at their ease, spectators of the fight. They could make out, however, in front of them, two or three batteries of guns. On came the Russians; every moment it seemed as if a general battle would begin.

"I wish we had rifles," cried Tom, "we'd go and join those brave fellows, and help to keep the Russians back."

"No, no," answered Archie, "that isn't our duty; the soldiers can do very well without us."

"Well, then, let's go to our left, where I see some bluejackets," said Tom, who had been looking through his telescope; "to my mind we ought then to be about-ship, and find our way to where we left our horses, or we shall be getting into a scrape."

To reach the spot at which Tom pointed they had again to descend into another valley, and to climb up some steep height; but this was a feat they easily performed. Scarcely, however, had they got there than they caught sight of a body of redcoats farther down the glen, firing rapidly as they retired before a dense mass of Russians. The English soldiers they made out in a short time to be Guardsmen, who, though retreating, were doing so with a definite object, and were certainly not running away. The midshipmen soon saw, a little in the rear of where they were standing, a trench towards which apparently the Guards were making their way. Archie suggested that they also should get behind the trench, and there do their best to help the Guards in resisting the enemy. Tom agreed that it was the wisest thing they could do. Scarcely had they got behind it than the English soldiers, numbering no more than sixty men, who had hitherto been retreating, came to a halt; and, getting behind the trench, stood shoulder to shoulder, as if determined to bar the farther progress of the Russian column. In vain the Russian officers endeavoured to get their men to advance; whenever they did so, they were met by a rattling fire, and a bristling line of bayonets. Thousands might have been in their rear, but they could make no impression on the gallant little band.

Scarcely had the Guards come to a halt than from the very midst of the Russian column two persons sprang out, and were received in their midst with a shout of joy. They proved to be one of their captains and a sergeant, whom they supposed had been taken prisoners or killed by the Russians. The officer advised the midshipmen to go, as they could do no good where they were.

"But before we wish you good-bye, sir, may we ask how you managed to get out alive from among so many Russians?" inquired Tom.

"In a very unexpected manner," answered the officer. "I had gone on with the sergeant to some distance ahead of the men, when, on turning an angle, we found ourselves confronted by a whole mass of Russians hurrying up at a great rate, apparently intending to effect a surprise. The first men we saw fired at us, and, after we had retreated up the hill, several followed, intending to make us prisoners, but we knocked them over with the butts of our rifles. We then found ourselves hurried along by the advancing masses of the enemy. As we had on our greatcoats, the fresh men did not recognise us, and, by taking care not to keep near the same persons longer than we could help, we were carried on till we caught sight of our own men directly in front of us; and the Russians thinking we were going to lead them against their foes, we were able, without a blow aimed at us, to leap into the midst of our friends."

"It was indeed a wonderful escape," said Tom; "but I wish you would let us stop and help you; we could use our rifles as well as your men."

To this the officer would not consent, again urging them to make good their retreat while they could do so without risk. After going a little way up the valley, they began to ascend the steep side of the hill to a place where they were protected from the shot which flew high over the heads of the gallant band below. On reaching the summit, they saw before them a battery manned by English sailors. They made their way into it, and as it was upon high ground, they could see, on their right, vast masses of Russians, who, having driven back the English skirmishers, now crowned the top of a high hill. The enemy soon afterwards, bringing up several field-pieces, began to fire at the English brigade in their front. Scarcely had they begun to do so than the English guns rapidly replied, their shot taking fearful effect upon the closely-pressed body of Russians, which seemed rent and torn in every direction by the iron showers hurled into their midst. For some time the Russians stood their ground bravely, and, more masses coming on, they threatened not only to cut off the gallant little band in the valley below, but to surround the battery in which the midshipmen were posted, and towards which several of the enemy's guns were now directed. The shot came flying into and around it; the bluejackets who manned the guns returned the fire with interest. But first one was struck, then another and another, and there appeared every probability that the battery would be overwhelmed.

Dangerous as was the position into which the midshipmen had got, they were ashamed to retreat. Several more men had been killed, when a sergeant hurried into the battery, ordering the naval officer in command to spike his guns and retreat. "When my captain directs me to do so, I will obey," was the answer. "In the meantime, this gun will be of service." As he spoke, the Russians, who had been driven from the hill on the right, were seen climbing up the sides of the valley, threatening to take the battery in reverse. Not a moment was to be lost; by immense exertion part of the parapet was thrown down. "Lend a hand, all of you," cried the naval officer. His appeal was responded to. The gun being slued round by the sailors and a few soldiers, the midshipmen exerting themselves with hearty goodwill, it was fired directly down upon the enemy with such effect that they immediately abandoned their intention of making their way in that direction, and retreated with the rest of the attacking force towards Sebastopol.

"Hurrah! we've done for them," cried Tom, unable to restrain his feelings of satisfaction, while the gun continued to hurl its missiles into the midst of the enemy as long as they were in sight.

The midshipmen, on their way back, fell in with the officer whose acquaintance they had just before made, and found that he and his gallant little band, with the aid of another small party, had not only defeated their host of foes, but had succeeded in making several of them prisoners. They now hurried back, under the guidance of a brother officer of Sidney's, to the Guards' camp. Sidney himself soon after arrived; and after rowing the midshipmen for having unnecessarily thrust their noses into danger, and giving Tom a message for Jack, bade them hasten back to Balaclava as fast as their steeds would carry them. They got a slight glimpse of the field of Inkerman, on which, before many days were over, a desperate battle was to be fought. From the high ground on which they stood near the Guards' camp, they could look down into a deep valley covered with brushwood, with a line of lofty hills on the farther side.

By urging on their steeds they got back to the harbour before dark. On reaching the ship, they heard that Lord Raglan had given up his intention of abandoning Balaclava. Next morning the *Tornado* sailed for Constantinople with a number of sick and wounded men. Several poor fellows died on the voyage, and the rest were carried to the hospital at Scutari.

CHAPTER XVII

Storm in the Black Sea—Jack aids Vessels in Distress—Rescues Murray—The *Tornado* renders Assistance—Shipwrecked Crew on Shore attacked by Cossacks—The Latter are driven off.

THE *Tornado*, exerting her steam-powers to the utmost, was on her way back to Balaclava. On the 13th of November the glass fell; the weather, which had hitherto been calm and sunny, began to change, and there was every indication of a heavy gale. The commander knew that his safest course would be to run back to Constantinople, but his orders were to proceed to Balaclava without loss of time. Soon after sunset a heavy squall struck the ship, followed by fitful gusts, gradually increasing in strength, while the hitherto calm sea was covered with foaming waves, through which the *Tornado* forced her way. Most of the officers were on deck, for few felt inclined to turn in; the lieutenants stood near the commander, ready to carry out his orders, while the midshipmen were collected in a group on the quarter-deck.

"This seems likely to prove a pretty heavy squall," observed Tom.

"You may call it a hurricane, lad, and you won't be far out," observed Jos Green, who overheard him. "May Heaven have mercy on the unfortunate vessels caught by it outside the harbour! the holding-ground is none of the best."

During the remainder of the night the *Tornado* stood on, a bright look-out being kept for any vessels which might, rather than trust to their anchors, be endeavouring to haul off the land; though none but the most powerful steamers, or very well-handled vessels, could hope to do so successfully with the fierce gale now blowing. As morning broke, the high cliffs of the Crimean coast could be seen ahead, while the masts of numerous vessels were distinguishable rolling from side to side, or tossed wildly up and down amid the sheets of spray which flew off the troubled waters. Jack could trust to his engines, and Jos Green, who was thoroughly acquainted with the entrance to Balaclava harbour, undertook, if necessary, to carry in the ship, though there was a risk of running foul of some of the numberless vessels brought up before it.

"Our orders are to go in, and the despatches we carry may be of importance," observed Jack. The *Tornado* accordingly stood on; as she approached, the fearful danger to which the ships at anchor were exposed, became more and more evident. Over many of the smaller vessels the sea was making a clean breach, sweeping their decks fore and aft; several of the larger ones were dragging their anchors; and three or four vessels had already broken away from them, and were driving rapidly towards the threatening rocks which frowned under their lee. Steamers were endeavouring to get up their steam; but too many had been caught unawares, and before they could get their engines to work, might be driving helplessly towards the cliffs.

Such was the spectacle which presented itself when the *Tornado* was still at some distance off. As she drew near, it was seen that matters were even worse than had been anticipated.

"There are three vessels on shore already," cried Higson, who had been looking through his glass; "their masts are gone, but I can make out their hulls, with the sea breaking over them and flying high up the cliffs—and there goes another large craft, a screw from her appearance. Had she got up her steam in time, she might have worked off the shore, but as it is, no power can save her."

As he spoke, the vessel at which he pointed was seen, by those who had their glasses at their eyes, to strike an outer reef; the next instant her hull was scarcely visible from the mass of foaming breakers which dashed furiously over her, and ere another minute had passed, she looked as if utterly torn to pieces, her vast hull rapidly melting away, till scarcely a single dark spot remained to show where her stout timbers had lately been.

"Can any of the poor fellows have escaped?" asked Tom.

"Not one," answered Green; "and from the size of the ship her crew must have numbered upwards of a hundred. It is only to be hoped that her passengers had landed; she was, I suspect, a large screw we saw pass through the straits a few days ago with troops and stores. There must be a fearful loss of life."

Jack was consulting with Higson as to the best means of rendering assistance to the vessels most in peril. Several had signals of distress flying; he was steering towards one of the nearest, over which the sea was breaking with extreme violence; it would be impossible to run alongside her, but ropes might be hove on board as the *Tornado* passed within a comparatively safe distance. Jack stood on, intent on his mission of mercy, but when his ship was scarcely three cables' length from the hapless vessel, a heavy sea with a prodigious crest went hissing towards her, just as a previous one of less height passing on had lifted her stern. The mass of water rolled onwards; for an instant her masts could be seen inclining forward, but her bows never again rose, and the foaming waves leaped wildly over the spot where she had been. Not a human being could be discovered to whom a rope or life-buoy might have been thrown; the latter, indeed, would have been useless; for even had a struggling swimmer clung to it, he must ultimately have been driven towards the cruel rocks on which the sea was fiercely beating.

But another sight still more fearful was to be witnessed. A Turkish line-of-battle ship lay some way out, pitching heavily into the seas. Suddenly her cables parted, her vast bulk availed her not, the savage seas caught her on the broadside. An attempt might have been made to cut away her masts, but long before the task could be accomplished, she heeled over, till the water rushed in through her lee-ports.

"She's gone! she's gone! no power can save her," exclaimed Higson. She never again rose on an even keel; for a few minutes her dark hull could be seen, the waves dashing over it. It sank lower and lower; again her masts rose suddenly, but already the foaming waters were above her bulwarks, and ere another minute had passed, her mastheads had disappeared beneath the surface. Many a stout heart on board the *Tornado* uttered a cry of grief as they saw the catastrophe. Long before they could reach the spot, the strongest swimmers of her crew must have perished. Not a human being could be discovered amid the tumbling seas.

Jack was unwilling to run into port while he could hope to render assistance to any of his fellow-creatures. Several vessels had signals of distress flying, and others could be seen in the distance, either driving towards the shore, or pitching so heavily into the seas that it was evident they were in the greatest possible danger of going down. Jack had been looking at one some way off along the coast, when his attention was directed to another vessel to the northward. When he next turned his head, the first had disappeared suddenly. In those few short moments she must have gone down with all on board. They had now to decide whether they would run into the harbour or keep the sea. Green urged that they should not venture nearer the coast; for should anything go wrong in the machinery, the *Tornado* must inevitably be driven on shore. The difficulty of entering the harbour was increased in consequence of several vessels, some of which had brought up off it, others having been drifted in that direction. The *Tornado's* head was accordingly brought round during a lull, and with topgallant-masts on deck and yards pointed to the wind she stood off shore.

"We came round not a minute too soon," observed Green, as he watched the progress the ship was making; "we are going ahead scarcely half a knot an hour."

Another vessel still lay a considerable way out on the port bow. "She'll not keep afloat many minutes longer," observed Higson, who had been watching her, "unless she parts from her anchors, and then it will only be to get out of the frying-pan into the fire."

"We might reach her, and should she appear likely to go down, we might get the crew out of her," observed Jack.

"It will be no easy matter, but it may be done," answered Higson.

"We'll try it," cried Jack, giving directions to Green, who was standing by the men at the helm, to edge the ship off towards the transport. As they approached her, they saw that they were arriving not a moment too soon. Already the seas were sweeping over her deck, and it seemed that each plunge she made would be her last. Jack determined to steer up on her starboard side; picked hands were stationed in the rigging, and in every spot whence ropes could be hove on board to assist the crew in escaping. They could scarcely hope to save all, but some by activity might avail themselves of the assistance offered them; the chief danger in the undertaking was that the sides of the vessels might strike each other, or that the rigging might get foul. To guard against this as much as possible, the lower and topsail braces were "manned" ready to "brace round" smartly in the event of her yards fouling those of the other vessel, and men were stationed with axes and tomahawks to cut the ropes.

The *Tornado* stood on till she was nearly astern of the vessel she was about to assist. The faces of the crew could be seen, as they turned their eyes towards the coming succour, while they clung on to the rigging and bulwarks of their ship, ready to seize the ropes hove to them. The danger to the *Tornado* was very great; for should the cable of the vessel ahead give way at that critical moment, she might be hurled against her bows, when, in all probability, both vessels would go down together. The *Tornado's* progress in the teeth of the gale was very slow, and the fear was that the vessel ahead would go down before she could reach her. On the other hand, when once she got alongside, more time would be allowed to the crew to leap on board. At length the *Tornado's* bows were up to the transport's quarter, but not till she was completely alongside, and both vessels should rise and fall on the same seas, could any attempt be made to rescue the crew.

"Don't heave a rope till I order you; and take care that the men are secure before you haul in," cried Jack. More than another minute passed; Green, who with two hands to assist him was at the helm, skilfully brought her alongside. "Now heave," cried Jack, and twenty ropes or more were hove with a good will on board the sinking vessel. Most of them were eagerly seized by the almost despairing crew; some fastened them round their waists, others, grasping them tightly, attempted to leap on the *Tornado's* bulwarks. Some succeeded, and were seized by the hands of those on board; others missed their footing, and, with shrieks of despair, letting go their hold, dropped into the intervening space. Many still remained on board; more ropes were hove to them; of these several were officers. Warned by the fate of those who had failed to leap on board the *Tornado*, each of them, as he caught a rope, secured it round his waist; some springing into the main, others into the mizzen-rigging, thus attaining a greater height. Among them Jack observed one who wore a naval uniform, though he had as yet been unable to distinguish his features.

The risk the *Tornado* was running of falling on board the vessel was very great, and Jack was about reluctantly to give the order to sheer off from her, when he saw the remainder of those on deck prepare to make the desperate leap which would either terminate in their destruction or place them in comparative safety. Just at that moment, as his eye was fixed on the naval officer, he recognised Murray.

"I must save him, at all events," was the thought which

passed through his mind. Murray had grasped the rope, which he was fastening round his waist; he sprang into the main rigging of the ship, and stood waiting for a favourable opportunity to take the desperate leap. Jack pointed him out to Higson, who, securing himself in the same manner, sprang up on to the hammock nettings, and, stretching out his hands, stood ready to grasp him. In another instant the two vessels must either be separated or be hurled against each other. Murray stood calmly holding on to the rigging by one hand, while with keen eye he watched the movements of the *Tornado*. Now her side rolled away from him, now it again approached, and seemed to be sinking far lower down than the level on which he stood. It was the moment for which he had waited; letting go his hold, he sprang with outstretched arms towards the *Tornado*. The crew held the rope; hauling it in, Higson grasped his hand at the same moment that his feet touched the hammock nettings of the *Tornado*, which the next was separated several feet from the vessel he had quitted.

Those who had hitherto hesitated to leap now sprang overboard, and were dragged up the side of the *Tornado* by her crew. The master and one of his mates were thus saved, but nearly half a dozen people still remained on board. Jack had barely time to shake Alick by the hand, but not a moment to inquire how he happened to be on board. Jack's wish was, if possible, to save the poor fellows still clinging to the sinking vessel.

"We may do it," said Higson; "but we've run a fearful risk already of losing the ship."

"We will try it," cried Jack.

"She's sinking! she's sinking!" shouted several voices.

Such indeed was the case; a heavy sea came rolling up, which even the *Tornado* with difficulty breasted, while it ran clear over the other vessel lying at anchor. For some moments it seemed doubtful whether she would rise, but another sea came hissing on into which her bows plunged, not again to appear. Those on deck must have been washed far away, for no human power could have withstood the furious sea which assailed them. Ere another minute had passed, the masts of the ill-fated vessel had disappeared beneath the foaming ocean.

The *Tornado's* best chance of safety was now to stand out to sea, and to battle bravely with the storm while it should last; still, while there was a possibility of rendering assistance to others in distress, Jack was unwilling to go to a distance. Some way off was another vessel with signals of distress flying; he ordered Green to keep away for her, intending to try and get the people off if there was a risk of her foundering, as he had done from the first vessel. The sound of a gun came from her, as if to show her urgent necessity for help; another and another followed.

"We are doing our best," muttered Higson; "though it's little good, I fear, we can do you."

The sound of the last gun had just reached their ears when the vessel from which it came was seen to be moving; her cable had parted. Away she drove before the fierce gale; her crew were seen attempting to range another cable. The sea caught her starboard bow, and she drove bodily onwards towards the rocky shore on which the fierce breakers were raging savagely. To attempt getting nearer would have been worse than useless, for Jack saw that should he try to do so, he might involve his ship in her fate.

Though many others had signals of distress flying, Jack knew well that he could render them no effectual assistance, and therefore once more put the *Tornado's* head off shore. He now for the first time had leisure to inquire from Murray how he happened to be on board the vessel which had gone down. Murray briefly told him that he had been sent by the admiral, who had steamed on to the Katcha, with despatches on board the Turkish flagship, with directions afterwards to visit several other vessels, and then to run in to Balaclava. He had been detained on board the Turkish ship longer than he expected, and his boat being nearly swamped before he had finished his mission, he had gone alongside the nearest vessel, intending to remain on board till the morning. His boat had been lost before she could be hoisted up, and the gale having so rapidly increased, he had been prevented leaving in one of her boats. Three of his people had unhappily been lost, but the remainder succeeded in reaching the *Tornado*.

"I am indeed thankful that we came to you in time," said Jack; "though I little expected when I determined to run down to the assistance of that vessel, that I should be the means of saving your life."

"Not the first time that we have helped each other, and I am very sure that it will not be the last if we either of us require help and have the opportunity of rendering it," answered Murray. "I expect soon to be appointed to the command of a ship, as the admiral has offered me the first vacancy, which Hemming advises me to accept, as the smaller craft will in future have more to do than the line-of-battle ships."

As may be supposed, there was but little time for conversation. Jack still wished, if possible, to try and render assistance to some of the many other vessels at anchor off the coast, but both Higson and Green strongly expressed their opinion that the attempt to do so would endanger the ship; and Murray concurring with them, he was compelled to abandon his intention. The *Tornado* proved herself a first-rate sea-boat; indeed, had she not been so, she would have shared the fate of so many other vessels during that fearful gale. By keeping her head to the southward, she was able in a short time gradually to draw off shore.

For the greater part of the night the gale blew with unabated fury. Towards morning, however, the wind began to abate. Soon after daylight the ship's head was brought round, and she stood back towards Balaclava. A melancholy spectacle was presented to those on board, as she neared the harbour; the whole coast, as far as the eye could reach, was strewn with masses of wreck, while the entrance was nearly blocked up with shattered spars and pieces of timber; while numerous dead bodies floated about, or had been thrown by the foaming surges on the rocks on either hand. The *Tornado*, having not without difficulty made her way in, brought up; and Jack immediately sent his despatches on shore. The vessels in the harbour had not escaped. Brought up close together, they had been driven in one mass towards the head of the harbour, directly down upon the line-of-battle ship at anchor, carrying her upwards of a hundred yards, when she grounded by the stern; while few had escaped without more or less damage.

The gale considerably abated towards noon, when Jack received orders to run down the coast, to try and bring off any of the crews which might have escaped from the wrecked ships. Accordingly, he immediately got up steam and put to sea. A number of boats were already engaged in the humane object; but few of the people belonging to the vessels which had been wrecked in the immediate neighbourhood of Balaclava had escaped. Farther down the coast, however, two or three ships were seen on shore, from which it was possible the crews might have landed in safety. Jack kept in as close as he could venture, steering for the first wreck he saw. She lay with her masts gone broadside to the sea, which was sweeping fiercely over her. Not a human being was seen near the wreck.

"Not a man, I fear, could have escaped," said Jack, as he surveyed the coast with his glass; "and yet, from the position of the vessel, I cannot help thinking that they might have made their way to the shore—see, near yonder wreck farther south, a good number of people appear to be collected."

The *Tornado* was accordingly steered in the direction Jack pointed. Higson had been watching the group through his telescope.

"They appear to be expecting an attack," he observed; "there are fifty or more of them, and they are standing to their arms. Their ship is evidently a large transport, and from her position I should judge that they managed to land without much difficulty, and would carry their muskets and ammunition with them."

Directly afterwards a forest of lances were seen above the hill, and a band of Cossacks came galloping towards the wreck. Jack immediately ordered the port gun to be brought to bear on the advancing horsemen, who seemed not to be aware that they could be reached from that distance, and went on, making sure of being able to capture the whole shipwrecked crew. On seeing that the latter were armed, they levelled their lances, and were bearing down upon them, when Jack gave the word to fire. The first shot struck the horse of their leader, which came down, rolling over him; it seemed as if both rider and steed were killed. The next shot pitched into the midst of their ranks, emptying at least a couple of saddles. The third shot did still more damage; when the Cossacks, not knowing how many more might be coming, wheeled quickly round and galloped off into the interior; the crew of the transport, meantime, firing a volley which, though at a considerable distance, brought two or three to the ground.

As soon as he came abreast of the wreck, Jack sent three of his boats on shore to bring off the crew; Murray volunteered to take command of them. As he neared the beach, he saw the Cossacks still hovering in the distance, out of the reach of the guns, but threatening to pounce down again, probably still in the hopes of making some prisoners. The *Tornado* accordingly stood in as close as she could venture, to cover the boats, which soon reached the beach. The transport's crew stood ready to receive them; scarcely, however, had they begun to embark, than the Cossacks once more came galloping up. Murray immediately ordered those still remaining on shore to face about; while, just as the Cossacks reached the high ground above the beach, a couple of shells thrown from the *Tornado's* guns burst amid their ranks; when, once more wheeling about, they galloped off at a rapid rate, leaving the rest of the crew to embark without molestation.

Having carried them on board, Murray returned for the purpose of destroying the transport, that her stores might not fall into the hands of the enemy. He had for this purpose to pull round inshore. It was not without some difficulty that he, Higson, and Needham made their way on board. Such combustible materials as could be found were soon collected, and lighted in the hold of the transport; the boat then at once pulled away for the *Tornado*. She had got to some little distance from the ship, when the Cossacks were again seen coming down towards the shore, this time accompanied by a couple of field-pieces, which quickly opened fire. The first shot, however, fell short, and the party were soon safe on board the *Tornado*.

As the *Tornado* steamed off, the Cossacks were seen again coming forward, in the hopes possibly of still being able to plunder the wreck. Just then, however, the flames burst furiously forth from every part of the wreck, and in another minute a loud roar was heard, and a portion of her deck rose high in the air, while her sides, rent and shattered, flew out in every direction; and as the smoke from the explosion cleared away, a few burnt timbers of the wreck alone remained, while the Cossacks, disappointed of their booty, were seen galloping off in the distance.

The scanty remnant of another shipwrecked crew having been saved by the *Tornado*, she steamed back to Balaclava. During that fearful storm no less than forty vessels, with upwards of four hundred men, had been lost; one Turkish line-of-battle ship, and several transports, had gone down with all hands. The French lost one of their finest line-of-battle ships and a corvette, with nearly twenty smaller craft. The most severe loss was that of the *Prince*, with a crew of a hundred and fifty men; she had arrived two days before with troops, who had providentially landed—but the army was doomed to suffer terribly from the loss of her cargo, consisting of warm clothing, ammunition, medicine, and supplies of all kinds.

A few ships being left to watch Sebastopol, the remainder of the fleet and all the transports were sent back to the Bosphorus; and soon afterwards, Admiral Dundas having struck his flag, Sir Edmund Lyons became commander-in-chief.

CHAPTER XVIII

State of Affairs in the beginning of 1855—Murray in Command of the *Giaour*—Shelling Sebastopol by Night—Tom finds matter for Serious Thought—The *Tornado* chases a Russian Steamer—Attack on a Fort—Another Steamer sighted—Friend or Foe?—Proves to be the *Giaour*—The *Flash* appears—The Fort Stormed.

THE fearful Christmas of 1854 was over, and of the troops, which in gallant array had left England, more than one-half had died or been disabled by the shot of the enemy or the still more deadly pestilence. Sufferings, such as an English army had never before been called upon to endure, had been borne with fortitude. The siege, notwithstanding, had been carried on, and now reinforcements, and clothing, and stores, and provisions were arriving in the camp of the allies. Affairs looked brighter than they had done for many a day; the fleet, notwithstanding the battering some of the ships had received at the opening of the bombardment, was in as efficient a state as ever. It had rendered good service at Eupatoria in assisting the Turks to defend the place against a powerful force of Russians, which had been driven back with great loss. The naval brigade had been doing good service on shore, not only in the batteries, but by laying down a railway from Balaclava to the Chersonese, by which the transport of heavy guns, ammunition, and stores was greatly facilitated.

The *Tornado* had not been idle, though, in consequence of the straining her engines had received during the storm, she had been compelled to remain some time at Constantinople, to have them set to rights. Once more she was steaming across the waters of the Black Sea, with another vessel of similar size in company.

"The *Giaour* will beat us if we can't get up more steam," observed Jack to his first lieutenant, who was walking the deck with him.

"We have on our full power, and are doing our utmost,"

answered Higson; "the *Giaour's* engines are new, and we must make up our minds, I suspect, to let Commander Murray get ahead of us."

"I am always happy to follow wherever he leads," said Jack; "if there is work to be done, he'll find out the way to do it."

The *Giaour* was coming up slowly on the *Tornado's* quarter, gaining foot after foot but never losing an inch, so that at length she was abreast of her; both vessels were steering for Sebastopol. The land was soon afterwards made, and, as they approached, the admiral's flag was seen flying at the masthead of the *Royal Albert*, a magnificent three-decker of a hundred and thirty guns, to which Sir Edmund Lyons had shifted it from the *Agamemnon*. She, and several other English and French line-of-battle ships, lay across the entrance of the harbour, effectually preventing any of the enemy's ships from getting out.

"The admiral is speaking to us and the *Giaour*," said Tom, who was acting as signal midshipman.

"Let's see what he is saying," said Jack, looking at the signal-book; "it's 'Keep under weigh' and 'Commanders to repair on board the admiral's ship.' We are to be sent somewhere together, I hope."

The two steamers closed rapidly with the fleet, beyond which could be seen the frowning batteries on the other side of the harbour of Sebastopol; while on the right appeared thin curls of smoke, marking the course of the shells thrown from the lines of the allies into the city and those sent by the batteries in return: while the thunder of the artillery was heard with fearful distinctness. On reaching the flagship, Jack and Murray went on board, when they received directions to take a part in the work which had been going on nightly. Some time before, the boats of the fleet had set up signals on shore within reach of the French camp, and men were sent down soon after dark to light them. By their means every night an English and French steamer had stood in and shelled the town, greatly to the astonishment of the Russians, who were utterly unprepared for such a mode of attack. They of course fired in return; but as they could scarcely see their foes, the ships were but seldom struck; while not only did they commit a good deal of harm, but thus harassed the garrison by night as well as by day.

Jack was to take the lead that night, in company with a French ship. All hands were well pleased at the work cut out for them, and eagerly looked forward to the hours of darkness when they might begin shelling the enemy, little troubled by the thoughts of the shot which might be sent on board them from the Russian guns in return. Tom and Archie were especially in high glee at the thoughts of what they were to do.

"Who knows but one of our shells may burst in one of the enemy's chief magazines, or knock down some of their defences, and allow the allies to take the place?" said Tom.

"We shall not be much the wiser if we do do it," observed Archie; "and, depend upon it, they will insist that it was their own guns did the work."

Soon after dark the *Tornado* and her French consort steamed in towards the harbour, steering by the lights which had been placed on shore. The screws made but little noise, and perfect silence was maintained on board, so that the enemy could not discover their whereabouts till they opened fire. The lights were so placed as to enable them to know with terrible accuracy the position of the forts into which they were to fire. As they glided onwards through the darkness for some minutes together, not a sound was heard in the direction of the beleaguered city, which to all appearance lay in profound slumber. Then came from the far distance the reports of a few dropping shot, showing that the riflemen of both parties were awake. They again ceased, and the same silence as before reigned over the scene.

The *Tornado's* heavy guns were loaded, and elevated to throw their shot into the city, and their crews stood ready to fire at the word of command. Jack waited till his ship had reached the point he was directed to gain. "Fire!" he shouted. The next instant the loud roar of his guns echoed through the harbour, arousing many a weary sleeper in the Russian fortifications. The French ship immediately fired her guns in rapid succession, and then both vessels steamed round away from the spot they had previously occupied, towards which numberless Russian guns immediately directed their fire, though not a shot touched either of them. The *Tornado's* guns were reloaded, and, standing back, she rapidly discharged them, the French ship following her example. Again the shot from the forts came rushing through the air, falling around the ships, but without striking them. In this way they continued circling round, now firing from one point, now from another, and each time after firing taking different directions.

At length every gun which could be brought to bear on the harbour began to play upon them, but, by keeping ever on the move, for a considerable time not a shot took effect. At length, as Tom and Archie were standing close together, a shot from one of the heights whistled by close to their heads, and struck the bulwarks behind them.

"I say, Tom, if that shot had been a few inches on one side, where should you and I have been by this time?" said Archie.

"Not a pleasant subject for contemplation," answered Tom; "however, a miss is as good as a mile."

"I have been thinking seriously of the matter," observed Archie; "not that I am afraid, but I am very sure that we ought to be prepared to go out of the world, seeing that at any moment either of us may lose our lives."

"It doesn't do to think of that sort of thing," said Tom, not liking Archie's tone.

"Now there you're wrong. I believe that it is much wiser to think about it than to be taken unprepared," replied Archie. "My Cousin Alick thinks very seriously, and no one can say that he is not as brave an officer as any man in the fleet. I tell you honestly that I have been saying my prayers, and asking God to help me to take Him at His word, and to trust to His plan of salvation—that is what I want you to do, Tom, also. I should be very miserable if I saw you killed and could not feel sure that you had gone to heaven. I should be unhappy in either case; but it would be ten times worse if I thought that I should not meet you again."

"Do you really, Archie, think that I am so wicked that if I was to be killed I should not go to heaven?" said Tom.

"I only know what the Bible says about it, and I believe that," answered Archie firmly. "Just obey God, and you'll be all right, and it won't make you a bit less brave than you are now."

"I will," said Tom; "still I hope that neither you nor I will be hit to-night, though the shot are falling pretty thickly about us."

The moment after he had spoken, a loud cry was heard from one of the crew of the nearest gun, and the sound of a person falling heavily. They sprang to the spot, and found a seaman stretched on the deck. They tried to lift him up, but, inexperienced though they were, they both felt convinced that he was dead. Others, coming up, confirmed their opinion; the shot had struck his chest, and killed him in a moment.

Notwithstanding the heavy fire to which his ship was exposed, Jack continued at his post, firing away till the hour arrived at which he was directed to leave the harbour; and he and his French consort steamed away to rejoin the fleet. Tom was unusually serious during the following day.

"I say, Rogers, what's the matter with you?" asked Billy Blueblazes.

"He didn't quite like the fun we had last night," observed Dicky Duff.

"I'll tell you what, youngster," said Tom, "you wouldn't have thought it any fun if either of you had one of those Russian round shot walking into you, as poor Norris had."

On which Tom spoke to them as Archie had been speaking to him, much to the latter's satisfaction, for it showed him that his words had not been thrown away. Tom, indeed, afterwards came to him, and begged that he would get out his Bible, and more fully explain what he had been talking about on the previous night. Archie gladly did so. It was the beginning of many Bible readings they had together. Others joined them, and they then to their surprise found that several of the men had long been in the practice of meeting together to pray and study God's Word. They heard also that such was done on board many of the ships in the fleet, and that the men who thus occupied themselves were looked upon as the best and steadiest of their respective crews.

The next night Murray was directed to stand in and engage the forts, also accompanied by a French ship. Thus, night after night, the fleet harassed the unfortunate garrison, while the guns of the besieging army played on them in the daytime, giving them no rest during the four-and-twenty hours.

A short time after this a considerable squadron, composed of English, French, and Turkish ships, with some thousand troops on board, proceeded to the eastward, for the purpose of attacking Kertch, at the entrance of the Sea of Azov. Well might the garrison of Sebastopol have felt alarm when they saw the fleet sailing past the mouth of their harbour, for on the shores of that inland sea were placed the chief granaries from which they drew their supplies of provisions.

The *Tornado* and *Giaour*, with numerous other steam-vessels, accompanied the fleet. Passing along the rocky and picturesque southern shore of the Crimea, the expedition soon came off Cape St. Paul, in a small bay near which the troops were landed without a casualty; the steam-vessels scattering a body of Cossacks, the only hostile force that appeared to dispute the disembarkation. The line-of-battle ships continued their course along the coast, which at every available spot was strongly fortified. The ships were standing in to attack the batteries when a thundering roar was heard, the concussion from which shook even the vessels at sea. Another and another followed.

"The Russians are performing our work for us, and saving Her Majesty a considerable expenditure of gunpowder," observed Higson to his commander. "I am afraid if they play that trick, of which they seem so fond, they will leave us nothing to do."

"Never fear, we shall be too quick for them," answered Jack; "and, from what I hear, there are numerous magazines all round the coast."

"The inhabitants of Kertch must be glad to save their town from a bombardment, for really it is a much handsomer place than I expected to find in this part of the world, and those lofty stone houses give it a very imposing appearance," observed Higson.

"At all events, we shall not have injured them," observed Jack; "we are especially directed to do as little harm as possible to private property, and to let the Russians understand that we are not warring with them, but with the Emperor and his Government."

The fleet having thus gained a bloodless victory, the line-of-battle ships came to an anchor; the larger number of the steamers proceeded into the Sea of Azov, while the remainder were sent along the coast to look out for any vessels which might have been concealed in any of the inlets or deep bays with which it is everywhere indented. The *Tornado* was ordered on this service, greatly to the disappointment of her crew, who expected to have more stirring work within the Straits.

She had just lost sight of the fleet, when standing in as close as she could venture, Jos Green, who was forward, observed a light cloud of smoke ascending above a rocky point, the summit of which was feathered with a grove of lofty trees. It was a question, however, whether the smoke proceeded from a fire on shore or from the funnel of a steamer. Green inclined to the latter opinion. It had moved some distance since he first sighted it, he declared, so that it must come from a steamer on her way out to sea. The *Tornado* stood on, keeping as close inshore as possible, so that her presence might not be discovered till the other vessel had got well clear of the point;

after that, Jack hoped to get up to her before she could run in anywhere else for shelter.

A suppressed cheer from those on deck showed that Green was right, and the *Tornado* stood away after the stranger. The latter was no laggard, and it was soon evident that the *Tornado* must do her best if she was to come up with her. The chase, though a vessel of some size, showed no inclination to come to close quarters with her pursuer.

"If we can but keep her in sight, we shall catch her at last," said Jack; "and if she runs into any harbour, we must follow her, or send the boats in after her."

"We haven't had anything so exciting for a long time," said Tom; "I hope that we may have to cut her out with the boats."

"Her crew will blow her up sooner than let us do that," observed Archie; "the Russians seem to be fonder of that sort of thing than fighting."

The chase, however, kept well ahead, and there seemed a good prospect, should night come on, of her escaping altogether. Still the *Tornado* was really going faster than the Russian vessel, though so slight was the difference of speed, that at first it was scarcely discernible. At length, however, Jack considered that he had got the Russian vessel within range of his long guns, and was on the point of issuing the order to fire, when a shot from her came flying across the intervening space, but fell some twenty fathoms or so short of its mark.

"And now, let's see what we can do," cried Jack; "starboard the helm—steady—now, fire!" The *Tornado's* shot struck the Russian's counter, apparently committing a considerable amount of damage. This first specimen of the power of his pursuer's guns seemed to satisfy him that he had better not engage at close quarters. The dense volumes of smoke which issued from his funnel proved that he was endeavouring to get more steam, in the hopes of still keeping ahead. As the *Tornado* could not be made to move faster than she was then going, Jack had to content himself with the prospect of the chase's getting on shore, running short of coal, or of some accident happening to her machinery. Another shot was tried, but it fell short, showing that she had again drawn ahead. Some miles more had been run, when Green brought the chart on deck, and pointed out a fort situated on the shores of a bay a short distance off.

"The chase has evidently been making for that, and thinks that she will be secure under its guns," he observed.

"We'll stand on, and attack both ship and fort together," said Jack; "we'll sink the ship first, and then knock the fort to pieces."

In about ten minutes more the chase rounded a point, when a bay opened out, on the farther side of which appeared a strong-looking fort, guarding the mouth of a river which ran into the bay.

"She may escape us after all if she runs up that river," observed Higson, "unless we can first silence the guns of the fort, and then follow her."

"We must just do that same then; and if we can't knock the fort to pieces with our guns, we must land and storm it," said Jack.

His remark was received with universal satisfaction, as no one thought of the superior number of the garrison likely to oppose them. The chase was now more eagerly watched than ever, it being fully expected that she would run up the river to escape them; instead, however, of doing so, as she drew near the fort she let off her steam, and came to an anchor close under its guns.

"Now we've got her," cried Jack exultingly.

The *Tornado* stood on to within half a mile of the fort, when she opened fire on it, and now on the ship, which fired with some spirit in return; but as the *Tornado* kept moving about, their shot invariably missed her. She had been thus engaged for a quarter of an hour or more, her guns having told with considerable effect on the Russian vessel, when a column of smoke was seen ascending at some little distance behind the fort, apparently from the river.

"That must proceed from another steamer coming down to assist our friend," observed Higson; "and see, there is another rising just beyond it—we shall have no lack of enemies to fight."

"We must settle with the first, then, as soon as possible," cried Jack, in a cheery tone; "we'll then take the others in detail."

The crew cheered as they heard his remark, and worked away at the guns with redoubled zeal. Several shot had struck the vessel under the fort; first one of her guns ceased firing, then another and another; still she kept her colours flying, and in another minute the bows of a steamer were seen emerging from the mouth of the river. A shot was instantly fired at her; it struck her bulwarks, and evidently caused some damage. Instead, however, of running under the guns of the fort, she stood away up the bay, evidently not wishing to come to close quarters with the audacious stranger. A few minutes afterwards another vessel appeared, which, receiving one of the *Tornado's* shot, followed the example of the first. After getting nearly two miles away, they brought their broadsides round, and opened a brisk fire. The *Tornado*, however, moving rapidly about as before, escaped every one of their shot; while she fired her guns as they came to bear on her antagonists, and seldom failed to hull one or other of them. Still, their guns were of heavier calibre than hers, and their shot frequently went far beyond her, and she had to stand towards them to make hers tell with effect.

At length a shot came crashing on board just abaft the funnel, wounding one man severely, and another, Tim Nolan, slightly.

"Arrah, now, it's but a fleabite," he exclaimed, getting a shipmate to bind a handkerchief round his shoulder; "we've given them more than that already, and it's better than having the funnel shot away."

Still Jack had no intention of abandoning the attack, and, wishing to settle the first vessel before he attended to the other two, he directed his guns at her and at the fort, although the shot from the former continually hulled him. One, at length, went through the ship's side between wind and water, and the sea came rushing in like a mill-sluice. The midshipmen, who up to this time were enjoying the fighting, thought that things were beginning to look serious.

Dicky Duff, especially, expressed his apprehensions to his chum Billy. "If another shot comes in like that, we shall certainly go to the bottom; and I am not quite sure what will happen even now, for the commander has not told us to knock off firing. I wonder if he knows what has happened? He is such a plucky fellow, however, that I suppose he will go on fighting till the ship sinks below our feet."

The youngsters were somewhat relieved by seeing the carpenter and his crew going below with the means for stopping the shot-hole; while Ben Snatchblock, with a rope round his waist, allowed himself to be slung overboard to reach the injury still more rapidly from the outside. He had just performed his task, when another shot went right through the forepart of the ship; happily, without hitting anyone, and the damage it had caused was as quickly repaired as the other had been. Jack had carried on the unequal contest for half an hour or more, when a third steamer was seen gliding out of the river, and as she opened her fire, it was soon discovered that her guns were heavier than those of either of her consorts. The first shot she fired came crashing through the *Tornado's* side.

"I suppose we shall have to run for it now," cried Dicky.

"Not a bit of it," exclaimed Tom, who overheard him; "the commander wouldn't be turned from his purpose, even if a dozen Russian steamers came out on us, and we shall soon settle with our old friend—she has not fired a shot for the last minute." As he was speaking, a thick smoke rose from the afterpart of their antagonist, followed quickly by bright flames, which darted upwards through the hatchway. Directly afterwards a fire burst out in the forepart of the ship, and raged with a fury which it was clear the crew were incapable of overcoming. Her boats were lowered, and her people were seen dropping down into them with a rapidity which showed that they had abandoned all hope of saving their ship. As they could no longer offer any resistance, Jack humanely ordered his crew to refrain from firing on them. He directed, however, all his guns at the fort, for the purpose of silencing them before the other vessels should come up to take a closer part in the action, which he fully expected that they would do.

Though the damage he had received was considerable, there was nothing as yet, he conceived, sufficiently serious to make him haul off. Still he could not help wishing to see the flag of the fort come down, comparatively slight as was the damage he had received from its guns. Having destroyed the vessel he had chased, he might without any discredit haul off, considering the immense superiority of the force opposed to him; but Jack Rogers was not a man to haul down his flag, or get out of a fight, as long as he had a stick standing; and his spirit animating his officers and crew, the *Tornado* kept blazing away, throwing shells into the fort, and firing shot, as he could bring his guns to bear at the three steamers. They had now, however, drawn considerably nearer than they had hitherto ventured to approach, and there seemed considerable likelihood of Dicky Duff's apprehensions being fulfilled.

Jack now looked at the three vessels, now at the fort. "It might be done," he said, turning to Higson, "if the fort were stormed, and its guns turned against the steamers."

"I would undertake it," said Higson; "but with its own garrison and the crew of the vessel which has just been burnt, it would be a hard job."

"I would ask no one to lead it but myself," said Jack; "I will leave you to fight the vessel in the meantime; should I be killed, I give you orders to retire, for with a diminished crew you would have little prospect of doing more than has already been accomplished."

"I do not advise you to command the expedition," said Higson; "you know me, and that I am not likely to be stopped by any ordinary hazard."

Jack, without answering, still kept eyeing the shore, looking out for a place where his boats might land.

"There's a steamer in the offing, sir, standing in for the bay," said Archie, coming up to him.

"Another enemy," exclaimed Higson; "we shall have enough of them."

"We'll tackle them, notwithstanding," answered Jack; "they show no inclination, however, to come to close quarters."

Another shot from the enemy struck the *Tornado*.

"The commander is just a little o'er brave," observed Dicky Duff to Billy Blueblazes; "we've got terrible odds against us."

"He knows what he is about, and he'll manage to lick them all, one after another, depend on that," said Billy.

"I don't exactly see how he's going to do that," said Dicky. "If we could but tackle one at a time it would be fairer, and we should have a better chance of licking them."

"That's just what they don't want to give us," said Billy.

"Another steamer coming in from the southward, sir," said Archie, who had been looking out.

"Friend or foe?" observed Jack to Higson; "if the latter, we must stand out and meet her, and leave the three vessels in the bay till we can come back and settle with them."

Still Jack showed no inclination to quit the neighbourhood of the fort, into which shell after shell was thrown, till most of its guns had been silenced. Many an eye, however, was turned towards the approaching strangers, till at length the first showed English colours. A cheer rose from those of the crew not engaged at the guns, the only sign they gave of their desire for assistance. In another minute the number of the approaching steamer was made out,

"She's the *Giaour*," exclaimed Archie.

If Jack ever felt any inclination to be jealous of Murray it was now, as he was his superior officer; but the feeling which arose in his breast was speedily quelled. The *Giaour* came rapidly on; Murray signalised to Jack, "Remain where you are, and I will attack the vessels in the bay." Jack ordered the signal to be made, "They will attempt to escape up the river." "Stand on and stop them," was the answer from the *Giaour*.

The *Tornado* accordingly steamed on towards her three antagonists, which now began to turn their heads, as Jack had expected they would, towards the mouth of the river. They were thus unable any longer to fire at him, while he was still able to reach them with two of his guns, one firing shot and the other shell. The *Giaour* now signalised, "Steamer to the south, English."

"Hurrah!" exclaimed Tom; "we are now on equal terms, and can bag the whole of them."

The three Russian vessels were still half a mile away from the mouth of the river when Jack got off it, and by this time the *Giaour* was near enough to take a part in the engagement, her shot beginning to tell with considerable effect on the nearest of the enemy. The Russian vessels now swept round, apparently with the intention of running across the bay, firing their broadsides at the *Tornado*, but with little effect; and she, in return, as they exposed their sterns in flight, kept up a brisk fire at them with shot and shell. One of them now burst into flames, and in half a minute blew up, destroying the greater number of her unhappy crew.

The other two, however, still continued on their course, hoping, apparently, to get out of the bay ahead of the *Giaour*, not being aware, it was evident, that another English ship was near at hand to cut them off. Jack, knowing that they must both be intercepted, made a signal asking leave of Murray to pick up any of the Russians still floating on the wreck of the steamer. This request was at once granted; and, lowering two of his boats, of one of which Tom took the command, and of the other Ben Snatchblock, he again stood on in pursuit of the two steamers. They, however, had not got far when they made out a third vessel coming to attack them, and finding that all hope of escape was cut off, they both hauled down their colours.

Murray, who was nearest to them, at once sent a couple of boats to take possession of the two prizes; while Jack stood back to pick up his boats. Of the whole of the Russian crew they had saved but six men, two of whom were much burnt, and one died directly after he had been taken on board the *Tornado*. One of the survivors, a Fin, who, having served on board English merchantmen, spoke English perfectly, informed Jack that a considerable quantity of corn and other provisions were stored in warehouses on the banks of the river, some way from its mouth.

"It is our duty to destroy them," said Jack to Higson.

"I will undertake to do it," was the answer. An expedition was at once planned, the command of which Jack, with Murray's approval, gave to Higson; Archie was to accompany him, while Green and Tom were to go in another boat. The fort, however, still held out, and several of its guns had again opened fire on the English vessels. Murray determined to take it by assault as soon as the approaching steamer had come into the bay. She now made her number; the bunting flying from her masthead showed her to be the *Flash*.

"She can only lately have arrived in the Black Sea, and is probably on her way to join the fleet, for she was only building when we left home," observed Jack. "I wonder who commands her."

By the time the preparations for attacking the fort had been made the *Flash* had come close up to the *Giaour*. A gig from the former was seen to pull to the latter vessel; Murray now made a signal to Jack to come on board; he was soon alongside the *Giaour*. Stepping on deck, who should he see with his hand extended to greet him but Terence Adair; standing a little way behind him was Gerald Desmond. Archie, who had accompanied his commander, and Desmond were soon in eager conversation; while Jack, at Murray's invitation, went below with Adair. There was only just time for Jack to hear that Terence's former ship, having received some damage, had been sent home to be repaired, and that he in the meantime had been appointed to the command of the *Flash* destined for the Black Sea.

"I was glad to get her," he observed; "for, judging from our first year's experience in the Baltic, I suspected that we were not likely to have much to do in that part of the world; first, because the Russians showed no inclination to come out and fight us; and, secondly, because Charley Napier"—

"Never mind the second reason," interrupted Murray;

"here you are, and very glad we are to see you; and now let me hear what you say to our proposed attack on this fort."

"That I am perfectly ready to go in for it," answered Adair. "How many boats' crews do you require, or shall I send the whole of my ship's company?"

"Two boats' crews will be sufficient, and the sooner you send them off the better," replied Murray.

"In other words, you direct me to trundle on board as fast as I can," said Adair. "I should like to lead the expedition myself, and as we pull in I can take a sufficient survey of the fort for the purpose. As I have had no share in the glories of the campaign, you will not refuse me?"

Murray willingly agreed to Adair's request, and two of the *Flash's* boats being quickly manned, the three steamers stood towards the fort. As they approached, they were received by a pretty hot fire, which they returned, while still standing on, with shells from their guns; and, running close in, they brought their broadsides to bear on the fort, into which they forthwith poured a shower of shot and shell. The boats then cast off, and, led by Adair, pulled for a landing-place on one side, from which a road led up apparently into the interior. The ships meantime kept up a furious bombardment on the fort; and though one gun from it was brought to bear on the boats, none of them were hit. Adair, rapidly pulling for the shore, quickly landed, and without a moment's loss of time led the way up the hill. Every instant he expected to see the enemy, but none appeared. Turning to the right, and keeping under cover of some rocks and trees, he made his way towards the fort. Ben Snatchblock had been provided with a red flag, which he exhibited at the last point whence it could be seen from the ships; and it was calculated that in three minutes more after this the party would reach the rear of the fort. Directly that time had elapsed, the ships were to cease firing.

Adair and Higson led, followed closely by Ben, the two midshipmen being ordered to bring up the rear. Ben having showed his flag, the party rushed on, and directly afterwards a shower of bullets whistled over the spot where they had been; but by that time Tom and Archie were a dozen yards ahead. In less than three minutes they had reached the ditch in the rear of the fort. Not a Russian helmet was to be seen on that side; Adair and Higson had to restrain the ardour of their followers, who were eager to climb over the defences. They waited till the last shot fired from the ships came crashing into the fort; three or four seconds passed, and no others came. Adair began to count—"One, two, three, four, five, six—now, my lads, you may come on!" he exclaimed; and he and his party, springing forward, began, with the agility of cats, to climb over the defences.

Not a Russian soldier could be seen except those who were labouring at the guns, the rest of the garrison having wisely betaken themselves to their bomb-proof chambers. In consequence of the hot fire kept up by the ships, they had not expected that the party they had seen landing were about to attack them, and Terence and his men had actually jumped down into the fort before the garrison had mustered in sufficient force to resist them. They were, of course, quickly seen; the bugle sounded, and the troops rushed out of their bomb-proof chambers. A considerable body, headed by their commandant, at length drew up across the fort for the purpose of impeding the progress of their daring assailants.

"On, lads, on!" cried Adair, seeing that their best chance of victory was to attack the garrison before they had time to form into a compact body. They had indeed been completely taken by surprise, many having hurried out without bayonets fixed, others with unloaded muskets, some only with pikes or swords in their hands. Ben Snatchblock had brought an English ensign under his arm; keeping his eye on the flagstaff, he directed his course, with a few companions, towards it. As Adair and Higson led on the main body, the garrison gave way, some hurrying off to conceal themselves in the chambers from which they had just before emerged, while others made for a gate in the rear of the fort leading to the drawbridge, which was, however, up. Before they could lower it, Adair, with most of his men, was upon them, when, with a loud voice, he ordered them not to touch the chains unless they wished to be cut to pieces.

Meantime Ben and his companions were fighting their way towards the flagstaff; a few men who were collected were quickly put to flight.

"Now, up goes the British ensign and the fort is ours," cried Ben; and, suiting the action to the word, the Russian flag being hauled down, that of England was hoisted in its stead. The commandant, finding that the fort had really been captured by the English, came forward with a low bow, and presented the hilt of his sword to Adair, who took it in the most gracious manner he could assume, observing as he did so, "You have gallantly defended your fort, and deserve every consideration at our hands; but at the same time I must warn you that I cannot allow any of your garrison to escape from the fort. After they have laid down their arms, I will settle how they are to be treated."

The bugle on this sounded, and the garrison from all directions came out and piled arms in the centre of the fort. A few minutes afterwards, as Terence stood on the ramparts, he observed Murray with a couple of boats pulling to the shore. Adair, thinking it prudent not to lower the drawbridge, for fear any of the garrison might escape, called to Murray and his party to make their way over the walls into the fortress. Murray, having brought on shore some strong tackles, at once set to work to dismount the guns for the purpose of carrying them off, while the greater number of muskets, which were of no value, after being broken, were hurled into the sea below the fort. Murray highly approved of Adair's proceedings; and the commandant was politely informed that he and his garrison must be for the present content to remain prisoners within their own fort. He and his officers shrugged their shoulders, and observed that it was the fortune of war; while the garrison seemed very indifferent to the matter, probably very glad to have nothing to do, and to run no risk of being shot by their enemies.

Murray, however, took the precaution of shutting them all up in the bomb-proof chambers, to prevent them from running away, while at night a bright look-out was kept from the ramparts on all sides, and all hands ordered to be ready to turn out at a moment's notice, lest an attempt might be made by any Russian force in the neighbourhood to recapture the fort. The commandant was allowed to occupy his own quarters, to which he invited the English officers, who found a very welcome repast prepared for them. A remarkably pleasant evening was spent, and the commandant, expressing a hope that the war would soon be over, invited them, as soon as that happy event should occur, to his country-house, which he told them was only a few miles off up the river. They all promised gladly to avail themselves of the invitation, should circumstances allow them to do so.

CHAPTER XIX

An Expedition up the River—Attack on the Magazines—Burning Storehouses and Vessels—Higson and Archie have to run for it—Pull down the River—Higson and Tom have to recruit the inner Man—Russian Nightingales—Hospitable Reception—Higson succumbs to Beauty—The Old Tutor—Proves to be one of Green's Friends—Unpleasant Interruption by Cossacks.

AT early dawn the two boats, as had previously been arranged, shoved off from the side of the *Tornado*, on the proposed expedition up the river, for the purpose of destroying any Government stores or munitions of war which could be discovered.

"It is lucky we didn't attempt to come in till we had silenced the guns," observed Higson, pointing to the strong walls which frowned above them, from which the guns had been removed.

The country on one side was level; on the other, hills, some of considerable elevation, rose from the bank of the river, which twisted and turned, forming several short reaches, and prevented those going up from seeing to any considerable distance ahead.

"We must be prepared for anything that may happen," shouted Higson to Green; "for what we know we may meet another steamer coming down to look after her friends, or we may fall in with a troop of Cossacks or other soldiers, who may give us a somewhat warm reception, if they suspect what we are about."

"I suppose we shall board the steamer if she appears," said Green.

"Depend on that—and take her too," answered Higson; at which the men laughed, as if they thought there was no doubt about the matter. The boats pulled on, passing some pretty-looking country-houses, surrounded by gardens, and backed by orchards or vineyards planted on the hillside.

"A good style of country this to live in," observed Higson to Archie; "I always have my eye on pleasant spots, and amuse myself with the idea that I shall some day come and settle down there, when I have had enough of a sea-life. After knocking about for the best part of his days, a fellow longs to find himself quietly settled on shore."

"But surely, Mr. Higson, you wish to become post-captain, or an admiral?" observed Archie.

"That is more than I ever shall be, youngster, unless I'm a yellow admiral; indeed, I shall consider myself fortunate if I get made a commander, and after serving a year or two am allowed to retire from the service," said Higson. "Now, that is a place to which I should have no objection," he continued, as, having opened a fresh reach, he pointed to a house of greater pretensions than those they had before seen. "After we have performed the work we have been sent on, when we come down we'll look in there and request the inhabitants to provide us some dinner, for I am very sharp set, as I daresay you are."

Of course Higson shouted to Green, telling him what he intended to do, and, of course, the master and Tom very willingly agreed to his proposal. "We have, however, first our work to do," observed Higson; "to burn a few granaries and stacks of wheat, and as many vessels as we can fall in with; that won't take us long, however, if we meet with no opposition, and if we do we must fight, and get the matter over as soon as possible. We must finish it, as Shakespeare says we should a beefsteak."

"I don't think it's Shakespeare says that," observed Archie; "however, there's no doubt that unless we can do it quickly, we may miss doing it altogether, as those Cossack fellows who are in the neighbourhood will be coming down and trying to cut us off."

"Well, as they can't charge into the river, they'll have a hard job to do that," said Higson; "and when we land we must take care not to get far from the boats. It is to be hoped that Commander Adair will keep the garrison shut up in their fort, and so the people up the country, not knowing what has happened, will be unprepared for us."

As they pulled along the officers in the two boats kept a bright look-out on either bank, and, not having seen any horsemen, were in hopes that they might come suddenly upon the place they wished to reach, if no peasantry saw them; or, if they saw them, as they had no flag flying, the peasantry might easily mistake them for Russians, as they would scarcely suppose that two English boats would have ventured up so far from the protection of their ships.

The river rather narrowed as they proceeded, and they observed that the banks were fringed with wide belts of rushes, so that, should they have to run the gauntlet between foes on either bank, by keeping in the centre they should be a good distance from both of them. This was satisfactory; for the bravest of men do not find it pleasant to be shot at without the chance of getting at their enemies. Still Higson hoped that they should be able to accomplish their object, and make their escape again without loss. At length, having rounded a point over which the masts of several vessels were visible, they saw before them several long, high buildings, with a line of stacks in front of them, and a collection of, apparently, private houses and cottages beyond, while in front were between twenty and thirty vessels moored to the shore, and lying so closely together that by setting fire to two or three the rest must inevitably be burnt.

Without stopping the two boats pulled on, keeping close together, so that Higson could give his directions to Green. He ordered him to pull up alongside the farthermost vessels, and to board and set them on fire as quickly as possible; which beneficent work being accomplished, he was to come back and join him on the shore in front of the storehouses and stacks. It could scarcely be supposed that so much property would be left without protection; still no soldiers had been seen, and Higson hoped that they might accomplish their object before any could come down to oppose them.

"The truth is, I suspect," he observed to Archie, "the Russians have depended on their fort at the mouth of the river, and it did not occur to them that an enemy could force his way past it. The steamers may have been lying much nearer the entrance than this, and had not time to communicate with the village before they came down to attack us; the chances are that the people on the banks, who saw them go down, fancy that they sent us long ago to the bottom, and have no idea that we have taken their fort."

"They must have heard, however, the sound of the vessel blowing up," observed Archie.

"If they did, they may have thought it was one of ours," answered Higson, who had made up his mind that all was to go smoothly. The boats soon got up to the place, when Green pulled away to perform his part of the undertaking; while Higson steered for the shore. As he did so, a rattling fire of musketry was opened on him from behind a small fort, or earthwork, which he had hitherto not perceived. Probably the Russians had only just then discovered that the approaching boats belonged to their enemies. Not a man, however, was hit, though several bullets struck the boat; and the next instant she was alongside the wharf. Higson, springing on shore, followed by Archie and most of his crew, two only remaining to take care of the boat, made a dash at the earthwork; from which the defenders, if so they could be called, rushed out as their assailants leaped in.

"Don't follow them, lads," cried Higson; "small-arm men, just pepper them and prevent them coming back. And now we'll fire the storehouses."

The men had been provided with matches and torches, and more quickly than it can be described they threw their burning brands into the open windows of the storehouses, which the instant after were in a blaze from one end to the other. They then with equal rapidity lighting the huge stacks close to the water's edge, they also were soon blazing away, with a fury which would have defied all the attempts of the Russians, had any appeared, to save them. As the wind blew on the shore, the dense volumes of smoke which were driven in the faces of those on the other side completely concealed the perpetrators of the deed from their sight.

Green and Tom had, in the meantime, not been idle. A slight opposition only was made by the crew of the first vessel they boarded; finding it useless to defend her, they made their escape across the intervening craft to the shore. The English then set fire in succession to all those on the outside, the flames from which quickly caught the masts and rigging of the rest; and before the master's boat rejoined Higson's, every vessel was blazing away with a fury which secured the destruction of the whole. Higson, believing that the work was done, ordered Green to follow him down the river; he, however, had only just got clear of the line of burning stacks, when he perceived that another storehouse standing a little farther back than the others had not as yet been set on fire.

"We must not leave the work unfinished," he exclaimed. "Come, Archie, you and I and Tim Nolan will soon do the job;" and, springing on shore with a torch which he had just lighted, followed by Archie and Tim, each with a musket as well as a torch, he made his way towards the storehouse. As the party ran on they caught sight of several people in the distance, and Archie thought he saw some horsemen with long lances; but they believed that they could reach the building, and get back to the boat, long before the latter could be down upon them. As they arrived at the storehouse, they found that the door was closed, and that the windows were too high to enable them to throw in their torches. A piece of timber lay near at hand.

"We must make a battering-ram of this," cried Higson; "here, Gordon, you and Tim lay hold of it on one side, and I'll take the other, and we'll soon knock in the door."

The first blow failed in its intended effect. "Now, lads, heave with a will," cried Higson, and the door gave way.

Picking up their torches, as well as their muskets, which they had put down to handle the battering-ram, they sprang in; and Higson, running to the farther end, ignited some woodwork and a pile of sacks; while Tim, leaping up a ladder, left his torch burning on the upper floor. In a few seconds Higson came back, and, throwing Archie's torch as far as he could into the building, they all rushed out again. As they were making their way as fast as their legs could carry them to the boat, Archie, turning his head over his right shoulder, saw the horsemen he had before observed galloping at full speed towards them.

"Here come the Cossacks, Mr. Higson," he shouted out "run, Mr. Higson, run, while Tim and I keep them at bay."

Higson, having grown somewhat stout, was not as active as formerly; and Archie knew that he and Tim could soon overtake him. Higson, aware of this, did as he was advised, while he shouted out to the rest of the people in the boat to cover the two who remained behind.

"Oh, Mr. Green, Archie and the man with him will be cut off if we don't pull in and help them," cried Tom, who, just as the boat got clear of the smoke, caught sight of the Cossacks.

Green on this pulled to the shore, and part of the two boats' crews landing, just as the Cossacks got within twenty yards of Archie and Tim, they opened fire, which emptied two of their saddles, and made the rest of the troop wheel quickly round; while Archie and Tim, having also fired their muskets, took to their heels and soon joined their shipmates.

"Give way, my lads," cried Higson, as he once more took

his seat; "we've done the work effectually, and there's no use stopping to get fired at as we pull down the river."

The dense volume of smoke which rose up from the bank of the river completely concealed the Cossacks, and of course prevented them from seeing the boats, which they possibly might have supposed were still lying off the place, ready to commit other mischief. Higson had received orders, however, on no account to injure private property, and he could only hope that the flames had not reached the buildings he had seen beyond the storehouses. Just as they got a little way beyond the point there came the thundering sound of an explosion.

"That must be a magazine blown up," observed Tom.

"Perhaps one of the vessels has powder on board," said Green; "I think I caught sight of some spars through the smoke, but they may have been fragments of timber."

Just then there came another explosion as loud as the first, and scarcely had its echoes died away among the hills on the left when a third occurred.

"No doubt about it now," said Green; "some of the vessels we set on fire must have been laden with powder."

"I hope no unfortunate people were on board them. A pretty considerable amount of mischief we have done this morning," said Tom; "but I suppose it was our duty, so we mustn't think too much about it."

"Of course it was," answered Green; "if people will go to war, they must take the consequences."

"But perhaps the people didn't want to go to war," said Tom; "it was all their Emperor's doing."

"Then they ought not to live under such an Emperor," said Green.

"How can they help themselves?" asked Tom; "I daresay, if they had been asked they would have preferred remaining at peace."

"I confess that I don't feel any animosity against them; I would much rather be fighting the French; but they, by a sort of hocus-pocus, are our allies," remarked Green. "In reality we are not making war on the Russian people; we are expressly ordered not to injure any of their property; our business is only to destroy Government stores."

"Well, that's some comfort," said Tom, "though it may not always be easy to distinguish one from the other."

This conversation took place as the boats were pulling

away, as hard as the men could lay their backs to the oars, down the river. As yet they had seen no Cossacks or foot-soldiers on either bank; possibly they might have remained to try to put out the fire, or the nature of the ground on the left bank, on which the stores were situated, prevented them from making rapid progress over it. As the boats had come up, Green had observed an extensive marsh with a wide stream, which, unless there was a bridge over it, would have alone proved an effectual barrier to the progress of cavalry. To the right, on which the houses had been seen, were high and picturesque hills, some rising almost directly out of the water, with fertile valleys, groves, orchards, and vineyards. Had any number of armed men been in the neighbourhood, they might greatly have annoyed the boats as they went down. The tide, however, was with them, and they made rapid progress.

They could still see a cloud of smoke collected over the stores and vessels they had set on fire, which convinced them that any attempt which might have been made by the soldiers to extinguish the flames must have proved unsuccessful. They were pulling along, as has been said, at a rapid rate, when, in order to take the shortest course, they kept close round a wooded point on the right bank, the current, which was very strong, helping them along. Scarcely had they rounded the point when both boats struck with great force on a rocky ledge, the existence of which had not been perceived.

"We have made a pretty big hole in our boat, sir," observed Archie.

"Why, the water's running in like a mill-stream! Back all!" cried Higson; "now pull round the port oars."

The men gave way with all their might. Higson steered the boat to the shore. The water was almost up to their thwarts before they reached it; they all leaped out on the bank, or she would have sunk with them. Green's boat had also received considerable damage, and he, not without difficulty, followed them.

"We are in a pretty plight," exclaimed Tom; "what are we to do now?"

"Repair the damages as fast as we can, and continue our course," said Higson.

To do this, however, it was necessary to haul the boats up; as they were full of water, this was a very difficult matter; they had to tow them along for some distance to a convenient spot, where the bank, shelving gently down, enabled them by degrees to get them up and bale the water out. Should the enemy find them while thus employed they would all be taken prisoners; Higson felt considerable anxiety on this score, his only consolation being that they might be exchanged for the commandant and garrison of the fort. By all working together they first hauled one boat up and then the other. Though the men got pretty wet in the operation, Higson and Green and the midshipmen kept tolerably dry.

"I say, Archie, are you not very hungry?" said Tom.

"Yes," answered Archie; "Mr. Higson said he would go up to one of the houses on our way down, and try and get some food; I vote we ask him."

"He has probably forgotten all about it; I'll remind him," said Tom; "I know what will make him as eager as we are for something to eat. Mr. Higson," he said, going up to him, "don't you think, sir, it would be pleasant if we had a dish of Irish stew, with a few bottles of porter to discuss, while the boats are being put to rights?"

"What made you think of that, youngster?" asked Higson; licking his lips, however, at the bare thoughts of his favourite dish.

"You told Gordon, sir, when you came up, that you thought of putting in to try and get something to eat," answered Tom; "he and I are almost starved; and I should think you and Mr. Green and the men must be pretty sharp set also. Now would be a good opportunity, and Gordon says that the cottage we saw a quarter of a mile or so off is the one which you thought so pretty, and where you said you would like to spend the remainder of your days."

"What business has he to be telling you what I said?" exclaimed Higson; "I don't approve of you youngsters chattering about me."

"Of course not, sir," said Tom; "but it was the thought of the Irish stew, or some other nice dish, which the good people of the house might be inclined to set before us, made us propose asking you to let us go up and try what we could get."

"Well, I have no objection to make an excursion to the house," said Higson, "provided we can ascertain that the coast is clear, and I will take one of you with me. As you can talk French, I shall take you and leave Gordon to assist the master."

"Thank you, sir," said Tom; "I am pretty sure that there are no Russians in the neighbourhood, or they would have been down on us some time ago."

Before starting, however, Higson, accompanied by Tom, took the precaution of climbing to the top of a hill, from whence they could look up and across the river, and over a considerable part of the right bank. Not a human being was visible moving anywhere, nor was a boat of any description to be seen floating on the surface of the stream. Had it not been for the houses and the cultivated ground, they might have supposed that they were in some wild country; the fact being, probably, that the male part of the population had been drawn off either to garrison the forts or to serve in the army, while the women were attending to their household duties within doors.

Higson, directing Green to launch the boats as soon as they were repaired, and to fire a musket should any enemy appear, and promising to bring the party some food if he could obtain it, set off with Tom in the direction of the country house he had thought so attractive. The first part of their way was over wild ground, without any beaten track; but as it was tolerably open, they were able to get along without difficulty. At length they came upon a path which led apparently from the house to a landing-place, near which a small, gaily-painted boat was hauled up, and a boathouse, which they concluded contained a larger craft.

"Now, this looks as if the people in the house yonder are well to do," observed Higson, "and are likely to have a good store of provisions."

"That is of the chief consequence to us just now," said Tom; "shall we go up to the front entrance and tell them our errand, or find out the back door, and get a servant to go in and say what we want?"

"Go in at once and explain what we require," answered Higson.

While speaking they were making their way along the path they had discovered. In a short time they reached a small gate, and seeing the roof of the house over the shrubbery, they concluded that by going through the gate they could make a shorter cut through it. As time was of consequence, they accordingly proceeded on by the pathway which led through the shrubbery, when, just as they were about to emerge from it, they heard the sound of a female voice singing in an accomplished and very sweet manner. Higson put his hand on Tom's arm, and signed to him to stop.

Those who have for many months been accustomed to the roar of guns, the howling of the tempest, and the gruff voice of the boatswain, may conceive what effect such dulcet notes were likely to produce on the lieutenant and midshipman. They stopped for some time listening with delight.

"I would not for the world run the risk of frightening her, whoever she is," said Higson, when at length the lady ceased singing; "if we go on, we shall come directly in front of the room in which she is sitting; the window is open, or we should not hear the sound so plainly. We must try and find some other way of approaching the house."

"If you will let me, sir, I'll creep forward and try to get a look through the trees without being seen," said Tom, who was highly delighted with the adventure, which promised, as he hoped, to be of a romantic character. He was more of an age to enjoy the sort of thing than his lieutenant. Higson, however, preferred looking for himself, as he was, in reality, quite as much interested as Tom. They could just see that the path opened out on a gravel walk, which ran along the well-kept, smooth lawn, with flower-beds dotted about on it. Just at this juncture they heard a childish laugh, and caught sight of a little boy with a hat in his hand, running across the lawn in chase of a butterfly, presently pursued by a young lady in a white muslin dress, who, overtaking him, lifted him up in her arms, and was returning with him to the window, from which she had apparently issued, when her eyes fell on the two strangers. She stopped and looked at them, without exhibiting any particular sign of alarm, apparently wondering who they could be and what had brought them there.

The little boy, however, uttered a loud cry, which produced a question from another person who was yet invisible. As they were now discovered, they did the best thing that, under the circumstances, they could do. Taking off their caps, they advanced with low bows, when they saw another young lady who had just come through the venetian window which opened on to the lawn, under a broad verandah running along the side of the house.

"Pray do not be frightened, young ladies," said Higson, bowing first to one and then to the other; "we had no intention of intruding on you so suddenly, and I beg you ten thousand pardons."

As neither of the ladies replied, Tom thought that they probably did not understand English, and began repeating in French, as far as his knowledge of the language enabled him, what his lieutenant had said. The young lady who had just appeared at the window, and who was evidently the elder of the two, smiled as she listened to Tom's bad French. "You have not alarmed us, I assure you," she answered at length, in very good English. "Gentlemen, I know, would not act uncourteously. I am surprised, however, at seeing you, as our two nations are unhappily at war; but may I inquire whence you have come, and what it is you want?"

Higson, of course, did not think it necessary to say that they had been up the river burning the Russian granaries and vessels, and he merely therefore explained that they had landed from some men-of-war's boats, and, having come away without provisions, would be very much obliged if they could be informed where they could obtain food for themselves and their men.

"This seems very strange," said the young lady; "I thought that none of the enemy's boats could come up the river past the fort at its entrance, of which our papa is the commandant. We heard a great deal of firing yesterday evening, and were very anxious to know what it was about; but were assured by Herr Groben, our brothers' tutor, that some English vessels, which were attacking it, had been beaten off, and that no harm could have happened to the defenders; indeed, three of our war-steamers went out from the river, and we of course supposed assisted to put the English to flight. You have, I hope, therefore, come up with a flag of truce? Surely Herr Groben could not have been mistaken. Can you give us any tidings of our papa?"

"I am very glad to be able to assure you, young lady, that when I had the pleasure of seeing him he was perfectly well, though somewhat vexed at the loss of his fort, which we were under the painful necessity of capturing, as also the man-of-war steamers which came out of the harbour to assist him," answered Higson.

The young ladies spoke to each other for several minutes in Russian, so that Higson and Tom could not understand what they said.

"Though we have no enmity against the English, you bring news which is painful to us, as we know that our papa will grieve for the misfortune which has happened to him," said the elder of the young ladies. "We are, however, obliged to you for informing us of his safety, and should be glad to do our best to supply your wants."

Higson and Tom had been all this time standing with their caps in their hands, in front of the window. While the lieutenant was addressing the eldest of the two ladies, Tom was turning an admiring glance at the youngest, who still held the little boy in her arms, while he had thrown his round her neck, and was every now and then taking an alarmed look at the strangers.

"I am afraid that he is frightened at us," said Tom. "I must really apologise for our intrusion; I can assure you that it was not intentional, and we should have retired at once had we not stopped to listen to some delightful singing. Was it you or your sister we heard?"

"It was my sister; but we both sing," answered the young lady, "and we shall be very happy to sing to you by and by if you wish it."

Of course Tom thanked her very much, and felt quite at home in a minute. The elder sister then invited them to come in and sit down, while she ordered some supper to be prepared for them and their men. While she was absent, and the younger lady was sitting with the little boy in her lap, doing her best to entertain them, the door opened, and an old gentleman, in a sky-blue suit, with a periwig on his head, entered the room, making a profound bow as he did so. The young lady introduced him as Herr Groben. He probably had heard about the English officers from the elder sister, for he looked in no way surprised, and, at once coming forward, welcomed them with apparent sincerity. He made no remark about the capture of the fort or vessels; perhaps he thought it better to let the subject alone. On hearing that the party at the boats were in want of provisions, he at once volunteered to carry down a supply as soon as it could be got ready. Higson, who thought him a very agreeable person, at once accepted his offer; for he himself had been so much struck by the appearance of the elder of the young ladies, and by her sweet singing, that he was in no hurry to go away.

Herr Groben said he must apologise for the absence of the lady of the house, Madame Paskiewich being unable to make her appearance, as she was confined to her room by a slight indisposition; but she sent her compliments, expressing a hope that they would be satisfied with the treatment they might receive during the time they might think fit to remain. Higson, not to be outdone in politeness, begged to assure Madame Paskiewich that he was grateful for the kind reception he had met with, and should be happy to be the bearer of any message or more weighty articles which she might wish to send to her husband. On the return of Mademoiselle Paskiewich, who had gone to order supper and to superintend the packing of some baskets of provisions, Herr Groben made his bow, and was shortly afterwards seen crossing the lawn, followed by two long-shirted servants carrying a couple of hampers slung on a pole borne on their shoulders.

Tom had asked the young lady her name, which she told him was Feodorowna. "My eldest sister's," she added, "is Ivanowna. And have you any sisters?" she asked. Upon which Tom told her all about his family, and that he had several brothers, one of whom commanded the ship to which he belonged, and that another was in the Guards; all of which pieces of information considerably raised him in the young lady's estimation. He wisely thought it better to say nothing about Higson, except that he was the first lieutenant of his brother's ship. While supper was being prepared, Ivanowna, observing that the English officers were good enough to be pleased with her singing, went to the piano and sang several songs, with which Higson expressed himself highly delighted. Every moment his admiration of the young lady evidently increased. She was not, it must be acknowledged, possessed of what could be called classical beauty; she was fair, certainly, with blue eyes, but they were rather small; while her figure was too short and round to be graceful, and her nose differed considerably from that of the Venus de Medicis; but then she had smiling lips, and a good-natured expression altogether.

Her younger sister, Feodorowna, who was scarcely fifteen, was certainly very much prettier; indeed, Tom was inclined to pronounce her perfectly beautiful, and he was still more delighted with her when she sang, though her voice was not equal to that of her sister.

Supper being announced, they went into the dining-room without waiting for the return of Herr Groben. His two pupils, boys younger than Feodorowna, however, made their appearance.

They reported that they had gone down to the boats, and had seen Herr Groben shaking hands with the officer in command, having apparently found an old friend.

"That is not surprising," observed Higson; "our master, Jos Green, finds old friends everywhere, and I believe that if he were to go to the North Pole he would fall in with an acquaintance."

Higson and Tom had been now nearly two hours at the house, and it was high time that they should be off; but neither of them felt any inclination to quit such agreeable society. Still, Higson was too good an officer to forget his duty, and he at length told Tom that it was time to go; and they were on the point of wishing their fair hostesses good-bye, Higson promising with perfect sincerity that, if able, when the war was over, he would come back; and Tom, with equal honesty, saying much the same thing, when they saw Herr Groben hurrying across the lawn towards the drawing-room window, and panting for breath.

"I am sorry to say, gentlemen, that I bring you unsatisfactory intelligence," exclaimed Herr Groben. "As I was sitting on the point, enjoying my meerschaum with my old friend Green, I caught sight of a number of foot-soldiers and a troop of Cossacks, who had come over the hills farther down the river, and who, it was very evident from their gestures, had caught sight of the boats hauled up on the bank, and the English seamen around them. I advised Green to launch the boats, and to come round to the landing-place near the house to receive you on board. There is not a moment to be lost, for they outnumber your people as five to one, and can find plenty of shelter; and were they to discover you on shore, they would make you prisoners."

Higson and Tom smiled. "They are not likely to do that," answered Higson; "though we are very much obliged to you for your warning, and most unwillingly we must wish our kind hostesses good-bye."

"Oh, do go! do go!" cried both the young ladies in a breath; "we should deeply regret if you were to be made prisoners, and grieved still more were you compelled to fight the Cossacks."

"We must first thank you for your kindness, which, believe me, we shall never forget," said Higson, who, supposing that the Cossacks were still at a distance, did not feel that there was any necessity to be in a hurry. Tom was thanking Feodorowna in still more sentimental language, when the old tutor seized their arms.

"Come down, come!" he exclaimed; "even now I am afraid that you are too late. I hear the hoofs of the Cossacks' horses clattering along the road, and they will catch sight of you before you can reach the landing-place."

As he spoke, he went round to the front of the house, and quickly came back again.

"It is as I feared," he exclaimed; "your retreat is cut off, and if the boats come in to take you on board, they will to a certainty be fired on. I must go and warn them, and leave you to the care of the ladies."

"But if you can go, so can we," said Higson, preparing to accompany Herr Groben.

"Oh no, no! they will recognise you at once from your uniforms; but they will not suspect my object. Besides, you will have to show yourself," said Herr Groben, "as you try to get on board; but I can remain concealed, while I warn your friends to keep off the shore."

Higson and Tom still persevered in their intention of making their way down to the landing-place, and were on the point of hurrying off, when the young ladies seized their hands and entreated them, with tears in their eyes, to remain.

"You will both of you be shot, for you will have to pass within a dozen yards of the spot the Cossacks have reached, and it would be so dreadful to have you killed. Do stay, and we can easily conceal you till they have gone away, for they dare not search this house; indeed, they will not suspect that English officers are within it."

As the young ladies spoke, they led Higson and Tom to a side window, from whence they could see a troop of Cossacks, followed by a considerable number of foot-soldiers, passing along the road a short distance off beyond the garden. There could thus be no doubt that their retreat was cut off.

"You are perfectly safe here," said Ivanowna; "though, as a protection, we will shut the windows leading into the garden. I have great hopes that Herr Groben will reach the boat in time to warn your friends, so as to prevent bloodshed, which is our great object; there has been too much spilt already in a bad cause. We could not sympathise with those who are guilty of the massacre of Sinope, and we believe that this cruel war was unnecessary. It may seem strange to you that I should thus express myself," she continued, observing Higson's look of surprise; "but our mother is half an Englishwoman, and we have been taught to regard the English with affection."

"I am very glad to hear it," said Higson, a strange feeling taking possession of his heart; indeed, he was much inclined to ask whether she could regard an Englishman with affection, but he wisely forbore to put the question. He, indeed, just then had his thoughts occupied about the boats. "Could you allow us to go to a window from whence we could watch what is going forward on the river?" he asked. "I am afraid that my friends may be tempted to remain, in the hopes of receiving us on board, till the Cossacks are down upon them."

"Not if Herr Groben succeeds in carrying out his intention," she answered. "But come with us to a room in the second storey, and from thence you will have a view of the river, and be able to watch the progress of the boats. It is our boudoir, but under the circumstances we will venture to admit you."

Higson and Tom assured the young ladies that they very much appreciated the confidence placed in them, and forthwith accompanied them upstairs. Just as they entered the room, which they had time to see was prettily ornamented with pictures on the walls, an easel, ladies' embroidery frames, and numerous other elegant articles, the loud rattle of musketry reached their ears. The young ladies uttered a cry of alarm.

"Pray do not be over anxious about the matter," said Higson; "musket-balls do not always reach the object they are aimed at, and it does not follow that any harm is done."

As he and Tom and the young ladies looked out of the window, cautiously keeping concealed behind the curtains, they saw a party of Cossacks on the landing-place, and some foot-soldiers under shelter of a wall. The two boats, a hundred yards off or more, were pulling away out towards the middle of the river.

"Herr Groben has had time to warn them," said Higson; "and as far as I can judge, by the way the men are rowing, no one has been hit. We are deeply indebted to him, ladies, and to you also; and I have no doubt that when Green supposes that the Cossacks have retired, he will come back and relieve you of our company."

"Oh, do not say that," observed Ivanowna, "we shall be sorry to lose you; and I am sure we shall have done what our papa would wish by treating you with hospitality."

Higson and Tom watched the progress of the boats with

interest; they somewhat expected that Green would lie on his oars and wait till the Cossacks had gone away. Perhaps he might have thought that they were already made prisoners and that there would be no use in doing this; at all events, he continued his course down the river, till the boats were lost to sight in the distance. The Cossacks, disappointed in their hope of surprising the English, turned their horses' heads round, followed by the foot-soldiers, and marched back the way they had come, without even visiting the house.

The young ladies seemed highly pleased. "We are perfectly safe now," observed Ivanowna; "but to prevent surprise, we will send our young brothers to keep watch, and bring us notice should any of the officers take it into their heads to pay us a visit. They can be thoroughly trusted."

Soon afterwards they heard Herr Groben's cheery voice in the passage. "All right," he exclaimed; "I had time to warn Green, though I was nearly caught, I must confess; but the horsemen did not get as fast over the rough ground as I did. I fear, however, that Green did not understand that you were in safe keeping, and may possibly conceive that you have been made prisoners; though he will know that you are not likely to be ill-treated."

"I am sure that he must have thought that, or he would not have pulled away," said Higson. "However, we have no cause to complain; my only fear is that we shall be trespassing on the hospitality of this kind family."

"On that point I can answer with confidence that you are welcome," said Herr Groben; "they are all, as I am, devoted admirers of the English; I have great cause to be so, and especially have I reason to be grateful to my dear friend Green. You will be curious to know how I became acquainted with him; it happened in this wise. Many years ago I was making a voyage, when my ship caught fire, and I—with the officers and crew—escaped in three of the boats. The other boats were lost; and after several of my companions had died of hunger, we were picked up by a ship to which Green belonged. All the officers and crew treated us with kindness; Green especially took care of me, and pressed on me the use of his purse when we arrived in England, where I was also treated with great kindness. Such conduct can never be forgotten, and I have ever endeavoured to imbue the hearts of my pupils with a love for England, and for everything English."

"We are very much obliged to you and Green," said Higson, "since we have benefited so largely by your instructions."

As there was no longer any danger, Higson proposed going back into the drawing-room. The young ladies, however, first showed him and Tom their drawings and embroidery, and numerous other samples of their handiwork, which passed the time very agreeably. When they went downstairs, they found a huge samovar bubbling and hissing on the table, and such tea was offered them as they had never before tasted. Higson, indeed, in compliment to his hostess, begged to have his cup replenished again and again, till he had drunk six or eight cups-full; though, to be sure, they were not of any unusual size. Herr Groben undertook to take charge of Higson and Tom for the night, and to give them due warning should there be any danger of their being discovered, though he thought that this was not likely; still, he acknowledged that there were some persons who might prove treacherous should they hear of English officers being in the house; and he begged them on no account to make their appearance out of doors without him, a caution which they promised to observe.

CHAPTER XX

Green returns without Higson and Tom—Jack goes in search of them—Colonel Paskiewich's House—Higson and Tom captured by Cossacks—Tom's Escape—Miss Feodorowna's Joy—The Fort blown up—The Mosquito Fleet—Gallant Exploit of Captain Lyons—Jack heads Expedition Inland—Escape.

MURRAY and Rogers had been employed during the day in removing the guns from the fort, while Adair and his party watched over the prisoners. It was their intention to blow it up, but they were unwilling to do this until the return of the boats. Evening was approaching, and as they had not yet made their appearance, Jack became somewhat anxious as to what might have happened to them. The smoke rising from the conflagration of the stores and vessels could be discerned in the far distance, so that it was evident that they had accomplished their work; but it was possible that some disaster might afterwards have happened to them. Jack accordingly went on board the *Giaour* to consult with Murray, who agreed to send up a couple of his boats at daybreak the next morning to search for those under Higson, and to negotiate for his and his party's release, should they have been taken prisoners. Jack begged that he might lead the expedition himself, to which Murray willingly agreed.

Darkness had for some time set in, and still the missing boats had not appeared; as Jack, whose anxiety had increased, was walking the deck with Mildmay, the splash of oars was heard. The sentry hailed, and Green's voice replied; the boats were soon alongside, both of them half full of water.

"Where are the first lieutenant and Mr. Rogers?" asked Jack.

"I am afraid, sir, that they are in the hands of the Russians;" and Green gave an account of what had happened, adding, "Had it not been for an old friend of mine, who warned us of the approach of the troops, we should ourselves have been overpowered, or at all events have had a pretty hard tussle for it."

Green took care not to throw any blame upon Higson, who might have been accused of acting imprudently, if not of neglecting his duty, by remaining longer than was necessary at the house which he had visited to obtain provisions. Having heard Green's report, Jack again went on board the *Giaour*, and as some time would be required to repair his own boats, Murray arranged, as he had before promised, to send two of his half an hour before daylight, so that they might enter the river as soon as they could see their way.

Just as the ruddy streaks of dawn appeared in the sky, Jack shoved off from the *Tornado's* side. He took Green with him to pilot the boats, and also to communicate with the old German tutor, through whom he might be able to learn what had become of the prisoners. He carried also a flag of truce, in the hopes of gaining his object by pacific measures. As the boats passed under the walls of the fort, they were hailed by the sentry on the ramparts, by whose side Gerald Desmond directly afterwards made his appearance. Jack told him to inform Commander Adair where they were going, and that he hoped to be back again in the course of a few hours.

"The Russian commandant, sir, wishes to send a letter to his family to inform them of his safety, and he will be obliged to you if you will convey it."

"That is more than I can undertake to do," answered Jack; "but inform the commandant that if he will let me know where his family reside, I shall be happy to give them any message he may send."

Gerald disappeared, and quickly afterwards returned with the commandant and Adair. The commandant, in surprisingly good English, described his residence to Jack, and requested that he would tell his wife and daughters that he was well, and, as he was to be liberated on his parole, that he hoped to remain with them till the end of the war.

"This information will be more satisfactory to them, probably, than had I gained a great victory," he added; "so that they will be ready to receive you as friends rather than as enemies."

"I shall be happy to deliver your message, colonel," answered Jack; "and regret that I am unable to carry a written communication."

A few further compliments having been exchanged, Jack ordered his men to give way, and the boats proceeded up the river.

"Why, sir, that house must be the very one which Mr. Higson and your brother visited," said Green; "unless the Cossacks have carried them off to a distance, they may, I hope, be easily recovered."

"That is satisfactory," said Jack; "whether we recover them or not, we must be away from this early to-day, as there is work to be done in other places."

The boats pulled on some way, when they caught sight of a vessel stealing along on the opposite shore towards the mouth of the river. Jack immediately steered for her, ordering Archie to pull ahead, so as to cut her off should she attempt to slip by them. On seeing them approach, however, the Russian skipper immediately hauled down his colours.

Jack found, on stepping on board, that the Russian skipper was not aware that the English vessels were still off the mouth of the river, and had expected to get clear; he said that his was the only vessel that had not been burnt.

"Sorry to have to condemn yours to the fate you have escaped," said Jack.

"It is the fortune of war," answered the skipper, shrugging his shoulders; "I only wish the war had come to an end."

The operation did not take long; the unfortunate skipper and his crew were landed, to make their way home as best they could; when the vessel, being set on fire, drifted on to the bank, where she quickly burnt to the water's edge. Jack then pulled on, and in a short time the boats reached the landing-place near the colonel's house, which Green pointed out. Having, as far as they could from the water, examined the ground before them, they came to the conclusion that no enemy was in the neighbourhood. Green, who felt that some blame might have been attached to him for deserting his commanding officer, volunteered to proceed by himself to the house to ascertain how matters stood. He assured Jack that he could trust Herr Groben, who would give him warning should the enemy be near. Jack agreed to this, and Green set off.

In a short time he was seen returning to the boat, accompanied by the old German tutor, who, as he approached, appeared to be much agitated.

"Bad news, sir," said Green, as he came up to Jack; "the Cossacks have got hold of Higson and your brother."

"It was dere fault, it was dere fault," broke in the old tutor; "dey would go out walking vid de young ladies when I warned dem not to go, and a troop of Cossacks came galloping up to dem, and carry dem both off. It almost break de young ladies' heart, and dey have not done crying yet."

"Then they must be still in the neighbourhood!" exclaimed Jack, "and we may be in time to overtake them."

"Oh no, captain," answered Herr Groben; "I fear not, for dey mount upon two horses and gallop away."

"At all events, if you can supply us with a guide to show us the way they have taken, we will pursue them," said Jack.

"Perhaps one of my pupil vill go, for dere moder, Matame Paskievich, is very unhappy at the thoughts the officers were made prisoner, as she consider that they were under her protection; and as dey come as friends, dey should be allowed to go away as friends."

As there was no time to be lost, Jack, ordering Green to remain, with a couple of men in each boat, set off, accompanied by Archie and Herr Groben, who promised to find him a trustworthy guide, though he showed no inclination to go himself. The name of Paskiewich had struck Jack, and, on making inquiries from the old tutor, he found that the owner of the house was the commandant of the fort.

"I think, sir," observed Archie, who was walking by his side, "if that is the case, we shall be able to exchange the colonel for Mr. Higson and Tom."

"I would rather get them back without having to do that," said Jack; "the colonel is to be liberated on his parole; but, should we find it necessary, we shall be able, as a last resource, to recover them as you propose."

On arriving at the house they were met by Madame Paskiewich and her two daughters. Jack, fortunately recollecting the colonel's message, delivered it to his wife, who expressed herself very grateful for the kind treatment he had received, and assured them how grieved she was that, notwithstanding all her precautions, the Cossacks had captured the two officers. Jack, in reply, expressed his conviction that it was from no fault of theirs, and comforted them greatly by telling them that probably in the course of the day the colonel would be enabled to return to them.

On hearing of their want of a guide, Madame Paskiewich at once consented to allow her eldest boy to show them the way the Cossacks had gone, though she believed that by this time they were far beyond pursuit. Herr Groben's pupils soon made their appearance, and the eldest, Ivan, who spoke English very well, without hesitation undertook to guide them, and to make inquiries on the way as to where any troops were stationed, so as to prevent them from being surprised. Jack, though perfectly sensible of the risk he ran, resolved to persevere; and, accompanied by young Ivan, at once set off at the head of his party, who, as they were well armed, had no fear of the result should they meet three times their number.

They had gone some distance, when Jack learned, from Ivan's inquiries, that the Cossacks were already a long way ahead; he at length began to despair of recovering his first lieutenant or Tom; he felt, too, the imprudence of advancing farther into the enemy's country, when, before he could secure his retreat, the foe might gather between him and the boats. He was at last obliged unwillingly to confess that he must give up the pursuit.

"I am very sorry for it, sir," said their guide; "the English midshipman and I had become great friends; and though I don't think he will be treated ill, yet he will not like to be kept away from his ship. However, when my father returns, I promise to do my best to get him set at liberty."

"Thank you," answered Jack warmly; "I will trust you."

He now gave the order to his men to face about, and they began to retrace their steps. They had gone but a short distance, when the loud clattering of hoofs struck on their ears, and, looking round, they caught sight of a horseman galloping towards them at headlong speed.

"Hurrah! that's Tom himself!" cried Archie; and Tom appeared from amid a cloud of dust, riding as he had done many a day after the hounds in ——shire. He was within hailing distance, when a couple of hundred yards or so behind him were seen a number of Cossacks in hot pursuit. Jack ordered his men to fix bayonets, to be prepared to receive cavalry. As Tom came galloping along, they opened to let him pass, when, not without some difficulty, he pulled up at their rear.

"I've done them!" he exclaimed; "I was sure you would come to look for me, though I little expected to find you so near at hand."

The Cossacks, of whom there were scarcely more than a dozen, and who had by this time got within a hundred yards of them, on seeing the resolute bearing of the British sailors, pulled up, and, after a moment's hesitation, wheeling round their horses, galloped off, followed by a shower of bullets.

"The only thing you have done wrong was to fire without my orders!" exclaimed Jack; "reload, and now right-about face and march—double quick time." The party, without a moment's delay, hurried back on the road they had come.

"I'm afraid Mr. Higson's in for it," said Tom. "The Cossacks had halted for breakfast, when the thought came into my head that we might make our escape while the men were all dismounted, and eating some horrid mess or other, their horses being picketed some distance from them. I did my best to persuade him to come too, but he never was much of a horseman, and declared that he could not do it; though he told me to take my chance, and that he would try and prevent anyone from following me. I had already fixed my eyes on a horse. While the men were all engaged, I sauntered up to where their steeds were tethered, and, before anyone had observed me, I set a dozen or more of them at liberty, when, finding that the men suspected what I was about, I leaped on the back of the one I had fixed on, and, giving a loud shout, galloped off as fast as the wind, with a troop of riderless horses scampering at my heels. I had got a fine start, and intended to keep it, and it was not till just before I caught sight of you that I knew I was pursued; still even then I did not give up all hopes of escaping, though I little knew how near help was at hand; I only wish Mr. Higson had followed my advice."

As Jack had no wish to encounter the Cossacks, who were certainly not likely to bring Higson with them, he hurried on his men, and at length reached Colonel Paskiewich's house. The fair Feodorowna, in an artless manner, showed her pleasure at seeing Tom in safety; while Ivanowna could not restrain her tears on hearing that the lieutenant was still a prisoner.

As Jack considered it his duty not to delay a moment longer than was necessary, he was compelled to decline Madame Paskiewich's invitation to remain for breakfast, and, accompanied by Herr Groben, who wished to bid farewell to Green, he hurried to the boats. In a few minutes they were again pulling down towards the mouth of the river.

On arriving at the fort, Jack found that all the necessary preparations had been made for its evacuation. Colonel Paskiewich and his officers were liberated on their parole not to serve again during the war, while the men were transferred to the *Flash*, to be conveyed on board some of the larger ships of the fleet.

"I'll do my best to obtain the liberation of your first lieutenant," said the colonel to Jack, as he bade him farewell.

"We might arrange for exchanging you with him," observed Jack.

"Thank you, but I would rather not," answered the colonel significantly; "I should then be compelled again to fight in this detestable war, whereas at present I may remain as a non-combatant with my family; which I confess — though mention it not, my friend — much better suits my principles and taste."

"You are a brave man, and defended your fort gallantly," observed Jack.

"That was my duty," answered the colonel; "a man, I hold, may be physically brave, and yet abhor fighting. As long as it was my duty to fight, I fought; I can now with honour sheathe my sword, in the earnest hope that I may never again have to draw it, especially against Englishmen. There are many of my countrymen, who, I doubt not, feel as I do. Good-bye, my friend; may we meet again in happier times!"

Jack accompanied the colonel out of the fort, and, as soon as the last Russian had taken his departure, Jack fired the trains which had been laid to the mines in different parts of the fort, and, leaping into his boat, pulled away towards the *Tornado*. Before the boat had got half-way, the first explosion was heard, the stout walls trembling and shaking, while clouds of dust and smoke, and fragments of stone and timber rose in the air; and in a few seconds the spot where the fort had stood presented a mass of shapeless ruins.

"We've done for the fort, at all events," observed Tom; "I hope that before long our army will treat Sebastopol in the same way."

"I wish they were likely to do it at so slight a cost," said Jack, as he thought of Sidney, from whom he had not heard for some time; for he knew what sorrow his loss would cause to his family at Halliburton.

The three commanders, having delivered over their prizes to the admiral, proceeded to carry out their instructions, in conjunction with the Mosquito fleet, engaged in the destruction of the vast magazines of corn and other provisions accumulated at numerous places on the shores of the Sea of Azov, as well as the fleets of vessels loaded with supplies for the Russian army in the Crimea.

"It seems to me a wanton destruction of property," observed Jack when he first received his orders.

Murray, to whom he spoke, smiled. "Sagacious commanders have to take into consideration the appetites of their men, as well as those of the enemy, quite as much as their battlefields and the weapons they use," he observed; "if we can cut off the supplies of the garrison of Sebastopol, we shall render as effectual service as the guns of the besiegers, and quickly bring the war to a conclusion."

"Then I'll set about it with all my heart!" exclaimed Jack; "though I wish, instead of burning the wheat, we could ship it off to our people at home."

"That would prove a somewhat too long operation," observed Murray; "and if we remember that every stack we burn will perhaps shorten the war by as many hours, any scruples we may feel on the subject will soon vanish."

Jack and his brother commanders, remembering this, set energetically to work to perform what would have been otherwise a very disagreeable duty. The gallant Lyons, who in the *Miranda* had been some days in the Sea of Azov, had already inflicted immense damage on the enemy; on his arrival off Genitchesk at the entrance of the Putrid Sea, he found a large fleet of merchantmen at anchor, protected by a strong force of infantry and a battery of field-pieces on the mainland. On sending in to summon the flotilla to surrender, his demand being refused, he despatched his boats under the command of his first lieutenant, Mackenzie, through the strait, covering their advance with a heavy fire of shell on the town and troops. In spite of all opposition, thus protected, the brave lieutenant set fire to seventy-three vessels and several corn-magazines. On returning to their ship, the party discovered that some of the vessels had escaped the conflagration; on this, Captain Lyons despatched a second expedition with three other officers, Lieutenants Buckley and Burgoyne, and Mr. Roberts, a gunner of the *Ardent*. On approaching the shore, and discovering that the enemy were prepared to give them a warm reception, the three latter officers determined to land by themselves, so that their men might escape the risk of being cut off; while Mackenzie undertook the destruction of the shipping. The vessels were quickly set on fire, and the magazines had shared the same fate, when a troop of Cossacks bore down on the three officers who had landed. They, accordingly, had to take to their heels; and, keeping well ahead of their pursuers, were received in safety by Mackenzie on board the boats, which pulled back to the ships without the loss of a single man, one only having been slightly wounded.

Thus he went on from place to place, destroying stores and vessels in the same daring manner, his two lieutenants frequently landing in a four-oared gig, and setting fire with their own hands to different Government buildings. Taganrog, a place of great strength, was attacked, and though the town was protected by some heavy batteries, and above three thousand troops, who kept up a hot fire on the ships and boats, every Government building and magazine was destroyed. In this way Captain Lyons sank or burnt upwards of two hundred and fifty vessels laden with supplies and provisions and stores, to the value of many thousands of pounds, and at the present juncture of immense importance to the Russian army and the beleaguered city. His brave career was, however, drawing to a close; rejoining the squadron off Sebastopol, at the end of a fortnight, he was shortly afterwards struck by a shell, while running into harbour at night to annoy the enemy, and in a few days breathed his last at the hospital at Therapia, to which he had been removed.

He was succeeded in the command of the squadron by Captain Sherard Osborne, an officer of equal determination, courage, and sagacity, who was not likely to leave any of the work he had undertaken undone, or half-done. Our three commanders proceeded in the same spirit to the execution of their duty. On revisiting several places where a few weeks before they had destroyed all the then existing supplies, they found that the Russians, supposing they would not return, had rebuilt their storehouses, and completely replenished them, giving a proof of the productive power of the neighbouring districts. All the work before them was not, however, accomplished with the same ease; hitherto they had had only to dash boldly on shore, protected by the guns of the ships, set fire to the stores, and to be off again as fast as they could. Spies were not wanting, who brought them information of the position of stores; from one of these men, Jack, who was stationed off the spit which separates the Putrid Sea from the Sea of Azov, gained intelligence that some large stores, situated on the Crimean shore, had lately been replenished, and that the grain was only waiting the means of transport to be removed to Sebastopol.

Jack asked the spy whether he would lead a party to the spot; this, however, he declined, but gave so exact a description of the country, that Jack felt convinced that he could find it out without the man's aid. Plenty of volunteers were ready to go; but having, as he said, got every inch of the way into his head, he determined to lead the expedition. He did not, however, hide from himself the dangers to be encountered. "If I destroy these stores, the siege may be shortened by one or two days, or it may be more, and the lives of several of my fellow-creatures saved; then it is my duty to go."

Had Higson been on board, he might have entrusted the expedition to him; Green would be very likely to carry it out; but he feared that Mildmay would fail. He had perfect confidence that Tom would obey his orders; he accordingly fixed on him, with Dick Needham and Jerry Bird, in addition to his gig's usual crew. Standing in at nightfall as close to the spit as the water would allow, he pulled on shore. The boat had now to be dragged across the sands, and launched on the opposite side. He and all hands uniting their strength, accomplished it, however, and away they pulled with muffled oars across the Putrid Sea. A mist lay on the placid water, which would have shrouded them from the view of any boats which might have been passing, even at a hundred yards' distance. Not a word was spoken above a whisper; it was impossible to see the shore, and difficult to know when they might come upon it; indeed, had not the boat been provided with a compass, the commander would have been unable to steer a direct course.

The men gave way with a will, as the success of the expedition depended on the rapidity with which it was carried out. On a sudden, as Jack fancied they were still a considerable way from the shore, he felt the boat's keel passing over a soft bottom; directly afterwards she remained fixed. In vain the men pulled away with might and main, endeavouring to force her over; the water appeared shallower ahead even than astern, and at length all hands had to jump overboard, including the commander and Tom, when they sank almost up to their knees in mud.

"Pretty condition we shall be in if daylight finds us here!" said Tom.

"No fear of that," answered Jack; "off the boat must come."

Needham, with boat-hook in hand, went ahead to ascertain the depth of water, and on his return reported that after some yards it deepened considerably, whilst, as he could see nothing of the land, he concluded that they were on a mudbank.

"No doubt about it," said Jack; and all hands together lifting the boat, they bore her along for fifty yards or so, when, washing the mud off their legs, they tumbled on board, and again gave way.

"Pretty mess we're in," observed Tom.

His brother laughed. "We shall be in a worse mess before long, as we have a couple of rivers and a marsh or two to wade through before we reach our destination. Needham, you are in good wind, I hope?"

"Ay, ay, sir," answered Dick; "I doubt whether any Russian would overtake me if we have to run for it."

"I wish that I was to go with you," said Tom.

"No, you must remain by the boat, and keep a bright lookout that you are not surprised," answered Jack; "have your muskets ready for instant use; and should we at the last be pursued, be ready to cover our retreat; you don't know at what time we may come. We may be turned back before we reach our destination, or we may succeed, and still be hard pressed to escape capture; the last is most likely to occur: at all events, be on the watch."

Jack had previously made all his arrangements; the gunner and Jerry Bird each carried match-boxes in waterproof cases, and small torches which they could easily ignite, so that the moment they stepped on shore they could proceed on their expedition. A sense of the importance of the work to be accomplished made Jack enjoy it, otherwise an act of incendiarism would not have been to his taste. The gunner and Jerry Bird, it must be confessed, did not trouble their heads much about the matter.

At length a group of trees, seemingly of unusual magnitude, standing apparently on the top of a hill, appeared ahead, but almost an instant afterwards the bows of the boat touched a bank with a few willows or alders growing on it. As far as Jack could judge, it was the very spot he would have chosen for landing, as the bushes would afford sufficient concealment to the boat during his absence.

"Remember my orders," said Jack, as he sprang on to the bank, followed by Dick and Jerry. They had not gone many yards when they found themselves floundering in the mud, at which the two latter began to grumble, as seamen will grumble, not at the work before them, but at the mud, which prevented them from advancing as rapidly as they desired.

"Never mind," said Jack, as he led the way, "we shall get on the firm ground presently; those in the boat are much less likely to be taken by surprise than they might have been by the side of a hard bank."

The marsh, however, was broader than Jack expected, but, as they ran lightly over it, their feet did not sink down very deep. They at length reached firm ground. According to the commander's calculation, they had about two miles to go before they could get to their destination. A pocket compass, and a small lantern which threw its light on it, enabled him to steer a direct course. The country was unpopulated and open, the chief impediments in the way of the party being the streams and marshes and rivers. They got on rapidly over the hard ground, but found it heavy work wading amid the expanse of rushes which bordered the streams.

"No crocodiles or alligators about here, I hope, sir?" whispered Jerry to the gunner.

"If there are, it's our business not to mind them," answered Dick, with a low growl, intended as a rebuke to Jerry; "if there was a shoal of sharks, either, we should have no business to cry out till we were caught."

They dropped a few feet behind while thus speaking, but quickly again overtook the commander, who was wading across the stream, the water gradually getting deeper and deeper, till it rose up to his waist.

"Maybe we shall have to swim for it," whispered Dick; "but where's the odds, provided we get across at last?"

Jack led on, not listening to the low, whispered remarks of his companions. One river was thus crossed; still there was another, on the farther bank of which were situated the stacks of wheat destined to destruction. The ford was some way above the stacks, so that they would have to cross the river by it, and then descend the bank, taking the same route on their return. Jack had been unable to ascertain what sentries were likely to be posted in the neighbourhood, or what guards protected the stacks. An extent of open ground had now to be passed over, and there was then a tolerably extensive wood, with more open ground between it and the river. Jack was able to recognise each feature of the country from the description given to him by the spy; he thus felt sure that he was on the right road. He went on and on till the bank of the river was reached, and he could see a town or village on the opposite side. He now led the way up the stream till he discovered the ford, which he and his companions crossed without difficulty, though he had some fears that he might find a guardhouse on the opposite side.

No one, however, appeared; the Russians undoubtedly supposing, from the numerous impediments in the way, that no enemies would venture to attack the place. They had now to make their way along the bank of the river for some distance before they could reach the stacks destined to destruction. It was necessary to proceed with the greatest caution, for the slightest noise might betray them to the enemy, and ensure their capture. They had gone part of the distance when they heard a dog bark, and they could make out, a few yards from the river, the roof of a cottage, from the neighbourhood of which apparently the sound came. They could only hope that the dog was chained, for, should he be loose, he might rush out upon them, and though they might kill him with their cutlasses, the noise they might make would, in all probability, bring his owners on their track.

The mist had cleared away and the stars were shining brightly overhead, so that they had to keep under cover as much as possible. Jack hoped, however, that all the inhabitants of the place would be in bed. Again the dog barked. Jack, in a whisper, ordered the gunner and Jerry to crouch down and remain perfectly quiet for a few minutes, when immediately the dog became silent. After waiting a minute or two, he again led the way forward till he could see the tops of the lofty stacks rising high above the houses against the sky. They had made some way, when again the dog barked fiercely, and they could hear the animal leaping and rolling about, as if trying to break his chain.

"Here comes the brute!" cried the gunner, stepping forward; and they caught sight of the animal, a huge mastiff, bounding towards them. Dick held his drawn cutlass ready in his hand, and as the creature sprang up to seize him by the throat, with one sweep of his weapon he laid it dead at his feet, with its head almost severed from the body.

"Well done, Needham!" exclaimed Jack.

"It was necessary, sir, but I was sorry to kill the poor brute!" answered Dick.

"We have no time to think about that," said Jack, "for we must set the stacks on fire at once;" and they again crept forward. Brave as he was, and fully convinced of the importance of the act he was about to do, he could not help reflecting that it was not the sort of work in which he, as an English officer, would wish to be discovered. However, it was to be done, and the sooner it was done the better. As he got close to the stacks, he looked to either side, to ascertain whether any sentry was posted in the neighbourhood, but discovering no one, he placed his two companions, one at one end, and the other at the centre of the stacks, with directions to strike their lights immediately they saw him ignite his, so that they might fire them at the same moment. He then crept forward to his post, and waited a few seconds to listen; not a sound was heard from the neighbouring village, and, quickly obtaining a light, he set fire to a bundle of stalks which he pulled out of the stack, strewing it along the side. His companions imitating him, in one instant the whole of the immense pile was in a blaze, the flames ascending with unexpected rapidity.

"We must put our best foot foremost," said Jack, suiting the action to the word; and off they set running as hard as they could. Fortunately there was a tolerably well-beaten path along the bank of the river, by which they had come, but concealment was hopeless, and Jack observed the glare of the fire falling on the backs of his two companions as he followed at their heels, feeling it his duty, as he had led the advance, to bring up the rear.

Shouts and cries were presently heard; every moment he expected to see a body of the enemy in hot pursuit. At first he thought of plunging into the stream and swimming across; but, fully clothed as they were, it would have been a difficult undertaking, and they might get over by the ford quite as quickly. They accordingly kept on till it was reached, and then, wading across, they returned down the opposite bank, Jack considering it important to keep in the road they had come. By the time they had got opposite the stacks, the whole were blazing fiercely up, throwing a ruddy glare on all the objects around to a considerable distance. They thus stood revealed to the inhabitants on the opposite side, who appeared not to be aware till then who were the perpetrators of the deed.

Just then they saw a large body of Cossacks galloping up towards the fire, some of whom by their gestures had, it seemed, at that moment caught sight of them.

"We must put on all our steam, or these fellows will be at our heels," said Jack; and again they set forward. One glance he cast over his shoulder showed him the Cossacks making for the ford; he could not help feeling very doubtful whether he and his party could keep ahead of them. The bank of the first river they had crossed was again reached, and plunging in, partly by swimming, and partly by wading, they boldly pushed across, thus avoiding the loss of time by going round by the ford.

Scarcely, however, had they got over, when through the gloom of night they distinguished the Cossacks galloping towards them. They did not stop long to shake themselves, but dashed on, still hoping to keep ahead, as the Cossacks would have to go some distance up the stream to cross the ford.

"I only wish the fellows would try to swim," said Dick; "their horses would stick in the mud and rushes we've had a hard job to get through. Keep up, Jerry, keep up," he continued, observing that his companion was flagging; "we've a clear road before us, and we mustn't let our legs play us false."

Thus encouraged, Jerry made fresh efforts to keep alongside his companions. Jack felt his own legs moving somewhat heavily, and could not help acknowledging to himself that there was every probability of their being overtaken; once across the stream, the Cossacks on their fleet steeds would soon be up to them. The thought of being speared in the back by a savage horseman, and left to die like dogs, was too terrible.

"No; if we are overtaken, we must fight for it, and die like men, with our faces to the foe," said Jack aloud.

"Ay, ay, sir, that we will!" exclaimed Dick; "maybe, however, they'll miss us; and if we can get anywhere near the boat, Mr. Rogers and our fellows will help us by peppering them."

At length Jack was compelled to stop for a moment to draw breath; he took the opportunity of casting a look behind him, to ascertain in what direction the Cossacks were coming, but he could nowhere see them.

"I hope that you are right, Needham," he whispered; "and now, on we go, and we may get up to the boat before we are discovered."

Scarcely had he spoken, than a shout was heard, and the

figures of the horsemen, with their long lances, were perceived against the sky.

"On! on!" cried Jack; "they see us; no matter, we are still well ahead of them."

Dick, seizing Jerry's arm, again sprang forward; on came the Cossacks clattering in their rear; the boat was still at too great a distance to enable them to make themselves heard by Tom. The ground was hard and level, and, straining every nerve, they ran faster than they had ever before done in their lives. No mercy could be expected from the Cossacks, should they be overtaken.

Again Jerry began to slacken his pace. "Cheer up, mate, cheer up!" cried Dick; "the Cossacks' lances are not within a good many inches of us yet, and it will be time enough to cry out when they get inside our waistcoats."

Jack, though he might have gone faster than either of his men, would not leave them behind; if he sprang ahead, it was merely to have time to look round and ascertain how far off were their pursuers. He calculated that they were approaching the boat, and that if they shouted loudly Tom would hear them; once more he looked round; the horsemen were within a hundred yards of them; they might have stopped them with their carbines; possibly, however, they were unloaded, when they hurriedly threw themselves on horseback. Jack, as he sprang forward, felt the ground very soft beneath his feet, and recollected that they must have reached the marsh they had crossed on leaving the boat. To run across it seemed scarcely possible, as their feet had before sunk in every few yards they trod; there appeared to be no hope of escape.

Just at this moment down came poor Jerry—who had for some few seconds been floundering along, though doing his best to keep up—with his face in the mud.

"Go ahead, sir, go ahead!" cried Dick; "don't stop for us; I'll do my best to set Jerry on his legs."

"I will not desert him," answered Jack, stooping to lift up the fallen seaman, while Dick lifted him up with the other arm, and quickly again set him on his feet.

"Heave out that quid of mud from your mouth, and give your eyes a rub over, and you will be all to rights," said Dick; "don't say die yet; now on we go;" and suiting the action to the word, dragging Jerry along with him, they began moving forward in a "hop-skip-and-a-jump" fashion, which enabled them to get over the soft ground with tolerable rapidity. They were scarcely more than a quarter of the way across, when the Cossacks reached the edge of the marsh, of the existence of which they were apparently not aware, for, without pulling rein, they plunged in; the consequence being that, with the impetus they had attained, and the weight of their horses, they sank deep down in the soft mud.

Jack, with infinite satisfaction, saw that they were floundering about, but he did not allow his companions to slacken their speed, for the horses would still, probably, be able to make their way across it. He, therefore, assisting to support Jerry, moved on as fast as his weight and the nature of the ground would allow. Jerry's fall, however, had given an advantage to their pursuers, who were now making their way across the morass, sometimes stopped by a soft portion, and again moving faster where the ground was comparatively firmer. Still the Cossacks had somewhat gained upon them, and were scarcely fifty yards off, when Tom's welcome shout reached their ears.

"We see you, we see you; and we see your pursuers too!" he cried; "we've got our muskets ready to cover you."

"Then fire!" cried Jack; "and reload quickly."

A volley from the boat somewhat staggered the Cossacks, for though none of them were seen to fall, yet the bullets whistled pretty close to their ears. It might have made them less eager in spurring on their steeds; still, on they came. The sound seemed to revive Jerry, who, though nearly done up, again made an effort to push on. A few shots were fired at them by their disappointed pursuers, who might have guessed that they would soon be beyond their power.

Tom had kept the boat ready to shove off at a moment's notice; the latter part of the ground was somewhat higher and harder; across it they rushed as hard as they could pelt, for the Cossacks had already passed the softer portions, and, once upon it, they would be up to them. The points of their long lances were couched not many yards behind, and Jack again shouted to Tom to fire, while he, with the gunner and Jerry, almost the next instant sprang into the boat.

"Shove off!" cried Jack, seizing an oar; Dick and Jerry imitated him, while the rest were reloading their firearms. The boat was but a few yards from the bank when the Cossacks reached it, and had to pull up sharp to avoid plunging into the water.

"Good-bye, old fellows!" shouted Dick; "you've had a hard scamper, and now you may go back and look after your cornstacks."

That these had not been put out was evident by the ruddy glare which suffused the sky in the distance. On receiving another volley from the boat, the Cossacks wheeled about and made their way over the marsh, where, had Jack thought fit, they might all have been picked off in detail; but he had from the first seen the wickedness of killing a single human being unnecessarily, and now that they could no longer impede their flight, he was glad to let them escape. Lest, however, they might give notice to any armed Russian boats to proceed in chase of the daring Englishmen, Jack ordered his crew to pull away as hard as they could, so that they might possibly regain the ship before daylight.

They were not, however, free from danger, as the burning stacks would put the people on the shores for miles round on the alert, and they could scarcely expect to escape pursuit. Jack, by steering rather more to the northward, escaped the bank on which they had before run, and he hoped now to make a straight course across the water. The sandpit had then to be passed before the boat could be launched into the more open sea. Poor Jerry was so exhausted that it was some time before he could handle an oar, so he employed the interval in trying to wash the mud out of his eyes and nose.

The mist had again come down, and but a few yards could be seen ahead; thus the crew were pulling on as hard as ever, when, before Jack was aware that they were near, the boat's bows grated against the sand, which fortunately yielded easily or they would have been stove in.

"All hands leap out!" cried Jack; and the men, seizing the boat, began hauling away, without stopping an instant, across the sand.

They had got very nearly to the water's edge on the other side, when Tom shouted out, "See, sir, here come some Cossacks!"

It was fortunate that Tom had observed them; in another minute they would have been up to the boat, but the men, giving her a shove which sent her skimming away over the calm surface, leaped on board, and, getting out their oars, pulled away at a rapid rate, leaving the Cossacks to shake their lances at them in vain.

After pulling some way, they caught sight of the *Tornado's* light, when the commander and his party were welcomed with a hearty cheer on board, the crew having felt very anxious when they heard of the dangerous character of the expedition on which he had gone.

CHAPTER XXI

Dick Needham's Expedition—Dick and Archie captured—Attack on the Caravan—Unexpected Meeting with Higson and Midshipmen—Higson's unwillingness to return—Jack's Solution of the Difficulty—The Young Ladies' Grief—Tom, against his will, joins the *Flash*—Captures a Fort and Guns—The Sleeping Beauties—The *Flash* Aground—Attacked by Russians—Fate of *Flash*—Desmond thinks of Emigrating—Tom's "Prior Engagement"—Capture of Kinburn.

THE Mosquito fleet had been employed for many weeks in destroying almost immeasurable quantities of provisions and stores, effectually crippling the resources of the Czar's armies. Private property had invariably been spared, so that the inhabitants of the country did not exhibit any ill-feeling towards the English. The few men who by chance fell into their hands were treated with considerable kindness.

Jack's usual plan was, after having ascertained the whereabouts of the magazines or stacks, which were nearly always placed on the seashore, to steam up to the spot just before daybreak, and immediately to send in one or two boats, the officers of which, landing with torches, quickly set the stores on fire, and scampered back before they could be pursued. Night after night, now in one place, now in another, stores and magazines were destroyed; and as there were upwards of a dozen vessels thus engaged, it may be conceived what mischief was committed.

There is an old saying, however, that the pitcher which goes often to the well gets broken at last. Jack had heard from his faithful spy, Niuski, that some large stores existed on the shores of a lake about a mile from the coast, the river communicating with which was too shallow to allow of the boats proceeding up it. He had intended going himself, but an attack of illness made him feel that it would be imprudent to venture, as he might break down on the way. Dick Needham, hearing of what was required to be done, at once volunteered to lead an expedition, and Jack gladly accepted his offer. Tom and Archie, who had been burning to distinguish themselves in some exploit of the sort, begged that they might be allowed to go.

"There are no fellows on board who have better wind or can run faster than we can," observed Tom; "Archie, with his long legs, gets over the ground at a great rate, and I can keep up with him by making my short ones move so much the faster."

Jack, believing that there was no greater risk than usual, consented, greatly to the midshipmen's delight. Billy Blueblazes was ordered to go in the boat, to remain in charge of her while the rest of the party were on shore. The spy had informed Jack that there were no enemies in the neighbourhood. Tom and Archie were in high glee. Dick Needham had settled to take only one man with him, besides the midshipmen, leaving the rest under the command of Billy Blueblazes to cover their retreat. The boat, with muffled oars, pulled in for the shore, when, no one being seen, Dick and his companions landed.

"Remember, Billy, the commander's orders are that you are on no account to leave the boat; and should by chance the enemy come down upon you, you are to pull off to the ship, and obtain further orders," said Tom; "not that there's much chance of that."

"Good-bye, my laddie," said Archie, as he and Tom leaped on shore; "we'll be back in little more than half an hour, and you will know when to look out for us by seeing the jolly bonfire we are going to light."

There was no moon, but the stars shone brightly forth, enabling them to steer their way by them. The country being pretty level, they hoped, should they have to run for it, to make rapid way; it was also tolerably open, with here and there copses composed of trees of moderate height, by advancing along the side of which Dick expected to be able to keep concealed till they had gained their destination.

"We may reserve our strength for the run back after we have set the stores on fire," he whispered to the two midshipmen; "we learned a lesson about that in our other expedition."

Whenever they had to cross an open space, they bent down like North American Indians on a war-trail, keeping perfect silence, so that they might have passed close to an enemy without being discovered. Thus on they went, Dick calculating that it would take them about half an hour to reach the magazines, and they expected to return in half that time. Dick led, Tom and Archie followed, and Tim Nolan brought up the rear. Each one of them knew beforehand what they were to do, and there seemed no risk of failure.

The magazines and stores were at length reached, presenting much the same appearance as those which had before been destroyed. Not a sound which could indicate that any human beings were in the neighbourhood was heard; not a dog barked. In less than a minute they all had their torches lighted, and effectually set fire to the buildings and stores, which blazed up so rapidly that had any people been out of doors at the time the flames would have quickly betrayed them. Their task being accomplished, they set off at a rapid speed towards the boat, Dick as before leading. The midshipmen enjoyed the scamper, and they had every reason to believe that they should get back in safety. They had not got far, however, when they heard the voices of people from the neighbouring cottages, who had been, it was evident, aroused by the glare, and who would soon, from the nature of the conflagration, suspect that it had been the work of incendiaries. Unless, however, they could throw themselves on horseback, there was no risk of their overtaking the nimble seamen; still concealment was difficult, for as the fire increased its glare fell upon them and betrayed their whereabouts.

They had passed over the widest extent of open ground, and had made their way along under the shelter of a copse, when they were again exposed to view. As they were passing another copse a short distance on their right, several shots whistled by them.

"Push on, Needham!" cried Tom; "they're not very good marksmen."

A cry from Tim Nolan made Tom turn his head, when he saw a party of the enemy, who had rushed out from the copse, close upon him, while Tim, by actively dodging, tried to escape. "Arrah, never mind me!" he shouted; "though I'm after being made a prisoner, you'll get off if you keep going."

Archie, who was some little way behind him, endeavoured to escape, when his foot struck against a stone, and the cry he uttered made Tom again look round and spring back to help him get on his feet. In his hurry he also fell; the cry he had uttered made Dick also look round, when, believing that one or both of the midshipmen were wounded, though he was so far ahead as to have been able to reach the boat without difficulty, he immediately turned back to assist them. As he did so, he saw the Russians hurrying up. Drawing his cutlass, he threw himself between them and the midshipmen, hoping to drive back their foes, and allow them to make their escape. Tom and Archie were quickly on their legs, but before they could do as Dick told them and run for their lives, they were surrounded by a party of helmeted Russians.

Dick, however, laid about him so lustily with his cutlass, that had the midshipmen been willing to leave him, they, at all events, might have made their escape. They were endeavouring to draw their swords, when the Russians, throwing themselves on them from behind, seized their arms; and Dick received a wound from a bayonet in his sword-arm which made him, very much against his will, drop his weapon. In an instant, more Russians coming on, they were completely overpowered and dragged away; not, however, till Dick, in a stentorian voice, had let Billy Blueblazes know what had happened, and directed him to pull back to the ship with the news.

Billy had caught sight of the party in the distance just as the enemy rushed out on them, and had seen Dick turn back to help Tom and Archie. Had he not been ordered to remain in the boat, he would have landed, and tried to assist them. Fortunately, perhaps, he did not make the attempt, as his men could not have fired at the Russians for fear of hitting their friends, and he and his party would, in all probability, have been captured, with the loss of their boat. As soon as he heard Dick's voice, he shoved off and pulled away for the ship, in the hopes of getting assistance.

Jack, however, saw that it would be useless to send a party on shore, as the Russians would to a certainty carry off their prisoners to a distance. As Billy stated that he saw a large number of men, the fresh party might very likely be overwhelmed. Jack naturally felt very much grieved at the loss of the midshipmen and gunner, although they were not likely to be otherwise than kindly treated; still the war might last for some time, and they would lose the advantage of the experience they were gaining — while he could ill afford to dispense with Needham's services, or lose Tim Nolan, a good seaman on whom he could always depend.

"The midshipmen are pretty sure to fall on their feet wherever they are carried," observed Mr. Mildmay, "so we need not, I hope, be over-anxious about them."

Next morning, Jack sent a flag of truce on shore to inquire what had become of his captured officers and man, and to offer to send them any necessaries they might require. Before the boat returned, another steamer hove in sight, which proved to be the *Giaour.* Murray had orders to summon the *Tornado*, with any other vessels he might fall in with, in order that their boats might form an expedition up the river—across which ran the great highroad leading to the Crimea. Information had been received that a large amount of stores and provisions were on their way to the garrison of Sebastopol.

"If we can cut them off, we shall commit incalculable damage —perhaps starve the garrison into surrender," Murray observed. He was, of course, sorry to hear of Archie's capture, but the two commanders agreed that they need not make themselves very unhappy about the matter. Green, who had gone on shore with the flag of truce, returned, saying that he had been unable to fall in with anyone who could communicate information about the prisoners; and they had therefore to be left for the present to their fate.

A few hours afterwards the *Flash* appeared, and the three commanders proceeded to the rendezvous, a short distance out of sight of land. It had been arranged that they were to stand in at nightfall, and immediately to send their boats up the river, so as if possible to take the enemy by surprise. In the meantime several of the fleet were sent to different parts of the coast, to burn all the Government stores they could discover, and thus to assist in misleading the enemy. The squadron was delayed longer than had been expected, but at length information was received that a caravan was on its way, and might be expected near the mouth of the river the next night. Jack settled to take command of one of his boats, while Green took command of the other. Adair went in one of his, and Desmond, greatly to his delight, had charge of the second. Murray also despatched two of his, and the other ships sent the same number.

The squadron came off the mouth of the river about an hour and a half after dark, when the flotilla of boats, without a moment's delay, proceeded up the stream, with muffled oars. A mist lay on the water, though the stars could be distinguished overhead, which, as they kept directly in the centre, would, they hoped, conceal them from any persons on the banks. The crews were ordered to keep perfect silence; the larger boats were armed with guns in their bows, capable of throwing shot and shell, so that they were well able to compete with any force which might appear, even though accompanied by field-pieces. It was known, however, that the enemy possessed but few in that part of the country.

The boats at length got up within about a quarter of a mile of the ferry at which the caravan was expected to pass. Either bank of the river was lined with a broad belt of tall rushes, in which they were directed to conceal themselves, while Adair in his gig pulled up to try and ascertain whether the waggons had reached the bank. The commodore had settled to wait till some had crossed, so as to attack as many as possible close to the edge of the water, making sure of destroying them as well as those actually crossing.

The crews of the boats were waiting in anxious expectation for the order to dash out of their places of concealment. Day at last dawned; the startled wildfowl flew up from among the rushes, screaming loudly at the intruders; while, as the light increased, the dark water assumed a brighter hue, though a mist still lay on the surface, which greatly assisted in the concealment of the boats. At length Adair's gig was seen dimly through the mist, pulling at a rapid rate down the stream. In an instant the crews of the boats, jumping into their seats, got out their oars ready to give way as soon as the order should be received. Adair soon reached the commodore's boat; he said that the provision-waggons had begun to cross, and that several were already on the opposite or western bank. The boats had been ordered to pull up in two divisions, the larger to attack the east bank, the other the west; Jack's and Adair's boats belonged to the latter.

The welcome order to advance was heard, and the boats, emerging from their cover, pulled away in two lines, as fast as the men could bend to their oars, moving along like two huge serpents darting on their prey. Not a word was uttered; so that the boats, still shrouded by the mist, were close up to the ferry before they were discovered. The Russians were taken completely by surprise; the waggons on board the ferry-boat were at once captured. The small body of troops sent to convoy them fired a volley from the east bank, on which side the greater number of waggons were still advancing to cross, and then, seeing the strong forces approaching to the attack, retreated; while shouts and shrieks and cries resounded on all sides, the drivers endeavouring to turn round their animals and escape—while the seamen, who sprang on shore, set to work to cut the traces, to prevent them from so doing.

Jack and Adair, with their men, had landed on the west bank, where the drivers of the waggons were doing their utmost to urge on their beasts. The sailors were getting quickly up to the nearest of them to put a stop to their progress, while the others ahead still endeavoured to escape; some in their hurry getting off the road upset. The wildest uproar and confusion ensued, the drivers shrieking to their beasts, the seamen shouting as they rushed forward.

One of the leading waggons, as it dashed forward, overtook a carriage which had apparently been on its way down to the ferry, when the postillions, alarmed by the sounds which reached their ears, turned it round to escape in the opposite direction. A waggon coming against its hinder wheel, had upset it on one side of the road. Just at that juncture, Adair and Desmond, who with their men had gone ahead, arriving at the spot, heard cries for help from female voices proceeding from the carriage. At the same moment they saw a gentlemanly-looking personage in a travelling-dress emerging from one of the windows, and several others, who had evidently been on the outside, endeavouring to pick themselves up in a field into which they had been thrown.

"If that isn't Tom Rogers, I'm not an Irishman!" exclaimed Desmond; "and there's Archie Gordon, too—hurrah! provided they haven't broken their legs or arms, they'll be all to rights after all;—and that's no other than our friend Colonel Paskiewich."

Hurrying forward to assist Colonel Paskiewich in extricating himself from the overturned carriage, they perceived that there were several ladies in the inside, who, although they every now and then uttered screams, were wisely remaining quiet, holding each other in their arms.

"Thank you, gentlemen," said the colonel; "I must now ask you to help out my wife and daughters, who are naturally fearfully alarmed at what has occurred."

"We regret to have been the unintentional cause of their disaster," said Adair politely; while he and Gerald, climbing up on the side of the carriage, caught hold of one of the young ladies, who proved to be Mademoiselle Feodorowna. They were quickly joined by Tom and Archie, the former of whom took the fair Feodorowna in charge. Another person now made his way up from the field into which he had been thrown.

"Why, Higson, my fine fellow, I am very glad to see you!" exclaimed Adair; "where do you come from?"

"I'll tell you all about it by and by," answered Higson, "when we have got out the ladies;" and he lending a hand, Mademoiselle Ivanowna was next hauled up, Higson taking her in his arms with the most affectionate solicitude and carrying her to a place of safety by the side of the road; while the rest dragged out her mamma, who, if not much hurt, was greatly alarmed. The coachman, who had also been thrown off his box, had in the meantime been assisting the postillions in cutting the traces; which, having been done, the latter galloped off, under the impression, probably, that should they remain they would be made prisoners with their master.

While this scene was taking place, Jack, with Jos Green, and their men, had advanced towards the posthouse, in front of which a small body of troops were drawn up, waiting an opportunity, apparently, to attack the English as soon as they were still more scattered in their pursuit of the waggons, as it was evident they would quickly be. No sooner, however, did they perceive Jack's compact party of seamen in well-ordered array advancing towards them, than, without even firing their muskets, they went to the right-about, and scampered off as fast as their legs could carry them.

Just as they disappeared, a window in the posthouse was thrown open, and out of it jumped Dick Needham, followed by Tim Nolan. "Erin-go-bragh!" shouted the latter; "it's ourselves have gained our liberty."

"There's no time to tell you how it all happened, sir," said Dick, as Jack welcomed him; "we were not badly treated by the Russians, but I am main glad to get out of their hands—I only wish there was as good a chance of your brother and Mr. Gordon getting set at liberty; but I am sorry to say they gave their parole, as they called it, to the colonel; and when I told them that Tim and I had got a plan for getting off from the Russians and making our way to the coast, they told me that they could not join in it, as they were bound to stay till the war was over."

Commander Rogers, however, had no time to listen further to what his gunner had to say, as he had to set to work at once to destroy the captured waggons. Having examined the posthouse to ascertain that no enemies lurked within, he set fire to the leading waggons; and, upon his way to the river to destroy the remainder, he came upon the overturned carriage, near which he found the colonel's family, with Higson and the midshipmen. The colonel expressed his pleasure at seeing him, and informed him that he was on his way to visit an estate, remote from the seat of war, in the eastern parts of the country, when he heard that some English officers and seamen who had been made prisoners were in the neighbourhood, and that on visiting them he discovered that they belonged to the *Tornado*. Upon making application to the governor of the district, he had succeeded in obtaining the release of the officers on their parole, though the men had to continue in charge of their guard. "I am afraid, therefore," he added, "that I cannot restore the former to you, unless you choose to consider me your prisoner."

"As you are a non-combatant at present, we certainly cannot capture you or your family," answered Jack; "but with regard to my lieutenant and the two midshipmen, I am somewhat in doubt whether or not to do so."

Greatly to Jack's surprise, Higson and Tom both expressed their decided opinion that as men of honour they ought to remain; though Archie seemed much less confident on the subject.

"We'll get your carriage on its wheels and then think about this matter, colonel," said Jack; "and if you will send your coachman to bring back the runaway postillions and their steeds, we will escort you across the river, and see you on your journey to the eastward."

As there were no enemies to contend with, the plan proposed by Jack was quickly carried into execution; the horses were brought back; the carriage, which was an old-fashioned family coach, had not received much damage. Jack consulted Adair as to how he should act towards the lieutenant and midshipmen.

"As they are in our power, we are bound to lay hands on them whether they like it or not," answered Adair; "if they go unwillingly, their parole is not broken;" whereupon Jack told Higson and the midshipmen that they must consider themselves under arrest, and prepare to return in the boats to their ship.

On hearing this, both the young ladies began to evince signs of agitation.

"Surely you are not going to take away Lieutenant Higson!" exclaimed Ivanowna.

"You cannot be so cruel as to carry off our dear Tom!" cried Feodorowna.

"We had all sorts of pleasant schemes to make them contented during their exile," added Ivanowna.

"I must be very hard-hearted, and perform my duty," answered Jack.

It was pretty clear that both Higson and Tom had no objection to remaining, but he was firm; though Archie seemed happy enough to get back.

"I'll tell you how it is," he whispered to Desmond; "the first lieutenant and Tom are spooney on the young ladies; it is my belief that they expect to marry them some day. The colonel and his wife seem to have taken a great fancy to Higson."

"Oh, oh!" said Jack; "that makes it doubly important to keep them out of harm's way."

In vain the young ladies again and again pleaded, supported by their mamma and the colonel; Jack was inexorable. The remains of the waggons burnt on the banks of the river having been cleared away, the colonel's carriage was escorted to the ferry-boat, which conveyed it across to the opposite bank. Here, however, so many more waggons had been destroyed that some time was spent before it could proceed. Higson and the midshipmen now got leave to pay their farewells to the ladies. Ivanowna could with difficulty restrain her feelings, as the gallant lieutenant approached to shake hands; and Archie declared to Desmond that he heard him vowing unalterable affection, and making a promise that as soon as the war was over he would come back and marry her, with her parents' permission.

The more impulsive Feodorowna threw her arms round Tom's neck and kissed him on both cheeks. He, in return, made the same promise as his lieutenant, with a proviso that he should obtain his papa's permission.

"All right," said Jack, when he heard of it; "he's very safe."

A considerable amount of damage had been inflicted, but the waggons proved only to be a leading detachment, a second and larger portion being some miles in the rear, and they, getting timely notice of the raid of the English, retreated to a safe distance. The commodore, receiving information that troops with some field-pieces were advancing, prudently conducted his boats down the river, to avoid an engagement which could have produced no satisfactory results.

Tom Rogers was at first very much downcast, but in the company of his old friends quickly regained his spirits; and he and Archie were loud in their praises of the hospitality with which they had been treated. Higson did not say much, but Jack could not help suspecting that he no longer relished being engaged in hostile operations against the countrymen of his charmer. He confessed as much: "Still, you've known me long enough to be sure that though it may be against the grain, I'll do my duty whatever happens."

Higson kept to his word, and no man was more active in the operations which soon afterwards took place off Gheisk, Vodnia, and Glofira. Strange as it may seem, considering that the places had before been attacked, the Russians had accumulated along the shore in their neighbourhood enormous rows of stacks, several miles in extent. They had, however, four thousand troops to protect their property, while they were aware of the small force possessed by the English, who could not muster more than two hundred men for boat service. The larger vessels, from want of water, had to remain in the offing, while the gunboats towed the other boats as near as possible to the shore, and then covered them by their heavy fire. They pulled in, when their crews, springing to land, drove back the enemy, and set fire to the stacks in succession; proving that it is much easier to commit harm than to prevent it.

These attacks being made simultaneously at different points, so distracted the enemy, that they knew not in which direction to proceed; scarcely had the flames burst out at one point than they saw fires blazing up at several others. The stores at Vodnia and Glofira having been destroyed, the squadron proceeded off Gheisk. Here, for full four miles, stacks of corn and hay were arranged close to the water's edge; while under the protection of the forts around the town were vast piles of timber, cured fish, naval stores, and a number of boats. Here again the shallowness of the water prevented the larger vessels from approaching; even the gunboats could not get in nearer than long range; such boats as could carry heavy guns, being distributed in four divisions, were sent in to cover the landing parties in the smaller boats, about a mile from each other. As they approached, they saw that the Russians had thrown up light breastworks along their front, from which they kept up an unremitting fire on their invaders. Fortunately the wind blew on shore, and carried the smoke from their own and the

British guns in their faces; the landing-parties, rapidly advancing, sprang on shore, and, dashing with bayonet and cutlass over the Russian breastworks, speedily put the enemy to flight.

The stacks along the whole of the line, being simultaneously lighted, blew so dense a cloud of smoke into the eyes of the Russians, that, though they rallied and opened a hot fire, they were unable to take aim or ascertain what their persevering foes were about. In six hours every stack, as well as the timber and naval stores and boats, were destroyed, with no other loss to the British than five men wounded.

These proceedings, unheroic as they might appear, tended greatly to bring the war to a conclusion. The *Flash*, with several other vessels, had in the meantime been despatched to different parts of the coast to carry on a similar work. Tom had a short time before been sent to serve on board her. After he had been brought back to the *Tornado*, he appeared a changed being; unless when compelled, he spoke to no one except Higson, and they two seemed to have much interesting conversation together. Jack observed it, and came to the very natural conclusion that Tom was over head and ears in love with the Russian colonel's daughter; he consulted Murray on the subject.

"Send him on board the *Flash*," was Murray's answer; "Adair and young Desmond will soon knock all that sort of nonsense out of him. It never does for midshipmen to be falling in love; it is bad enough for a lieutenant—except under some circumstances," added Murray, recollecting how both he and Jack had acted.

"At all events my father would not approve of his marrying a Russian, even putting her religion out of the question," said Jack.

The *Flash* being in company at the time, Jack pulled on board her and soon arranged the matter with Adair, who very readily consented to take charge of Tom. That young gentleman was somewhat astonished at finding that he was thus to be disposed of, but he could not venture to expostulate with his commander, even though that commander was his brother. With a deep sigh he wished Higson good-bye.

"Perhaps if you are sending a letter on shore you will put in a word from me to Feodorowna, and assure her that I shall ever be faithful," said Tom.

"As to that, Tom, I don't think there is much chance that I shall have an opportunity of writing to anyone living in the enemy's country," answered Higson, who could not help perceiving the absurdity of the thing. "You, with the interest you possess, have certain prospects of promotion, and you will be giving them all up, and be separated from your family, if you were to marry a Russian and settle down in this part of the world. My case is very different; I have no interest—am getting on in life, and shall probably not get my next step till I am old enough to retire from the service. The young lady has, I'll allow, a fancy for you, but she'll soon get over it; and if I ever come out and marry her sister, I'll persuade her that it is the best thing she can do."

Tom did not quite fancy this advice, but, like many another midshipman, he had to grin and bear it; and was two minutes afterwards proceeding with his chest on board the *Flash*. Gerald welcomed him warmly, and, having received the cue from Adair, said not a word for some time about the fair Feodorowna. The *Flash* being actively engaged, Tom had plenty of work, and very little time to think about his lady-love. His conscience was not at all troubled when he was sent in to burn stacks of corn and hay, and other Government property; indeed, had he been so, as he had heard Jack observe that by doing so the war would be the sooner brought to a conclusion, he would have considered that he was doing what would be well pleasing to the colonel and his family.

Although Adair thought Tom a goose for falling in love, he yet placed great confidence in his gallantry and discretion. The *Flash* had been sent to the eastern end of the Sea of Azov. She was cruising one day close inshore, when her commander observed a fort which mounted six guns, but could see no gunners to fight them. He accordingly came to the conclusion that they had been withdrawn to garrison Taganrog, or some other important fortress.

"We must have those guns," observed Adair. "I intend sending you, Rogers, and Desmond, in to-night to bring them off, should I find, as I suspect, that they are undefended," he said to Tom. "You will be supplied with a scaling-ladder, with which you can take a peep in and ascertain the state of affairs. If there are only three or four soldiers, you must secure them; then shut the gates of the fort, to prevent anyone getting in, while you hoist the guns into the boat."

Tom and Gerald were delighted with the thoughts of the proposed expedition, and undertook faithfully to carry out their commander's orders. The *Flash* continued steaming on till she was out of sight of the fort, when, as soon as it was dark, her head was put inshore, and she ran back to within a short distance of the fort. Tom and Gerald were ordered to burn a blue light should they require assistance, but if not, to carry out the work as quietly as possible.

"You may trust us, sir," they said, as they stepped into the gig, which had a crew of six hands, and a supply of tackles for lowering the guns.

"This is just the sort of fun I like," observed Tom, as they were pulling for the shore.

"Much better than sighing your breath out for the Russian damsel," answered Desmond; "I am sure of that." It was the first time he had ventured to touch on the delicate subject.

"What, have you heard about my little affair?" asked Tom; "I suppose, then, the whole fleet have been talking about it?"

"Don't trouble yourself as to that," whispered Desmond; they were both speaking in a low voice, so that neither their own men nor the enemy could hear them; "however, it is time, unless we want to be discovered, to clap a stopper on our jaw-tackles."

"You are right," said Tom; "we shall soon be up to the fort." They pulled on till they came under the walls, which rose sheer out of the water. Landing on one side, and leaving a couple of hands in the boat, they carried the scaling-ladder to a wall which offered a fair prospect of their being able to mount to the top. Tom claimed the post of honour for himself, the rest of the party being prepared to mount as soon as he should summon them. The instant after the ladder was placed he was on the top of it. On looking down, not a human being could he see, either awake or asleep. Making the signal to his companions, they speedily followed him, and dropped down noiselessly into the fort.

Their first care, as ordered, was to secure the gate; and then, lighting their lanterns, they began to search the various chambers in the fort. They had not gone far when they heard voices from what appeared to be a guardhouse. "At all events, we shall have no great difficulty in securing them," said Tom. As they opened the door, they found four soldiers, a flagon of vodka before them, and their heads resting on the table.

They were excessively astonished to find their arms seized by a party of Englishmen, who signified by their gestures that the less noise they made the better. They were then lashed to their seats, and almost immediately afterwards dropped off to sleep again.

"At all events, we are not likely to meet with much opposition," said Tom; "though, if we had had some fighting, we might have gained more credit."

No other persons being found in the fort, they immediately set to work to unship the guns and to lower them down into the boat, which was brought under the wall for the purpose. They were of brass, and not very heavy considering their size, but it was soon found that three were as many as the gig could carry. Having secured these, they pulled back to the *Flash*, which now stood in as close as she could venture, when they returned for the other three. They looked in as they arrived at the drunken garrison, who were still fast asleep and unconscious of what was taking place. The remaining guns were then removed as the first had been.

"Faith, those Russian fellows will be astonished when they wake to-morrow morning and find themselves minus their guns," exclaimed Gerald, laughing.

"I only hope that they won't be shot in consequence," said Tom. "I think we ought to have left a notice of the way we surprised the fort, with a request that the brave garrison may not be punished."

On returning to the ship, they received due commendation from their commander for the way in which their exploit had been performed. The next day Adair himself determined to undertake a still more hazardous expedition, very similar to that in which Tom and Desmond had been captured. He had to proceed north, two miles from the coast, to the banks of a river, where he burned a large number of stacks. On his return he was chased by a body of Cossacks; he fortunately got within fire of his men in the boats just as the Cossacks were up to him. He acknowledged on getting on board that he had never had a harder run in his life.

Thoroughly knocked up, he turned in, leaving orders that the ship should be kept along the coast, so as to draw off their attention from other places which were to be attacked. Adair was in a deeper sleep than a commander under such circumstances generally ventures to enjoy, when suddenly he was startled by a shock, accompanied by an ominous grating sound, the meaning of which he too painfully knew.

"The ship's on shore!" he exclaimed to himself, starting up

and with the practised rapidity of a seaman putting on his clothes. An officer entering his cabin, he found his worst apprehensions realised. The *Flash* had struck on a reef, not a quarter of a mile from the beach. He was on deck in a moment; the hands were turned up, and the boats immediately lowered to lay out an anchor astern to haul her off. The day was just breaking, and as the light increased rocks were seen inside of the ship, with a sandy beach and a wide extent of level country.

In vain the officers and crew exerted themselves; the tide had been falling, and every instant made the task of getting the ship off more difficult. Adair had once before lost his ship under circumstances when the best of seamanship could not have saved her; but he now felt that she had been got on shore by inexcusable carelessness, and this thought made him inclined to become almost frantic. He restrained his temper and feelings, however, in a wonderful way for an Irishman, and with perfect coolness bent all his energies to the task of getting her off. His first lieutenant was on the sick list; the second had a short time before been relieved by a mate who somewhat resembled Mr. Mildmay, without the sterling qualities of that officer, and for the sake of being better able, as he thought, to examine the coast, had kept the ship just a point or two, as he said, to the northward of the course given to him. However, had he even steered directly for the shore the commander was answerable, Terence knew too well.

In vain the crew laboured away at the capstan till the hawser was taut as a fiddle-string; not an inch would the ship budge. The master suggested that by heaving the guns and stores overboard she might be got off.

"And perhaps even then we might stick fast, or before she is afloat the enemy might make his appearance and find us at his mercy," answered the commander; "no, no—we'll keep our teeth, and show them too, to some effect, as long as the ship holds together."

Tom and Desmond were not very complimentary to the stupid old mate who had been the cause of the disaster. Tom, who was acting as signal-midshipman, had been for some time examining the shore, when he caught sight of some figures moving along in the distance. Presently, as they approached, he could see that they formed a small body of Cossack cavalry; two of them galloped on ahead, till they got near enough to ascertain the condition of the ship, A shot from one of her long guns, though it missed them, sent them to the right-about, and the whole body soon afterwards disappeared. No long time, however, had elapsed when they were again discerned coming in the direction of the ship, accompanied by a body of infantry and several field-pieces.

"We must be ready for those fellows," observed Terence, "and do our best to dismount their guns."

While one portion of the crew were sent to their quarters, the others were kept employed in endeavouring to haul off the ship. On came the infantry, looking out for such imperfect shelter as could be found on the coast; and the guns, which had remained some way behind them, opened their fire on the ship. They were not ill served, and their shot fell pretty thickly about her. Terence immediately ordered his guns to be fired in return, when the Cossacks, wheeling about, retired to a safe distance.

"I can't say much for the gunnery of those fellows," said Tom; "not a shot has struck us yet."

"Wait a bit, my boy," answered Desmond; "they'll get the range presently. It's more easy for them to hit a big object like our ship, than it is for us to reach those little gimcracks of guns."

The Russian riflemen having in the meantime advanced, their bullets kept whistling through the air, close to the heads of the crew, who, however, took no more notice of them than had they been pellets from pop-guns. At last a shot from the *Flash* struck the earth directly in front of one of the Russian guns, which at the same instant was fired, and the next, when the dust and smoke had cleared away, it was seen upset with its carriage broken, and several gunners lying stretched on the earth on either side of it. The other guns, however, still kept their position, and fired away as briskly as before.

"They'll be after getting tired of that," observed Desmond, "if we can manage to send another of our pills down their throats like the last."

The firing was kept up for some time on both sides without intermission, no apparent effect being produced on the enemy, while the ship was frequently hulled by their shot. Still Adair did not despair of getting her off, and as soon as the tide began to rise, he set to work with renewed energy. He and his crew seemed to bear charmed lives; for though the shot caught the rigging above their heads, and came plunging into the ship's side, not one of them had been hit.

"There's a fresh body of the enemy coming down, sir," said Tom, pointing to the north-east.

"If they are only Cossacks they'll not harm us," answered Adair, taking a look in the direction Tom pointed through his telescope. "I am not quite certain about that same," he observed to his first lieutenant.

"They appear to me to be artillery," answered that officer.

In a few minutes more this became evident; up came the officers, galloping at full speed, with four more guns.

"They are not of very heavy metal, or they would not come along so fast," observed Adair. "We'll be ready for them," and he ordered one of the after-guns to be trained so as to give them a warm reception as soon as they came within range. As they approached, however, the guns separated, and took up positions a considerable distance from each other, while those which had already been engaged followed their example.

This, of course, increased the difficulties of the *Flash*, as each of her guns could only engage one opponent at a time. Her heavy sixty-eight pivot-gun was, however, worked with such rapidity and skill that the enemy were frequently compelled to abandon their guns, and many of their men and horses were killed. Still fresh horses were brought up to move them to new positions, not allowing the crew of the *Flash* a moment of rest from their labours. Every time one of their shot was seen to tell with effect they cheered lustily; and as they worked away they seemed to enjoy the fun, laughing and joking as if no round shot and bullets were whistling through the air near their ears.

The master had just reported that the water had risen another inch, and Adair had begun to entertain fresh hopes of getting the ship, ere long, afloat, when the smoke of a steamer was seen in the offing.

"I hope she's the *Tornado* or *Giaour*," observed Desmond; "they'll be for sending the boats on shore and putting the enemy to the rout."

Adair naturally hoped pretty much the same, but, on consideration, he could not help suspecting that the ship in sight was the *Anaconda*, commanded by Commander Allport, his superior officer, for whom, on account of previous circumstances which need not just now be mentioned, he had no special regard.

"At all events, he is a brave fellow, and will stand by me," he said to himself.

As the stranger drew near, Adair found that his surmises were correct. He had, in the meantime, been continuing his efforts to get the *Flash* afloat, the crew working away as energetically as at first.

"She's the *Anaconda*, sir," said Tom, who had been watching the signals as they appeared at the masthead of the approaching vessel.

"Say the ship's ashore, but I hope to get her off, and beg *Anaconda* to stand in and support me," said Adair.

The signals were hoisted. It was possible that the wreaths of smoke which circled round the ship might have prevented them from being seen clearly. The enemy continued firing away at her as if hoping to secure her destruction before support could reach her, while her crew worked her guns with the same ardour as before. Adair calculated that, in another hour, she would be afloat, perhaps in less time. The *Anaconda* stood in nearer, and began again to make signals. Adair looked over the signal-book.

"It can't be that!" he exclaimed, as he read, "Abandon ship, and come on board me with your crew."

"There must be some mistake," he added in an undertone. "I wish that I was blind of one eye and not able to see it. Answer it," he said at length, "'Before we quit the ship, we'll try what we can do.'"

With reluctant heart he gave the order to heave the pivot-gun overboard, taking care to secure a buoy to it, hoping that he might yet get it up. The engine was set going, once more the capstan was manned, but still the *Flash* did not move.

"If that Commander Allport would stand in like a true man and lend us a hand, we might get off even now," exclaimed Desmond. "Arrah, my poor uncle, 'twill be after breaking his heart to leave the barkey here."

The *Anaconda* now fired a gun and made fresh signals, ordering Adair immediately to quit the ship. The boats, all of which had escaped injury, were hoisted out, and the crew were ordered to leave the ship they had fought so bravely. Adair was the last man to quit her.

"Well, I am the most unfortunate fellow alive!" he exclaimed.

He was thinking of Lucy and his promotion stopped, and all the other unpleasant consequences of the loss of his ship.

The only thing which kept up his spirits was the hope that he might persuade Commander Allport to stand in and make fresh efforts to get her afloat. It was a wonder none of the boats were struck as they left the ship. They, however, at length succeeded in getting on board the *Anaconda*. Commander Allport, who was standing on deck, received Adair with a supercilious air. He had been many years a lieutenant, and his temper had been considerably soured before he had got his promotion; indeed, some of those whom he had known as midshipmen were now admirals, and he seemed to take especial pleasure in acting in a dictatorial manner towards all those under him.

"Well, Commander Adair," he observed, as Terence stepped on deck, "you have made a pretty business of this somehow or other; young officers are, however, not always the best navigators, and the *Flash* has been lost to Her Majesty's Service. It won't bring much credit on those concerned."

Adair bit his lip, but, though ready enough to retort, he wisely restrained his temper, and answered, "If you will let me have your boats, or will stand in and give us a tow while we keep the enemy at bay, we may get the *Flash* off before many hours are over; she has not a shot-hole in her to signify, as we plugged them all as soon as they were received."

"Impossible, Commander Adair," answered his superior officer; "the only thing we can do is to prevent the *Flash* from falling into the enemy's hands. I cannot uselessly expose the lives of my crew in so hopeless an undertaking. Those who have the advantage of experience know that it is the duty of an officer to watch with a father's care over his people. We'll stand in closer, and then see what is to be done."

Adair still urged the possibility of saving the *Flash*.

"I am your superior officer, and it is my duty to act as I think fit, without taking your opinion," answered Commander Allport.

Adair turned away with no very affectionate feeling in his heart towards his "superior officer."

The *Anaconda* stood on till, when still at a safe distance from the enemy's shot, she brought her broadside to bear upon the unfortunate little *Flash*, and commenced practising with her heavy guns. A groan escaped from Adair's bosom, echoed by many others from his crew, as he saw one huge missile after another strike his devoted craft, and in a short time commit more mischief than the enemy had inflicted on her during the gallant fight he had waged for so many hours.

"We must take care, should she fall into the hands of the Russians, that she is reduced to an utter wreck," observed Commander Allport.

"You are certainly setting about the right way to make her so," observed Adair.

He even now was strongly inclined to urge the old martinet to desist, as he saw shot after shot strike the hull of his vessel. The enemy, seeing that the English were engaged in destroying her, wisely saved their own powder by ceasing to fire, and allowed them to finish the work which they had commenced.

While the *Anaconda* was thus employed, another vessel hove in sight, steaming up from the westward.

"She's the *Giaour*," observed Commander Allport, looking at the signal-book; "Murray will assist us in knocking her to pieces."

"I very much doubt whether he will do anything of the sort," answered Adair, unable to restrain himself; "I only wish he had come an hour ago, to save her from destruction."

"You are forgetting our relative positions, Commander Adair," observed Commander Allport, beginning now to fume.

"I only expressed my opinion that Murray would not have tried to knock the *Flash* to pieces, till he had assisted me in making further efforts to get her off," answered Adair; "and I only ask you to desist from firing till you have his opinion."

Now Commander Allport did not recollect that Murray was his senior. The latter had been promoted a few weeks before him, and would have power to decide the question. Instead of desisting, however, he directed his guns so as to concentrate their fire upon one portion of the *Flash*, thus more completely to ruin her. Adair knew that it would be useless to plead any longer; his only regret was that he had obeyed his superior officer's command, and quitted the vessel, instead of remaining on board and taking the consequences. Had he remained he felt that he would certainly have run the risk of censure for disobeying orders, but he would have saved his ship, and that alone would have proved a sufficient excuse had Commander Allport brought him to a court-martial; which it was very likely he would not have dared to do. Terence consoled himself with the reflection that he had fought his ship gallantly, and would have continued to fight her till she had been knocked to pieces, and that he had acted in obedience to the orders of a superior in quitting her.

"Well," he said to himself, "as Murray always used to advise, 'Do right and take the consequences.' I have done right in obeying, but the consequences are not less unpleasant. I shall be reprimanded for losing my ship, and shall be sent on shore with a black mark against my name, and all my prospects in the service ruined; and Sir John will be less likely than ever to allow me to marry Lucy. I *am* the most unfortunate fellow alive." This was about the twentieth time poor Terence had uttered the expression since he had been compelled to leave the *Flash*. As long as he continued on her deck, fighting her bravely, he had not cared half so much about her having run on shore; besides which, he had never abandoned the hope of getting her off. So completely did his feelings run away with him that he even began to contemplate, though his calmer moments would have forbidden him doing so, the idea of calling out Commander Allport, as the only way of avenging the injury he had received; but he, happily, had strength to banish the thought almost as soon as it was conceived, and, walking to the other side of the ship, he anxiously watched the approach of the *Giaour*.

As soon as she drew near, he ordered his gig, and, without holding any further communication with Commander Allport, pulled on board her.

"Why, Adair, what have you been doing with the *Flash*?" asked Murray, as he sprang up the side. Terence briefly explained what had happened, and declared his conviction that the ship might have been saved by the adoption of proper measures.

"Instead of that, old Allport is expending powder and shot in making a target of her, for no earthly reason beyond that of showing that he is my superior officer, though of equal rank. I wish to goodness he had been laid on the shelf, the only position he is fit for."

"We must try what can be done," said Murray. "Happily, I am *his* superior officer, which he will find out by looking at the *Navy List*, if he does not know it already;" and Murray directed a signal to be made to the *Anaconda* to "Cease firing." Commander Allport, who still had not discovered that Murray was his superior, was at first inclined to pay no attention to the signal; till his first lieutenant, happening to know the true state of the case, brought him a *Navy List*, and pointed out to him Murray's date of promotion.

"The old fellow is in the wrong box," whispered Desmond, he having observed what was taking place; "there's a chance after all for the little barkey."

"Cease firing," cried Commander Allport. Directly afterwards Murray sent his second lieutenant to the *Anaconda*, with a request that the commander would come on board his ship to consult with him as to the best means of saving Her Majesty's ship *Flash*, now in sight on the rocks. The request, of course, amounted to an order, which Commander Allport, however unwillingly, obeyed.

"Save her?" he exclaimed; "surely you mean destroy her as soon as possible. I have done my best for the last two hours to knock her to pieces."

"I am very sorry to hear it," answered Murray; "we should never abandon a vessel while there is the slightest hope of saving her; and the enemy might easily have been kept at a sufficient distance to prevent them from interfering with us, when getting her off. I must ask you to stand in towards the shore, as close as you can venture, and keep the enemy in check with your guns."

For the first time for some hours Adair's heart began again to beat with hope, as the two steamers, with the lead going and a bright look-out kept ahead, stood towards the shore. The artillery were seen to limber-up and gallop off, while the infantry scampered away, as fast as they could go, to a safe distance; judging correctly that as they had made no material impression upon a single ship, they were unlikely to impede the proceedings of two.

Murray, accompanied by Adair, and followed by the whole of the boats of the *Flash*, immediately pulled on board her. Groans, and expressions which were certainly not groans, however much they were like growls, proceeded from the crew, as they observed the damage committed by the *Anaconda's* shot. A very brief inspection satisfied Murray and Adair that she was too completely ruined to allow of any hope that she could be got off.

"It can't be helped," exclaimed poor Terence; "the only thing now to be done is to prevent her falling into the hands of the enemy. I would sooner have gone down in her to the bottom of this wretched pool than this should have happened. We must blow her up; I know it—I am the most unhappy fellow alive—I shall never get another ship, and Lucy is farther off than ever."

"We must set her on fire, of course, or the enemy will boast that they have captured her; but as to any blame being attached to you personally at a court-martial, I don't believe it," answered Murray, in a tone calculated to soothe the feelings of his friend. "From what I see, I am pretty sure that, had old Allport not taken it into his head to knock her to pieces, we should have got her off and put her to rights in a few hours. The side exposed to the enemy is but slightly damaged, and he allows that you must have fought her bravely, and that he only ordered you to desert her for the sake of preserving the lives of you and her crew. The first thing, however, we have to do is to weigh her guns."

Murray, having formed his plans, summoned the larger boats of the squadron, when, after much labour, the guns were weighed, and conveyed on board the *Giaour*. The Russian troops had taken their departure, and a good many parties of the peasantry were seen on the shore, spectators of what was going on, probably hoping that the wreck would be deserted, and that they should find a rich booty on board her. They were to be disappointed. Now came the scene most trying to Adair; everything of value, and that time would allow, was removed; the *Flash* was set on fire, and the boats pulled away, leaving her in flames fore and aft.

"There goes our little barkey," exclaimed Desmond; and in a short time she blew up, covering the sea on every side with the fragments of wreck. "I am glad, Tom, it was not you or I got her on shore; I don't envy old Fusty his feelings, if he's got any; perhaps he hasn't. If Uncle Terence doesn't get a ship, he'll be for cutting the service and going out and settling in Australia; and I intend to go with him, to keep sheep and ride after wild cattle, and lead an independent sort of life. I say, Tom, won't you come too?"

"Oh no; I am bound to come out here, and marry my little Feodorowna," answered Tom; "though perhaps she'd like to come out to Australia with me."

"You be hanged, Tom! that's all nonsense," answered Desmond. "I thought you had forgotten all about that affair."

"Of course not!" exclaimed Tom indignantly; "if she's faithful to me, I am bound to be faithful to her."

"Always provided Sir John approves of your faithfulness," put in Desmond.

"Let's change the subject," said Tom. "It's time that you

and I and Gordon should pass for seamanship, and as soon as we go home we shall get through the college and gunnery, and then, I hope, before long get our promotion."

Castles in the air erected by midshipmen are apt to fall to pieces, as well as those built by older persons. They serve, however, to amuse their architects, and after all, as they do not exhaust the strength or energy, are not productive of any harm.

The squadron continued their depredations along the coast, till not a Russian vessel, or any craft larger than a cock-boat, remained afloat, and every storehouse and stack of corn or hay which could be got at by the British seamen had been destroyed. As no private property was intentionally injured, these proceedings produced scarcely the slightest ill-will among the inhabitants, though they might have thought the perpetrators somewhat impious for thus daring to offend their sacred Emperor. History tells how gallantly the naval brigade behaved before Sebastopol, and how at length, the night before that proud fortress fell, the Russians sank their remaining line-of-battle ships; and how the English and French admirals, to prevent a single keel from escaping, placed their fleets across the mouth of the harbour, when the garrison, despairing of saving even their steamers, set them on fire with their own hands; and after proud Sebastopol had fallen, how Kinburn, not far from the mouths of the Boug and the Dnieper, a strong casemated fort, armed with seventy heavy guns, supported by well-made earthworks, each furnished with ten guns more, was attacked by the combined fleets. Its best defence, however, existed in the shallowness of the surrounding water and the intricacy of the navigation, so that ships of the line could not approach it; while the smaller vessels ran the risk of getting on shore when attempting to do so.

The fleet consisted of between thirty and forty steam-vessels, and numerous transports conveying four thousand troops. The French had as many troops, but fewer ships of war; among them, however, were three newly-invented floating batteries, from which the Emperor Napoleon expected, it was said, great things. Difficult as was the navigation, every inch of ground was well known to the commanders of the fleets, it having been thoroughly surveyed by Captain Spratt of the *Spitfire*.

Early on the morning of the 15th the troops were thrown on shore, to the south of the principal fort, when they immediately entrenched their position, to cut off the retreat of the garrison. The next day proving too rough for the ships to co-operate with the troops, the attack was postponed; but on the 17th the work was begun in earnest by the English mortar-boats, which first opened fire on the devoted fort. The French floating batteries followed suit, throwing their shot and shell with effective precision, while the enemy's round shot dropped harmless from their iron sides, their shells shivering against them like glass. After this game had been carried on for about a couple of hours, the ships of the line stood in on the southern side of the forts, till they got within twelve hundred yards.

"Now comes our turn!" exclaimed Jack Rogers to Adair, who was serving as a volunteer on board the *Tornado*, which ship, following close astern of the *Giaour*, formed one of a large squadron of steamers which had been directed to approach the forts on the northern side.

The two squadrons reached their destined positions at the same time, when they both opened a tremendous fire, literally raining down shot and shell upon the hapless garrison. Stubborn as were the Russians, human endurance could not long withstand such a fire.

"Faith, I'm very glad I'm not inside those walls," said Gerald to Tom, as they watched the effects of their shot, hundreds of shells bursting in the air together, and raining down fragments of iron on the heads of the unfortunate garrison; "if each round shot and shell only kills a single man, there won't be one left alive in the course of a few minutes."

"Fortunately, I fancy that it takes fully five shot to kill a man," answered Tom, though he may not have been perfectly correct in his estimate.

"I should doubt if even a cat could escape, unless she hid herself in a cellar," said Desmond; "it is tremendous."

His last remark correctly described the scene; from the two lines there issued, without intermission, flashes and wreaths of smoke, each denoting the passage of an engine of destruction against the fortress; the shells forming continuous arches in the air, the shot flying with more direct aim, till the whole atmosphere became filled with dense clouds of smoke, amid which the walls of the fort and dark hulls of the ships, with their masts and rigging, could only be indistinctly seen. At the end of ten minutes there appeared, in a conspicuous part of the fort, a white flag. In an instant, as if by magic, the wild uproar ceased, and the only sounds heard were the cheers of the seamen at their speedily-gained victory.

The admirals at once proceeded on shore, when the governor and his officers, coming out of the fort, presented their swords, which were politely returned to them, when a French garrison was left in the fort. Two generals and a large staff of officers thus became prisoners, besides which a large number of guns, ammunition, and stores were captured.

As the Government still held out, the fleet proceeded to the attack of Oczakov, but, greatly to the disappointment of the allies, the Russians evacuated it, and blew it up. This was almost the last action of any consequence during the war; though the Mosquito fleet still continued their depredations on the shores of the Sea of Azov till the winter compelled them to retire, when, before the return of spring, peace with Russia was concluded.

CHAPTER XXII

Adair acquitted for Loss of *Flash*—Appointed to *Gleam*—The *Tornado* in the Bosphorus—Arrival of Herr Groben—Higson obtains Leave of Absence—Tom asks for it, and is sent on board *Gleam*—Higson Promoted—His Marriage with the Fair Russian—Ball on board the *Tornado*—The *Gleam* in a Storm—Tom and Adair lost overboard—Desmond's Grief—The Admiral's Home—Appearance of the Missing Ones—Joy of the Admiral—Adair narrates their Adventures—Jack and Adair married—Generosity of Admiral Triton.

ANTECEDENT to the events mentioned in the last chapter, one of considerable importance to Terence Adair occurred. He had to undergo a court-martial for the loss of the *Flash*. She had been run on shore, of that there was no doubt; but when there he had fought her with the greatest gallantry, and had done his utmost to get her off. The result of the investigation was that, having been admonished for the loss of his ship, his sword was returned to him.

"Really, my dear Adair, I don't think you need break your heart about the matter," said Jack to him when he returned on board the *Tornado*, which he had joined as a volunteer; Tom and Desmond were already on board her. "Depend upon it, it won't stand in the way of your getting another ship or promotion. I hear that the admiral highly approves of your conduct, and that he has stated he will give you solid proof of his opinion as soon as a vacancy occurs."

These remarks raised poor Terence's spirits, and he wrote a very hopeful letter to Admiral Triton, which he hoped might be shown to Lucy rather than the one he had penned some time previously. Still some weeks went by, and Adair remained without a ship; he at length got a cheery reply from his old friend in answer to his letter, urging him to keep up his courage, and prophesying that all would turn out well at last.

"There is a young lady by my side who fully agrees with

me, and who is as ready as I am to admire the gallant way in which you fought your ship, and to appreciate your merits, whether the Admiralty do so or not. I am the last man to advise a promising young officer to leave the service; but should you be compelled to come on shore, and turn your sword into a reaping-hook, I have made such arrangements as will enable you to do so without having to depend solely upon your pittance of half-pay," wrote the admiral.

"What can the kind old man mean?" asked Terence, when he showed the letter to Jack.

Jack smiled. Perhaps he had heard something about the matter.

"It is evident that he has your interest at heart," he answered, "and intends to give you substantial proof of his regard; however, my opinion is that you will not be laid on the shelf, and that if you remain out here the admiral will give you the first vacancy that occurs."

Jack was right; a few days afterwards, on the return of the *Tornado* to the fleet, the admiral sent for Adair, and, complimenting him on the gallant way in which he had fought the *Flash*, informed him that he was appointed to the *Gleam*, the commander of which had just been invalided home. Adair's heart bounded as if a load had been taken off it. Without loss of time he went on board his new command. His natural wish was now to do something by which he might gain credit.

"Let me advise you, my dear fellow," said Murray, who paid him a visit on board, "not to trouble yourself about that, but just go straight forward and do your duty, and you'll gain all the credit you can desire in doing that."

Terence followed his friend's advice, and was warmly complimented by the admiral for his zeal and activity in carrying out the orders he had received, although he had done nothing to fill a page in history.

The *Tornado* was lying in the Golden Horn, having made her last trip to the Crimea, when a caïque came alongside, an old gentleman in somewhat quaint costume seated in the stern. Green, who happened to be near the gangway, on looking down recognised his old German friend, Herr Groben. "Glad to see you," he exclaimed, as he ran down to help him up the accommodation ladder.

"Ah, my friend Green, I am delighted to see you," answered Herr Groben, shaking his hand warmly with both of his. "I come on a very delicate and important matter, and you can help me greatly."

"Very glad to help you to do anything you wish," answered Green, "provided it doesn't amount to treason or petty larceny."

"Ah, no, my friend, this is no treason," answered the old tutor, looking over his shoulder as if he expected to see a Russian spy there; "it relates entirely to another sort of affair. You know that Mr. Higson, the first lieutenant of this ship, fell in love with the eldest sister of my pupils; and, to confess to you the truth, the young lady fell in love with him, and she has been expecting now that the dreadful war is over that he would go back and claim her hand."

"So I suppose he intends doing when the ship is paid off; but, till then, he is not his own master, and he could not get away however much he might wish it," answered Green.

"Ah, Mademoiselle Ivanowna does not understand that sort of thing, and began so to pine and fret that she became very ill indeed; and, seeing her state, I volunteered to come to Constantinople, where I heard your ship was likely to be found, to bear a message to Lieutenant Higson; and I have been greatly anxious till I got on board lest the ship should have sailed away. Where is your first lieutenant, that I may deliver myself forth of my message?"

"For a wonder he has gone on shore," answered Green, "but he will be off again soon; and, in the meantime, we will take good care of you; so come down at once into the gun-room, and we shall have luncheon on the table immediately."

Herr Groben was warmly received by the officers when they heard who he was, and soon had out of him the whole history of the loves of Lieutenant Higson and the fair Ivanowna. Lieutenant Mildmay expressed his intention of writing it in verse; the doctor proposed their healths during luncheon, in conjunction with that of the Queen of England and the Emperor of Russia, now the best friends in the world. After luncheon, as Higson did not appear, Herr Groben expressed a wish to go round the ship, and Green at once offered to conduct him. As he was going round the lower deck, he popped his head into the midshipmen's berth, when, whom should he see seated directly before him but Tom Rogers.

The recognition was mutual; Tom started up. "Oh, Herr Groben, I am delighted to see you!" he exclaimed. "Do tell me, how is Miss Feodorowna? Have you just come from there?"

"Not very long ago," answered Herr Groben; "and I can tell you they have not forgotten you, and she told me if I saw you to give her very kind remembrances."

"Is that all?" asked Tom.

"Of course," exclaimed Paddy Desmond, who was seated in the berth; "what more could you expect from a young lady?"

"Then doesn't she care about me?" cried Tom, forgetting that several of his messmates were within hearing, and that they were not likely to forget his question.

"As to that I must be discreet," answered the old tutor, laughing; "if you ever come back to Russia in peaceable guise, not in one of your ships with big guns to batter down our forts, you may depend upon it Colonel Paskiewich and his family will be very happy to see you."

The conversation was cut short by Green, who had gone away, returning to conduct Herr Groben into the gun-room. Soon after he was seated there, Higson returned on board, little expecting whom he was to find. Though he had never been known to exhibit the slightest signs of nervousness, he looked excessively agitated on seeing the old tutor; who, after telling him that he had lately come from the family of Colonel Paskiewich, requested a private interview. The old German had evidently something of importance to communicate beyond what he had told Green. Higson's agitation as he proceeded increased; he, however, at length came to a decision, and Herr Groben returned on shore, saying that he should expect to see him the next day.

When Jack, who had gone on board the *Gleam* to see Adair, just on the point of sailing for England, returned to his own ship, Higson begged to have a few minutes' talk with him. Jack, of course, granted it, and, begging him to come into his cabin, sat down to listen to what he had to say.

"We have been shipmates a good many years, Commander Rogers, and I am going to ask a favour of you," he began. "You know how I fell in love with a young lady in Russia, and she has fallen desperately in love with me, it seems. I don't say it as a boast, and cannot account for it, and, what is more, her mother sends me word that she is dying for fear I should go away and forget her, or, at all events, not come back again. Now, I have no thoughts of doing anything of the sort; though the young lady may believe what I will write to her, I would rather give her practical evidence of my affection by paying her a visit at once. I could be there and back in a week or ten days, and if you could manage to give me leave for that period, I would run over and see them, and I trust that neither the service nor the ship will suffer from my absence."

Jack reflected on the request made to him, and considering that Higson merited all the favour he could grant at his hands, and that the duty of the ship could be carried on in the meantime, gave him the leave he asked. Higson expressed himself very thankful, and set about making arrangements for his intended journey.

Scarcely had Higson left the cabin when Tom entered, and begged to have a few minutes' conversation with his brother.

"What is it?" asked Jack.

Tom went into the whole story of the kind treatment he had received from the family of Colonel Paskiewich; "And you must know," he continued, "that I fell in love with Miss Feodorowna, and promised to go back and marry her as soon as the war was over."

"Really, Tom, I hope with the proviso that you should obtain the permission of Sir John," remarked Jack.

"I don't know about provisionally," answered Tom; "I promised to go back and marry her as soon as peace was settled; and as you wouldn't wish me to break my promise, I hope you will give me permission to do so at once."

Jack burst into a loud fit of laughter.

"I'll tell you what, Tom, I am much more likely to marry you to the gunner's daughter," he answered.

"That is very cruel treatment," exclaimed Tom; "you'll drive me to quit the service and expatriate myself for ever."

Jack only laughed louder.

"Do you mean to say that you are going to deprive the country of your valuable services, bid farewell to your father and mother and sisters, or perhaps take service in the Russian navy, should they ever launch any fresh ships, and turn your sword against your countrymen, simply because I refuse to let you go and make a fool of yourself by marrying this little Russian girl? though my belief is that, even should I let you go, as soon as her father finds out that you haven't a sixpence to bless yourself with, he'll send you about your business with a flea in your ear. Come, Tom, think the matter over; you used to have some brains in your head, and I hope you have not left them all behind you in the Sea of Azov."

Still Tom was obstinate; he really had a midshipman-like amount of attachment for Feodorowna, but though it was very disinterested and sincere and romantic, it was not the less foolish. Nothing Jack could say would induce him to promise to give up all thoughts of her, and to write a kind note pointing out the impossibility of their marrying, and bidding her farewell.

"She mayn't see the impossibility of it," answered Tom; "her father is the owner of thousands of acres, and country-houses, and serfs; and she told me that all he wanted was to get gentlemanly, intelligent sons-in-law, who could live in his houses and superintend the cultivation of his estates."

"Well, well," said Jack, "that doesn't sound so badly; but still, you have no right at your age to go and marry without our father's and mother's sanction; and until you have got it I'll be no party to your giving up the service and settling down for life in an out-of-the-way corner of Russia. With regard to Higson, the case is very different; he is twice your age, has very little prospect of promotion, and no friends that I know of to give up; besides which, I am pretty certain that nothing would induce him to take service in the Russian navy, with the chance of being employed against England."

"I don't see that our cases are so very different," answered Tom; "and you may put me in irons, and do what you like, but I'll not promise to give up Feodorowna, nor write the cruel letter you propose, to bid her farewell. There, you've got my answer, and I've in no way infringed the articles of war by saying that, though you *are* my commander."

"I am not quite certain that you have not, by the tone in which you speak," answered Jack; "however, I am very sorry for it, Tom, and warn you that as you are obstinate, I must take measures accordingly."

What those measures were, Jack did not tell his brother. Having dismissed him, he sent for Dick Needham, and desired him to keep a watchful eye on the youngster, lest he might take French leave and quit the ship.

"Ay, ay, sir," answered Dick; "though they're not a bad sort of people in the main, I shouldn't like Mr. Tom to turn into a Russian—it won't be my fault if he gives leg-bail."

Satisfied on this point, Jack, ordering his gig, pulled on board the *Gleam*, which ship was to sail the next day for England. The *Giaour* had gone home some time before, and Murray hoped to pay her off and to be allowed to remain on shore with his beloved Stella. Jack explained his anxieties about Tom to Adair, who at once agreed to take him home, and not to lose sight of him till he had handed him over either to Admiral Triton or Sir John and Lady Rogers.

"Take him in the first instance to the admiral," said Jack, "he will consider his opinion as less biassed than that of our father and mother, and be more likely to yield submission to it."

On his return to the *Tornado*, Jack ordered Tom's marine to pack up his chest, and have it lowered into his gig alongside; he then summoned Tom, and, allowing him to wish his messmates good-bye, told him to follow his chest. Tom looked, as he felt, very unhappy; Dicky Duff and Billy Blueblazes, especially, thought him a hardly-used individual—though his older messmates were more inclined to laugh than to sympathise with him. Adair received him on board in a very kind way, and Desmond acted the part of a true friend by listening to all he had to say—though he avoided giving him any encouragement, and when Tom declared his intention of making his escape in the first caïque which came alongside, he warned him that he could not possibly succeed.

Next morning the *Gleam* steamed away down the Bosphorus. Tom had not been many hours at sea before he recovered his spirits, and was able to admire the beautiful scenery amid which the ship was steering her course.

Having now settled this matter to his satisfaction, Jack turned his attention to the affair of his first lieutenant. Higson's interview with the old tutor had confirmed him in his resolution to abandon the service and marry Ivanowna; and Jack, though sorry to lose him, promised to do his best to forward his views. Jack gave him leave of absence, and Higson was engaged in packing up to accompany Herr Groben in a steamer which was to start the next day for the Crimea, when the commander of the *Tornado* was sent for on board the flagship. Greatly to his satisfaction, Jack found that he had to return to Balaclava on an affair relating to the evacuation of the place, and afterwards to visit other places to the eastward which had been captured by the allied squadrons and restored to the Russians.

"This is a most fortunate circumstance for you, Higson," he said, when he returned on board; "you will have an opportunity of visiting your friends, and if you take my advice, you will go home in the ship, and, as I hope, obtain your promotion."

Higson, thanking Jack, promised to be guided by circumstances. The *Tornado* had got her steam up, when the mail from England was signalled, and Jack waited for its arrival. He received several letters—one from his sister Mary, replete, as was usually the case in her letters, with scraps of news. The most important, as far as he himself was concerned, was that Julia Giffard was somewhat out of health, and that her father had taken her to Malta, where they intended to pass the winter. Sir John and Lady Rogers were as averse as ever to Lucy's marriage with Adair, not from any objection to him, except on account of his want of means; and they were annoyed at the encouragement Admiral Triton and Miss Deborah appeared to have afforded the young people. The admiral had actually written to Sir John on the subject, but neither he nor Lady Rogers could understand his meaning, except that he thought him unwise in objecting to a fine promising young officer, who was certain if he remained in the service to become an admiral some day. "Poor Lucy is sadly perplexed about it," said Mary; "she has given her heart to Adair, and is certainly not a person likely to bestow it on anyone else; so that her fate will be a hard one if she is not allowed to marry." Sidney had returned home very much improved by his Crimean campaign, having dropped all his Guardsman's airs, and become, Mary observed, very like Jack himself.

Jack would have been more deeply concerned about Julia, had he not received a letter from her, assuring him that the voyage had done her a great deal of good, and that she was looking forward to the happiness of seeing him shortly on his arrival at Malta. Murray had reached England, but, much to his disappointment, the *Giaour* had not been paid off, and he had been directed to hold himself in readiness to sail immediately. He spoke of the admiral as very much broken, while Mrs. Deborah was also ailing. He could not sufficiently express his gratitude for the kindness with which the old people had treated Stella and his two children; she was still residing with them at Southsea—they insisted on their remaining there till his return, to which he had consented, as he hoped not to be long absent from home. "I shall then," he said, "not seek for employment, and, as I have some hopes of my promotion, I may become an admiral some day. I had expected to have been back at Bercaldine and to have been able to receive you and Mrs. Jack Rogers on your wedding tour; perhaps even now I may be home in time, and, at all events, my dear Jack, I look forward to the pleasure of seeing you and Terence Adair there as one of the greatest in this sublunary world."

Jack had read his letters, when Higson entered the cabin, with an official-looking despatch in his hand.

"Congratulate me!" he exclaimed. "I have received what I little expected, my promotion; and, as there is small chance of my being employed, I think you will agree that I should be wise in taking advantage of the good fortune offered me."

"I congratulate you heartily," said Jack, "and I won't say a word to dissuade you."

Higson, after considerable trouble, succeeded in obtaining a commander's full-dress uniform, with which he expressed himself highly delighted. He had just time to get on board when the *Tornado* steamed away for Balaclava, with the worthy tutor, to whom Jack had offered a passage on board. The duties with which he had been charged at Balaclava having been performed, Jack continued his course to the eastward, and the *Tornado* soon arrived off the fort with which he had had so gallant a contest. Jos Green having undertaken to carry the *Tornado* up the river as far as the depth of water would allow, she entered its mouth, keeping the lead going, and proceeded on at half speed till she came off Colonel Paskiewich's house. Her approach had been perceived; gay flags, that of England being the highest, were hoisted on the flagstaff near the house, and numerous persons were seen collected at the landing-place.

Jack agreed to accompany Higson, who of course had put on his commander's uniform, on shore; the two other boats followed with most of the officers, all in full dress. The colonel was the first person to greet them. He welcomed them cordially, and invited the whole party up to the house, where the ladies sat ready to receive them. The eyes of the fair Ivanowna beamed with pleasure as they rested on the gallant commander, though she cast them down modestly as he approached to take her hand, which he lifted gallantly to his lips.

The eyes of poor little Feodorowna wandered in vain among the group of officers in the background in search of Tom, and her countenance fell on discovering that he was not among them. Unable to restrain her anxiety, she asked Herr Groben, who was compelled to inform her of the truth, on hearing which she burst into tears.

"How very, very cruel to send him away!" she exclaimed

"I don't see why my sister's lover should have been allowed to come and mine been sent off to England."

Herr Groben tried to explain that the one was a commander, and the other only a midshipman; and that while one might be allowed to act as he thought fit, the other was still under the direction of his parents. Nothing, however, would comfort her; it had, however, the effect of making her look very interesting; and just at that moment any one of the officers would have been perfectly ready to take Tom's place, especially Dicky Duff and Billy Blueblazes; indeed, they both determined to make her an offer in the course of the evening, and to toss up which should first do so. Perhaps the attention she received somewhat consoled her, for she soon dried her tears, and to all appearance became perfectly happy.

After a magnificent banquet, when the table literally groaned with viands of all descriptions, a dance was got up, several young ladies arriving from various houses in the neighbourhood, while for a couple of hours after it had begun, others, to whom notice of the coming of the English ship had been sent, arrived from greater distances. As a natural consequence, all the unmarried and unengaged officers lost their hearts to Russian young ladies, and it was said that Feodorowna received certainly two if not three offers before the evening was over. Jack, when he found the state of affairs, began to consider whether he had not made a mistake in coming to the place.

Not till morning dawned did they return on board. Honest Higson was, of course, the hero of the evening, and it was very evident, from the attention the colonel paid him, that he was well pleased with his intended son-in-law. At breakfast the next morning, Higson begged Jack to wait till his wedding, which he told him had been fixed for the next day.

"Rather sharp work," observed Jack.

"Why, the fact is," answered Higson, "Madame Paskiewich is anxious to give the marriage éclat by having the advantage of your presence, and that of my late shipmates, and, as the young lady did not object, of course I was delighted, and I hope you will be able to stay."

Jack of course agreed, and the news, soon spreading round the ship, afforded infinite satisfaction. It would take more space than can be allowed to describe the magnificence of the fête. As many of the officers as could be spared were invited on shore, while an abundance of good viands were sent off to those who had to remain on board to take care of the ship. The whole neighbourhood were assembled in their gayest costumes. The upper classes were entertained either in the house, or in a large marquee erected on the lawn, and tables were spread in the neighbouring field for the peasantry and seamen, who, though they could not exchange many ideas, became nevertheless on excellent terms. Everyone, indeed, seemed to forget that a few months before their respective nations had been engaged in a fierce and bloody struggle.

The marriage ceremony was performed in a neighbouring church. Though Jack, who acted as Higson's best man, did not admire the style of service, and the pictures of saints, and bowings and singing, he came to the conclusion that his friend was as firmly spliced as he would have been in a quiet English country church; and that, after all, as he remarked to him, was the chief point to be considered.

The officers and crew of the *Tornado* made all the preparations in their power to do honour to their former first lieutenant's marriage; the ship was decked with flags, and the boats' crews who had attended the wedding requested the honour of escorting the young couple round the ship. A barge having been got ready for their reception accordingly, Higson, leading his bride down to the water, embarked, and was rowed three times round the ship; while the crew manned yards, the band played "Haste to the wedding," and the guns fired a salute.

Jack and his officers had also arranged to give a ball on board, and invitations had been sent out through Madame Paskiewich to all her acquaintances. The ship for the purpose had been housed in, and by an extensive use of bunting the deck had been converted into a perfect ballroom, while a handsome supper was laid out in Jack's cabin and the gun-room. The ship's boats, aided by a few from the shore, were employed in bringing off the guests; and as they danced away merrily to the music of the ship's band, few recollected that a few months before the big guns on that deck had been busily engaged in firing on their countrymen. It was one proof of many how slight an interest the nation at large had felt in the war, which they had looked upon as an imperial affair, with which they themselves had nothing to do beyond sending, as in duty bound, their quota of friends and relatives to be slaughtered. Altogether, the ball was pronounced a success, and the officers and their guests parted mutually satisfied with each other.

Feodorowna, who suspected that Jack had been the cause of Tom's being spirited away, could not help at first exhibiting her displeasure, but by degrees he calmed her anger, assuring her that Tom would have proved a very unsatisfactory husband, as he was much too young for her, and would in a few months have got heartily sick of an idle life on shore, and have either taken to drinking, or run away; and that she would do much more wisely to choose an older partner for life; on which she naïvely inquired whether his second lieutenant was disengaged.

Jack assured her that he was wedded to the muses, and that he doubted much whether even for her sake he would be induced to break off his engagement, but that he would ask him. On Mildmay's begging to be excused, she begged Jack to select one of the officers; but he told her that notwithstanding his wish to oblige her, such not being the duty of a captain of a man-of-war, he must decline interfering in the matter. The result was, that, having bade Higson and his bride farewell, and wished them every happiness, Jack ordered the fires to be got up, and steamed away down the river.

Greatly to his satisfaction, on his return to Constantinople, he was ordered off to Malta, where he found Julia Giffard and her father. Jack thought Julia looking as blooming as ever; she acknowledged that the voyage had done her so much good that she thought she should be ready to go back again, should he be ordered to England.

"Then your father will, I hope, take a passage on board my ship," said Jack; "the admiral will not now object to your doing so; but had I the happiness of calling you my wife, it would be against the rules of the service, and I should very likely be compelled to let you come home by some other vessel."

Julia raised no objection to this proposal, and the colonel very kindly said he wished to do whatever his daughter liked. Jack, therefore, waited with some anxiety to hear the admiral's decision as to his future proceedings. To assist in deciding the point, he directed the engineer to make a report as to the state of the engines; while the carpenter sent one in respecting the condition of the ship. Both were of opinion that though her safety would not be endangered by the voyage home, she was in a condition to require such a thorough repair as could only be obtained in England.

"In fact, Commander Rogers, you have no objection to go home and pay off your ship, I presume?" observed the admiral;

"you certainly have not had much opportunity of allowing the weeds to grow on your keel since she was commissioned, and I shall therefore send you home with despatches; when the Admiralty will decide whether or not to pay the ship off."

Jack, highly pleased, came back with the news to Julia, who the next day took possession of the cabin Jack had fitted up for her accommodation.

"This is indeed perfect," she exclaimed, as she admired the neat chintz curtains and furniture, vases and flowers and pictures, which adorned the bulkheads; "I had no idea that a cabin could be made so nice and pretty."

The colonel was equally well pleased with the accommodation provided for him, and Jack felt a proud satisfaction at being able to carry home his intended bride on board his own ship. We must leave them to make the passage, forgetful of the possible storms, and the many other dangers to which those who voyage upon the fickle ocean are exposed, and follow Adair on board the *Gleam*.

On touching at Gibraltar, Adair saw by the papers that the *Giaour*, instead of being paid off, was ordered to proceed to the Cape; and, as far as he could make out, Murray still commanded her.

"Poor Alick!" he exclaimed; "I thought he would now be allowed to remain on shore, and enjoy the society of his wife; there are plenty of other fellows who are not so blessed, who would have been delighted to supersede him."

Adair was beginning to sympathise with his benedict friend, hoping as he did, in spite of adverse circumstances, ere long to belong to that fraternity.

While in harbour, he had a strict eye kept on Tom, who, though by this time he had regained his usual temper, might, he thought, if possible, take it into his head to try and make his way back to the Crimea.

After getting through the Straits, and when to the northward of the latitude of Cadiz, the ship encountered unusually bad weather. Instead of improving, it became worse and worse; two of her boats were washed away, the wheel and the steering apparatus damaged, and numerous other injuries were received. She would, indeed, have been compelled to put in to Cadiz, had not the wind shifted to the southward; when, setting her close-reefed topsails, she ran on before the gale.

"Well, old fellow, our sweethearts and wives have got hold

of the tow-ropes, and are hauling us along at a famous rate," observed Desmond to Tom.

"Don't talk about that sort of thing to me," answered Tom gloomily; "I have no sweetheart or wife in England to tow me along—I am only getting farther and farther from all I hold dear."

At hearing this, Gerald burst into a hearty fit of laughter. Tom at first felt inclined to quarrel with him, but a poke in the ribs from his messmate, and the word "humbug," made him instead join in Desmond's cachinnations. Adair had invited his midshipmen to dine with him, and had by his kind remarks succeeded in driving Tom's absurd notions out of his head. Tom, who really felt grateful to him, talked cheerfully of home, and of the pleasure he expected to enjoy on returning there.

It was Tom's first watch. Shortly after sunset he and the second lieutenant, who was officer of the watch, were seen standing on the bridge; the weather had somewhat moderated during the evening, but it had now come on to blow harder than ever, and the ship seemed suddenly to have entered a wild region of tossing, tumbling waves. Adair had left the deck for a few minutes to obtain some refreshment, for he saw that the night was likely to prove a boisterous one, and he intended, as every good commander will do under such circumstances, to remain on deck. He hurried over his meal; indeed, there was no temptation to spend any longer time over it, as even the puddings and fiddles could scarcely keep the articles on the table. He had rung for his steward to clear away, to avoid that operation being performed by the eccentric movements of the billows, and was going towards the door of the cabin, when the ship received a tremendous blow, which made her quiver from stem to stern. At the same time loud cries reached his ears; he sprang on deck, when, glancing towards the bridge, he saw his second lieutenant alone standing there.

"Man overboard!" shouted several voices.

"Who is it?" he asked.

"Mr. Rogers, sir," was the answer; "he was on the bridge a moment ago, and he isn't there now."

"There he is, there he is," shouted someone; and a figure was seen struggling on the foaming crest of a sea. Adair had made his way aft to the lifebuoy, and, pulling both the lanyards, as it dropped into the ocean, a bright light burst forth from its centre. For one moment he gazed at it; he recollected that Tom was Lucy's brother,—he had been committed to his charge,

—without aid he would be unable to reach the buoy. Can I allow him to perish without an attempt to save him? These thoughts flashed through his mind far more rapidly than it has taken to record them; and, without considering the fearful risk he was running, shouting to his first lieutenant to lower a boat, he plunged overboard, and was seen buffeting the tumbling seas and making his way towards the midshipman; who, catching sight of him, cried out, "All right—I see the lifebuoy, and shall soon be up to it."

Adair, believing that he said this to prevent him from exhausting himself by making efforts to assist him, contented himself by treading water and throwing off his coat, that he might be able to swim to Tom's assistance, should he prove after all unable to reach the lifebuoy. The ship, meantime, was running on before the gale, and minutes which seemed hours passed by before her canvas could be reduced and she could be rounded to, to enable a boat to be lowered. Besides the regular boats' crews who stood collected between two of the guns, ready for instant service, numerous volunteers had come forward, as is always found to be the case whenever there is work to be performed; the two lieutenants stood together.

"We shall sacrifice the boat's crew and boat if we make the attempt," observed the first lieutenant; "still, I wish to obey the commander's orders."

The first lieutenant and master were both of opinion that a boat could not live in such a sea; the discussion was brief, but it lost time, and every moment was of consequence.

"Surely, sir, you're going to lower a boat," cried Desmond, who observed the hesitation of his superiors; "you can't be after letting my uncle and Tom Rogers drown without an attempt to save them; it's myself would go in her, even if I go alone;" and without further remark he sprang to the lee side, where several of the crew were already collected.

"I'll go also, at all risks," cried the boatswain. "Who'll go with me and Mr. Desmond?"

The crew were standing ready with the falls in their hands; he selected six of the best men; but, as they were on the point of leaping into the boat, a sea struck her, and, lifting her bows, unhooked the forward fall, and the next instant she was dashed to fragments against the side.

"I should be throwing away your lives, my lads, to lower another boat," cried the first lieutenant, as he saw the crew running to the after-quarter boat. "Very sad, but it can't be helped; we must look after the ship, or she'll be in a scrape presently."

By this time the light from the lifebuoy was no longer visible, and even had a boat been lowered, it would have been difficult, if not almost impossible, to find it. The order was given to brace round the headyards, the helm was put up, and the ship was kept on her course running before the wind. Several seas struck her, carrying away two more of her boats and committing further damage. Had not the hatches been battened down, so tremendous was the quantity of water which flooded her decks that she would in all probability have foundered.

Still the men talked and grumbled, and asked whether all had been done that was possible to save their commander and the midshipman. Poor Desmond was in a fearful state of grief; he declared, perhaps unjustly, that all had not been done, and that the ship ought not to have left the spot without, at all events, searching for the lifebuoy, and endeavouring, should the commander and Tom have been found clinging to it, to get them on board. The night was unusually dark, so that had the light not continued burning this would have been impossible. The weather, contrary to expectation, again moderated; Desmond thought that even now they ought to put back, and try to find the lifebuoy. He expressed his opinion very strongly to the first lieutenant.

"You are using very unwarrantable language, young gentleman," was the answer; "I overlook it, as you naturally feel grieved at the loss of your uncle and friend, but I am the person to judge what it is right to do, and I should not have been warranted in risking the lives of the crew, even to attempt saving that of the commander."

Poor Desmond was silenced, and though quite indifferent to the consequences, he felt that he had already gone further than he ought to have ventured. He was unable to recover his spirits during the remainder of the passage; he could scarcely say whether he was most sorry to lose his uncle or Tom Rogers, who was to him more even than a brother. From their earliest days, with slight intervals, they had been shipmates and friends; then, again, he thought of the grief Tom's death would cause at Halliburton; and he had a slight inkling of the engagement between Lucy Rogers and his uncle, and having faith in the tender nature of young ladies' hearts, he fully believed that hers would be broken. He had read Falconer's *Shipwreck*, and remembered the lines, "With terror pale unhappy Anna read," as she received the news of Palæmon's loss.

At length the ship reached Portsmouth, and was ordered at once to go into harbour. Desmond, to whom the first lieutenant had been very civil during the remainder of the voyage, asked leave to go on shore, that he might communicate the sad news to Admiral Triton, should he be at Southsea, and get him to break it to Tom's family. The first lieutenant, who also knew of Adair's engagement to Miss Rogers, very willingly gave him leave; for though he had acted according to the best of his judgment in not making further efforts to pick up his commander, he could not help reflecting that censorious remarks might be made on his conduct, and he was anxious to avoid any bad construction being put upon it.

Gerald hurried on shore, and made his way as fast as he could to Southsea; on reaching the admiral's house, he was at once admitted, and ushered into the drawing-room, where he found Mrs. Deborah and Mrs. Murray seated at the tea-table; and almost before he had time to open his mouth, the admiral stumped into the room.

"Who are you?" he asked, examining his features; "I know you—you need not tell me; you are my old friend Paddy Adair's nephew. I remember him when he was much younger than you are, and your jibs are cut much alike. He sent you up with a message, I suppose—paying off his ship, and couldn't come himself? We shall see him soon, however; he'd have come fast enough had he supposed that a certain young lady was staying here."

Not till now could Desmond get in a word.

"I am sorry to say, sir, that I bring very sad news," answered Gerald; and he briefly described what had occurred. The admiral, who had been standing up, tottered back into a chair as he heard it.

"I won't believe it!" he exclaimed at last; "your uncle and Tom can't be lost—poor, poor Lucy! and my friend Sir John and Lady Rogers, they'll be dreadfully cut up at the loss of that fine youngster, Tom. It mayn't have been your fault, Desmond, but I wonder you didn't try and save him."

"I'd have risked my own life to do so, sir," answered Gerald; and he explained more fully all that had taken place.

"I must go on board and make inquiries about the affair!" exclaimed the admiral. "Deb, help me on with my greatcoat."

25

"Pray don't think of going, admiral; it is too late in the day, and you are not fit for such a walk," said the old lady, without moving from her chair.

Desmond had remarked the wandering way in which the admiral had spoken, as also that there was a great change in his appearance. He assured him that there was no possible use in going on board, and persuaded him at length to give up the idea. He grew more quiet and reasonable after he had taken a cup of tea, and observed with a sigh that it was high time he should slip his cable, since so many of his younger friends were losing the number of their mess.

"And now, youngster," he asked, "what are you going to do with yourself when your ship is paid off, which I suppose she will be in a day or two? Have you any friends to go to?"

Desmond owned that without his uncle he should be very unwilling to return to Ballymacree, and he thought that the best thing he could do would be to get afloat again as soon as possible.

"You are right, youngster, depend on that," said the admiral; "but in the meantime you must come and hang your hammock up here, and my sister Deborah will take care of you."

Desmond of course accepted the admiral's kind offer, and made himself very useful by walking out with the old man, who was now unfit to go out by himself, while he also made an excellent listener to his long yarns.

The next day, Mrs. Murray, who sympathised greatly with poor Lucy, and Sir John and Lady Rogers, wrote to Mary that she might break the intelligence to them, which they thus fortunately heard before they saw it in the papers. Desmond found that Murray had sailed but a short time before, but was expected back again shortly, when Mrs. Murray hoped that the ship would be paid off.

Some time passed away; though Desmond frequently spoke of trying to get a ship, the admiral always replied that there would be time enough by and by, and that a spell on shore would do him no harm. They were one day walking across Southsea Common, intending to go to some shops in the High Street, when Desmond caught sight of three officers, whom he saw by their uniforms were commanders, walking along at a rapid rate towards them. A fourth, in a midshipman's uniform, at that moment came up from behind them. The admiral had just before stopped to take a breath, while he leant upon

Desmond's arm. The astonishment Gerald felt made him gasp almost as much as the admiral, when he recognised Commanders Murray and Rogers and his Uncle Terence, with Tom Rogers, both of them as alive and hearty as they had ever been. He could not restrain a shout of joy as the fact burst on his mind, though the admiral's arm prevented him from rushing forward as he was inclined to do.

"I knew it, I was sure of it," cried the admiral, as he shook the hands of the whole party. "Now let me hear all about it. We'll not go into Portsmouth to-day, Desmond; come back with me; come back with me. You'll make the ladies as happy as crickets, and restore my little friend Lucy to life; by the last account she was in a sad way. Sir John and Lady Rogers are very little better; grieving over you, you rascal, Tom; poor Mary had enough to do in looking after them. Now I think of it, Lucy was to be with us this very day; so you are in luck, Adair; though we must break the news to her gently, or we shall be sending her into hysterics, and doing all sorts of mischief. As you, Murray, I am pretty sure, are eager to see your wife, we'll let you go on first, for, as she expects you, it won't have the same effect on her."

Murray gladly followed the admiral's advice, and hurried on to his house, leaving the rest of the party to stroll slowly along. Adair then narrated the wonderful way in which he and Tom had been preserved. Tom, though a good swimmer, was almost exhausted when Adair made his way up to him and assisted him to reach the lifebuoy, over which they both managed to get their arms. To their dismay they saw the ship running away from them till she disappeared in the darkness. At length, however, they again caught sight of her as she rounded to a long way to leeward. The light burned but dimly amid the mass of spray which surrounded it, and they knew that their voices would be drowned in the loud howling of the tempest, should they exert them ever so much. They waited, therefore, still hoping against hope that the ship would make her way up to them. Adair well knew the difficulty she would have in finding them, and the fearful danger there would be in lowering a boat; he even doubted whether he would have made the attempt himself.

Still neither he nor Tom gave way to despair. They both hung on securely to the lifebuoy, and felt little or no exhaustion. They kept their eyes fixed on the ship, believing to the last that she would stand down to them. At length she disappeared in the darkness, and Adair knew that his first lieutenant, despairing of finding them, had borne up.

"I did not blame him, for I knew he had done his best," he said; "my only fear was that an attempt had been made to lower a boat, and that some of my poor fellows might have lost their lives in trying to save us.

"Hour after hour went by. Tom kept up his spirits wonderfully; and I did my best to keep up mine and to cheer him. I thought of a good many things during that period; indeed it seemed to me that I was living my life over again.

"We were looking out anxiously for morning, in the hopes that we might be seen by some passing ship, when Tom cried out that he saw a steamer standing right for us. She came near; we shouted at the top of our voices, which were still pretty strong. When not half a cable's length from us, what was our joy to see her stop her way and alter her course so as to avoid running us down. When just abreast of us a boat was lowered, and, on being taken on board, great was our surprise to find ourselves on the deck of the *Giaour*. It was only equalled by that of Murray at seeing us.

"We had no opportunity of sending home information of our merciful preservation, and, as Murray had to sail again at once, we, as you see, were the first to bring home intelligence of our safety."

"And thankful I am, my boy, that you have escaped," exclaimed the admiral, again wringing Adair's and Tom's hands. "Well, Commander Jack, and what have you to say for yourself? I suppose you will be starting immediately for Halliburton?"

"That must depend upon the arrangements of Colonel Giffard and his daughter, who took a passage home in my ship," answered Jack; "my belief is that they will return home shortly, to make arrangements for an event which is to come off early next month, which is no other than my marriage with Julia Giffard. Adair has promised to be my best man; and I know I may trust to your coming, admiral."

"Not unless Sir John and Lady Rogers consent to allow Adair to take a leading part in another event of the same description; and I will now tell you, Adair, what I've done. I have left you half my property, provided you marry Lucy Rogers within six months—that is to say, if she wishes to have you; or, in case you should decline, I have left it to her to console her for your ill-treatment."

"You are indeed most kind and generous," exclaimed Adair, wringing the admiral's hand.

"As to that, I don't know that it is any great exertion of generosity," answered the admiral; "considering that I can't take my money away with me, and that I have no relative except Deborah to whom I am bound in any way to leave it. She'll do what she thinks fit with the other half; either will it away to a hospital for dogs and cats, or leave it to those whom she thinks it may most benefit."

The meeting of Adair and Lucy need not be described. Murray and Jack paid off their ships; when the former, instead of returning immediately, as he had intended, to Bercaldine, accepted an invitation to spend some weeks at Halliburton. The double marriages took place, when, after the pleasantest time they had ever spent together, the three commanders separated, Murray going with his wife and family to his Highland home, where shortly afterwards Jack and Terence, who were on their wedding tours, paid them a visit.

Ben Snatchblock, who had been appointed to the charge of the *Stella*, had got her trim and taut as ever; and many a pleasant cruise did the old shipmates take together on board her, sometimes accompanied by their wives, and sometimes alone. Which proved the pleasantest trips of the two we cannot venture to say, but undoubtedly on the latter occasions there was more fun and frolic on board the craft; while many a yarn of old days was spun, in which Ben took his part. They were all, indeed, supremely happy, with no cares or responsibilities to trouble them; but the pleasantest of times must come to an end, and again the old friends parted, Jack and Terence going south with their brides, to finish their promised round of visits, while Alick and Stella remained at Bercaldine, very naturally hoping that nothing for a long time to come might compel them to leave it.

CHAPTER XXIII

A Hard Trial for Jack and Terence—The *Dragon* and *Eolus* sail for the Pacific—The Straits of Magellan, Valparaiso, Callao—Peruvian Kidnappers—A Strange Tale—Sail for Tahiti—Fall in with a Kidnapper—A Fearful Atrocity—A Coral Island—Tahiti—Its present state—Samoa.

"THOSE Lords of the Admiralty are the most horribly cruel, tyrannical, hard-hearted set I ever heard of. Why could they not have appointed another officer who is not just married? There are numbers of single men who would have been delighted to take command of the *Dragon*; and to think of their sending you, my dear, dear Jack, all the way out to the Pacific, for I don't know how many years, among coral reefs and cannibals, and all sorts of fearful dangers;" and Mrs. Jack Rogers put her handkerchief to her eyes and sobbed as if her heart would break. Her husband, who held an official-looking letter, which he had just read, in his hand, looked as he felt, much distressed; but at the same time, it never occurred to him that he could possibly refuse the appointment to the fine new screw-steamer which had just been offered him, although her destination was the Pacific, and she might be kept out there three or four years. It was the first trial of his married life—a very great one—and he had had no other as yet to break him in. He in vain tried to comfort his young wife; it was very, very hard to them both; and, indeed, it was very difficult to discover any sort of comfort, and the more he said the more poor Julia wept.

"Could you not say that, under your circumstances, you would rather be appointed to the coastguard?" she exclaimed at length; "then you might stay at home, and I should not be separated from you in the unnatural way the Admiralty propose."

"It would be equivalent to desiring to be shelved, and I aspire to become a post-captain and to get my flag some day," answered Jack. "Our case is not worse than that of many others. Some friends of mine have been sent off to sea a few days only after they have been married."

"It was a shame, then, and they had no business to go," answered Julia indignantly. "I wonder how those horrid lords themselves would like being separated from their wives, unless, as is possible, they are incapable of feeling the slightest love for them."

"I assure you, my dear Julia, that, though in the aggregate they are somewhat inconsiderate of the feelings of naval officers, they are individually as amiable gentlemen and affectionate husbands as any other men," said Jack. "My friend, Tom Somers, one of the most lucky dogs in the service, who was a post-captain at five-and-twenty, tells a capital story on the subject. He is, I must confess, impudence personified. He was one day at the Admiralty, complaining to one of the lords, much in the way that you are now doing, of their want of consideration for the feelings of junior officers. The lord heard him out, and then asked him to come and dine with him, which Tom condescended to do; and a very good dinner, with a number of excellent wines, he enjoyed. His host produced one bottle after the other of different descriptions, and of the choicest. 'And you like my wines?' he asked. 'Excellent, all of them, sir,' answered Tom. 'I shouldn't mind dining with you once a week while I remain on shore.' 'Very well,' answered the lord: 'but as I am leaving home, and cannot have the pleasure of seeing you, I'll send you a bottle, and you shall tell me how you like it.'

"The next day Tom received a bottle, tied significantly round with red tape, for his host was somewhat of a wag. On tasting it, Tom poured out a glass and drank it off, but the instant afterwards regretted his precipitancy, for he declared that he had never tasted anything so execrable. Just then his friend looked in upon him. 'Well, Somers, how did you like my wine?' he asked. 'I can't say that I ever wish to take another drop of it,' answered Tom. 'Well, I sent you exactly the wines you tasted at my house,' answered his visitor. 'You, however, drank them separately; I mixed them together, and you complain of the result. Now if you take each of us lords by ourselves, you will find us as well-disposed and amiable as most other men; but when we act together we put aside all the gentle feelings of our nature, and form the stern, unrelenting body you and others find us.' I believe, Julia, Tom gave a very exact description of the

Admiralty; and however much some of the lords might be disposed to befriend me individually, I should ruin myself in the service were I to plead that I have just married a wife, and would rather not go to sea."

"Then is there no chance of your getting some other appointment?" asked Julia, in a faltering tone.

"Not the slightest, I am afraid," answered Jack; "however, we must make the best of a bad case. Some weeks may pass before the ship is ready for sea, and perhaps before that time you will have got tired of me."

Julia gave a melancholy smile, as she looked up in her husband's face. "I am jealous of Lucy," she said after some time; "I suppose the Admiralty will not also be appointing Commander Adair to a ship."

"I am not so certain of that," said Jack; "I know that they talk of sending out several to put a stop to the kidnapping system which has of late prevailed in the Pacific, as also to keep some of the black and brown island-chiefs in order, and they may fix on Adair as likely as on anyone else."

"Poor Lucy!" said Julia; "I am sure I don't really wish her to share my fate."

This conversation took place at Colonel Giffard's, where Jack and his bride were staying. The very next day he got a letter from Adair, who with Lucy was at Southsea, saying that he had been appointed to the *Eolus*, to proceed forthwith to the Pacific station.

"Lucy behaves capitally, like a sailor's wife, and says she knows I ought to go—though it is a cruel affair to us both. However, Jack, I know that you will compassionate us, and that your wife will do her best to comfort her when I am away. I tell her that I have hopes of coming back in a couple of years, as I will try at the end of that time to get superseded, which, with the help of the admiral, I hope I may succeed in doing."

"Poor Lucy!" said Julia, "we must support each other; but when we married, I little thought such would be our fate."

Jack, of course, took his wife down to Southsea, as, fortunately for him, the *Dragon* was fitting out at Portsmouth, as was also the *Eolus*. The young ladies, having got over their first sensations of grief when they met, wisely determined to make the most of their husbands during the time they remained with them. The *Eolus* was almost ready for sea, and sailed about a fortnight after Adair had commissioned her. Curiously enough, Desmond had been previously appointed to her; so he once more accompanied his uncle.

The *Dragon* was not ready till the week afterwards. Jack was glad to get Jos Green as master, with Mr. Mildmay as his first lieutenant. His brother Tom, who had been taking a spell on shore, was appointed to her, and, just before she sailed, Archie Gordon joined her. Dick Needham, though eligible for a much higher rate, had joined as gunner, with Mr. Large, who had been with Jack in the *Gauntlet*, as boatswain. When it was known that Jack was to command the *Dragon*, several old shipmates volunteered, Jerry Bird and Tim Nolan among them. Tom was much pleased to have his old messmate Billy Blueblazes. Dicky Duff had joined the *Eolus*. Altogether Jack was well satisfied with his officers and ship's company.

We cannot venture to describe the parting, as it might be too touching to the feelings of our fair readers. Lucy, having had to undergo the same ordeal just before, was able to console her sister-in-law. Jack's manly heart felt very full, but he tore himself away, and, hastening on board, ordered the ship, which was at Spithead, to be got under weigh. Round went the men at the capstan, the merry pipe sounding, and under all sail the *Dragon* stood down Channel. She was directed not to use her coal except in case of necessity. Having touched at Madeira, where she took in a cask of wine for the admiral, and oranges enough to keep scurvy at bay for many a month, and having sighted the Cape de Verdes in the distance, she stood across to Rio. That city had improved greatly since Jack was last there, the enlightened Emperor being the advocate of liberal institutions, which have done much to advance the social as well as the material interests of the inhabitants. Mildmay, who still, notwithstanding he was first lieutenant, indulged his poetical fancies, wrote a sonnet on the benign rule of the Emperor, which, unfortunately, having been blown overboard, cannot be given.

Touching at the Falkland Islands for a supply of fresh beef and vegetables, the *Dragon* steered for the Straits of Magellan, which Jack had determined to run through. She called off Sandy Point, near the eastern entrance of the Straits, where the Chilian Government have formed a settlement for the purpose of working a coal mine. Some copper-coloured natives, with broad faces and high cheek-bones, and dressed in guanaco robes and skin boots, came off to the ship, principally to obtain some liquor, though they brought some ostrich, fox, and guanaco skins to exchange for guns and gunpowder or spirits. The passage of the Straits being broad and well known, the ship steamed rapidly on till she reached Cape Pillar at the western end, beyond which the Pacific Ocean burst on their view. Instead, however, of entering it, she steered north into Smith's Channel, the southern end of a passage which runs due north between the mainland and a chain of islands, two hundred miles in length. Nothing could be grander than the scenery which those on board the *Dragon* beheld, as the ship threaded her way through this intricate channel, with the islands on the left hand, and lofty snow-capped mountains towering up on the right. As she proceeded northward, their bases appeared covered with trees, reaching almost to the water's edge, deep bays and gulfs running up far inland; indeed, the whole scenery was grand and beautiful. It required careful steering and a bright look-out ahead to avoid running on shore, a hot tide being frequently met with which might quickly have whirled the ship round on the rocks.

At length, a heavy gale blowing outside, in order to avoid it she ran through a narrow passage, and entered a small harbour known as Connor Cove. The mountains, thickly covered with trees for some distance up, rose around the harbour, their snowy summits towering to the sky. The scene was grand and sombre, a few sea-birds only appearing, who, with their loud, wild shrieks increased its melancholy character. Though several of the officers landed, they could make no progress through the dense forest, the whole ground being one mass of rotten timber, amid which grew ferns and moss of various descriptions. Here, though the gale raged overhead, she lay as securely as in a dock, moored by the stern with a hawser to a large tree on shore. The gale having ceased, steam was again got up, and about forty miles on she entered the open sea, and passed several Chilian towns, the most northern being Lota and Coronel, at both of which places extensive coal-mining operations were carried on. At the latter, the *Dragon* took in a fresh supply of coal, which would carry her, if properly husbanded, across the Pacific. Steaming northward, she entered the bay of Valparaiso, which Tom, as he looked at the barren, red, and bare hills surrounding it, with scarce a bush except the cactus to be seen, pronounced a very odd sort of Paradise. The town stands partly on the shores of the bay, and chiefly on a number of hills separated by valleys, with the mighty Cordilleras rising beyond, giving the scenery, in spite of the barren aspect of the foreground, a grand and picturesque character. The bay was full of vessels, showing that a considerable amount of trade is carried on in the place. Jack and his officers received numerous invitations both from the English merchants and the native residents of rank; a ball being given by them in honour of the *Dragon's* officers, at which Tom lost his heart, as did several of his companions theirs.

"What, you don't mean to say you have forgotten the fair Feodorowna?" said Archie, as Tom was expatiating on the beauty of the black-eyed damsel who had attracted his admiration.

"Well, as you know, she is in another hemisphere, and as I never expect to see her again, and she has probably forgotten me, I don't think I ought to wear the willow for her any longer," said Tom; "and Doña Seraphina is, you'll allow, very beautiful."

"Granted," answerered Archie; "but as the ship sails to-morrow, and Doña Seraphina will probably forget you in the course of a day or two, even if she happens to distinguish you from the rest of us, you'll not, I hope, break your heart about her."

"Not if we happen to touch at another port soon, and a ball is given to us there," said Tom, with a demure look; "provided I have the luck to meet a partner with attractions equal to Doña Seraphina's."

"You're all right, my lad," said Archie, clapping him on the back; "and Mr. Mildmay won't have to write your epitaph, '*Hic jacet* Tom Rogers, who died of a broken heart, etc. etc.'"

About three weeks after this the *Dragon* entered the bay of Callao, passing round the barren island of San Lorenzo, long the burying-place of Protestants, who were denied sepulture on the mainland. At the farther end of the plain, between the lofty Cordilleras and the shore, could be seen the spires and fanes of Pizarro's "City of a thousand towers and a hundred gates," while on the island were basking numbers of drowsy seals and sea-lions with sleek skins and shaggy manes. The ship came to an anchor about a mile from the mole, outside the merchant vessels. Jack had been looking out for the *Eolus*, and was somewhat disappointed at not hearing of her at any of the ports at which he had touched. As they had been ordered to cruise in company, he determined to wait here for her. This gave an opportunity to several of the officers to visit Lima. Those who went there pronounced the city a very fine one, and declared that it was more worthy to be called the Vale of Paradise than the Chilian town to the southward.

The ship had been there some days, when some time after sunset a schooner was observed gliding into the harbour. She came to an anchor among several other vessels which concealed her from sight. Jack, who had been on deck enjoying the cool air of the evening, was about to turn in, when the sentry hailed a small boat which was seen approaching. An English voice answered, and asked leave to come on board; it was granted, and a middle-aged seafaring man stepped up the side.

"Who are you, and what do you want, my man?" asked Jack.

"Please you, sir, I am an Englishman; my name is Ralph Hake, of Plymouth; and I belonged till half an hour ago to a Peruvian schooner, the *Saltador*, which now lies inside of us; but I've taken French leave of her, and don't want to go back," answered the man.

"A very clear statement of yours; but what brought you on board this ship?" asked Jack.

"Because I had nowhere else to go to, sir, and that's why. I'd like to enter with you, sir; I'm sick of the craft I was serving aboard, and of the work she was carrying on," answered the man.

"What was that?" asked Jack.

"Just kidnapping poor natives in the different islands away to the westward whenever she could get hold of them, and bringing them here as slaves, to labour in the mines, or at any other task their masters may think fit to put them to," answered Hake. "You see, sir, I was left on shore sick, from a whaler, which, as she never came back for me, was, I suppose, lost, and as I was starving, not knowing how this craft was to be employed, I shipped on board her, being promised high wages and thinking I should like the trip; but when I came to see the sort of work she was carrying on, I made up my mind to leave her on the first opportunity, though I never found that till to-night, when, getting hold of the dingy which was alongside, I slipped my bag into her, and pulled away before anyone found me out. I can tell you, sir, I never saw more cruel work than that craft carried on. When the skipper could, he enticed the natives on board, and clapped them under hatches. Sometimes he pretended to trade with them, and got them below under the pretence of looking at his goods; at others, he asked them into the cabin to have a bit of something to eat, and, making them drunk, slipped their hands into handcuffs before they knew what was happening. At some places where this did not answer he sent the boats' crews armed on shore, and seized as many as he could fall in with, and not unfrequently took the people out of fishing-canoes, which he sent to the bottom. I have known him run down three or four canoes one after the other, to get hold of some of the people in them, not minding what became of the rest. At one place the people must have been Christians, for when we went on shore we found a number of them in a large chapel, and a brown man preaching to them. We got hold of nearly a score, and when their friends attempted to rescue them, we shot or cut down all who interfered, and carried away a dozen or more. When we got them on board, instead of complaining, they sat together and sang psalms, and one of them, who I found knew a little English, talked to me, and told me that two of their number were elders of their church, and that he and all the rest were Christians. When I told the skipper, he only laughed, and said that they were only Protestants, and that when they got on shore the priests would make them into real Christians. The native, when I told him this, sighed, and said he hoped he and his friends would remain faithful. On another occasion we enticed a whole fleet of canoes some distance off the shore; when they, taking the alarm, were pulling back, he fired among them, and when they took fright and were paddling away, we sunk the whole of them, giving some the stem, throwing shot into others, and firing at the rest. We picked up as many people as we could, but not a few were drowned, and the remainder managed to swim on shore. At last, with a full cargo, though some died on board, we came in here. I found that this was not the first trip on this business the schooner had made, and that half a dozen more craft were employed in the same way, so that many hundreds of the poor natives must have been carried off from their homes to die up among the snowy mountains of cold, starvation, and hard work, or else of broken hearts."

"This is important information, my man; you should at once have informed the consul, who might have taken steps to get the natives liberated," observed Jack.

"If I had gone on shore, sir, I should have had a sharp knife stuck under my ribs before I was many hours older," answered Hake. "By that time, and long before the consul could have interfered, the whole cargo would have been miles away up the country; even now there is not one left in the schooner."

Jack reflected on what the man had told him, and, believing the account, gave him leave to remain on board during the night, resolving to look into the matter the next morning. A hand was sent to secure his punt; but it was found that when he stepped out of her he had given her a shove, and sent her drifting away, and she was nowhere to be seen.

The next morning Jack went on shore to communicate with the acting consul, who acknowledged that he had had information on the subject; but though aware that several vessels had been fitted out for the purpose mentioned, he had been unable to take any steps for putting a stop to their proceedings.

"Then I must see what we can do!" exclaimed Jack indignantly.

"If we can find out from what islands people have been taken, and the inhabitants ask for our protection, we shall have the right to afford them all the assistance in our power. You may be very certain, should you seize any vessels engaged in carrying off the natives, no one will interfere; for their Government, even should they be aware of their proceedings, will not dare to acknowledge that they are so, or protect them; and I am very sure that the French will be ready to assist in capturing the villains who may have ventured to visit any of the islands under their rule," observed the consul.

"Then I will go to Tahiti, and ascertain what the French Government knows about the matter," said Jack; "possibly on my way I may fall in with some of the kidnappers, and it will be a satisfaction to release the slaves they may have taken, and to put a stop to their proceedings."

That evening the ship sailed for the westward. A look-out was kept for any craft which might answer to Hake's description of the vessels engaged in the traffic. The *Dragon* had been nearly three weeks at sea when a vessel was seen ahead steering to the eastward. As she drew nearer, she was seen to be a brigantine, and Hake declared that she was one of the vessels sent out to collect natives. Hopes were entertained that she might have some on board, and that they should have the pleasure of releasing them and taking them back to their homes, if such could be found. As the *Dragon* drew nearer, Jack made a signal for the stranger to heave-to; and as she did not appear to understand it, he fired a shot across her bows, which had the desired effect. A boat was lowered, and Jos Green, with Tom and Archie, were sent to examine her, and should natives be found, to bring her close up to the ship, so that they might be transferred on board.

Jos and his companions pulled away in high glee, fully hoping that they should have the satisfaction of liberating some of their fellow-creatures.

"It is too bad," observed Green, "that we should be spending our energies on the West and East Coasts of Africa, and all the time that these degenerate descendants of Spaniards out here in the Pacific should be endeavouring to drag our fellow-creatures into a far worse slavery than the Africans have to endure. These poor islanders, accustomed to the perfect freedom of the breezes of the ocean, must perish miserably in the course of a few months if compelled to work in the mines, or even in the fields on the mainland."

"I think we should be right to hang up their captors at their own yard-arms, and send their vessels to the bottom!" cried Tom indignantly.

Archie, though he doubted the legality of the proceeding, perfectly agreed with Tom that it would be a just punishment for the kidnappers. Six ruffianly-looking fellows, one of whom appeared to be the master, most of them having their heads or arms bandaged up as if they had been wounded, received them on deck. The master pointed to the Peruvian flag, and inquired why he was stopped on his voyage.

"I'll tell you when we've examined your craft," answered Green.

"You'd better not go into the forecastle, where we have five of our men suffering from the smallpox," said the skipper.

"And how many have you in the hold?" asked Green, who knew Spanish sufficiently to carry on a conversation.

"We have no one there, but you had better not go into it, for some have died there of smallpox, and you may carry the disease on board your own ship," answered the skipper.

"We will run the risk," said Green; "take off the hatches, and I'll go below."

As no one seemed inclined to obey him, he ordered his own men to lift off the hatches. He and Tom, with two of the men, went below, while Archie, with the rest, remained on deck, keeping an eye upon the Peruvian crew, who, as Tim Nolan observed, "looked as if they were after mischief." The hold was empty, but it was evidently fitted for passengers, or rather for slaves.

"What are all those dark marks?" asked Tom.

"Bloodstains," answered Green, examining them; "and see, here are bullets sticking in the deck and timbers. The wood has been splintered in all directions; depend on it there has been some desperate work going on. I believe that the account of the smallpox was false, and was merely given to try and prevent us from examining the craft."

"You found no one, as I told you," said the skipper, when Green returned on deck.

"No, but we have found enough to convince us that you have murdered the unhappy wretches you induced to come on board," answered Green.

"You should rather say our passengers treacherously rose on us, and we had to fight in self-defence," said the skipper, forgetting what he had said about the smallpox.

"And your men forward are suffering from the wounds they received?" said Green.

"Such is the case, but I was ashamed to acknowledge how nearly we were defeated by the savages," said the master, with the greatest coolness.

Green accordingly went forward, and found five men in their bunks, all badly wounded, two being nearly at the last gasp.

"I will bring the surgeon to dress their hurts," said Green; "though, if what I suspect is the case, you all deserve to be sent to the bottom; and, depend on it, we shall endeavour to get at the truth of the story, and you will hear more of the matter by and by."

The master shrugged his shoulders; and Green, not thinking it prudent to leave anyone on board with such villains, returned with the midshipmen to the ship to make his report. Jack was doubting how to proceed with the brigantine, when her sails were let fall, and, the breeze freshening, she stood away to windward. As the *Dragon* had not even her fires lighted, there was but little chance of catching her, and Jack did not think it worth while to go in chase, as he felt pretty sure that she would not continue her kidnapping cruise.

The next day the look-out announced that he saw a fleet of

vessels ahead. "A grove of palm trees, rather," observed Green, laughing. As the ship rose and fell in the swell, the trees alternately disappeared and came into sight; and, on getting nearer, a coral island hove in view; it consisted of a ring a quarter of a mile or so in width, with a lagoon in the centre. First was seen a line of surf, then a white sandy beach, and beyond a belt of green ground, sparsely sprinkled with cocoa-nut and pandanus trees, and here and there with a few bushes of low growth. The ship stood along the shore at a respectful distance, a look-out being kept for inhabitants, as Jack thought it possible that if any of the people had escaped from the brigantine, they might have managed to effect a landing, the natives of these islands being generally first-rate swimmers. No one, however, was seen, and he feared that the whole of the kidnapped people must have perished. As he was unwilling to lose time by heaving-to to effect a landing, he stood on towards Tahiti.

All hands were somewhat disappointed with the appearance of that island when they first came in sight of it—jagged peaks and rugged mountains being alone visible; for the shady groves and waterfalls, the verdant meadows and fields, were not to be seen till the ship got close to the entrance of the harbour. Before them appeared a line of breakers dashing in snow-white foam on the encircling reef of coral, with a lagoon of calm blue water within, out of which rose the shore, covered with the richest tropical vegetation; numberless vines and creeping plants making their way up the hillsides, amid which sparkling cascades came falling down from the rugged mountains above.

"Well, after all, Tahiti does present a highly picturesque and beautiful landscape," exclaimed Mildmay, taking out his notebook; "and I hope that we shall find the inhabitants living in that Arcadian simplicity appropriate to so lovely a region."

Alas! they found but little Arcadian simplicity when they reached the shore; guns frowned from the surrounding heights down on the harbour; the French flag flew from the battlements of the forts; French soldiers were everywhere seen. It was soon evident that the once free Tahitians were a conquered race.

Jack lost no time in communicating with the French governor, who had already heard that many of the natives of the outlying islands under French protection had been carried off. He had already sent out two men-of-war to try and catch the kidnappers, and he expressed his wish heartily to co-operate with the English in putting a stop to so abominable a system. Jack, being satisfied that the French would attend to that part of the Pacific, determined to proceed to the westward, where the appearance of an English man-of-war might effect some good.

The fires were lighted, and preparations were being made for weighing, when a column of smoke was seen in the distance, announcing the approach of a steamer. A French officer on board said that she must be direct from Europe, as none of their own cruisers were expected. Jack, hoping to obtain some news, accordingly waited for her arrival. As she approached, she made the number of the *Eolus*. Soon coming to an anchor, visits were exchanged between the two ships' companies. Adair told Jack that he had arrived at Callao the day after the *Dragon* had left, and that as soon as he could obtain fresh provisions and water, he had again sailed in search of him. The *Eolus* had come round by the Cape, and had not entered the Pacific till three weeks after the *Dragon*.

Jack agreed to wait till the *Eolus* could take in provisions and water. The feeling with which the unjustifiable capture of Tahiti by the French had been regarded by the English had by this time subsided; and, the officers of the two ships having been treated with all the civility the French were able to show, they left the harbour with some regret, as they were not likely to meet with any place so advanced in civilisation before they reached Sydney.

A voyage across the Pacific sounds very romantic; but there are often long distances to be traversed when no land is in sight, and there is nothing to break the monotony of the voyage. The midshipmen of the two ships voted it very dull, and began to believe that they should meet with none of the wonderful adventures which they had anticipated. Mr. Mildmay confessed that he had been dreadfully disappointed; he had expected everywhere to see bevies of graceful nymphs, dressed in gossamer robes, their glossy hair decked with wreaths of bright flowers, and their necks and arms adorned with coral and precious stones; instead of which, he declared that he had seen only a set of dowdy women with brown skins and without a particle of beauty to boast of.

"One thing, however, can be said of the inhabitants of these islands," observed Jack; "whereas a few years ago they were in heathen darkness, now, thanks to the exertions of the missionaries, heathenism has disappeared from all the islands to the southward; and if the people are not perfect Christians, they are at all events as much so as the great mass of people in Christendom."

Jack was right; indeed, they found missionaries established at all the principal islands at which they touched, with large chapels, well-built schoolhouses, and neat villages; the inhabitants being universally able to read and write, and many of them being well informed on various important subjects. After touching at several islands to the south and west of Tahiti, where not a single heathen remains, the ships steered for a harbour in one of the islands of the Samoan group. It was here that a boat's crew of the French navigator, La Perouse, were massacred. As they approached the islands, no sign of a harbour could be perceived—lofty cliffs towering up before them to the sky without apparently a break. Still the *Dragon* stood on, followed by the *Eolus*, two rocks appearing, one called the Tower Rock, and another on the opposite side, the Devil's Point, so well defined that Jack had no fears of mistaking the entrance. The sails were furled, and the steam got up. At length the ships entered a passage between the cliffs, about a third of a mile in width, till they reached a basin, completely surrounded by lofty precipices, from 800 to 1000 feet in height. The lower portion of the rocks was bare, but their summits were clothed with the most luxuriant vegetation — magnificent tree-ferns and cocoanut-trees growing high up in situations in which they are seldom seen in other latitudes.

No sooner had the ships dropped their anchors than they were surrounded by canoes full of natives, who, though they appeared to be merry fellows, were remarkably well behaved; all of them being also decently clothed. Several chiefs and others came on board, some of whom spoke English; and from them it was ascertained that the whole of the people were Christians, having long been under missionary influence. One of Jack's chief objects in entering the harbour was to ascertain whether any of the natives had been carried off. A strange vessel had appeared off the coast, and had attempted to entrap some lads fishing in a canoe, but they had been too wary to be so caught; and when a boat put off in chase of their canoe, they had made their way to the shore, though only just in time to escape capture.

Jack issued a notice which he desired might be sent among all the islands of the group, warning the people against the various devices practised by the kidnappers. After a short time the two ships again put to sea.

CHAPTER XXIV

Santa Cruz—Its Unattractive Inhabitants—A Schooner chased by the Boats—Suspicious Characters—The Schooner allowed to proceed—A Gale—Run for Shelter under the Lee of an Island—A Volcano bursts forth—Driven away—Breakers ahead—An Opening in the Reef—Pass through—Land on an Island—Food found—Natives appear—Hostile Demonstrations—Green's Old Shipmate—Peace established—Escape from the Island.

THE *Dragon* and *Eolus* had been for some weeks at sea; the latter was to touch at various islands of the New Hebrides group, after which she was to proceed to the Loyalty Islands, to visit the Isle of Pines and Norfolk Island, and thence to go on to Sydney. The *Dragon*, meantime, was to continue her course to the north-west, visiting Santa Cruz, the Solomon Islands, New Ireland, and New Britain; and she also was to visit Sydney. Thence the two ships were to recross the Pacific, to touch at the Sandwich Islands, and to go on to Vancouver's Island and British Columbia; after which, all hands heartily hoped that they might be ordered home. The projected cruise was being discussed in the midshipmen's berth, with the chart on the table.

"It doesn't look so very far," observed Billy Blueblazes; "though, considering that we are to perform the distance under sail, it will take us some time, I suppose."

"I rather think so, laddie," observed Archie, who had a pair of compasses in his hand, and was measuring off the distances; "we shall have run over between sixty and seventy thousand miles of salt water before we drop anchor in Portsmouth harbour,—not an inch less according to my calculation,—it would be enough to wear the sheathing off the ship's bottom if it was not pretty thick to begin with."

Most of the islands the ship visited were lofty, the hills covered thickly with trees to their summits. They were surrounded by coral reefs, through which, in many instances, no passage was to be found; others had openings affording secure harbours within them. After visiting several small islands in the neighbourhood, the ship came to an anchor in a sheltered harbour in the island of Santa Cruz. Canoes quickly gathered round her, full of the ugliest-looking natives they had yet met with. Their skin was nearly black, their heads covered with thick woolly hair, their foreheads low and receding, their faces broad, with high cheek-bones, their noses flat, and their mouths large. They had adorned their bodies with various colours, and ornamented themselves further with rings through their noses and ears, as also with armlets and necklaces of human teeth; the rest of their dress consisting only of a string round the waist, to which a small apron was secured. These unattractive-looking personages were considerably under the ordinary size, but appeared, notwithstanding the character bestowed on them of being the most cruel and treacherous in the Pacific Ocean, to be a good-tempered, merry race. They brought off large quantities of cocoa-nuts, bows, arrows, and mats, which they were willing to exchange for empty bottles, old clothes, and tobacco. As yet, no missionaries having ventured among them, they were in the same savage state in which they had for centuries existed.

In the evening, those who had been allowed to come on board were turned out of the ship, and a bright look-out was kept against any treacherous trick they might have attempted to play. The fires had been let out, as Jack intended to remain during the day for the purpose of obtaining water. Early the next morning, a schooner was seen passing close in with the land. As the wind was light, Jack despatched two boats to overhaul her; one was commanded by Green, who was accompanied by Archie—the other by Tom, who had Billy Blueblazes as his companion. They pulled away, hoping soon to overtake the stranger. When, however, they were about half a mile from her, a breeze sprang up; but, as the boats had their sails, the masts were stepped, and they stood on after the chase. She took no notice of the musket which Green fired as a signal for her to heave-to, but, instead of doing so, she set more sail and stood on. This making him more suspicious than ever of her character, he determined to persevere; Tom and his companion being equally ready to continue the pursuit.

"Perhaps she is a pirate," observed Billy, "and when she finds that she cannot get off she will try to defend herself, and we shall have some fighting—something to vary the monotony of the voyage."

"As to that, I doubt whether such craft are to be found in these seas at the present day," answered Tom; "and I rather think, if we can manage to get up to her, that she will strike without firing a shot."

The question was, however, whether the boats would come up with her; the breeze was freshening, and she was walking away from them. Still Green kept on, hoping that the wind might head her, or that it might fall calm, when they would soon be alongside. She was steering towards a lofty conical island, which rose sheer out of the sea, with a thick cloud of smoke rising above its summit, which showed it to be an active volcano. The day was drawing on, but the schooner did not gain sufficiently on the boats to make Green abandon all hopes of overtaking her. Her persevering efforts to escape convinced him that something was wrong, and made him the more eager to overhaul her. At length, her sails were seen to flap against her masts, and, though the boats still had the breeze, it was very evident that she was becalmed. The sky had for some time been wearing a threatening aspect, and had not Green been so eager to overhaul the stranger, he would have endeavoured to make the best of his way back to Santa Cruz. At length the wind dropped altogether, and, the sails being lowered, the crews of the boats gave way, with a certainty that they should at length get up with the chase. Each boat had four muskets; the officers had stuck their pistols in their belts, and the men had their cutlasses—weapons on which British seamen always place more reliance than on firearms. They were now within gunshot of the schooner, but she did not fire, nor were any signs visible that she intended to offer resistance. Green steered for the starboard quarter, and directed Tom to board on the port side. They were soon up with her; Tom and Billy, with six men, scrambled up on deck, which Green and his party gained at the same time; but, except the man at the helm, and one other forward, none of the crew were visible. The man at the helm looked very much astonished, and asked with cool effrontery what they wanted. Green replied that he must know where the schooner was from, whither she was bound, and what cargo she had on board.

"The master will tell you all about it, sir," answered the man, "but he is at present below, sick with a bad leg."

"Then I must pay him a visit, and get him to show his papers," said Green; who, telling Tom and Billy to keep a watch on deck, went into the master's cabin with Archie, and a couple of armed men. The master was sitting up in his cot, with a black boy attending on him.

"Well, gentlemen, what do you want?" he asked, as Green and Archie entered.

"Why did you run away from us," asked Green, "when you must have seen that our boats were those of one of Her Majesty's ships-of-war?"

"How could I tell what you were?" said the master; "you might be pirates. At all events, I have no wish to be stopped in my voyage."

"Well, at anyrate, show me your papers, and inform me how many people you have on board; for as yet I have only seen a couple of hands," said Green.

"We have upwards of eighty, including passengers," answered the master. "I suppose the crew got out of the way lest you should fire at us, and for the same reason the passengers thought it prudent to keep below. Boy, take that tin case out of the the locker there, and give it to the officer."

Green examined the document brought him. It set forth that the schooner *Expert*, Captain Toby, belonging to Brisbane, Queensland, had a licence to trade for sandal-wood, and to carry a hundred passengers.

"Well, your papers seem all very clear; and if your passengers came on board with their own free will, I can have nothing to say to you, but wish you a good voyage," he remarked; "but I should have been better pleased had you hove-to when I made a signal to you to do so, as you would have saved us a long pull."

Captain Toby only grinned, as if he was well pleased at the trouble he had caused the man-of-war's officers. As they were speaking, two other men, who were apparently mates, came out of a side cabin, yawning and stretching themselves in a way which somewhat tried Green's patience.

"Well, I must beg your officers to show me your passengers, and the rest of your crew, before I quit you," he said, addressing the master.

"I suppose you've got legal authority for what you are doing?" said Captain Toby.

"Certainly; and as we are in a hurry to be off, I must beg

you to be smart about it," said Green; turning to the mates, "Come, my lads, I am only performing my duty, and that duty I intend to carry out."

The two mates, seeing that the officer was not to be trifled with, went forward and summoned eight ruffianly-looking fellows who had been stowed away in the forecastle. Three or four were apparently Englishmen, the others black or brown men, one a Kanaka, the other a New Zealander. By the mate's orders they lifted off the hatches, and went below. Archie observed that they had the butts of pistols sticking out of the breasts of their shirts, and that all of them wore long knives in sheaths by their sides. There was some talking below, and one by one sixty black-skinned natives made their appearance on deck, and were ranged on either side. None of them had any other clothing besides a piece of matting or sail-cloth round the waist. Unfortunately, Green had come away without an interpreter; but he did his best to try and ascertain from the natives if they were on board of their own free will. No one uttered a complaint, but he observed that the mates kept their eyes fixed on the blacks, who seemed to cower under their glances. He was still not satisfied, but he was unable to find any sufficient reason for detaining the vessel. On returning to the cabin he found another individual, who had not before appeared, seated at the table, busily employed in writing.

"Our doctor, sir," said the master; "he has come with us for the sake of science, to gain a knowledge of the wild inhabitants of this region. He is a perfect slave to science; are you not, doctor?"

"It is the sole object of my life," answered the person who had been addressed, without rising from his seat.

Though the man spoke with the accent of a gentleman, Green thought that he had seldom seen a more ill-looking individual.

"Well, I hope you are satisfied, Mr. Officer," said the master at length; "and, if so, that you will allow us to fill our sails and stand on; for my mate tells me he doesn't like the look of the weather, and I'd advise you to make the best of your way back to your ship."

Green saw indeed that it was important to get back, and did not therefore waste words with the master or his ill-mannered surgeon. On returning on deck, he found that the mates had sent the blacks below again, while the crew were shortening sail

The weather had become rapidly worse; he could not help regretting that he had come so far from the island, with the prospect of a pull back through a heavy sea. He could not hoist the boats on board, or, under the circumstances, he might have compelled the schooner to beat back to Santa Cruz. Had he attempted to do so, and to tow the boats, they would, in all probability, have been swamped.

"We must make the best of it," he said to Tom, who had for the last few minutes been feeling anything but comfortable about the matter.

"A safe voyage to you, my friends," he said, as he leaped into his boat.

The mates made no reply, but as he shoved off he fancied that he heard a laugh, and at the same time he caught sight of the ill-favoured visage of the scientific doctor looking over the quarter, while the schooner stood away to the southward. Scarcely, however, were they a quarter of a mile apart than the wind came down with greater force than before, and he found that it was impossible to make any headway against it. The nearest island was that of Tinakula; by running under its lee he might get shelter for the night; but should an eruption occur, it would prove a dangerous neighbourhood. There were other islands beyond, but they were surrounded by reefs which might prevent the possibility of landing upon them, while, from the savage character of the natives on the inhabited ones, they could only expect a hostile reception.

"We'll try it a little longer, Rogers," sang out Green; "perhaps the weather will moderate; and if it grows worse, we must run under the lee of that burning mountain; we can only hope that it will remain quiet for a few hours."

The weather did not moderate, and when the men had been pulling hard for a couple of hours without gaining ground, the boats' heads were put round, and with reefed sails they steered towards the eastern side of the mountain, Green intending to haul round it, so as to be able to anchor during the night under its lee. Night rapidly came down over the stormy ocean; the wind increased, and the seas came roaring up astern, threatening every instant to swamp them. Green led, Tom following in his wake.

"I wish we hadn't been sent after that abominable slaver!" exclaimed Billy, who was feeling more uncomfortable than he had ever before been in his life. "I wonder whether the ship will come to look after us?"

"Not likely," answered Tom; "as well hunt for a needle in a bundle of hay; she wouldn't know where to find us if she did. My brother trusts Green, who always knows what he's about, and he will not be unhappy on our account. We shall soon be under the lee of the island, and then we shall be snug enough; though, for my part, I would rather have been comfortably stowed away in my hammock."

"You take things very coolly, Rogers!" cried Billy. "Oh, look at that big sea! it will tumble aboard us in a moment."

"If it does, you must stand by to bale it out," answered Tom; "hold on though, in case it should wash you overboard."

Tom, who was grasping the helm with a firm hand, received the sea on the quarter; a portion of the crest broke over the boat; she, however, went gliding forward, while the sea roared on till it caught Green's boat, which appeared for a moment to be overwhelmed, but was seen directly afterwards rising on the summit of another wave; while Billy and the rest of Tom's crew baled away with might and main, knowing the importance of freeing their boat before another sea broke into her. Thus on they rushed amid the dark, foam-crested waves; several times they were treated in the same manner, but as quickly as the water entered it was hove out again. The darkness increased, and the dim outline of the mountain alone could be seen, its lofty summit towering to the clouds. Green was unwilling to keep farther off the island than was necessary; but, at the same time, he thought it possible that a reef might extend some distance from it, on which, should the boats strike, they must inevitably be lost. A keen look-out was kept ahead, but nothing could be seen besides the dark, tumbling, foam-crested seas. It was a time to try the hearts of the stoutest. Gradually the island grew more and more distinct.

"Haul aft the sheet!" cried Green, and the boats sailed on with the sea abeam.

Now was the most dangerous time, for a sea striking the side might in an instant, without allowing anyone a chance of escaping, have capsized the boats, and sent them to the bottom. The seas seemed to rush forward with greater fury even than before, as if eager to seize their prey before it had escaped them. Happily it did not last long; on shooting under the lee of a lofty precipice which rose sheer out of the water, they were almost immediately becalmed, though still fearfully tumbled about by the waves as they swirled round the base of the cliff.

"Get out your oars, my lads, and give way," cried Green.

The order was quickly obeyed, and after pulling for a few hundred yards, the boats lay in comparatively calm water. The island mountain rose like a dark spectre above their heads, without any beach that could be discovered on which the boats could be hauled up, or any cove to afford them shelter. Green had a lead-line on board; it was let fall over the side, but no bottom was found.

"Perhaps by pulling on a little farther we may find some place in which we can bring up for the night; if not, we must keep the oars moving," said Green.

They pulled on accordingly.

"Hilloa!" cried Tom; "what's that?"

The moment he spoke a bright light appeared on the summit of the mountain; it rapidly increased, and presently a vast stream of incandescent lava came flowing down the side, now moving in a broad sheet, now rushing down in a cataract of fire, again to unite at the foot of a precipice, as it rushed down in a dozen different streams, some close to where the boats lay, till reaching the water they suddenly disappeared.

"Very fortunate that we were not on shore, or we should have been all burnt into cinders," said Tom; "we are even now nearer than is altogether pleasant."

"If we get farther off we shall be in the middle of a cross-sea which will quickly swamp us," observed Green; "I see the crests of the waves dancing about, not many cables' lengths away, with the light from the mountain reflected on them. We will pull back a short distance to the eastward and lie on our oars."

The boats' heads were turned round, but the men had not pulled many strokes when the lava again rushed out from the crater, rising far above it in a fountain of fire; then down it came, covering over the whole side of the mountain with a vast sheet of liquid flame, sending its glare far over the ocean, and rendering the night as bright as the day.

"Grand!" exclaimed Billy Blueblazes; "magnificent! superior to anything I ever saw at Vauxhall!"

"I should rather call it awful," said Tom; "how those huge black cliffs stand out! Why, they positively look as if they were about to topple down over us; it will give us an idea of what the world will be like when it is on fire."

The men gazed at the burning mountain, their countenances expressing their feelings, though none of them spoke. The hardy seamen could scarcely believe that they should escape destruction; the water hissed and bubbled as the hot lava reached it, and sent wave after wave towards the boats; which, as they rushed on board, were found to be perceptibly warmed. Green, who had been watching the summit of the mountain, began to doubt whether it was prudent to remain in the neighbourhood; at any moment it might send up not only lava, but ashes and stones, and huge rocks, which might in an instant overwhelm the boats. Now came a fearful rumbling noise, louder than a thousand Woolwich infants roaring together. Tom declared that the whole mountain seemed to shake, while the summit appeared covered with a crown of ruddy flame.

"This will never do," cried Green; "better be swamped at sea than be buried under a shower of rocks. Pull round and give way, my lads; stand by to hoist the sail the instant we feel the wind."

The men dashed their oars into the water, and pulled away as fast as they could stretch their arms, eager to get to a distance from the fearful scene; but though they were really going at a rapid rate, it seemed as if the mountain was still as near as ever. Even the most dull and ignorant must have been conscious of their utter helplessness; at any moment the fiery shower might descend on their heads; indeed, the farther they got off, the more clearly they saw the fearful work going forward on the summit of the mountain; the flames seemed to spout higher and higher and higher, and amid them every now and then appeared huge fragments of solid rock, which, cast up to a great height, again fell down into the crater; while similar fragments came toppling over the edge, and rolled crashing down the cliffs into the ocean. Though the sea was rough, the wind, affected apparently by the outburst of fire, seemed greatly to have abated, and it was not till they had got some distance from the island that Green ordered the sails to be hoisted. He was on the point of hauling up, intending to beat back to Santa Cruz, when once more the gale was upon them.

"We must stand on," he cried to Tom; "we shall never be able to pull back against this wind, our best chance is to run before it."

"Ay, ay, sir!" said Tom; "I'll follow you;" and the two boats flew on as before, over the tumbling seas. They were well built, and well managed too, or they would to a certainty have been swamped.

They had, by this time, got to a considerable distance from the mountain, but still it appeared almost as clear as at first, the dark cliffs projecting far out from amid the sheets of fire which almost enveloped its sides, while the summit appeared in a still more fearful state of eruption than at first. Vast flames came spouting upwards, the fiery masses which were thrown out spreading over on every side, while overhead appeared a dark canopy of smoke, from which a shower of ashes continued to fall without intermission; and Tom declared, as he looked astern, that he saw huge pieces of rock descending into the sea. They had indeed reason to congratulate themselves that they had not delayed longer under the mountain, and even as it was they were conscious that they were still not free from danger. Their anxiety had hitherto prevented them from feeling hungry, or indeed from recollecting that they had brought but a small supply of food. In each boat was, however, a breaker of water, and Billy had slipped some biscuits into his pocket, as had also several of the men, just before they shoved off. After some time, when he believed that he had only the danger of the ocean with which to contend, Billy pulled a biscuit out of his pocket and offered part to Tom, who, beginning to feel very hungry, accepted it. The crew were sharing their portions among each other; and then the breaker of water was broached, for the biscuit had made the men feel very thirsty.

In Green's boat the men were not so well off, Archie and one of the men only having had sufficient forethought to bring a couple of biscuits apiece. This afforded but a scanty meal to all hands; and they knew that it might be very long before they could hope to get a further supply of food. The gale had still further increased, and the sea was rougher than ever. They thus ran on for some hours; Tom manfully sat at the helm, assisted by Billy, his anxiety keeping him broad awake; for he well knew that the slightest carelessness on his part might lead to his own destruction and that of all with him. Unhappily, they had come away without a compass in either boat, and as the sky was completely overcast, Green had not even the stars to steer by. The wind, he felt sure, had shifted several points while they lay under the island, and he was thus uncertain in what direction he was running. He could only tell by looking astern at the mountain, which, like a huge beacon, blazed away all night. There were other islands, he knew, ahead, surrounded by reefs; and, when morning approached, he judged that they could not be very far from the nearest. The atmosphere, however, was too dense to enable him to see the land at any distance. Still he could not venture to heave-to; his only hope of keeping the boats afloat was to run on, and he trusted that day light would return before they could reach the neighbourhood of the reefs. It was too dark to see the hands of his watch, even when held up so that the light from the mountain could fall on it.

"I think the sun will rise in about half an hour," he observed to Archie; "and then I trust that we shall be able to look out for an opening in the reefs, so that we may run in and take shelter till the gale is over."

The men in both the boats were all this time employed in baling, for the crests of the seas came toppling over, now on the quarter, now running up alongside over the gunwales, wetting the people through and through. Tom, with his lips closely pressed together, his hand firmly grasping the helm, excited the admiration of the men, who knew well that their lives depended on his coolness and judgment.

"He's a regular chip of the old block; as like the commander as two peas," observed the bow-man to the man sitting next to him. Tom, indeed, had always been held in respect by the crew, but that night's work raised him still higher in their estimation.

They had been running on for some minutes, when a shout reached them from the master's boat. "Breakers ahead, and land beyond them." Tom steered straight on, waiting to see what Green would do, still following in his wake. Green deviated slightly to port.

"There is an opening," he shouted; "follow me."

Tom peered through the mass of blackness surrounding them, and made out a line of white foam, rising like a wall on the starboard bow, while beyond he could just distinguish the outline of a still darker mass which he knew must be land. His heart did not sink, nor did his hand tremble. The crew turned their heads over their shoulders as the roar of the breakers reached their ears, becoming louder and louder as the boat rushed on. The seas came rushing up astern more furiously it seemed than ever, catching them now on the port quarter; should the wind fail them, or a rope give way, they must be lost. They all knew that, and each man grasped his oar ready to throw it out and give way as a chance for life. The breakers became more and more distinct, leaping high above the tumbling ocean;

but ahead was a blacker patch, though even that was streaked with foam. There must, however, be depth for the boats to pass over, though the passage was a fearfully narrow one; for away on the port bow the breakers were seen rising as high as on the starboard side. Green stood on; he did not again hail, but he knew that he could trust Tom, and that he was following. In another minute they would be safe, or the boats dashed to pieces on the coral reef. Still on they flew; a vast surge came rolling up, lifting the stern of the boat, and Tom, for an instant, thought that she would broach to; but with all his might putting the helm hard a-port, she went rushing on before it. The foaming, roaring breakers were leaping up on either hand. He had lost sight of Green's boat. Could she have met with the fate he had expected to overtake his boat? No! there she was, safe inside the reef, with her sail lowered. The next instant he was gliding forward in comparatively smooth water.

"Lower the sail," he shouted, "and get out the oars."

He was soon alongside Green's boat.

"We will lie on our oars, and wait till daylight to find a safe place for landing," said the master. "Let us thank God that we have escaped thus far. Should there be natives on the island, we must try and keep on friendly terms with them, and we shall the better do that by not landing till they invite us. In the meantime, we will look to our arms, for they must have got wet, and are pretty sure to miss fire."

The boats accordingly pulled along the lagoon till they reached a part where, sheltered by a higher line of the reef, the water was perfectly calm. Even there, as they looked in the direction from whence they had come, they could see the burning mountain blazing away as furiously as at first; the upper portion, which appeared above the horizon, presenting the appearance of a vast shining cone, with a crown of fire rising towards the sky. Far off as it was, the light it cast had enabled them to see the breakers much sooner than they otherwise would have done, and had been the means thus of saving their lives.

Daylight now appeared, and a glimpse was caught of the sun through an opening in the cloud just above the horizon. His rays fell on a hilly country, richly wooded, with streams flowing down at the bottom of the valleys, one of which emptied itself directly opposite the break in the reef by which they had entered. As yet no natives had appeared, nor were any huts seen, but it could scarcely be supposed that so fine a region was destitute of inhabitants. Green, therefore, pointed out to his men the importance of acting cautiously. Their hunger and thirst, however, must be satisfied; he therefore pulled in towards the mouth of the stream, where, at all events, they could obtain water. As they approached, Billy's sharp eyes detected some cocoa-nuts growing on several tall trees a short distance from the beach; these would afford them food till more substantial fare could be obtained. The difficulty, however, was to reach the trees where the fruit grew.

"I'll manage to do it," cried Billy, "in a way I have read of somewhere, with a rope round my waist."

Some rocks near the mouth of the stream afforded sufficient shelter to the boats, and enabled the party to land without the necessity of beaching them. The arms had all been made ready for use, and Green ordered one half of the men to remain in the boats under Tom's command, while he led the other, who carried the breakers to fill with water. Billy, in the meantime, with Archie to assist him, prepared to climb up a cocoa-nut tree. He had brought a long piece of rope, which he formed into a large grummet, or hoop, round the tree. He made several attempts, however, before he could succeed in getting up even a few feet. Though Archie laughed at him, he was undaunted.

"Practice makes perfect," he answered, again working his way upwards till he got several feet higher.

His plan was to hold tight with his knees while he jerked the grummet as high as it would go, and then to swarm up again and rest. Higher and higher he got, till at length he was able to catch hold of a branch by which he held himself up, when, highly delighted, he quickly broke off all the fruit on the tree, and threw them down to Archie. His success encouraged the bow-man in Green's boat, who, being a light, active lad, succeeded even better than he had done, and a supply of nuts for all hands was thus obtained. By this time Green's party with the breakers had returned, and the hungry crews eagerly commenced breakfast.

"We must look out for more substantial fare than this though," observed Tom; "if we can't get any animals on shore, we shall, at all events, be able to find shell-fish in the water, and we can easily light a fire and cook them."

Till, however, the men had satisfied their hunger with the cocoa-nuts, no one felt disposed to hunt for shell-fish, or for animals on shore. It was, indeed, doubtful whether it would be prudent to allow any of the men to go inland till they had ascertained what inhabitants were in the neighbourhood, or whether they were likely to be friendly. From the character of the natives on the surrounding islands Green very much doubted whether this would be the case; and he wished, if possible, to avoid bloodshed, even although his party might prove victorious. He had also heard that they used poisoned arrows, even a slight wound from which might prove fatal. As the gale still continued blowing outside, it was absolutely necessary that more substantial food should be found. As soon, therefore, as they had somewhat taken the edge off their appetites, he allowed a small party under Tom to proceed along the beach in search of shell-fish, while the boats pulled slowly along close in to the shore, so as to be able to take them off immediately should any natives appear. No officer could have acted more wisely and cautiously. Tom and his party collected a good supply of shell-fish, his last find being a bed of oysters. Two of the men, having stripped off their clothes, waded up to their necks and dived for them. They were thus employed when Green caught sight of a dark triangular fin, which rose for an instant to the surface and disappeared. He shouted at the top of his voice to the men, telling them of their danger, and ordering his own crew to pull in, and to splash the water as much as possible with their oars. The men sprang towards the shore, fully aware of the danger they were in. They were not a moment too soon, for the monster, having caught sight of their white legs, dashed forward and almost grounded itself on the beach before, giving a whisk of its tail, it darted off again, startled by their shouts and cries, and escaped.

Tom now cried out that he had seen some birds, and that if he might use small shot he was certain that he could kill several. Green, seeing no signs of natives, thought there would be no risk, and gave him leave. Tom was a good shot, and the birds, a species of pigeon, being unaccustomed to firearms, were not frightened, so that he very quickly made a heavy bag, without having had to go far for it. There appeared to be now no reason why the party should not land to cook their provisions, and, finding a clear stretch of beach, they pulled in and hauled up the boats. Some of the men set to work to gather sticks, and a blazing fire was soon lighted; while others plucked the pigeons and prepared them for the spit. These were placed on forked sticks round the fire, while the men sat down on the ground to enjoy themselves. A few cried out for grog, but not a drop of spirits had been brought, so they were obliged to go without it, but the smokers had their pipes and tobacco, and Green had put his cigar-case into his pocket, so that they were able to pass the time pleasantly enough while the birds were cooking.

"After all, we've no great cause to complain," observed Tom, as he lighted one of Green's cigars. "I suppose when the gale abates the ship will come and look for us, or if not we shall have no great difficulty in getting back to Santa Cruz, while in the meantime we may make ourselves happy where we are," he observed.

Billy Blueblazes, of course, echoed the sentiment, but Archie was somewhat doubtful whether they might not miss the ship, as it would take them the best part of two days to pull back, and before that time she probably would have come out to look for them. Green was rather inclined to be of Archie's opinion, and was considering what under the circumstances it was best to do.

"Dinner ready, sir," said Jerry Bird, who had dished up the pigeons with some large leaves. "We have broiled oysters and mussels, and cocoa-nut for dessert, and as much milk and water as we like to drink; a feast fit for a king."

Green and the midshipmen preferred the pigeons, leaving the shell-fish to be divided among the men, who had their share also of the birds. No one had cause to complain of want of sufficient food. After dinner, their spirits being raised, they amused themselves by playing rounders, varied by a game of leapfrog on the beach, till Green reminded them that they might have a couple of nights or more at sea before they could get back to the ship, and that it was as well to take some rest while they could obtain it. The difficulty was to find shade, as the sun was beating down with intense heat on the sand, though while they were in exercise they did not think of it. The palm trees afforded but a scant shelter; however, by going a little way inland they obtained some enormous fern-leaves, with which they quickly built several huts, sufficient to shelter all the party, with the exception of two, who were stationed on the top of the bank to keep watch; Green deeming it prudent not to run any risk of being caught napping. It fell to the lot of Archie and Tim Nolan, who belonged to Green's boat, to keep the first watch. Green directed them to remain in the shade under the trees with their muskets in their hands, and to keep a bright look-out inland, so as to be able to arouse the party in good time should any natives appear.

There was an opening in the valley just where the party were encamped, extending an eighth of a mile or so inland, leaving the trees on either side some distance apart. Archie took one side, and directed Tim to get into the shade on the other, so that they might thus, without having to step far out into the sun, command the whole of the open ground. Archie felt very tired and sleepy, and was longing for his watch to be over, but nevertheless, obedient to orders, he kept a bright look-out, seeing also that Tim did the same. They had been on the watch for nearly two hours, when Archie, as he stepped out a few paces from where he had been standing, caught sight of three or four black figures at the farther end of the glade. They stopped as they saw him, regarding him with looks of astonishment, each man seizing an arrow, and fixing it in his bow. Archie shouted to Tim, and told him to awaken the sleepers, while he himself advanced into the centre of the glade, and while he held up his musket in one hand to show the blacks that he was armed, made signs with the other to them to keep back. Green had heard his voice, and was on his feet in an instant, calling out to the rest of the party to show themselves. The blacks, seeing that the strangers were much superior to them in numbers, did not advance. They were savage-looking fellows, with their hair tied up in a huge bunch at the backs of their heads, and destitute of any clothing with the exception of a short kilt of matting tied round their waists. They appeared rather surprised than alarmed, and after watching the strangers, apparently to see what they would do, for some minutes, they darted off among the trees, and were hid from sight.

"We will get the boats into the water and be ready to shove off, in case those fellows should come down in overwhelming numbers; for though we might keep them at bay, I am anxious to avoid bloodshed," said Green.

Tom agreed with him, and the men immediately began to launch the boats; but the tide had fallen, and it was no easy matter, as they had to shove them over the rough beach for some distance. While they were thus engaged, loud shrieks and shouts reached their ears, proceeding out of the forest, and in another minute a whole host of blacks armed with bows and arrows, spears and clubs, poured into the open, and came rushing down towards them. It seemed scarcely possible to get the boats afloat before the savages would be upon them. Green waited till the last moment, then, calling the men, drew them up on the beach, and ordered them to present their muskets, but not to fire till he should give the word. The blacks, who apparently were well acquainted with the power of firearms, on seeing the force opposed to them, not only halted, but drew back several paces, bending their bows, however, as if they were about to shoot. Green, on seeing this, made signs to them to retire, pointing at the same time to his men's muskets, to let the savages understand that they only waited his command to fire. The blacks evidently understood him, for they at once relaxed their bow-strings, turning their heads over their shoulders as if about to beat a retreat. Just then, however, a chief made his appearance and began to harangue them, urging them, it seemed, to attack the strangers who had ventured to land on their shore. The moment was a critical one. Green saw that he might be compelled to order his men to fire, and should the savages have sufficient courage to rush out and attack them before they had time to reload, they must be clubbed or speared. He knew, too, that the blacks' arrows were poisoned, and that every person wounded by them would die. He would gladly have retreated to the boats and made another effort to get them afloat, but should he show any sign of fear, it would to a certainty encourage the blacks to come on.

"Stand steady, my lads!" he cried; "I'll try once more to make the savages understand that we don't wish to quarrel with them;" and, taking up a bough which had formed part of one of the huts, he waved it slowly backwards and forwards.

The effect at first appeared to be satisfactory, but just then the voice of the old chief, who had before incited them to attack the strangers, was again heard, and the savages, encouraged by him, once more drew their bows; while he, flourishing his club, came forward at their head, leaping and bounding in the strangest fashion, his followers imitating his example.

"Tim Nolan," shouted Green, "as soon as I give the word, pick that fellow off; if Tim misses, do you, Bird, give an account of him. Don't throw a shot away, my lads, and we'll make them repent interfering with us."

Green wisely said nothing about the deadly effect of the poisoned arrows, hoping that the men would not think about them. Just as Green was about to sing out "Fire!" feeling that it was useless any longer to entertain hopes of maintaining peace with the savages, a strange-looking being leaped out from their midst, armed only with a club, which, placing himself in front of the chief, he whirled round and round in his face, shouting, at the same time, at the top of his voice. He was a white man, though scarcely better clothed than the blacks, his body being tattooed all over with strange devices, while his long carroty hair hung down over his shoulders. No one attempted to interfere with him; even the chief came to a standstill, while he bounded backwards and forwards in front of the horde of savages, shouting and gesticulating in the most vehement manner conceivable. Having thus succeeded in stopping the advance of the blacks, he turned round and rushed forward towards where Green was standing.

"Arrah, shure, Masther Green, it's meself, Paddy Casey, is delighted to see ye; though little was I after thinking, when I last set eyes on ye, that the next time ye'd see me I'd be turned into a wild savage!" he exclaimed.

"What! Pat Casey, my man," cried Green; "of course, I remember you right well; though I confess I shouldn't have expected to see you, one of the smartest hands on board the *Tudor*, in your present style of dress."

Pat, looking at himself, gave a broad Irish grin.

"Shure enough, yer honour; and bad luck to them who left me here, thinking I'd be killed and cooked and eaten, about which I'll be after telling yer honour when there's more time than at present. I've just been informing these black friends of mine that they were fools to come and attack you, seeing that you belong to a mighty big ship, which would come and blow them and their island right out into the sea in a quarter less than notime; and now I've got them to be peaceable, it will be as well to take advantage of the opportunity to get the boats afloat, for, by my faith, they're not the most dependable of people, and in another moment they may again change their minds."

"I am much obliged to you, old shipmate," answered Green; "and if you can manage to keep the blacks quiet, we will have the boats in the water in a few minutes. Tell them that we were driven by the storm on their island; that we wish to be good friends with them, as with all the people in these parts, and, provided they behave well to us, we will do them no harm."

"Shure, yer honour, I'll tell them all that, and just anything else that may come into my head at the same time, and I'll answer for it that they'll be decently behaved as long as you stay," said Pat.

"Just keep them in play, then, while we get the boats afloat;

and make them understand that we go away because it is our good pleasure, and not because we are afraid of them," said Green.

"Shure, yer honour, I'll do that," answered the Irishman, with one of his inimitable grins, which possibly had been the means of enabling him to preserve his life.

While he went back to his black friends, the two crews, uniting their strength, got first one boat afloat and then the other. Green felt greatly relieved, for, whatever turn events might take, he and his party would be able to get away without having to fight for their lives.

Casey now returned.

"The savages say, sir, that if you like to stop and be friends, they'll be friends with you; but I'm after thinking that the sooner you can get away from this the better, for they're not altogether trustworthy gentlemen. Not long ago a sandal-wood trader put in here and sent her boat ashore, when they knocked every mother's son of the crew on the head, and ate them afterwards. To be sure the Englishmen hadn't behaved altogether properly, for once before when they had been here they employed the natives to cut a cargo of sandal-wood for them; and when they had got it on board, they refused to pay what they had promised, saying that they would come back again, and that it would then be time enough to talk about payment. When they saw you they thought that you were people of the same sort, and so were going to treat you as they had done the others."

"I must confess," said Green, "that the Englishmen met their deserts. But how did you manage to escape, my man; and what brought you to the island?"

"Arrah, yer honour, it's a long story; and about the escaping, it was a narrow squeak I had for it. You see, when I was paid off from the *Tudor* at Portsmouth, I went up to London, when I entered on board an emigrant ship bound out to Sydney. While I was on shore there one day, and had been taking my grog pretty freely, a chap I had never set eyes on before hailed me as an old chum, and telling me he was now skipper of a fine schooner, axed me if I would join her, and promised that I should fill my pockets with gold in a few months. As they were just then turned clean inside out, and I had had my spree on shore, without more ado I closed with him; and before I knew where I was going, I found myself stowed away on board the schooner, which at daybreak next morning sailed out of Sydney Harbour.

The craft, I discovered, was engaged in the sandal-wood trade, cruising among the islands, and getting it as best she could, sometimes in one way, and sometimes in another, and very curious ways they were. We made several trips, and each time came back with a full cargo. At some places we got the natives to cut the wood and bring it off, paying them with beads and trinkets when they were content with such things; at others with rum, muskets, and powder and shot. When no natives appeared, we went on shore ourselves to cut the wood.

"At last the skipper took a new dodge, for he was in no ways particular. Having put in to a harbour where the natives were friendly, he enticed above three dozen off, making them large promises if they would cut wood for him, and undertaking to bring them home again as soon as they had done the job. All seemed very fair and above board; we at once sailed for one of the islands to the westward, which is inhabited by blacks of a terribly fierce character, but where plenty of sandal-wood grows. Having landed our passengers, we went on shore, well armed, to keep the natives at bay, while they were employed in cutting the wood. They worked well, and we quickly got a full cargo. Now, as the wind was from the eastward, and it would have taken us a fortnight or more to beat back to the island from which we had brought our labourers, while it was fair for Sydney, the skipper had no fancy to lose so much time. What did he do, therefore, but send the poor fellows back again, telling them that they must remain and cut another cargo while he went to Sydney, and that he would come back and take them off. Knowing the character of the natives, they did not like this at all, and begged hard to be taken on board, saying that they would go on to Sydney, or anywhere else, rather than remain. In truth, it was a terribly cruel thing the skipper was doing, and I and another man told him so, and declared that when we got to Sydney we would make the matter known. He replied that we had better not, but said nothing more. The long and the short of it is that the poor brown men were left behind, and it's my belief that one and all of them were killed and eaten, before many days were over, by the cannibal blacks.

"The night after we sailed it came on to blow hard, and the next morning when I came on deck to keep my watch I was told that Ned Mole, the man I spoke of, had been washed overboard. I had my thoughts about it, and couldn't help saying that I was sure there had been foul play. I had better have held my tongue. In a few hours it fell a dead calm, just as we were off this here island. The skipper observing that he thought there would be sandal-wood on it, had one of the boats lowered, telling me to come in her. I, of course, went, without thinking that any harm was intended me. As no natives were seen, we at once landed, when the skipper ordered me to accompany him with an axe, saying that we would have a look for sandal-wood. We had gone some distance when at length we discovered some trees of the sort we were in search of. 'Now, Casey,' says the skipper, 'do you cut as much as you think the boat's crew can carry, and I'll go back and fetch them up. I should like to have a sample of this wood, as it seems somewhat different to what we have got on board.' 'Ay, ay, sir,' I answered, and, taking off my jacket and tucking up my sleeves, I began chopping away. I thought the skipper was a long time in coming back, for I had cut even more than he was likely to want. I waited and waited, but still saw nothing of my shipmates; at last I began to have some uncomfortable feelings about the matter; shouldering my axe, I made my way down to the beach. I need not tell you, sir, how I felt when I could nowhere find the boat, and saw the schooner standing away to the southward, for the breeze had again sprung up. I shouted and shrieked, but she was too far off for those on board either to see or hear me, and I then felt sure that the skipper had left me behind on purpose, and had probably told his crew that I had been knocked on the head by the savages, or had met with some other fate. I was dancing about and shouting out, and tearing my hair with rage at being so treated, when, turning round, I saw standing close to me a dozen black fellows. They were all staring at me, wondering what I was about. I was too full of rage to feel frightened, and so, forgetting that they couldn't understand me, I began to tell them how I had been treated. They jabbered away in return; and I shouted louder and louder, thinking to make them understand what had happened; while, holding my axe in my hand, which I flourished in the air, I leaped backwards and forwards as if I was a madman—in truth I felt very like one.

"At last one of the blacks, who seemed to be a chief by the big rings he wore in his nose and ears, and the long feather stuck on the top of his head, came forward, waving a green bough, and then, putting out his hand, took mine, which he rubbed on his flat nose. It was a sign that he wished to be friends; and by this time, as I had begun to get a little cool, I saw that it would be wise to make the best of a bad matter; so I took his hand and rubbed it on my nose, and behaved to all the party in the same manner. From that time the blacks treated me with great respect. Whether they had seen any other white man before that I cannot tell; but at all events they saw that I was superior to themselves; and maybe they took me for a prophet or a great medicine-man, or something of that sort. The chief had fixed his eyes on my axe, but I gave him to understand that I would not part with it; however, wishing to please him, I took off my jacket, and made him put it on, which pleased him amazingly, and bound him to me as a friend. It is my belief, from what I saw of them afterwards, that if they had found me sitting down and bemoaning my hard fate, they would have knocked me on the head and cooked me before the day was over—so I had reason to think myself in luck.

"The natives, I found, lived on the other side of the island, and, for some reason or other which I could never make out, seldom came over to this side. They at once took me with them; and when we got to their village, which consists of a number of small huts not much bigger than beehives, the chief introduced me to his wives, who made me sit down on the ground and brought me out some food, which I was very glad to get, seeing that I was pretty hungry by this time. In return, having nothing else to offer the chief lady, I took off my shirt and put it on her, which pleased her as much as my jacket had her husband. It was not pleasant to go without clothing, though I still held on to my trousers, but it was better than being killed; and I thought that if I could make the chief and his wife my friends, I might be able to live pretty pleasantly among the people. I succeeded even better than I had expected; and from that day became a sort of prime minister to the chief, and general of his army. I found, however, that another of his wives was jealous of the first who had got the shirt; so, thinking to please her, I made myself this here petticoat, and presented her with my trousers. As she didn't fancy putting them on the right way, she threw them over her shoulders, and wears them in that fashion to this day."

"Well, Pat, you have had indeed a narrow escape of your life," observed Green. "Do you wish to live on with your friends?"

"Arrah, no, yer honour, 'tisn't for a dacent man like me to

desire altogether to turn into a savage," said Pat. "I'm mighty eager to get back to the old country to see once more my brothers and sisters, and the rest of the Casey family; so, if you will take me with you, and supply me with a pair of trousers and a shirt, I'm ready to go off at once—though I shouldn't just like to appear on board without some dacent covering to my skin."

"I shall be very glad to take you," said Green; "but will the chief be willing to part with his prime minister? I'm afraid the whole country will go to rack and ruin if you leave him."

"I'm afeard, yer honour, that I must leave the country to look after itself," answered Pat, with one of the broadest of his grins; "and as to axing the chief about the matter, I'm after thinking it will be better to take French leave, lest he may try to stop me. The weather, I see, is moderating, and if yer honour will take my advice, you'll shove off as soon as it is calm enough to put to sea."

"We can't go without food, and it will take us some time to collect enough to last till we find the ship," said Green.

"Then I'll tell my friends that they must bring us some, for not a rap of salary have I had since I became prime minister, and if they were to load the boats up to the thwarts, I shouldn't be overpaid for the good I have done the state," said Pat; and, flourishing his axe in the fashion he had found so effective, he made his way back to where the blacks were now seated on the ground, discussing apparently some important matter or other. The chief listened to him for some time, and he and his people then getting up disappeared among the trees in the distance.

"I've done it, yer honour," said Pat, who quickly returned; "they'll soon be back with as much we can require for some days to come."

While the savages were away, a fire was lighted, and the remainder of the shell-fish and the birds which Tom had shot were cooked. The boats were also got ready, so that they might put to sea as soon as the provisions arrived, or, in case the natives after all should prove treacherous, shove off at a moment's notice. Green knew well the danger of an encounter with savages armed with poisoned arrows; a shower of such arrows might wound every one of the party, and he was aware that even slight hurts might prove fatal. At length the blacks made their appearance, carrying baskets containing taro, cocoa-nut, several other roots and fruits, and some fish of various sizes. By Pat's directions they were placed on the ground, when Green, not wishing to take them without payment, collected some handkerchiefs and clasp-knives and a few other articles, which he desired Pat to convey to the chief. This unexpected gift afforded intense satisfaction to the savages, who would have rushed forward and rubbed noses with the strangers, had not Pat hinted to his friends that such a proceeding would not be appreciated by the white men. The blacks, having set down their baskets, retired, and they were forthwith conveyed to the boats. While the natives were absent, Tom had wisely refilled the breakers.

"Now's your time, yer honour," cried Casey, who feared that his friends might suspect his intention of leaving them. The men, by Green's directions, retired quietly to the boats, Pat trying to keep himself concealed among them; and while they were embarking, he also jumped in and stowed himself away in the sternsheets of Green's boat.

"Shove off, yer honour," he shouted out, "or they'll be coming down to stop me."

Before the boats had got half a cable's length from the shore, the chief discovered that his prime minister had disappeared, and, suspecting that he had gone off with the white men, he and his tribe came rushing down to the beach, shouting vociferously to him to come back.

"That same is more than I intend doing," cried Pat, from the bottom of the boat.

The surf had by this time considerably gone down, and the sea was sufficiently smooth to enable the boats to steer a direct course for Santa Cruz; Green could, therefore, only hope that the ship might not have left the harbour to look for them, as, in that case, they would in all probability miss each other.

CHAPTER XXV

Jack's Anxiety—Search for the Boats—A Wreck discovered—The Mate brought off—Mr. Large attacked by Savages—The Natives punished—The Boats recovered—Sydney—The Ships sail for the Sandwich Islands—A Visit on Shore—Visit Hawaii—Scene of Cook's Death—Trip to the Crater of Kilauea—Magnificent Scene—Tom nearly lost—Return on board—Again at Sea—Vancouver's Island—Doings there—News from Home—Jack and Terence superseded—Reach England—Future Career of the Three Commanders—Conclusion.

JACK's anxiety became very great when, after the boats had gone away in chase of the schooner, he saw the threatening state of the weather. He waited for some time, expecting them to return, and then ordered the steam to be got up, intending to go in search of them; the gale, however, increasing, and night coming on, he had but slight hopes of success. At length the engineer reported that the steam was up, and in spite of the risk he ran, he stood out of the harbour, steering in the direction he supposed they had taken. Scarcely had he got outside than the weather became worse than ever. All night long the ship continued standing backwards and forwards over the ground where he expected to find the boats, while, as they happened at the time to be under the lee of the burning mountain, he of course could not see them. At daylight he steamed back into the harbour, hoping against hope that they might have returned, but his fear was that though the natives had behaved well in the presence of a big ship, they might conduct themselves very differently should a couple of boats only take shelter in their harbour. His doubt, therefore, was whether he should remain to wait for their arrival, or go in search of them. He did not, on his return, bring up, but, after remaining for a short time under way, he again put to sea and stood to the southward. A bright look-out was kept for the boats, as also for the schooner they had chased, for it was thought possible that, finding bad weather coming on, they might have remained on board. The island where they actually were at the time was sighted, but no signal being made from it, he stood on. He then visited several islands farther to the south, on which he thought it possible they might have landed.

Towards evening the *Dragon* came off a small island, the character of the scenery being similar to that of those in the neighbourhood. As she approached the coast, a vessel was sighted on shore with her masts gone, and it was very evident that she was a complete wreck.

"Should any of the people have escaped, we must do our best to help them," observed Jack to Mildmay, as they stood looking at the wreck through their glasses.

"I am afraid there is very little chance of that," answered Mildmay; "but if they should have reached the shore alive, the natives are nearly sure to have clubbed them."

"We shall soon ascertain the state of the case," said Jack; "in all probability she was cast away during the gale last night, and we may still be in time to rescue any who have remained on board."

The *Dragon* stood on, with the lead going, as close as it was prudent to venture, when her head was put round, and a boat was sent away under charge of Mr. Large, who was directed to board the wreck if he could, but on no account to venture on shore should any considerable number of natives make their appearance. The boat pulled away, first making for the wreck; the boatswain's proceedings were watched from the deck with great interest. He first visited the wreck, and after he had been some time on board, he was seen with the assistance of his men lowering a person into the boat. He then pulled for the shore, but just as he reached the beach, a number of savages rushed out from among the trees, and sent a flight of arrows at their visitors. He immediately pulled away, and came back at a rapid rate to the ship.

"Two of the men are hit, sir, I am afraid," he said, as he came on deck; "and an arrow has gone through the arm of the poor fellow we took out of the wreck, who was before almost dead of hunger and wounds. There seems now but little life in him of any sort. All I can make out about the vessel is, that she is the *Expert*, of Sydney; and from the look of her hold, I should think that she had a number of slaves on board, though what has become of them is more than I can tell."

No time was lost by the surgeon in looking after the

wounded men; his great aim was to neutralise the effects of the poison. The man taken from the wreck, notwithstanding Mr. Large's report, recovered considerably, and was able in a faint voice to answer the questions put to him. He said he was mate of the vessel; that she was wrecked the previous night, when the master and several of the hands had been washed overboard; that the passengers had broken loose and made their way to the shore, where, however, they had been attacked by the natives, who, to the best of his belief, had killed or captured every one of them.

"Then what became of the rest of the crew?" asked Jack.

The mate said he thought it possible that they had got away in the boat with the doctor and second mate, during the night when there happened to be a lull, but of this he was uncertain. He confessed that the vessel had been boarded by two man-of-war's boats, but the officer in command, finding nothing to detain her, had allowed the schooner to proceed; while they, he concluded, had returned from whence they came. Mr. Large, who was present at the examination of the mate, thought it just possible that the boat might have left the wreck, and if so, that she was in all probability driven on shore, when those in her must have shared the fate of the so-called passengers. Mr. Large, however, volunteered to go on shore to try and ascertain what had really become of the people. The ship was by this time about half a mile from the beach, so that through a glass everything going forward on shore could be seen.

Soon after the boat had shoved off, a considerable body of natives issued from among the trees, and stood gazing at her and at the ship. They were all armed with clubs and spears and bows and arrows, but, as they did not by their gestures show any hostile intentions, the boat continued her course; the boatswain still hoping, apparently, to establish friendly relations with them. As there was little or no surf, the boat ran on to the beach; Mr. Large stepped on shore, waving a white flag in his hand, and holding out several articles which he had carried with him as presents. On seeing this, two of the natives, placing their weapons on the ground, advanced towards him, when he gave each of them a present, and signed to others to come forward and receive the remainder. As he was all the time covered by the muskets of the men in the boat, he did not appear to consider that he was in any danger. As soon as the natives had received their presents, they retreated to a little distance and sat down, he imitating their example. He then, by signs, endeavoured to make them understand that he wished to know what had become of the people who had landed from the vessel on the rocks. They seemed to understand him, and replied by signs that the people had gone away into the interior. He, on this, tried to make them understand that he wished them to be brought back. They made no reply, but talked eagerly among themselves, and he could not tell whether they intended to comply with his demands. Still they appeared to be as friendly as at first. He was still sitting on the ground, waiting for their answer, when their party was increased by several other persons, who advanced from the larger body in the background. They were all young men, who, though they had laid aside their bows and spears, still retained their clubs. Having seated themselves, they made signs that they also wanted presents; when they found that they were not forthcoming, they got up, and, approaching the boatswain, who had also risen to his feet, one of them tried to snatch his cap, while another seized a cutlass which he had buckled round his waist. On this, with a blow of his fist, he knocked the savage down, and was in the act of drawing his weapon to defend himself, when another black, who had sprung behind him, dealt him a blow on the head with a club, which felled him to the ground.

So rapidly had this taken place that the boat's crew were not prepared to fire till they saw him fall. They instantly poured in a volley, which killed two of the savages, while the rest bounded off towards their companions. The seamen, then reloading, sprang on shore, in the hopes of bringing off the boatswain, whom they supposed to be killed. All that had occurred was seen from the ship, and Jack immediately ordered two shells to be thrown in the direction of the savages, which, falling into their midst, just at the moment that they were drawing their arrows to shoot at the seamen, drove them back into the forest. The arrows thus flew wide of their mark, and the seamen were able to convey Mr. Large to the boat, and to shove off without molestation. Several other shells were fired in the direction taken by the natives, who immediately scampered off, leaving several dead behind them.

On the return of the boat alongside, Mr. Large was seen sitting up, when with some assistance he managed to get on deck, notwithstanding an ugly gash he had received at the back of his head.

"I'll never trust those black rascals again!" he exclaimed; "they very nearly did for me, just as I thought I was getting on so well with them. I only hope our boats won't have landed on their shores, or they'll receive an unpleasant welcome."

"I trust not, Mr. Large," said Jack, who, on having such evidence of the savage disposition of the natives, was becoming more and more anxious about Green and the midshipmen; "however, you did your best; and now you must let the surgeon look after you, for that wound in your head is an ugly one."

The boat was, after this, again despatched to bring off any arms or articles of value which could be found on board the schooner, and then, as she was a perfect wreck, she was set on fire to prevent the savages from benefiting by her loss. This done, the ship proceeded along the coast, when a little farther on she opened a village which there was every probability belonged to their late treacherous assailants. A couple of rockets fired into it quickly set it in flames, and another village in the neighbourhood was treated in the same manner. Jack considered that this punishment was necessary to teach the natives that they could not attack white men with impunity.

Jack was by this time almost in despair of recovering the boats, but would not yet abandon the attempt to find them. If they had escaped foundering or being driven on a reef, they must have reached the shores of one of the neighbouring islands; he resolved therefore to go back to Santa Cruz, and then to steam round every island in succession, narrowly examining their shores. The ship accordingly stood back to Santa Cruz, though Jack scarcely expected to find the boats in the harbour. A look-out was kept on every side, and at night blue lights were burned frequently to attract their attention should they be in the neighbourhood.

In the morning watch, just before daybreak, as the ship was gliding smoothly on with a light breeze, a hail was heard on the weather bow. It was so faint, that had the screw been going at the time, it would not have been noticed. Mr. Mildmay, who was officer of the watch, ordered the yards to be braced up, and kept the ship in the direction from whence the hail came. Again it was heard louder.

"There's no doubt about it," he exclaimed; "that must come from the boats—call the commander."

In a minute Jack was on deck. At length the two boats could be seen under sail, running down towards the ship. She was immediately hove-to, and in another minute they were alongside. Instead of the woebegone, half-starved beings Jack expected to see, he was delighted to find them all in good condition and excellent spirits. Green and Tom gave a rapid account of their adventures; after leaving the island they had gone to Santa Cruz, where, not liking the manners of the natives, after obtaining a fresh supply of water, they immediately put to sea again in search of the *Dragon*, which Green felt pretty sure would not be far off. No one was at all the worse for the adventure, and Green's old shipmate, Pat Casey, from being able to speak the language of the natives, proved of great assistance during the remainder of the cruise. He, to be sure, did not always make himself understood, but that might have been because the natives spoke a different dialect to the one he had acquired. Numberless atrocities were brought to light, some committed by the sandal-wood traders and kidnappers, who were generally the aggressors; but others by the natives, who had treacherously cut off several boats' crews and murdered numerous individuals, who had been surprised much as was Mr. Large. Where the crime could be brought home to the natives, they were punished by the destruction of their villages and canoes. In one or two instances in which the chiefs had been implicated, they were carried off and left on other islands at a distance, from whence they were not likely to be able to return. It was a far more difficult matter to get the white men convicted and punished for the foul deeds of which they had been guilty in these regions.

At length the *Dragon's* course was shaped for Sydney, where Jack had the satisfaction of finding the *Eolus*, which had arrived a short time before him. Adair had numerous adventures to recount, very similar to those which the *Dragon* had met with. The chief satisfaction they experienced on their arrival was to receive letters from home. Their wives were bearing their separation as well as could be expected, and gave them very minute accounts of all their doings. Julia was living at Halliburton, and Lucy had been paying a long visit to the admiral and Mrs. Deborah, both of whom were somewhat ailing. The admiral could rarely do more than take a few turns on the esplanade, sitting down between each on one of the benches facing the sea, to watch the vessels as they ran in and out of the harbour.

The officers of the two ships were received with much hospitality by the inhabitants of Sydney. They were made honorary members of a club equal to any in London, and balls, dinner-parties, and picnics were got up for their entertainment. Indeed, after their long absence from civilised life, they very naturally thought Sydney a magnificent city, as indeed it is; rising as it does gradually from its superb harbour, and thus exhibiting to advantage its fine public buildings and substantial residences; in the suburbs were seen a number of beautiful villas, many of considerable size, while cabs, omnibuses, and other public conveyances, and handsome private equipages, abounded. Indeed, carriages were kept by families who would not have dreamed of maintaining them at home.

Not a few of the officers made up their minds to return and settle in the country. The midshipmen, for a wonder, did not lose their hearts—possibly on account of the small encouragement they received from the young ladies, who literally and metaphorically looked down upon them, being as a rule much taller than they were, and well able to distinguish beween the various ranks in the service. Indeed, some little disappointment was felt when it was discovered that the two commanders were married men.

The ships, having filled up their coal bunks, shaped a course for the Sandwich Islands. As it was important to husband their coal, the greater portion of the passage was performed under sail. Numerous islands were seen, several of them being regular coral islands, with lagoons in the centre, not more than a couple of miles in circumference, and some even much smaller, and rising within a few feet out of the water. About six weeks after leaving Sydney, Oahu, in which Honolulu, the capital of the Sandwich Islands, is situated, was sighted. The ships ran on and came to an anchor in the outer roads, opposite the city, which is very conspicuous from the sea, and has a somewhat imposing appearance, with its numerous public and private edifices spread out along the shore, and churches and tall spires in their midst. The coast had a barren appearance, very unlike the beautiful region everyone had expected to find it, far behind the town the land rising into high ridges, divided by deep and narrow ravines, amid which but little vegetation was visible; while the surf in a succession of long rollers broke along the reefs on each side of the inner anchorage, threatening any vessel with destruction which might have parted from her anchors.

The next day a portion of each ship's company got leave to go on shore. Tom, Desmond, and Archie were once more together. As they pulled in, they were highly delighted at seeing a party of the natives sporting in the surf on their surf-boards; now they swam out through the breakers, amid which it seemed impossible any human being could exist; then, mounting to the summit of a huge roller, one of them would leap up on his board in a standing posture, and glide down the side of the watery hill, balancing himself in a wonderful manner. Another would perform the same passage while sitting, or a third would throw himself full length along his board. In the same manner they would return to the shore, fearlessly approaching the surf, through which they made their way to the beach. Some twenty or thirty young men and lads were thus sporting together.

On landing, the midshipmen were assailed by the owners of horses, much in the same way that people landing in European cities are by porters or drivers of vehicles. The Kanakas, as the natives are called, were habited in every variety of costume, some fully clothed, others with little more than pieces of native cloth round their waists; though the women were all decently if not elegantly clad in long calico gowns, reaching from the shoulders down to the feet, generally of gay colours. Both men and women appeared good-natured, and ready to laugh and joke with their visitors. There was no quarrelling about the horses; the midshipmen were soon suited with steeds, on which they hoped to enjoy a pleasant ride. Their party was increased by Green, who had taken charge of another set of youngsters. All being mounted, away they galloped across the plain at the back of the town. They had not gone far when they overtook a cavalcade of fair damsels, seated on men's saddles, with long skirts fastened round their waists, and their heads adorned with wreaths of flowers. They answered the midshipmen's salutations with shouts of laughter, and either supposing that they had had an invitation to do so, or, which is not improbable, not thinking it necessary, they joined company, and away midshipmen and maidens galloped with a speed which would have tried less hardy steeds. Before long they overtook other parties of girls; on they went till a hill was reached, over which they scampered, descending at breakneck speed into a plain of still larger dimensions, on the other side. Here the road compelled them to keep closer together, as it passed between several sugar plantations. Tom had fixed upon a pretty Kanaka as his companion, who could speak a few words of English, as was the case with many of the others; indeed, most of the young ladies, though not very rigid in their manners, were fairly educated, and remarkably intelligent. Away they went for several miles, till one of the elder damsels, looking at the sun, declared that it was time to go back again; and, wheeling round their steeds, they returned as fast as they had come. On nearing the town, they made signs to the young officers to fall into the rear, while they advanced at a more sedate pace, when they scattered in various directions to their different homes. This was only one of their many excursions on shore.

Honolulu is a capital city, though a small one; few cities of its size contain more churches and schools; but, unhappily, they are not all of one denomination, for Protestants, Episcopalians, and Roman Catholics have of late years entered the field with the Presbyterians or Independents, by whose means the natives were converted to Christianity. It now boasted of a cathedral and an English bishop, who, while the ships were there, headed a grand procession, with banners, and bands playing, terminated by a display of fireworks and healths drunk in champagne opposite the king's palace; but whether it was of a religious or merely social character, our midshipmen's friends were unable to determine.

A considerable amount of trade is carried on, the chief export being sugar to the United States. There are merchants and inhabitants of all nations, but by far the greater number are Americans, who hold also some of the chief offices of State. There was a theatre, in which not only plays but operas were performed, and there were various other places of amusement. It was, indeed, difficult to believe that comparatively a few years ago the country was sunk in heathen darkness; especially when it was reported that few kingdoms are better governed, and no people, taken as a whole, more orderly and contented. Happily for itself, having no harbours of sufficient size to afford shelter to men-of-war, or which are capable of being defended, it is likely to remain as heretofore independent, unless republican principles should prevail, and the people involuntarily join themselves to the United States. The then king was said to be an amiable and enlightened gentleman, as well educated as most of the European sovereigns were but a few years ago; and the young Dowager Queen Emma, who has English blood in her veins, was pretty, sweet-tempered, sensible, and altogether a most excellent and attractive person. Still, notwithstanding the attention the officers received from the inhabitants, they agreed that Honolulu was not a place at which they would wish to remain for any length of time.

"Hurrah!" cried Tom, rushing into the berth one afternoon, "we are to be off to-morrow morning for Hawaii; and if there's time, some of us will have a chance of visiting the volcano of Kilauea, and the very spot where Captain Cook was killed. The commander told me I might tell you. And I advise you fellows who haven't got your clean linen off to send for it without delay, or you may chance to have to wait for it till our return, which I hope may be never."

Several of Tom's messmates jumped up on hearing this to follow his advice, as the Kanaka washerwomen were not likely to prove more honest than those of other places, or to return "wash-clothes" before the time agreed on.

The next morning the two ships were steaming out of the roads. For a few hours they brought up in the far-famed bay of Kealakeaku, on the north side of which was a rock, protected from the swell by a point of lava rocks, thus affording a convenient landing-place. Near it, at the foot of a cocoa-nut tree, is the spot where the celebrated navigator breathed his last; and on the still remaining stump of the tree was nailed a sheet of copper, on which was inscribed an account of the event. Most of the officers having visited the spot and inspected its surroundings, with such copies of Cook's *Voyages* in their hands as were to be found on board, the ships steamed out again for Hilo Bay, on the other side of the island. Round the shores appeared groves of tall cocoa-nut and richly-tinted bread-fruit trees, with extensive plantations of sugar-cane beyond; while amid them flowed numberless murmuring streams. Above this lower level rose a succession of pasture lands, surmounted by belts of trees, changing their character from the vegetation of the tropics to that of the more northern regions of the world. The country indeed sloped upwards twenty miles or more, forming the side of an elevated tableland in the centre of the island, out of which sprang towards the sky two mountains of prodigious height—that of Mauna Loa, the nearest, in the form of a smooth dome; and Mauna Kea, surmounted by nine snow-covered cones. Above the tableland appeared a silvery cloud, showing the whereabouts of the fearful crater of Kilauea, which it was the intention of the two commanders to visit on the following morning. As night closed in, its position was rendered still more visible by the glare of the ever-burning fires within the crater reflected on the cloud.

At early dawn, Jack and Adair, with a party of their ships' companies, and as many of the officers as could be spared, and who wished to go, started for the shore. Jack took Tom and Archie and Mr. Mildmay, who undertook to narrate the events of the expedition in verse. The second lieutenant declared that he had no wish to toil up a steep mountain for the sake of seeing a huge pit full of fire and smoke, so that he willingly remained on board instead of the first lieutenant. Several others, however, had more curiosity. Adair took Desmond, and three or four of his gun-room officers and midshipmen.

"Now, recollect that none of you must run the risk of being turned into cinders by tumbling into the crater," observed Jack, as they were setting off.

"I rather think that gas would be the product of such an immersion," observed the doctor; "there wouldn't be so much solid matter of you left in five seconds as I could put into my snuff-box—so look out for yourselves."

Horses and guides were in readiness, for of late years the once mysterious residence of the goddess Pelé has become one of the lions of the world.

"Forward!" cried the commander, and the party trotted on, headed by their guide. Eight miles on they passed a vast chasm, after which they began to ascend more rapidly than before. In a short time they entered a region of black lava with hollows in it full of water, into which the natives on foot plunged to cool themselves. Trees, however, were still seen which had sprung up amid the once burning mass, and bushes of various sorts, among them strawberries, not here low plants, but vines of large size bearing delicious fruit. Just below the edge of the plateau was a forest, and, on rising above it, the vast dome of Mauna Loa, of a bronze hue, rose before them, against the deep blue of a tropical sky. They had barely time to reach the edge of the crater and to pitch their tents, which had been sent on before, when the sun set, and the surrounding darkness revealed two lakes of liquid fire down in the depths of a vast basin, with perpendicular sides several miles in circumference, and an apparently level bottom. For some time they gazed at the scene; not a word was uttered—even the midshipmen failed to cut a joke. No loud sounds were heard; no reports, as many of the party had expected; but, instead, there came up from the bottom of the abyss a low, bubbling murmur, like that emitted by a thick liquid when boiling—for to nothing else could it be likened. Guided by some of the natives, Jack and Terence, with the three midshipmen, climbed down to the ledge some hundred feet below the plateau, when they found themselves apparently not much above the margin of the largest of the two lakes of fire.

"There are a good many things I would dare to do, but I shouldn't like to jump into that," said Tom, as he watched the mighty volume of lava in a furious state of ebullition, forming fiery waves which ran ceaselessly across the lake towards a wide abyss to the southward. Sometimes the whole seemed rising, and suddenly, at the distance of scarcely three hundred yards, a vast column spouted up to the height of sixty or seventy feet, almost as quickly subsiding; and the next instant another rose still nearer to them, which made even Jack spring back, for so near did it appear that he could not help fancying that it might fall upon them.

After watching this wonderful phenomenon for some time, the rest of the party were very glad when Terence proposed that they should climb up from whence they came; an operation which took them the best part of an hour. The early part of the night was spent before they could manage to go to sleep, and even then few of them could get the terrific scene they had witnessed out their heads. They had not been long asleep when all hands were aroused by a report like thunder, which came up from the vast lake boiling beneath them. Everybody started up; Billy Blueblazes, seizing hold of Desmond, alongside whom he was sleeping, exclaimed—

"Is the volcano going to burst out and smother us? Won't it be better to run for it?"

"Arrah, sure it will be running faster than we can," answered Desmond, who wasn't quite comfortable, though he didn't wish to show it.

On looking over the cliff, however, the lake was seen boiling away as before, sending up here and there spouts of fire, which at the distance they were below them looked like flashes from firearms at night, though probably fifty or sixty feet in height. No one, however, felt inclined to turn in again for some time, in spite of the cool air which circled round them. As they looked over the crater, the shadows from its mighty walls were cast upwards, reaching, it seemed, to the sky, and giving it the appearance of being clothed in a dark cloud.

"It is very fine," cried Terence at length; "but if we wish to enjoy our ramble to-morrow, we shall be wise to get a little more sleep."

His advice was followed. After breakfast next morning several of the party started off to walk round the crater, while the more adventurous ones, including the two commanders, Tom, and Desmond, with a couple of Kanaka guides, again descended another part of the cliff to the ledge. On looking at the spot where they had stood on the previous evening, a thrilling sensation came over them as they observed that it had disappeared in the burning lava below—the cause undoubtedly of the noise which had startled them during the night. Still they were anxious to get close down to the boiling lava, and obtain some of it in a state of fusion. Their guide confessed that many had gone and come back safe, but that he considered it an expedition of no slight danger. Probably at that moment neither Jack nor Terence were thinking of their wives at home.

They had gone some way, when suddenly the whole mass surged upwards, and the lava on which they were walking began to crack, while terrific reports were heard.

"Back! back!" cried the guide. They needed no second warning, but, keeping apart, made for the upper ledge. All had gained it, except Tom, who, being at a distance from the rest, made for a part which when he got up to it he found inaccessible. Close behind him at that moment the crust was rent asunder by a terrific heave, and a vast jet of molten lava, with a fearful noise, rose high into the air. Almost roasted by the heat, he cried out for help; in another moment it would have been too late, when the guide, hearing his voice amid the uproar, leant over, and, just able to grasp his arm, though his own face was burnt in the attempt, jerked him up with a strength few of Tom's companions could have exerted, and placed him in comparative safety. Not a moment was to be lost, for the seething mass was fast gaining on them. Up the cliffs they climbed till they gained a place of safety.

"We've had enough of the inside of the crater," said Jack, as he thought how nearly Tom had been lost; and they made their way again to the upper rim of the vast basin. The larger lake, they calculated, was 1190 yards long and about 700 wide; the smaller nearly circular, and upwards of 300 yards across. The lava continued rising till it overflowed a large portion of the hitherto black surface, in some places appearing like a vast sheet of liquid fire, in others running along in serpentine courses. As their time was short, as soon as the party who had gone round the crater arrived, the tents were packed up, and they commenced their descent by the way they had come.

The next day the ships weighed, and shaped their course for Vancouver's Island, under sail. Jack and Terence were eager to reach their destination, in the hopes of finding letters awaiting them there from England. In about little more than three weeks they entered Fuca Straits, up which they ran for about sixty miles, with magnificent scenery on both sides, though desolate in the extreme, till they reached Esquimault Harbour, in Vancouver's Island; about three miles from which stands Victoria, the capital.

Jack and Terence eagerly awaited the letter-bag, which, as soon as their arrival was known, would be sent off to them. Jack was reading his letters, when Adair came on board.

"Jack," he said, "the kind old admiral and Mrs. Deborah have both gone, and have left Lucy and me the whole of their property."

"Our good old friends dead!" exclaimed Jack, in a tone of grief; "I can scarcely realise the fact. I can remember him from my earliest days; always the same—kind and wise, and hearty and full of spirits. I saw a great change in him before we left, but still hoped to be greeted by his cheery voice on our return. How my father and mother will miss him!"

"I especially must ever hold his memory in grateful remembrance," said Adair, with feeling. "For Lucy's sake, I am most thankful that he and his kind sister have left us their property, as indeed I am for my own. I must be off for England as soon as I can get superseded, as it is absolutely necessary to settle their affairs. I wish you had as good an excuse as I have."

"I heartily congratulate you, Terence," said Jack; "but I am not sure that I shall not also have to go home before long, for Julia writes me word that her father is very ill, and much wishes to see me. As we have already served two years, I don't think that the Admiralty will object to supersede us, as it will give them an opportunity of obliging some of their friends."

After the two young commanders had somewhat got over the sorrow they naturally felt at hearing of the admiral's death, their spirits recovered; and, when together, they could talk of little else than their proposed return. They hoped to be sent down to Panama, where their ships could wait till their successors arrived. They possibly, on this account, took less interest in Vancouver's Island than they might otherwise have done, though present at a naval regatta at Esquimault, when the quiet harbour assumed a wonderfully gay appearance by the arrival of numerous steamers and boats of various descriptions from Victoria, and also at several cricket-matches played between the settlers and the officers of the ships' companies, and at a ball at Government House. The midshipmen voted the ball a decided failure as far as they were concerned, in consequence of the small amount of attention they received from the fairer portion of the guests; though they considered the cricket-matches and regatta very good fun.

At length the *Dragon* and *Eolus* were ordered to Panama. Soon after their arrival, two officers, who had come across the isthmus by the railway, made their appearance on board with the welcome information that they were to supersede them. They were both old shipmates, in whom they could place thorough confidence; they therefore left those who had so long sailed with them with less regret than would have been the case had they confided them to the charge of strangers. Notwithstanding the distance they had to pull, their respective midshipmen begged leave to man the boats which conveyed them on shore; and a few minutes after landing they were seated in the railway-car, which rattled on through the rich vegetation of the tropics, across the famed Isthmus to Colon, the port on its eastern side. Thence proceeding by the mail steamer, they safely reached Southampton, where Julia and Lucy were waiting to receive them.

The important affairs which had brought them home took some time to settle, and, Colonel Giffard soon afterwards dying, Jack found himself in possession of a comfortable income, which few people were better able to enjoy. He frequently heard from Tom, who liked his new commander, and gave an amusing account of the subsequent adventures he met with in the Pacific. That young gentleman never alluded to the fair Feodorowna, and in a letter Jack received from Higson, he learned that she had married, not long after her sister, a Russian gentleman of good fortune; though she never failed to inquire after her youthful admirer, hoping that in ten years or so he would find an English wife to suit him.

THE THREE COMMANDERS

Dick Needham got charge of a ship in ordinary, and nothing gave him so much delight as to receive a visit from his old shipmates, who never failed to go and see him when they went to Portsmouth.

Ben Snatchblock remained in charge of the *Stella*, and every summer when Murray was at home she was to be seen trim and taut at her old moorings off Bercaldine. The three commanders paid their wives the compliment not to apply in a hurry for employment, though they all at different times had commands offered them, which, however unwilling they were to leave home, they felt it their duty to accept. They were in due time posted, and all three are now admirals.

FINIS.

Richard Clay & Sons, Limited, London and Bungay.

SOME BOOKS FOR BOYS AND GIRLS

PUBLISHED BY

HENRY FROWDE and HODDER & STOUGHTON

BOOKS FOR BOYS
By HERBERT STRANG

> "Boys who read Mr. Strang's works have not merely the advantage of perusing enthralling and wholesome tales, but they are also absorbing sound and trustworthy information of the men and times about which they are reading."—DAILY TELEGRAPH.

Humphrey Bold : His Chances and Mischances by Land and Sea. Illustrated in Colour by W. H. MARGETSON. Crown 8vo, cloth elegant, olivine edges, 6s.

In this story are recounted the many adventures that befell Mr. Humphrey Bold of Shrewsbury, from the time when, a puny slip of a boy, he was befriended by Joe Punchard, the cooper's apprentice (who nearly shook the life out of his tormentor, Cyrus Vetch, by rolling him down the Wyle Cop in a barrel), to the day when, grown into a sturdy young giant, he sailed into Plymouth Sound as first lieutenant of the *Bristol* frigate. The intervening chapters teem with exciting incidents, telling of sea-fights with that redoubtable privateer Duguay Trouin; of Humphrey's escape from a French prison; of his voyage to the West Indies and all the perils he encountered there; together with an account of the active service he saw under that grim old English seaman, Admiral Benbow.

Glasgow Herald.—" So felicitous is he in imparting local colour to his narrative that whilst reading it we have found ourselves thinking of Thackeray. This suggests a standard by which very few writers of boys' books will bear being judged. The majority of them are content to provide their young friends with mere reading. Herbert Strang offers them literature."

Rob the Ranger : A Story of the Fight for Canada. Illustrated in Colour by W. H. MARGETSON, and three Maps. Crown 8vo, cloth elegant, olivine edges, 6s.

Rob Somers, son of an English settler in New York State, sets out with Lone Pete, a trapper, in pursuit of an Indian raiding party which has destroyed his home and carried off his younger brother. He is captured and taken to Quebec, where he finds his brother in strange circumstances, and escapes with him in the dead of the winter, in company with a little band of stout-hearted New Englanders. They are pursued over snow and ice, and in a log hut beside Lake Champlain maintain a desperate struggle against a larger force of French, Indians, and half-breeds, ultimately reaching Fort Edward in safety.

Glasgow Herald.—" If there had ever been the least doubt as to Mr. Herbert Strang's pre-eminence as a writer of boys' books, it would be very effectually banished by this latest work of his."

BOOKS FOR BOYS

By HERBERT STRANG

One of Clive's Heroes : A Story of the Fight for India. With Illustrations by W. RAINEY, R.I., and Maps. Crown 8vo, cloth elegant, olivine edges, **6s.**

Desmond Burke goes out to India to seek his fortune, and is sold by a false friend of his, one Marmaduke Diggle, to the famous Pirate of Gheria. But he escapes, runs away with one of the Pirate's own vessels, and meets Colonel Clive, whom he assists to capture the Pirate's stronghold. His subsequent adventures on the other side of India—how he saves a valuable cargo of his friend, Mr. Merriman, assists Clive in his fights against Sirajuddaula, and rescues Mr. Merriman's wife and daughter from the clutches of Diggle—are told with great spirit and humour. Mr. Strang lived for several years in India, and tells a great deal about the country, the natives, and their ways of life which he saw with his own eyes.

Athenæum.—"An absorbing story. ... The narrative not only thrills, but also weaves skilfully out of fact and fiction a clear impression of our fierce struggle for India."

Samba : A Story of the Congo. Illustrated by W. RAINEY, R.I. Crown 8vo, cloth elegant, olivine edges, **5s.**

The first work of fiction in which the cause of the hapless Congo native is championed.

Standard.—"It was an excellent idea on the part of Mr. Herbert Strang to write a story about the treatment of the natives in the Congo Free State. ... Mr. Strang has a big following among English boys, and anything he chooses to write is sure to receive their appreciative attention."

Journal of Education.—"We are glad that a writer who has already won for himself a reputation for good and vigorous work should have taken up the cause of the rubber slaves of the Congo."

Scotsman.—"Mr. Herbert Strang has written not a few admirable books for boys, but none likely to make a more profound impression than his new story of this year."

The Red Book for Boys. Edited by HERBERT STRANG.

A miscellany for Boys, containing a large variety of complete stories and articles by well-known writers; episodes and narratives of adventure; poems, etc.

288 pages, with 12 Plates in Colour, and many Illustrations in black and white. Picture boards, cloth back, **2s. 6d.**

Some of the Contents.

TRAPPED. By G. A. HENTY.
THE PUNISHMENT OF KHIPIL. By GEORGE MEREDITH.
A MODERN ODYSSEUS. By L. QUILLER-COUCH.
FOREST ADVENTURES. By HERBERT STRANG.
HIS FATHER'S HONOUR. By Captain GILSON.
THE HIGHWAYMAN. By ALFRED NOYES.
OCEAN LINERS, PAST AND PRESENT. By FRANK H. MASON.

BOOKS FOR BOYS

By HERBERT STRANG

Barclay of the Guides : A Story of the Indian Mutiny. Illustrated in Colour by H. W. KOEKKOEK. With Maps. Crown 8vo, cloth elegant, olivine edges, **5s.**

Of all our Native Indian regiments the Guides have probably the most glorious traditions. They were among the few who remained true to their salt during the trying days of the great Mutiny, vying in gallantry and devotion with our best British regiments. The story tells how James Barclay, after a strange career in Afghanistan, becomes associated with this famous regiment, and though young in years, bears a man's part in the great march to Delhi, the capture of the royal city, and the suppression of the Mutiny.

With Drake on the Spanish Main. Illustrated in Colour by ARCHIBALD WEBB. With Maps. Crown 8vo, cloth elegant, olivine edges, **5s.**

A rousing story of adventure by sea and land. The hero, Dennis Hazelrig, is cast ashore on an island in the Spanish Main, the sole survivor of a band of adventurers from Plymouth. He lives for some time with no companion but a spider monkey, but by a series of remarkable incidents he gathers about him a numerous band of escaped slaves and prisoners, English, French and native; captures a Spanish fort; fights a Spanish galleon; meets Francis Drake, and accompanies him in his famous adventures on the Isthmus of Panama; and finally reaches England the possessor of much treasure. The author has, as usual, devoted much pains to characterisation, and every boy will delight in Amos Turnpenny, Tom Copstone, and other bold men of Devon, and in Mirandola, the monkey.

School Guardian.—"Another of Mr. Herbert Strang's masterful stories of adventure and romance."

Swift and Sure. The Story of a Hydroplane. Illustrated in Colour. Crown 8vo, cloth. **2s. 6d.**

What the aeroplane is to the air the hydroplane promises to be to the sea. This story is a companion volume to "King of the Air" and "Lord of the Seas," a forecast of what may be expected from the progress of mechanical invention in the near future.

Lord of the Seas : A Story of a Submarine. Illustrated in Colour. Crown 8vo, cloth extra. **2s. 6d.**

The present day is witnessing a simultaneous attack by scientific investigation on the problems of aerial and submarine locomotion. In his book "King of the Air" Mr. Strang gave us a romance of modern aeronautics. In "Lord of the Seas" we have a companion volume dealing with the marvels of submarine navigation.

By HERBERT STRANG

King of the Air: or, To Morocco on an Airship. Illustrated in Colour by W. E. WEBSTER. Crown 8vo, cloth extra, **2s. 6d.**

In this story (Mr. Herbert Strang's second half-crown book) the young hero, having a strong turn for mechanical invention, contrives a machine that represents a great advance on what has previously been accomplished in the direction of aerial navigation. He has nearly perfected his invention when a British diplomatist is captured by tribesmen in Morocco, and his assistance is invoked in order to rescue the captive without negotiations that may involve international difficulties. The story tells of the exciting and amusing adventures that befell him and his companions in their perilous mission.

Morning Leader.—"One of the best boys' stories we have ever read."

Jack Hardy: or, A Hundred Years Ago. Illustrated by W. RAINEY, R.I. Crown 8vo, cloth extra, **2s. 6d.**

The old smuggling days! What visions are called up by the name—of stratagems, and caves, and secret passages, and ding-dong fights between sturdy seamen and dashing King's officers! It is in these brave days of old that Mr. Herbert Strang has laid the scenes of his story "Jack Hardy." Jack is a bold young middy who, in the course of his duty to the King, falls into all manner of difficulties and dangers: has unpleasant experiences in a French prison, escapes by sheer daring and ingenuity, and turns the tables on his captors in a way that will make every British boy's heart glow.

Athenæum.—"Herbert Strang is second to none in graphic power and veracity. . . . Here is the best of characterisation in bold outline."

HERBERT STRANG'S HISTORICAL SERIES

This new series is quite unique. Its aim is to encourage a taste for history in boys and girls up to fourteen years of age by giving all the important events and movements of a reign or period intermingled with a rousing story of adventure. While the stories are worth reading for their own sakes, they are also worth reading—especially on the eve of an examination—by a boy or girl who in class or in school text-book has worked up the "dry history" of the period. Each volume contains, besides the story, a general summary, a chronological list of important events, and a map. Much care has been devoted to the "get-up" of these books. They contain about 160 pages each, with four beautiful illustrations in full colour. Cloth, **1s. 6d.** each.

In the New Forest: A Story of the Reign of William the Conqueror.

Lion Heart: A Story of the Reign of Richard I.

Claud the Archer: A Story of the Reign of Henry V.

One of Rupert's Horse: A Story of the Reign of Charles I.

BOOKS FOR BOYS

HERBERT STRANG'S HISTORICAL SERIES *continued*

With the Black Prince : A Story of the Reign of Edward III.

A Mariner of England : A Story of the Reign of Queen Elizabeth.

With Marlborough to Malplaquet : A Story of the Reign of Queen Anne.

Practical Teacher.—"These Stories, which are bright and stirring, are sufficiently simple to be within the grasp of the children, the descriptions of life and manners are accurate, and the history of the period is interwoven in a skilful manner."

By CAPTAIN CHARLES GILSON

The Lost Empire : A Tale of Many Lands. Illustrated in Colour by CYRUS CUNEO. With Map. Crown 8vo, cloth elegant, olivine edges, 6s.

To found a great Empire in the East was one of the designs of Napoleon Bonaparte, and he might possibly have carried it out, had not certain events happened, which are related in this story. Amongst these were the Battle of the Nile, and the discovery of Napoleon's plans of campaign, in each of which incidents the hero, Mr. Thomas Nunn, Midshipman, was concerned. He was captured and taken to Paris, and it was here that the plans of campaign fell into his hands; what he did with them forms the material of an exciting story.

Daily News.—"It is a magnificent story, with not an error of phrase or thought in it. . . . This book is not only relatively good, but absolutely so."

The Lost Column : A Story of the Boxer Rebellion. Illustrated in Colour by CYRUS CUNEO. With Map. Crown 8vo, cloth elegant, olivine edges, 6s.

At the outbreak of the great Boxer Rebellion in China, Gerald Wood, the hero of this story, was living with his mother and brother at Milton Towers, just outside Tientsin. When the storm broke and Tientsin was cut off from the rest of the world, the occupants of Milton Towers made a gallant defence, but were compelled by force of numbers to retire into the town. Then Gerald determined to go in quest of the relief column under Admiral Seymour. He carried his life in his hands, and on more than one occasion came within an ace of losing it; but he managed to reach his goal in safety, and was warmly commended by the Admiral on his achievement. The author has found opportunity in this record of stirring events for some excellent characterisation, and, among others, the matter-of-fact James, Mr. Wang, and Mr. Midshipman Tite will be found diverting in the extreme.

Outlook.—"An excellent piece of craftsmanship."

Ladies' Field.—"All the sketches of Chinese character are excellent, and we read the book with delight from the first page to the last."

By WILLIAM J. MARX

For the Admiral. Illustrated. Crown 8vo, cloth elegant, 6s.

The brave Huguenot Admiral Coligny is one of the heroes of French history. Edmond le Blanc, the son of a Huguenot gentleman, undertakes to convey a secret letter of warning to Coligny, and the adventures he meets with on the way lead to his accepting service in the Huguenot army. He shares in the hard fighting that took place in the neighbourhood of La Rochelle, does excellent work in scouting for the Admiral, and is everywhere that danger calls. The story won the £100 prize offered by the *Bookman* for the best story for boys.

Academy.—"It is much the best book of its kind sent in for review this season, and stands head and shoulders above its rivals."

By DESMOND COKE

The School Across the Road

Illustrated in Colour by H. M. BROCK. Crown 8vo, cloth elegant, olivine edges, 5s.

The incidents of this story arise out of the uniting of two schools—"Warner's" and "Corunna"—under the name of "Winton," a name which the head master fondly hopes will become known far and wide as a great seat of learning. Unfortunately for the head master's ambition, however, the two sets of boys—hitherto rivals and enemies, now schoolfellows—do not take kindly to one another. Warner's men of might are discredited in the new school; Henderson, lately head boy, finds himself a mere nobody; while the inoffensive Dove is exalted and made prefect. The feud drags on until the rival factions have an opportunity of uniting against a common enemy. Then, in the enthusiasm aroused by the overthrow of a neighbouring agricultural college, the bitterness between themselves dies away, and the future of Winton is assured.

Sheffield Daily Telegraph.—"Its literary style is above the average and the various characters are thoroughly well drawn."

The Bending of a Twig. Illustrated in Colour by H. M. BROCK. Crown 8vo, cloth elegant, olivine edges, 5s.

When "The Bending of a Twig" was first published it was hailed by competent critics as the finest school story that had appeared since "Tom Brown." Then, however, it was purely a story about boys; now Mr. Coke has enlarged and partly rewritten it, and made it more attractive to schoolboy readers. It is a vivid picture of life in a modern public school. The hero, Lycidas Marsh, enters Shrewsbury without having previously been to a preparatory school, drawing his ideas of school life from his fertile imagination and a number of school stories he has read. Needless to say, he experiences a rude awakening on commencing his new career, for the life differs vastly from what he had been led to expect. How Lycidas finds his true level in this new world and worthily maintains the Salopian tradition is the theme of this entrancing book.

Outlook.—"Mr. Desmond Coke has given us one of the best accounts of public school life that we possess. . . . Among books of its kind 'The Bending of a Twig' deserves to become a classic."

BOOKS FOR BOYS

By DESMOND COKE

The House Prefect. By DESMOND COKE, author of "The Bending of a Twig," etc. Illustrated in Colour by H. M. BROCK. Crown 8vo, cloth elegant, olivine edges, 5s.

This story of the life at Sefton, a great English public school, mainly revolves around the trouble in which Bob Manders, new-made house prefect, finds himself, owing to a former alliance with the two wild spirits whom, in the interests of the house, it is now his chief task to suppress. In particular does the spirited exploit with which it opens—the whitewashing by night of a town statue and the smashing of certain school property—raise itself against him, next term, when he has been set in authority. His two former friends persist in still regarding him as an ally, bound to them by their common secret; and, in a sense, he is attracted to their enterprises, for in becoming prefect he does not cease to be a boy. It is a great duel this, fought in the studies, the dormitories and upon the field.

World.—"Quite one of the books of the season. Mr. Desmond Coke has proved himself a master."

By A. C. CURTIS

The Voyage of the "Sesame"
A Story of the Arctic. Illustrated in Colour by W. HERBERT HOLLOWAY. Crown 8vo, cloth elegant, olivine edges, 5s.

The three Trevelyan brothers receive from a dying sailor a rough chart indicating the whereabouts of a rich gold-bearing region in the Arctic. They forthwith build a craft, specially adapted to work in the Polar Seas, and set out in quest of the gold. They do not have things all their own way, however, for a rival party of treasure seekers have got wind of the old sailor's El Dorado, and are also on the trail. In the race and fighting that ensue, the brothers come off victorious; and after a voyage fraught with many dangers, the *Sesame* returns home with the gold on board.

Educational News.—"The building of the stout ship *Sesame* at Dundee is one of the best things of the kind we have read for many a day."

The Good Sword Belgarde: or, How De Burgh held Dover. Coloured Illustrations by W. H. C. GROOME. Crown 8vo, cloth elegant, olivine edges, 5s.

This is the story of Arnold Gyffard and John Wotton, pages to Sir Philip Daubeney, in the days when Prince Lewis the Lion invaded England and strove to win it from King John. It tells of their journey to Dover through a country swarming with foreign troops, and of many desperate fights by the way. In one of these Arnold wins from a French knight the good sword Belgarde, which he uses to such good purpose as to make his name feared. Then follows the great siege of Dover, full of exciting incident, when by his gallant defence Hubert de Burgh keeps the key to England out of the Frenchman's grasp.

Birmingham Post.—"Evidently Mr. Curtis is a force to be reckoned with. He writes blithely of gallant deeds; he does not make his heroes preposterously wise or formidable; he has a sense of humour; in fine, he has produced a book of sterling quality."

By GEORGE SURREY

A Northumbrian in Arms. A Story of the Time of Hereward the Wake. Illustrated in Colour by J. FINNEMORE. Crown 8vo, cloth, olivine edges, 5s.

Harald Ulfsson, companion of Hereward the Wake and conqueror of the Wessex Champion in a great wrestling bout, is outlawed by the influence of a Norman knight, whose enmity he has aroused, and goes north to serve under Earl Siward of Northumbria in the war against Macbeth, the Scottish usurper. He assists in defeating an attack by a band of coast-raiders, takes their ship, and discovering that his father has been slain and his land seized by his enemy, follows him into Wales. He fights with Griffith the Welsh King, kills his enemy in a desperate conflict amidst the hills, and, gaining the friendship of Harold, Earl of Wessex, his outlawry is removed and his lands restored to him.

School Guardian.—"With this story the author has placed himself in the front rank of writers of boys' books."

By FRANK H. MASON

The Book of British Ships. Written and Illustrated by FRANK H. MASON, R.B.A. Crown 8vo, cloth, olivine edges, 5s.

The aim of this book is to present, in a form that will readily appeal to boys, a comprehensive account of British shipping, both naval and mercantile, and to trace its development from the earliest times down to the Dreadnoughts and high-speed ocean liners of to-day. All kinds of British ships, from the battleship to the trawler, are dealt with, and the characteristic points of each type of vessel are explained.

British Weekly.—"Mr. Mason has given us one of the best histories of English ships that exist. It is admirably written and full of information."

By Rev. J. R. HOWDEN

Locomotives of the World. Containing 16 Plates in Colour, 5s. net.

Many of the most up-to-date types of locomotives used on railways throughout the world are illustrated and described in this volume. The coloured plates have been made from actual photographs, and show the peculiar features of some truly remarkable engines. These peculiarities are fully explained in the text, written by the Rev. J. R. Howden, author of "The Boy's Book of Locomotives," etc.

Daily Graphic.—"An absolutely safe investment for every boy who loves an engine."

Nation.—"The large coloured pictures of the world's engines are just the things in which the young enthusiast delights."

BOOKS FOR BOYS

THE ROMANCE SERIES
Crown 8vo, illustrated, 5s. each.

By EDWARD FRASER
The Romance of the King's Navy.

"The Romance of the King's Navy" is intended to give boys of to-day an idea of some of the notable events that have happened under the White Ensign within the past few years. There is no other book of the kind in existence. It begins with incidents afloat during the Crimean War, when their grandfathers were boys themselves, and brings the story down to a year ago, with the startling adventure at Spithead of Submarine B4. One chapter tells the exciting story of "How the Navy's V.C.'s have been won," the deeds of the various heroes being brought all together here in one connected narrative for the first time.

Westminster Gazette.—"Mr. Fraser knows his facts well, and has set them out in an extremely interesting and attractive way."

By A. B. TUCKER
The Romance of the King's Army.

A companion volume to "The Romance of the King's Navy," telling again in glowing language the most inspiring incidents in the glorious history of our land forces. The charge of the 21st Lancers at Omdurman, the capture of the Dargai heights, the saving of the guns at Maiwand, are a few of the great stories of heroism and devotion that appear in this stirring volume.

By LILIAN QUILLER-COUCH
The Romance of Every Day.

Here is a bookful of romance and heroism; true stories of men, women, and children in early centuries and modern times who took the opportunities which came into their everyday lives and found themselves heroes; civilians who, without beat of drum or smoke of battle, without special training or words of encouragement, performed deeds worthy to be written in letters of gold.

Bristol Daily Mercury.—"These stories are bound to encourage and inspire young readers to perform heroic actions."

By E. E. SPEIGHT and
R. MORTON NANCE
The Romance of the Merchant Venturers.
Britain's Sea Story.

These two books are full of true tales as exciting as any to be found in the story books, and at every few pages there is a fine illustration, in colour or black and white, of one of the stirring incidents described in the text.

BOOKS FOR GIRLS

By CHRISTINA GOWANS WHYTE

The Five Macleods. Illustrated in Colour by JAMES DURDEN. Crown 8vo, cloth elegant, gilt edges, 6s.

Nina's Career. Illustrated in Colour by JAMES DURDEN. Crown 8vo, cloth elegant, gilt edges, 6s.

The modern Louisa Alcott! That is the title that critics in England and America have bestowed on Miss Christina Gowans Whyte, whose "Story-Book Girls" they declare to be the best girls' story since "Little Women." Mrs. E. Nesbit, author of "The Would-be Goods," in likening Miss Whyte to Louisa Alcott, wrote: "This is high praise—but not too high." "Nina's Career" tells delightfully of a large family of girls and boys, children of Sir Christopher Howard, the famous surgeon. Friends of the Howards are Nina Wentworth, who lives with three aunts, and Gertrude Mannering. Gertrude, because she is the daughter of *the* Mrs. Mannering and grand-daughter of a peer, is conscious of always missing in her life that which makes the lives of the Howards so joyous and full. They may have "careers"; she must go to Court and through the wearying treadmill of the rich girls. The Howards get engaged, marry, go into hospitals, study in art schools; and in the end Gertrude also achieves happiness.

Outlook.—"We have been so badly in need of writers for girls who shall be in sympathy with the modern standard of intelligence, that we are grateful for the advent of Miss Whyte, who has not inaptly been described as the new Miss Alcott."

The Story-Book Girls. By CHRISTINA GOWANS WHYTE. Illustrated in Colour by JAMES DURDEN. Cloth elegant, 6s.

This story won the £100 prize in the *Bookman* competition.

The Leightons are a charming family. There is Mabel, the beauty, her mature strength and sweetness mingled; and Jean, the downright, blunt, uncompromising; and Elma, the sympathetic, who champions everybody, and has a weakness for long words. And there is Cuthbert, too, the clever brother. Cuthbert is responsible for a good deal, for he saves Adelaide Maud from an accident, and brings the Story-Book Girls into the story. Every girl who reads this book will become acquainted with some of the realest, truest, best people in recent fiction.

By WINIFRED M. LETTS

The Quest of the Blue Rose.

Illustrated in Colour by JAMES DURDEN. Crown 8vo, cloth, olivine edges, 5s.

After the death of her mother, Sylvia Sherwood has to make her own way in the world as a telegraph clerk. The world she finds herself in is a girls' hostel in a big northern city. For a while she can only see the uncongenial side of her surroundings; but when she has made a friend and found herself a niche, she begins to realise that though the Blue Rose may not be for her finding, there are still wild roses in every hedge. In the end, however, Sylvia, contented at last with her hard-working, humdrum life, finds herself the successful writer of a book of children's poems.

Daily News.—"It is a successful effort in realism, a book of live human beings that beyond its momentary interest, which is undoubted, will leave a lasting and valuable impression."

BOOKS FOR GIRLS

By ELSIE J. OXENHAM

Mistress Nanciebel. Illustrated in Colour by JAMES DURDEN. Crown 8vo, cloth, olivine edges, 5s.

This is a story of the Restoration. Nanciebel's father, Sir John Seymour, had so incurred the displeasure of King Charles by his persistent opposition to the threatened war against the Dutch, that he was sent out of the country. Nothing would dissuade Nanciebel from accompanying him, so they sailed away together and were duly landed on a desolate shore, which they afterwards discovered to be a part of Wales. Here, by perseverance and much hard toil, John o' Peace made a new home for his family, in which enterprise he owed not a little to the presence and constant help of Nanciebel, who is the embodiment of youthful optimism and womanly tenderness.

By E. EVERETT-GREEN

Our Great Undertaking. Illustrated. 5s.

Miss Evelyn Everett-Green is one of the first favourites with girls and boys. This is how she tells about the beginning of "Our Great Undertaking." The children have been asking granny for a story:—"Well, my dears, I will see what I can do. You shall come to me at this time to-morrow night, and I will tell you the story of how, when I was a little girl, we children undertook what seemed to many people at the outset a labour of Hercules, and how we learned from it a number of lessons, which have lasted us through life." The grandmother smiles as the happy children troop off to bed, and in these pages Miss Everett-Green tells us the delightful story that grandmother told next day.

By M. QUILLER-COUCH

The Carroll Girls. Illustrated. 5s.

The father of the Carroll girls fell into misfortune, and had to go to Canada to make a new start. But he could not take his girls with him, and they were left in charge of their cousin Charlotte, in whose country home they grew up, learning to be patient, industrious, and sympathetic. The author has a dainty and pleasant touch, and describes her characters so lovingly that no girl can read this book without keen interest in Esther's housekeeping and Penelope's music, Angela's poultry-farming, and Poppy's dreams of market gardening.

By E. L. HAVERFIELD

Audrey's Awakening. Illustrated in Colour by JAMES DURDEN. Crown 8vo, cloth, olivine edges, 3s. 6d.

As a result of a luxurious and conventional upbringing, Audrey is a girl without ambitions, unsympathetic, and with a reputation for exclusiveness. Therefore, when Paul Forbes becomes her stepbrother, and brings his free-and-easy notions into the Davidsons' old home, there begins to be trouble. Audrey discovers that she has feelings, and the results are not altogether pleasant. She takes a dislike to Paul at the outset; and the young people have to get through deep waters and some exciting times before things come right. Audrey's awakening is thorough, if painful.

Glasgow Herald.—"Very pleasantly written and thoroughly healthy."

BOOKS FOR GIRLS

By E. L. HAVERFIELD

The Conquest of Claudia.
Illustrated in Colour by JAMES DURDEN. Crown 8vo, cloth elegant, olivine edges, 3s. 6d.

Meta and Claudia Austin are two motherless girls with a much-occupied father. Their upbringing has therefore been left to a kindly governess, whose departure to be married makes the first change in the girls' lives. Having set their hearts upon going to school, they receive a new governess resentfully. Claudia is a person of instincts, and it does not take her long to discover that there is something mysterious about Miss Strongitharm. A clue upon which the children stumble leads to the notion that Miss Strongitharm is a Nihilist in hiding. That in spite of various strange happenings they are quite wrong is to be expected, but there is a genuine mystery about Miss Strongitharm which leads to some unforeseen adventures.

School Guardian.—" A fascinating story of girl life."

Dauntless Patty.
Illustrated in Colour by DUDLEY TENNANT. Crown 8vo, cloth extra, olivine edges, 3s. 6d.

The joys and sorrows, friendships and disappointments—all the trifles, in fact, which make the sum of schoolgirl life—are faithfully delineated in this story. Patricia Garnett, an Australian girl, comes over to England to complete her education. She is unconventional and quite unused to English ways, and it is not long before she finds herself the most unpopular girl in the school. Several times she reveals her courage and high spirit, particularly in saving the life of Kathleen Lane, a girl with whom she is on very bad terms. All overtures of peace fail, however, for Patty feels that the other girls have no real liking for her and she refuses to be patronised. Thus, chiefly owing to misunderstanding and careless gossip, the feud is continued to the end of the term; and the climax of the story is reached when, in a cave in the face of a cliff, in imminent danger of being drowned, Patty and Kathleen for the first time understand each other, and lay the foundations of a lifelong friendship.

Schoolmaster.—" A thoroughly faithful and stimulating story of schoolgirl life."

Glasgow Herald.—" The story is well told. Some of the incidents are dramatic, without being unnatural; the interest is well sustained, and altogether the book is one of the best we have read."

By ANNA CHAPIN RAY

Nathalie's Sister.
Illustrated in Colour by N. TENISON. Crown 8vo, cloth, olivine edges, 3s. 6d.

Nobody knows—or cares—much about Nathalie's Sister at the opening of this story. She is, indeed, merely Nathalie's Sister, without a name of her own, shining with a borrowed light. Before the end is reached, however, her many good qualites have received the recognition they deserve, and she is Margaret Arterburn, enjoying the respect and admiration of all her friends. Her temper is none of the best: she has a way of going direct to the point in conversation, and her words have sometimes an unpleasant sting; yet when the time comes, she reveals that she is not lacking in the qualities of gentleness and affection, not to say heroism, which many young readers have already learned to associate with her sister Nathalie.

Record.—" 'Nathalie's Sister' is written in Miss Ray's best style and has all those bright breezy touches which characterise her work."

By ANNA CHAPIN RAY

Nathalie's Chum. Illustrated in Colour by DUDLEY TENNANT. Crown 8vo, cloth extra, olivine edges, **3s. 6d.**

By her stories, "Teddy" and "Janet," Miss Anna Chapin Ray has already made English readers familiar with many of the distinctive features of boy and girl life in America. The present story, which is cast in the same mould, deals with a chapter in the career of the Arterburn family, and particularly of Nathalie, a vivacious, strong-willed girl of fifteen. After the death of their parents the children were scattered among different relatives, and the story describes the efforts of the eldest son, Harry, to bring them together again. At first there is a good deal of aloofness owing to the fact that, having been kept apart for so long, the children are practically strangers to each other; but at length Harry takes his sister Nathalie into his confidence and makes her his ally in the management of their small household, while she finds in him the chum of whom she has long felt the need.

Teddy: Her Book. A Story of Sweet Sixteen. Illustrated in Colour by ROBERT HOPE. Crown 8vo, decorated cloth cover, olivine edges, **3s. 6d.**

World.—"Teddy is a delightful personage; and the story of her friendships, her ambitions, and her successes is thoroughly engrossing."

Yorkshire Daily Post.—"To read of Teddy is to love her."

Janet: Her Winter in Quebec. Illustrated in Colour by GORDON BROWNE. Crown 8vo, decorated cloth cover, olivine edges, **3s. 6d.**

Outlook.—"The whole tone of the story is as bright and healthy as the atmosphere in which these happy months were spent."

Lady's Pictorial.—"The sparkle of a Canadian winter ripples across Anna Chapin Ray's 'Janet.'"

BOOKS FOR CHILDREN
By LUCAS MALET

Little Peter: A Christmas Morality for Children of any Age. New Edition. Illustrated in Colour by CHARLES E. BROCK. Crown 8vo, cloth elegant, gilt edges, **6s.**

This delightful little story introduces to us a family dwelling upon the outskirts of a vast and mysterious pine forest in France. There are Master Lepage, who, as head of the household and a veteran of the wars, lays down the law upon all sorts of questions, domestic and political; his meek, sweet-faced wife Susan; their two sons Anthony and Paul; and Cincinnatus the cat—who holds as many opinions and expresses them as freely as Master Lepage himself; and—little Peter. Little Peter makes friends with John Paqualin, a queer, tall, crook-backed old charcoal-burner, whom the boys of the village call "the grasshopper man," and whom every one else treats with contempt; but this is not surprising, since Little Peter makes friends with every one he meets, and all who read about him will certainly make friends with *him*.

BOOKS FOR CHILDREN

By CHRISTINA GOWANS WHYTE

The Adventures of Merrywink: Illustrated by M. V. Wheelhouse.
Crown 4to, cloth elegant, 6s.

This story won the £100 prize for the best children's story in the *Bookman* competition. It tells of a pretty little child who was born into Fairyland with a gleaming star in his forehead. When his parents beheld this star they were filled with gladness and fear, and in the night they carried their little Fairy baby, Merrywink, far away and hid him. Why was it necessary to carry Merrywink away so secretly? Because of two old prophecies: the first, that a daughter should be born to the King and Queen of Fairyland; the second that the King should rule over Fairyland until a child appeared with a gleaming star in his forehead. Now, on the very day that Merrywink was born, the long-promised little Princess arrived at the Royal Palace; and the King, who was determined to keep his throne to himself, sent round messages to make sure that the child with the gleaming star had not yet been seen in Fairyland. The story tells us how Merrywink grew up to be brave and strong, and fearless and truthful; how he set out on his travels and met the Princess at court, and all that happened afterwards.

By E. M. JAMESON

The Pendleton Twins. Crown 8vo, olivine edges, Coloured Illustrations, 5s.

A great number of little readers now look forward eagerly to the appearance of further volumes telling of the adventures and misadventures of the Pendletons. This year the family's Christmas holidays furnish material for another bright and amusing story. Their adventures begin the very day they leave home. The train is snowed up and they are many hours delayed. They have a merry Christmas with plenty of fun and presents, and in the middle of the night Bob gives chase to a burglar. Nora, who is very sure-footed, goes off by herself one day and climbs the cliffs, thinking that no one will be any the wiser until her return. But the twins and Dan follow her unseen and are lost in a cave, where they find hidden treasure left by smugglers buried in the ground. Len sprains his ankle and they cannot return. Search parties set out from Cliffe, and spend many hours before the twins are found by Nora, cold and tired and frightened. But the holidays end very happily after all.

Peggy Pendleton's Plan. Illustrated. 5s.

The Pendletons. Illustrated. 5s.

Two further stories dealing with the fortunes of the entertaining Pendleton family.

Schoolmaster:—"Young people will revel in this most interesting and original story. The five young Pendletons are much as other children in a large family, varied in their ideas, quaint in their tastes, and wont to get into mischief at every turn. They are withal devoted to one another and to their home, and although often 'naughty,' are not by any means 'bad.' The interest in the doings of these youngsters is remarkably well sustained, and each chapter seems better than the last. With not a single dull page from start to finish and with twelve charming illustrations, the book makes an ideal reward for either boys or girls."

BOOKS FOR CHILDREN

By AMY LE FEUVRE

Robin's Heritage. Illustrated by GORDON BROWNE. 2s.

Robin, the little hero of Miss Amy Le Feuvre's latest book, is a charming creation. He is certainly one of the most lovable of the boy and girl characters in her books, whose adventures have given delight to so many thousands of little readers.

Christina and the Boys. Illustrated. 2s.

This is a splendid story for boys and girls. All who have read Miss Le Feuvre's other books will want to read this. It is a story of three children; one from England, another from Scotland, the third from Wales. They are all so jolly that it is difficult to say which of the three will be the favourite with young readers.

Roses. Illustrated. 2s.

This story introduces us to Mrs. Fitzherbert, a dear little old lady with snow-white hair, as she moves among the sweet scents and sounds of her rose garden. She lives in a quaint old-fashioned house with casement windows and deep window seats, old oak staircase and panelled rooms. And into the midst of this secluded scene comes Dimple—her real name is Isabella, but she will not allow anybody to call her by that name on any account—whose father, owing to ill-fortune, has had to go abroad. How Dimple wins the hearts of all in her new home is told by Miss Le Feuvre in this little book.

His Big Opportunity. Illustrated. 2s.

The two principal characters in this book are Roy and Dudley—two cousins. Both are anxious to become heroes, and they are constantly on the look-out for an opportunity to do some good. This leads them, one day, to pay a friendly visit to a sick man. They cannot get in by the door, so they clamber in by the window, greatly to the alarm of the invalid, who takes them for house-breakers. The story tells how, when their big opportunity does arrive, they are able to seize it and turn it to account.

Brownie. Illustrated. 2s.

A Cherry Tree. Illustrated. 2s.

Two Tramps. Illustrated. 2s.

The Buried Ring. Illustrated. 2s.

BOOKS FOR CHILDREN

The New Line upon Line. Revised Edition of "Line upon Line" (containing Parts I and II of the original work), edited by J. E. HODDER WILLIAMS, with a Preface by the BISHOP OF DURHAM. Illustrated in Colour. Leather, **2s. 6d.** net; cloth, **1s. 6d.** net; picture boards, **1s.** net.

The New Peep of Day. Revised Edition of "The Peep of Day," edited by J. E. HODDER WILLIAMS, with a Preface by the BISHOP OF DURHAM. Illustrated in Colour. Leather, **2s. 6d.** net; cloth, **1s. 6d.** net; picture boards, **1s.** net.

These new editions of two well-known children's books retain all the features that made the previous issues so popular, but they have been thoroughly revised with a view to making them more easily understood by the children of to-day.

THE CHILDREN'S BOOKCASE
Edited by E. NESBIT

"The Children's Bookcase" is a new series of dainty illustrated books for little folks which is intended ultimately to include all that is best in children's literature, whether old or new. The series is edited by Mrs. E. Nesbit, author of "The Would-be Goods" and many other well-known books for children; and particular care is given to binding, get-up, and illustrations. The pictures are in full colour.

The Little Duke. By CHARLOTTE M. YONGE.

Sonny Sahib. By SARA JEANNETTE DUNCAN (Mrs. EVERARD COTES).

The Water Babies. By CHARLES KINGSLEY.

The Old Nursery Stories. By E. NESBIT.

Cap-o'-Yellow. By AGNES GROZIER HERBERTSON.

Granny's Wonderful Chair. By FRANCES BROWNE.

The volumes in "The Children's Bookcase" are issued in three styles of binding: in paper boards, at **1s. 6d.** *net; cloth,* **2s. 6d.** *net; and art cloth with photogravure panel,* **3s. 6d.** *net.*

Scotsman.—"In point of artistic beauty and general excellence, these volumes, costing only 1s. 6d. each, are a marvellous production."

www.ingramcontent.com/pod-product-compliance
Lightning Source LLC
Chambersburg PA
CBHW022108300426
44117CB00007B/630